CW01662151

THE PEOPLE OF GOD HAVE SPOKEN

Continental Ecclesial Assemblies within the Synod on Synodality

Edited by
Myriam Wijlens and Vimal Tirimanna CSsR

columba
BOOKS

Published in 2023

Columba Books
Unit 3B, Block 3, Bracken Business Park,
Sandyford, Dublin 18, Ireland
www.columbabooks.com

Production Copyright © Columba Books 2023

Official Synod documents available from Synod 2021-2024 website www.synod.va

All authored material is copyright © authors

All rights reserved. Without limiting the rights under copyright reserved alone, no copyrighted part of this publication may be reproduced, stored in or introduced into a retrieval system, or transmitted, in any form or by any means (electronic, mechanical, photocopying, recording or otherwise) without the prior written permission of both the copyright owner and the above publisher of the book.

ISBN: 9781782184010

Set in Adelle and Adelle Sans
Cover design & book design Paula T Nolan | PEN GRAPHIC DESIGN

Printed by L&C Poland

columba
BOOKS

CONTENTS

Foreword 5
Cardinal Oswald Gracias

Introduction 10
Myriam Wijlens and Vimal Tirimanna CSsR

Adsumus, Sancte Spiritus: The Prayer of the Synod 19
Martin Klöckener

The Method is the Message: Method of Spiritual Conversation 24
Christina Kheng

'Enlarge the Space of your Tent' (Is. 54:2) Working Document for the Continental Stage 29
Secretariat for the Synod

Africa

The Church Family of God: The Continental Synodal Assembly of Africa 69
Marie-Laure Josée Abotcha-Boni

The Report of Africa 84

Asia

Tapping the Voice of the Holy Spirit in a Multi-Religious and Multi-Cultural Context: The Continental Synodal Assembly in Asia 99
Vimal Tirimanna CSsR and Jessica Joy Candelario

The Report of Asia 111

Europe

A Profound Spiritual Experience of Listening: The Continental Synodal Assembly of Europe 145
Myriam Wijlens and Arnaud Join-Lambert

The Report of Europe 161

Latin America and the Caribbean

The Call to 'Enlarge our Tent' (cf. Is. 54:2): The Continental Assembly of Latin America and the Caribbean 196
Birgit Weiler MMS and Ricardo González Sánchez

The Report of Latin America and the Caribbean 208

Middle East

'And the Word Became Flesh and Pitched his Tent Among Us' (Jn 1:14): The Continental Synodal Assembly in the Middle East 238
Souraya Bechealany and Mirna Abboud Mzawak

The Report of the Middle East 253

North America

A New Experience of Discerning Together: Opportunities and Challenges in the North American Continental Meetings 278
Kristin Colberg and Gilles Routhier

The Report of North America 290

Oceania

Care for People and Planet: Discernment from the Continental Synodal Stage in Oceania 314
Susan Pascoe and Ormond Rush

The Report of Oceania 328

Contributors 364

Acknowledgements 369

FOREWORD

Cardinal Oswald Gracias

Most of the bishops who participated at the historical Second Vatican Council (Vatican II) were so overwhelmed with their first-hand experience of being together during the conciliar sessions as a College of Bishops, that towards the end of the Council they requested Pope Paul VI to establish an ecclesial structure that would ensure the continuation of the worldwide collegiality of bishops with, and under, the Bishop of Rome. On his part, the Pope himself was also very keen to have a similar mechanism that would enable him to frequently get the pulse of the bishops from around the world. Thus, in the very year that the Council ended (1965), through a special Motu Proprio, *Apostolica Sollicitudo*, he established the post-Vatican-II ecclesial institution of the Synods of Bishops. In a sense, this was nothing new, but a return to the ancient venerable Church tradition of synods. Interestingly, the Pope already then visualised how, with the passage of time, this concept could further evolve, as he stated in the Motu Proprio itself: 'This synod, which, like all human institutions, can be improved upon with the passing of time'.[1]

The above-mentioned Motu Proprio of Pope Paul VI specified that this post-conciliar concept of the Synod of Bishops – whereby bishops chosen from various parts of the world were to offer more effective and tangible assistance to the Bishop of Rome in carrying out his office – was to be constituted in such a way that it would be: 'a) a central ecclesiastical institution; b) representing the whole Catholic episcopate; c) by its nature perpetual; d) as for structure, carrying out its function for a time and when called upon.' (Art.1) Since 1965 to-date, there have been twenty-nine synods altogether – fifteen ordinary synods, three extraordinary synods and eleven special synods, all of which were limited to attendance by bishops.[2] These post-Vatican-II synodal events have not only assisted successive Popes in their functioning in the Petrine Office, but also have enabled the worldwide Catholic Episcopate to experience their own communion as a College of Bishops.

Since he was elected as the Successor of Peter in 2013, our present Holy Father Pope Francis has tirelessly endeavoured to revive the teachings of Vatican II in almost every sphere of ecclesial life. Invoking the conciliar ecclesiology as

1 Paul VI, Motu Proprio *Apostolica sollicitudo* (1965), https://www.vatican.va/content/paul-vi/en/motu_proprio/documents/hf_p-vi_motu-proprio_19650915_apostolica-sollicitudo.html

2 Of course, there have been non-Bishop members, such as major religious superiors, representatives of various ecclesial groups and movements, and theologians (*periti*) and other experts who participated as non-voting observers.

taught in particular by *Lumen gentium* (LG), he has consistently sought to realise in concrete Church life the direct implications of the Church as the People of God. Basing himself on the fundamental Christian identity of Baptism, the Pope has sought to consider the concrete implications of a Church that consists of all the baptised, i.e., the bishops, priests, religious, lay men and women through all of whom the Holy Spirit speaks. As LG 12 so clearly teaches, thanks to the presence of the Holy Spirit, there is an inborn or innate intuition for the sense of the faith and morals (*sensus fidei*) among all the People of God as a whole:

> The entire body of the faithful, anointed as they are by the Holy One, cannot err in matters of belief. They manifest this special property by means of the whole peoples' supernatural discernment in matters of faith when 'from the Bishops down to the last of the lay faithful' they show universal agreement in matters of faith and morals. That discernment in matters of faith is aroused and sustained by the Spirit of truth.

Elaborating this conciliar teaching further, Pope Francis highlighted how this serves as a guide to the whole Church because it is but the voice of the Holy Spirit:

> In all the baptised, from first to last, the sanctifying power of the Spirit is at work, impelling us to evangelisation. The People of God is holy thanks to this anointing, which makes it infallible *in credendo*. This means that it does not err in faith, even though it may not find words to explain that faith. The Spirit guides it in truth and leads it to salvation. As part of his mysterious love for humanity, God furnishes the totality of the faithful with an instinct of faith – *sensus fidei* – which helps them to discern what is truly of God. The presence of the Spirit gives Christians a certain connaturality with divine realities, and a wisdom which enables them to grasp those realities intuitively, even when they lack the wherewithal to give them precise expression.[3]

In his address at the special ceremony in October 2015 to commemorate the 50th anniversary of the institution of the post-Vatican-II synods, the Pope declared: 'The *sensus fidei* prevents a rigid separation between an *Ecclesia docens* and an *Ecclesia discens*, since the flock likewise has an instinctive ability

3 Pope Francis, Apostolic Exhortation *Evangelii Gaudium* (2013), No:119. https://www.vatican.va/content/francesco/en/apost_exhortations/documents/papa-francesco_esortazione-ap_20131124_evangelii-gaudium.html

to discern the new ways that the Lord is revealing to the Church'.[4] In other words, as the Preparatory Document for the Synodal Process issued by the Vatican's Secretariat for the Synod of Bishops says, there exists an 'indispensable 'bond between the *sensus fidei* of the People of God and the magisterial function of the Pastors that the unanimous consensus of the whole Church in the same faith is realised.'[5] Hence the importance of listening to every person among the People of God:

> A synodal Church is a Church which listens, which realises that listening 'is more than simply hearing'. It is a mutual listening in which everyone has something to learn. The faithful people, the college of bishops, the Bishop of Rome: all listening to each other, and all listening to the Holy Spirit, the 'Spirit of truth' (Jn 14:17), in order to know what he 'says to the Churches' (Rev 2:7).[6]

Thus, by stressing the vital importance of listening to the voice of the Holy Spirit speaking through all the members of the People of God, Pope Francis, goes a step further to constructively use the present synodal structure introduced by Pope Paul VI in 1965 in such a way that the voices of all the baptised are heard though the decisions are to be taken by the bishops and the Pope:

> Although structurally it [Synod] is essentially configured as an episcopal body, this does not mean that the synod exists separately from the rest of the faithful. On the contrary, it is a suitable instrument to give voice to the entire People of God, specifically via the Bishops, established by God as 'authentic guardians, interpreters and witnesses of the faith of the whole Church', demonstrating, from one Assembly to another, that it is an eloquent expression of synodality as a 'constitutive element of the Church'.[7]

In fact, in order to promote new and deeper efforts to discern what the Holy Spirit is saying to the contemporary Church, Pope Francis used a type of a two-year consultation of the People of God when he called for two successive Synods on Family and Marriage in 2014 and 2015. A similar effort was in place with regard to the Synod on Amazonia in 2018. And with the Apostolic Constitution *Episcopalis Communio* in 2018, the Pope has officially and canonically established

4 Cf., The Address of His Holiness Pope Francis at the Ceremony Commemorating the 50th Anniversary of the institution of the Synod of Bishops, 17th October 2015. https://www.vatican.va/content/francesco/en/speeches/2015/october/documents/papa-francesco_20151017_50-anniversario-sinodo.html

5 Synod of Bishops, Preparatory Document *For a Synodal Church: Communion, Participation, and Mission* (2021) nr. 14. https://www.synod.va/en/news/the-preparatory-document.html

6 Address Pope Francis 50th Anniversary Synod of Bishops 2015 (fn. 4 supra).

7 Francis, Apostolic Constitution *Episcopalis Communio* (2018), nr. 6 https://www.vatican.va/content/francesco/en/apost_constitutions/documents/papa-francesco_costituzione-ap_20180915_episcopalis-communio.html

an institutional mechanism to consult the People of God in the preparatory stages of future synods.

This surely is a novelty (in the contemporary Church) that makes a conscious and concrete effort to deepen the ecclesiology of Vatican II as taught by *Lumen Gentium*, in the spirit of the ancient and venerable ecclesial practice of synodality. This papal initiative led to the beginning of the Synod on Synodality in local churches where all the faithful were invited to listen to what the Spirit is saying to the churches (Rev.2:7). The fruits of that listening process were collected in reports sent to Rome by 112 out of 114 episcopal conferences, and by 15 Eastern Churches. They formed the basis for the so-called 'Frascati Document', which is the Working Document for the Continental Stage, *Enlarge the Space of your Tent* (Is 54:2). In order to deepen further the listening process while studying the specific context in which the Church finds herself, seven continental stage meetings were organised. Most episcopal conferences responded favourably and enthusiastically to the question of the Secretariat of the Synod that they meet not just as bishops, but that the continental listening occurs together with other members of the People of God. These continental gatherings were therefore called 'Ecclesial Assemblies'. As the terms themselves literally indicate, while a Synod of Bishops consists of bishops, an Ecclesial Assembly consists of participants from all strata of ecclesial life, namely, bishops, priests, religious and laity. Such participation finds its *rationale* in the fundamental assertions that the Church and synodality are synonymous (as taught by St. John Chrysostom) and that synodality is 'a walking together' of all the People of God.

Although there are just six geographical continents in the world, in the current synodal process, so as to include every segment of the People of God spread all over the world, the Secretariat for the Synod has considered the world as comprising of seven groupings of episcopal conferences and Eastern Churches, namely, Asia, Africa, North America, Latin America and the Carribean, Europe, Oceania and the Middle East. In the months of February and March 2023, each of these 'continents' had their respective Ecclesial Assemblies using the Working Document for the Continental Stage, *Enlarge the Space of your Tent* (Is 54:2). In the history of the Church, this is the first time that such Ecclesial Assemblies were held. Also remarkable is that all continents were listening to what the Holy Spirit is saying to the churches almost simultaneously.

I was privileged to attend briefly the Frascati meeting and then participate in the Synodal Assembly for Asia. I thus had an inside view of the process and was deeply impressed by the seriousness of the preparation, the spiritual atmosphere that prevailed at the meetings of the Council of Bishops of the General Secretariat and the openness to amend displayed by the drafting committee at every stage. The Synod on Synodality gives great hope for bringing about a renewal of the Church under the guidance of the Holy Spirit.

Hence I am glad that Professors Myriam Wijlens and Vimal Tirimanna, CSsR have taken the initiative to capture the Spirit of the event at this historical moment of the Catholic Church in the form of a collection of essays based on the unique synodal experiences which each of the Continental Ecclesial Assemblies lived. The articles, written by persons who participated in these Assemblies, bear ample evidence to the richness of the gifts showered on the People of God all over the world through this continental stage of the synodal process. The Continental Ecclesial Assembly reports that are also published along with those respective articles enable the reader to compare, contrast and complement what the Spirit has been saying to the Churches spread all over the world.

I wish to congratulate Professors Wijlens and Tirimanna for this creative initiative which undoubtedly will serve as an indispensable reference work for those interested in the current process of synodality. I wish to thank them for their painstaking and generous efforts. The work they have produced is invaluable. I do hope they continue this initiative! We are just at the beginning of the Synod! Thank you and keep it up!

Cardinal Oswald Gracias
Archbishop of Mumbai
June 2023

INTRODUCTION

Myriam Wijlens and Vimal Tirimanna CSsR

The Synod is On!

The People of God have spoken. In October 2021, Pope Francis opened the Synod entitled *For a Synodal Church: Communion – Participation – Mission*. A week later, in their respective dioceses, the bishops inaugurated the opening of the synod in the context of celebrating the Eucharist. The Synod on Synodality, as it is commonly referred to, took off and indeed as results showed, it is really on!

It all began with an invitation to listen to 'what the Spirit is saying to the Churches' (Rev. 3:22). Around the world, the People of God responded in a remarkable way to the invitation to participate. They met in their local parishes, basic communities, associations, movements, institutes of consecrated life as well as on digital platforms. Together with other members of the People of God, they listened carefully and attentively. The findings of their deep listening were synthesised in reports composed, in particular, by episcopal conferences and Eastern Churches and submitted to the Secretariat for the Synod in Rome in the Summer of 2022.

In the Autumn of 2022 it became clear that the response to the invitation of the Pope to participate was overwhelming and surprising for three reasons: First, the number of reactions was unprecedented, because 112 of 114 episcopal conferences and 15 from 23 Eastern Churches, 18 Dicasteries of the Roman Curia, the International Unions of Male and Female Major Superiors (USG/UISG), and the Digitial Synod submitted reports. There were also approximately one thousand submissions containing responses, sometimes from individual persons, but usually from groups, that at times were rather large. Second, the content of the submissions showed that the people were extremely grateful that the leadership of the Church was finally asking what they themselves believe. For the first time, many said, they became aware of their baptism. They expressed that they had been pleasantly surprised and deeply moved that their own faith mattered to the Church. They reported not only that they discovered what it means to be a synodal church, but they also expressed a great desire to continue and deepen this experience. Third, in spite of the fact that the people live in very different contexts and circumstances, the reports surprisingly brought a remarkable convergence of topics to the fore. This is not to say that the reports did not express tensions, but wherever tensions were noticed, there too, the same or very similar points emerged all over the world. A team – called together by the Secretariat for the Synod – gathered just outside of Rome in Frascati (Italy)[1] at the end of September 2022 to pray with, read, analyse and discern all the responses from around the world. Having done so, they were moved when writing the Working Document for the Continental Stage (hereafter DCS), *Enlarge the Space of your Tent* (Is 54:2), to express with enthusiasm: 'The synod is on!' (DCS 1).[2]

Catholicity and the Sense of the Faithful

The first step of the listening phase occurred on the level of local churches. This is the place where the People of God hear the Word of God proclaimed, celebrate the Eucharist and live their faith. This is where they encounter God and other persons. This is where they experience joy and hope, sorrows and anxiety (GS 1). In the local churches the people shared with each other their deep experience of their encounter and journey with God and each other.

The People of God had thus spoken, but the Secretariat of the Synod after approval by Pope Francis, felt the need of a *restitutio*: a giving back to the people what had been collected, summarised and synthesised. It was felt to be indispensable to check and make sure that what was expressed in the DCS, *Enlarge the Space of your Tent* (Is. 54:2), did indeed resonate with the experience of all the faithful locally. It was also felt that the People of God locally should listen to what the People of God in other parts of the world had heard while listening to the Holy Spirit. A kind of becoming aware of the others and mutual reception between the different local churches in different continents should be provided for. It was felt to be necessary to go beyond the circularity between the church local and universal, and provide an opportunity to enter into the dynamics of what the notion of catholicity expresses.

In theological terms this can be expressed in the following way: In the first step, based on the teaching that the Church exists in and from the local churches (*in quibus et ex quibus* – LG 23) a circularity between the church local and universal came about. It was judged opportune that the second step should facilitate a listening of local churches to each other within a context beyond their own episcopal conference or Eastern Church, but yet within their specific (cultural) context. Really, there was a desire to enable and provide for a deep experience of catholicity as the constitution on the Church expresses it so well: 'By virtue of this catholicity the individual parts bring their own gifts to the other parts and to the whole Church, in such a way that the whole and individual parts grow greater through mutual communication of all and in their

1 The authors in this book refer to this meeting as the 'Frascati-meeting'. It was composed of approximately forty persons from around the world: bishops, priests, religious sisters, married and single lay women and lay men, some theologians and canon lawyers, others specialised in organisational management, communication or spirituality. Towards the end the Council of Bishops, composed of three bishops of each continent, joined the group and approved the work accomplished.

2 Secretariat for the Synod, *'Enlarge the Space of your Tent' (Is. 54:2). Working Document for the Continental Stage* https://www.synod.va/en/resources/official-documents.html. The Document can also be found in this book on page 29.

united efforts towards fullness in unity' (LG 13). The passage on catholicity not only speaks about the parts in the sense of local churches engaging in communication with each other, but also applies it to the different members of the body of the faithful in the sentence that follows the quotation: 'It follows from this that the People of God is not only gathered together from diverse peoples, but within itself is made up out of the union of different orders' such as laity, religious and clergy. The faithful, which includes thus bishops and other members of the People of God, need to be in an interaction that allows for an exchange of their faith so that it might edify the mission of the church. To quote from LG 13 again: 'As each has received a gift, employ it for one another, as good stewards of God's varied grace (1 Pt 4:10).'

When the catholicity of the Church is practiced and comes to life, the groundwork for determining the sense of the faithful is laid: 'The universal body of the faithful, who have received the anointing of the holy one (see Jn 2: 20 and 27) cannot be mistaken in belief. It displays this particular quality through a supernatural sense of the faith in the whole people when "from the bishops to the last of the faithful laity" it expresses consent of all matters of faith and belief.' (LG 12). The council teaches that the sense of the faith is aroused and sustained by the Spirit of truth. The doctrine on the *sensus fidei fidelium* is to be seen in conjunction with the specific ministry that the bishops and the Bishop of Rome hold. In light of their responsibility, the bishops that gather in the Synod of Bishops in Rome will discern what the Spirit is saying to the Church, and recommend to the Bishop of Rome which steps need to be taken. 'The Synod process culminates in listening to the Bishop of Rome, who is called to speak as "pastor and teacher of all Christians", not on the basis of his personal convictions but as the supreme witness to the *fides totius Ecclesiae*, "the guarantor of the obedience and the conformity of the Church to the will of God, to the Gospel of Christ, and to the Tradition of the Church".'[3]

The Synod on Synodality thus had to provide for a modality that would enable the Church to make these teachings of the Church into a lived reality. This Synod thus began with a listening phase in which the People of God were invited to speak. It will be followed by the XVI Ordinary General Assembly of the Synod of Bishops, in which its members will discern after the People of God have spoken.

Theology Governing the Continental Ecclesial Assemblies

The listening phase consisted of two steps: after listening in the local churches, there was a second round of listening in which the catholicity of the Church found expression. This time the listening took place within a continental context. In particular, the existing continental structures for cooperation of

3 Pope Francis, Address during the Ceremony Commemorating the 50th Anniversary of the Institution of the Synod of Bishops, October 17, 2015. Cf. https://www.vatican.va/content/francesco/en/speeches/2015/october/documents/papa-francesco_20151017_50-anniversario-sinodo.html

episcopal conferences within a continent such as CELAM, FABC, CCEE, SECAM, and FCBCO[4] were tasked with organising the meetings. The purpose of these meetings was a restitution in the sense of asking the People of God whether what had been said in the diocesan phase had been heard correctly, as well as to allow the People of God to engage in a conversation with others, including other local churches, about what had come from around the world, reflect about this within one's own context and identify further steps to be taken.

To prepare for all of this, seven continental meetings were organised: Africa, Asia, Europe, Latin America and the Caribbean, Middle East, North America, and Oceania. Each continent witnessed the celebration of a Continental Assembly which was composed of myriad contributions unique and new in the history of the Catholic Church. In the Autumn of 2022, the Secretariat for the Synod had asked the Episcopal Conferences and Synods of Eastern Churches whether they would prefer to have a meeting of bishops only, or whether some other members of the People of God should participate as well. From those who responded an overwhelming majority favoured not to hold merely episcopal continental meetings, but wanted 'representatives from the entire People of God to be involved in the Continental Stage. [Hence, it was asked] that all Assemblies be ecclesial and not merely episcopal, ensuring that their composition adequately represents the variety of the People of God: bishops, presbyters, deacons, consecrated women and men, laymen and women' (DCS 108).

It is remarkable that what more than fifty years ago had begun as a Synod of Bishops, composed of bishops only who merely met for a few weeks in Rome to discuss a draft document already prepared in advance in Rome, now has become a process in which the whole People of God from around the world, in one way or the other, participate from the beginning. Our times thus witness a new and unique feature: bishops and other members of the People of God meeting to listen together to the Word of God and the Holy Spirit. In doing so they give expression to the doctrine on baptism and the equality in dignity that flows from it, the teaching that revelation is a personal encounter of each and everyone with God, and not a mere receiving of doctrine, that God communicates with humankind as his friends (DV 2). From this flows the awareness that each and every person has something to say, is worth listening to and should thus be given an opportunity to speak and share. It is related to the awareness that the teaching and proclaiming Church is preceded by a Church that listens to the Word of God and to one another in the Spirit. It is deeply related to the doctrines on the working of the Holy Spirit in the whole community (LG 12), the need to attend to the sense of the faithful and that episcopal ministry stands in service to the community in its pilgrim journey towards fullness. These

4 Consejo Episcopal Latinoamericano y Caribeño (CELAM), Federation of Asian Bishops Conferences (FABC), Council of Bishops' Conferences of Europe (CCEE), Symposium of Episcopal Conferences of Africa and Madagascar (SECAM), Federation of Catholic Bishops of Conferences of Oceania (FCBCO).

are just some doctrinal aspects as articulated by Vatican II.

And yet more teachings found especially in the ecclesiology of Vatican II deserve being mentioned. Although many continents have structures that provide for a cooperation of episcopal conferences, the Continental Assemblies that occurred in February and March 2023 were rather unique on a few accounts: first, they implied that the existing continental structures somehow become part of the ecclesiological structure of the Church to an extent which had not been acknowledged before. Second, these structures imply a recognition of a particularity of each continent and thus an acknowledgment of a uniqueness and diversity between the continents. This uniqueness and diversity deserve appreciation in light of the teaching on the catholicity of the Church, as mentioned above. It challenges the Church to rethink as to how diversity and unity can be thought of both in terms of what the local churches offer to the church universal and how doctrines can be explained, applied and adapted in such a way that they can bear fruit in the soil where they are to grow and blossom.[5] Finally, and most importantly, what had not happened in the local churches or in the territory of e.g an ecclesiastical province or episcopal conference, occurred now in a continent: bishops and other members of the People of God engaged together in listening to what the Holy Spirit is saying to the Churches. The so-called Ecclesial Assembly was born.

The Task of the Continental Ecclesial Assemblies

The Synodal Continental Ecclesial Assemblies were invited to work with DCS *Enlarge the Space of your Tent* (Is. 54:2) 'through which the dialogue of the local churches among themselves and with the universal Church can take place during the Continental Stage. To pursue this process of listening, dialogue and discernment, the reflection [was] to focus on three questions:

- After having read and prayed with the DCS, which *intuitions* resonate most strongly with the lived experiences and realities of the Church in your continent? Which experiences are new, or illuminating to you?
- After having read and prayed with the DCS, what substantial tensions or divergences emerge as particularly important in your continent's perspective? Consequently, what are the *questions or issues* that should be addressed and considered in the next steps of the process?
- Looking at what emerges from the previous two questions, what are the *priorities, recurring themes and calls to action* that can be shared with other local Churches around the world and discussed during the First Session of the Synodal Assembly in October 2023? (DCS nr. 106)

5 The Peter and Paul Seminar, an international research group of Catholic theologians and canon lawyers, which attends to reforms of canon law in light of Vatican II, engaged in the project *Diversity and Unity: Rethinking the Teaching Office of Episcopal Conferences in a Worldwide Church*. Fourteen studies address the topic from different, but complementary perspectives. They are published in *Studia canonica* 53 (2019) 7-332.

Rather remarkable about the Continental Stage was the non-directive attitude of the Secretariat for the Synod, thus, allowing space for the Holy Spirit to speak through the believers. The continental gatherings were only invited to use the Method of Spiritual Conversation and 'pay special attention to the presence of women and young people (laymen and laywomen, consecrated men and women in formation, seminarians); people living in conditions of poverty or marginalisation, and those who have direct contact with these groups and persons; fraternal delegates from other Christian denominations; representatives of other religions and faith traditions; and some people with no religious affiliation' (DCS 108).

It was left to each continental meeting to decide how the listening and discernment process would take place. The centre did not determine how to give shape to the process in the periphery. This is an application of the decentralisation that not only Vatican II urged, but that also Pope Francis called for in his apostolic exhortation *Evangelium Gaudium* (nr. 16).[6] It implies that each continent had to find forms and ways that would enable a fruitful listening and discerning in light of the peculiarity of its own continent. The modality of the meeting was thus completely left to each continental organisation. From this follows that there is a great variety between the different continental meetings.

The Content of the Current Book

It was exactly the newness of the process and the variety between the different continental gatherings that prompted the editors to engage in a project that would capture this unique moment in history in which the People of God spoke not only through synodal continental ecclesial assemblies, but also did so while each one of them differs with regard to its composition, participation, method, mode of drafting etc. Yet, despite the diversity in modality, the seven continental reports reveal a remarkable convergence in their outcomes. In as much as the first round of the consultation in the local churches had revealed a remarkable convergence, the diversity of the synodal ecclesial continental meetings did not lead to a difference in outcome, but rather revealed a unity in how the People of God experience the Church, its mission, its opportunities and its challenges. The editors felt this uniqueness to be worthwhile to document, describe and capture.

Thus besides the seven continental reports,[7] this book presents seven articles that describe and inform the reader how the reports came about. All articles are written by persons who were personally engaged in their respective

6 Francis, Apostolic Exhortation *Evangelii gaudium*, 24 November 2013, in *AAS* 105 (2013), 1019-1137. See also https://www.vatican.va/content/francesco/en/apost_exhortations/documents/papa-francesco_esortazione-ap_20131124_evangelii-gaudium.html

7 The reports of the seven Continental Ecclesial Assemblies were taken from the website of the General Secretariat of the Synod on Synodality. https://www.synod.va/en/synodal-process/the-continental-stage/final_document.html For readability and future referencing a numbering of sections and paragraphs was inserted in those that did not have this.

continental ecclesial meeting. Many of them also participated in the drafting of the Working Document for the Continental Stages in Frascati and / or serve on a commission that serves the General secretariat of the Synod in the current Synod on Synodality. A good number of the authors will participate in the General Assembly of the Synod of Bishops in October 2023 either as a voting member or as a facilitator or expert.

A specific feature of this book is that the authors of the articles on the Continental Assemblies, as well as the editors engaged in writing their contribution, have done so in a synodal style. Not only the editors, but also the authors of the articles accomplished their task by cooperating with another person from a different country, expertise and vocation[8]: a lay woman cooperates with a priest from a religious institute, a sister cooperates with a diocesan priest, a diocesan priest cooperates with a married lay woman, a single lay woman cooperates with a married lay man. The authors are specialists in management or communication, scholars in systematic, fundamental, practical or liturgical theology or canon law. The articles do not describe who said what in the ecclesial assemblies, so that confidentiality is respected, nor do they enter into the content of the document as such. Each team of authors was invited to attend to the following topics, in a synodal way:

1. What is the nature of the episcopal continental structure that organised the meeting: e.g. when was the body first erected and how has it functioned so far? Describe the socio-economic and political situation, number of episcopal conferences involved, different kind and number of eastern churches, languages, religious background (multi faith or mainly Christian / Catholic etc.). What were the special challenges that the continent might meet e.g. wars, elections, natural disasters, visit of the Pope, etc.? In which languages was the DCS available to the participants?
2. Who organised the whole Continental Assembly? Was there a team? How was the continental meeting structured and prepared, e.g. diocesan and episcopal conferences submitted their reports on rereading the DCS? What material was distributed? What formats were chosen, e.g. online seminars, information, flyers, etc.? Were the meetings online, in person or hybrid? How were cultural and language barriers taken into consideration, e.g. were there translators (what languages) and how did this impact the communication? Who participated or was invited to participate in this preparatory process and who did not (compare this to list mentioned in DCS 108)?
3. Who decided who was going to participate in the continental consultation itself? What was the profile of the different participants (cf. DCS 108)? Where were the meetings held, e.g. in monastery, resort, hotel? Describe

8 Only the article on the Assembly in Africa is written by one person.

the programme. How were the meetings conducted? Was the Method of Spiritual Conversation used? How was it explained to the participants and how was it implemented?

4. Was there a spiritual imput by a speaker? Who was this speaker and what was being said, e.g. which biblical image was used? Was this a one-time presentation or a 'theme' throughout the meeting? Was there a commission for liturgy and / or spirituality? What scriptural passages were chosen and why? What kind of liturgies were celebrated? What kind of music and other art was used? How did the scripture readings and the liturgy impact the group? Anecdotes are welcome to let the reader sense how the gatherings were.
5. What method(s) was / were used to listen to each other, e.g. six-minute addresses by each episcopal conference? Were there plenary and / or group sessions? Were there online and in person meetings (simultaneously)? How were the groups mixed? How was reporting of group work organised?
6. Who participated besides Catholics or Christians and in what way? How were these people chosen? Did they have a right to speak or only to listen? How did this unfold? How did they participate in the liturgy?
7. Who was on the drafting team? How were these people chosen and what is their profile? When, how and where was the document written? Did all participants take part in the development of the document? How did the 'representatives' of the People of God 'approve' the document?
8. The bishops are invited to 'collegially reread the lived synodal experience from the perspective of their specific charisma and role. In particular, they are asked to identify appropriate ways to carry out their task of validating and approving the Final Document, ensuring that it is the fruit of an authentically synodal journey, respectful of the process that has taken place and faithful to the diverse voices of the People of God in each continent' (DCS 108). What was the role of the bishops? How did they validate the document? Why did they write a comment to it? Who proposed to have a separate meeting or proposed that this was not necessary? What was of particular relevance?
9. What was the role of the press and media? Were they invited? Was the meeting accessible to all, e.g by live streaming? Did the media people stay in the same accommodation? What did this mean for the interaction with the participants? Where participants free to speak with the press or did they have instructions not to speak?
10. Can you give a general impression of how the document was received in the continent by the People of God as well as the bishops of that continent?

11. Any quotations or outstanding remarks are welcome.

The seven studies describe that each synodal continental ecclesial assembly opened with the ancient Adsumus Prayer which invoked the Holy Spirit and each one used the Method of Spiritual Conversation. A short study on both the prayer and the method precede the continental reports. In order to present the results of the two steps of the listening phase, the decision was made to include in this book the DCS *Enlarge the Space of your Tent* (Is. 54:2) which expresses the findings of the diocesan consultation and which served as the main resource for each Continental Assembly.

Gratitude

We wish to express a special word of gratitude to the authors who generously and enthusiastically accepted the invitation to write their contribution and to do so in a very short time. Without their enthusiasm and commitment to the project we could not have published this book.

Thanks is expressed to Garry O'Sullivan of Columba Books who encouraged us to compose this book, generously assisted us in developing it and accepted to publish it. Without Paula T. Nolan of Pen Graphic Design, who meticulously assisted in the editorial process and provided us with ideas about its layout, this book would not have seen the day of light.

Finally, we wish to express sincere gratitude to Cardinal Oswald Gracias who from the beginning embraced the project, encouraged us in our efforts and generously offered to write a foreword to this book. We are also grateful to Cardinal Christoph Schönborn OP, who likewise supported us to publish this book. Their personal engagement in the Synod on Synodality as members of the Council of Bishops, their participation in part of the so-called Frascati meeting, as well as Cardinal Gracias' participation in the Continental Ecclesial Assembly in Asia, make them unique witnesses to and supporters of the synodal process.

August 2023

Erfurt, Germany — Kandy, Sri Lanka

Myriam Wijlens — *Vimal Tirimanna CSsR*

ADSUMUS, SANCTE SPIRITUS
THE PRAYER OF THE SYNOD

Martin Klöckener

The 2021–2024 Synod entitled *For a Synodal Church: Communion – Participation – Mission* shows time and again that such an ecclesial gathering is not just a place of exchange and discussion, but that it is above all a spiritual event from which the pilgrim church is to gain strength for its mission and its journey in this world towards fulfillment. Elements of worship and prayer are much more therefore than a framework around the gatherings. A look at the history of liturgy shows that to a certain extent synods have been understood as events of worship. Today's 'Ceremonial for Bishops' (1998) also argues along these lines when it says: 'The governance of the Church is never to be looked upon as a mere administrative act; under the influence of the Holy Spirit, its governing assemblies are gathered in the name of God and for God's glory, and they therefore are an expression of the unity of the Mystical Body of Christ, which shines with greatest clarity in the liturgy. It is right that those who bear the responsibility together also share in one prayer together.'[1] Trusting in the work of the Holy Spirit, numerous liturgical celebrations in connection with synods repeatedly encounter prayers and songs in which the Holy Spirit is invoked to assist. Scripture readings proclaimed on such occasions also attend to the mission of the Church prompted by the Holy Spirit.

The Origin of the Prayer of the Synod

Over the course of church history, the prayer *Adsumus, Domine Sancte Spiritus, adsumus* acquired special relevance for the opening of councils and synods. It appeared first in Spain towards the end of the 7th century, but it probably goes back to Isidore of Seville († 636) and was created in connection with the 4th Council of Toledo in 633. It is found, with only slight variations, in many sources for the liturgy of councils throughout the Middle Ages up to the present day. During the Second Vatican Council the prayer was recited at the opening of all general assemblies. The current liturgical order for the celebration of councils, synods and other church assemblies of both universal and particular churches, which can be found in the 'Ceremonial for

1 *Ceremonial of Bishops*. Collegeville: Liturgical Press 1989/1994, p. 321, no. 1169.

Bishops' (1998), recommends this prayer as a fixed element.[2]

Since the *Adsumus, Domine Sancte Spiritus, adsumus,* as it has been handed down, is rather extensive as well as not always easy to follow in its theological train of thought and linguistic duct, the Secretariat for the Synod saw in 2021 to the preparation of a shortened and slightly adapted version for the diocesan and regional assemblies, with the intention that the sessions of the synod within the particular churches would be opened using this prayer. The adapted version was prepared simultaneously in German and French, and numerous other translations were subsequently made. The reports from different particular Churches show that the prayer was and is widely used.

The Text of the Prayer of the Synod

The text of the Prayer is presented below in three major modern languages German, French and English.[3] The Latin text, which can be found on the Synod's website,[4] essentially corresponds to the version that has been handed down since the 7th century and therefore differs on a number of points from the slightly abridged and adapted translations into the modern languages. The jointly prepared German and French versions correspond to each other and also agree in fine nuances of individual formulations. There is only a slight deviation when the German version, following the original Latin text, additionally speaks of the 'gift of discernment'. The English version, on the other hand, remains more general in its pronouncements in some places. These linguistic variations cause deviations in further translations, depending on which modern language the respective translation is based.

2 The *Ceremonial of Bishops*, p. 322 offers a rather free English translation which in numerous places hardly allows for recognising the original Latin. The translation in the German edition of the *Zeremoniale für die Bischöfe in den katholischen Bistümern des deutschen Sprachgebietes*, Solothurn: Benziger 1998, p. 322f., is more faithful to the Latin and linguistically very good. For the history, the current editions in different languages and the theological meaning of the *Adsumus* see Martin Klöckener, *Die Liturgie der Diözesansynode. Studien zur Geschichte und Theologie des 'Ordo ad Synodum' des 'Pontificale Romanum'. Mit einer Darstellung der Geschichte des Pontifikales und einem Verzeichnis seiner Drucke*. Münster: Aschendorff 1986 (Liturgiewissenschaftliche Quellen und Forschungen 68), p. 146–154 and 274–277; Idem, 'Geistgewirkte Versammlung. Spirituelle Kommentierung des Konzilseröffnungsgebetes Adsumus, Domine Sancte Spiritus, adsumus', in: *Weizenkorn* p. 7. Stuttgart: Katholisches Bibelwerk 1986, 118–122; Idem, 'La prière d'ouverture des conciles "Adsumus": de l'Espagne wisigothique à la liturgie romaine d'après Vatican II', in: Achille Maria Triacca – Alessandro Pistoia (eds.), *La prière liturgique. Conférences Saint-Serge, XLVIIe Semaine d'études liturgiques, Paris 27–30 juin 2000*. Roma: Centro Liturgico Vincenziano 2001 (Bibliotheca Ephemerides Liturgicae. Subsidia 115), p. 165–198; Emanuele Borsotti, 'L'*Adsumus*: la sinodalità in preghiera,' in: *Rivista liturgica* 109 (2022) 47–75.

3 For the text see: https://www.synod.va/en/resources/the-adsumus-prayer.html [Access: 26.5.2023].

4 Latin version: https://www.synod.va/content/dam/synod/common/adsumus-new/latin/ADSUMUS-LATINA-MODEL01-PRINT.jpg [Access: 26.5.2023]. This text as it appears on the website contains typographical errors.

Adsumus, Sancte Spiritus

Wir stehen vor dir,
Heiliger Geist,
in deinem Namen sind wir versammelt.

Du, unser wahrer Ratgeber:
komm zu uns,
steh uns bei,
kehre ein in unsere Herzen.

Lehre uns, wohin wir gehen sollen;
zeige uns, wie wir das Ziel erreichen können.

Bewahre uns davor,
als schwache und sündige Menschen
die Orientierung zu verlieren.

Lass nicht zu,
dass Unwissenheit uns auf falsche Wege führt.

Gib uns die Gabe der Unterscheidung,
dass wir unser Handeln nicht von Vorurteilen
und falschen Rücksichten leiten lassen.

Führe uns in dir zur Einheit,

damit wir nicht vom Weg der Wahrheit und der Gerechtigkeit abkommen,
sondern auf unserer Pilgerschaft dem ewigen Leben entgegenstreben.

Das erbitten wir von dir,
der du zu allen Zeiten und an allen Orten wirkst,
in der Gemeinschaft mit dem Vater und dem Sohn
von Ewigkeit zu Ewigkeit.
Amen.

Nous voici devant Toi,
Esprit Saint;
en Ton Nom, nous sommes réunis.

Toi notre seul conseiller,
viens à nous,
demeure avec nous,
daigne habiter nos cœurs.

Enseigne-nous vers quel but nous orienter ;
montre nous comment nous devons marcher ensemble.

Nous qui sommes faibles et pécheurs,
ne permets pas que nous provoquions le désordre.

Fais-en sorte,
que l'ignorance ne nous entraîne pas sur une fausse route,

ni que la partialité influence nos actes.

Que nous trouvions en Toi notre unité,
sans nous éloigner du chemin de la vérité et de la justice,
en avançant ensemble vers la vie éternelle.

Nous te le demandons à Toi,
qui agis en tout temps et en tout lieu,
dans la communion du Père et du Fils,
pour les siècles des siècles.
Amen.

We stand before You,
Holy Spirit,
as we gather together in Your name.

With You alone to guide us,

make Yourself at home in our hearts;

Teach us the way we must go

and how we are to pursue it.

We are weak and sinful;

do not let us promote disorder.

Do not let
ignorance
lead us down the wrong path

nor partiality influence our actions.

Let us find in You our unity

so that we may not stray
from the way of truth and what is right,
but journey together to eternal life

All this we ask of You,
who are at work in every place and time,
in the communion of the Father and the Son,
forever and ever.
Amen.

Short Theological Commentary on the Prayer of the Synod

The *Adsumus* is addressed to the Holy Spirit both in its original version and in the version edited for the Synod. The Roman liturgy knows this only in very rare cases in the prayers said by the celebrant. The ancient Spanish liturgy, on the other hand, in which the prayer finds its origin, made more frequent use of this orientation of prayer. (Hymns and other chants, on the other hand, also reference the Spirit more frequently in the Roman liturgy.) The cause for the Church gathering, which depends on the help of the Spirit in its search for truth and the right paths forward, has led to preserving this prayer address in the Roman tradition. Also noteworthy is furthermore the opening of the prayer with the brief description of the praying person's own situation 'We stand before You', while the invocation of the Holy Spirit as a divine person follows only subsequently. This is an expression on the one hand of the presence of those gathered in synod *('adsumus')*, but on the other hand of their willingness to participate in God's work in the world.

The members of the synod confess that they have gathered under the guidance of the Holy Spirit and in His name. What according to Mt 18:20 is usually said of Christ, in whose name his disciples gather, is here predicated of the Holy Spirit. They ask for His help for the upcoming meetings.

The Spirit is described as the 'true guide' who is to direct those praying in all their doings and take up residence in their hearts, so that in this way they may reach the goal which does not spring from human reasoning alone, but which can ultimately be traced back to the Spirit of God and His inspiration. People appear as instruments of the divine will, without their own responsibility being denied. The probable background to this is biblical statements, above all the event of Pentecost (Acts 2), which reports the descent of the Spirit on the apostles, who are completely permeated by the Spirit, so that they become proclaimers of the Gospel of Jesus Christ. The fact that a synod is not only a gathering, but also a common journey, a process in which there is a growth of knowledge, is also addressed.

Human weakness and the resulting danger of misconduct are specifically emphasised, whereby both behaviour at the synod and inadequate decisions that may not fully correspond to God's will are to be considered. The experience of current synod members, as well as the experience of previous generations who have met at councils and synods, show the limitations and imperfections of all human activity, which carries the danger of losing one's bearings in the face of the complexity of the issues. In the theological tradition from which the prayer originates, self-inflicted ignorance was judged a sin. The text of the prayer makes petition to the Spirit that the synod may also be protected from this. When they pray in this sense, it becomes clear at the same time that imperfection and sin are not the all-determining reality of human existence, but that the Synod participants trust in the grace of God. Prejudices and false considerations also stand in the way of a sincere search. The gift of discernment is an indispensable charism so that divergent views can merge in the service of truth and in the search for God's will, and bring about what is true, good and right. Only in this way can the Synod be a service to the People of God as a whole; only in this way can it contribute fully to the building up of the body of Christ.

At the same time, the Synod is a place where the disciples of Christ experience themselves as the body of Christ, forming a unity. Each member makes its contribution to this, as Paul describes it in his letters (especially 1 Cor 12). The unity of the faithful, for which Jesus himself called upon his Father before his death (Jn 17:9-26), is a great good and should not be endangered by mutually exclusive opinions or even irreconcilable factions at the Synod. The ultimate goal of the earthly pilgrimage of God's people and all its members is eternal life in the unveiled vision of God.

Conclusion

The Synod prayer is based on a long and continuous prayer tradition of the Church and yet it perfectly and very realistically captures the concrete situation in which those find themselves who, in the name of Jesus Christ and under the impulse of the Holy Spirit, gather in the present to responsibly help shape the Church's journey into the future. The more significant the task to be accomplished, the more the Synod members place themselves under the guidance of the Spirit in order to realise the truth and justice willed by God in the best possible way.

Translation: Myriam Wijlens

THE METHOD IS THE MESSAGE: METHOD OF SPIRITUAL CONVERSATION

Christina Kheng

One of the notable observations from the Synod continental assemblies was the effectiveness of the Spiritual Conversation Method in fostering dialogue and discernment. Indeed, since the launch of the Synod in October 2021, it seemed that the Spiritual Conversation, when carried out well, was frequently a profound turning point for participants in groups, fostering a deep listening leading to a synodal conversion from 'I' to 'we'. It is thus fitting here to take a close look at the Spiritual Conversation Method, how it came about, why it was included in the Synod *Vademecum*[1], and how it might foster the Church's on-going growth in synodality.

The Origin of the Spiritual Conversation

The term 'spiritual conversation' is sometimes used in a general sense to refer to conversations about faith, religion, and spirituality. However, in the context of the Synod, it is more often used to refer to a particular method of group dialogue characterised by several rounds (usually three) of active listening, intentional speaking, pausing for silence in between, and discerning the voice of the Holy Spirit in the group. Thus Spiritual Conversation as a particular exercise characterised by this method implies that the group puts itself in the presence of the Holy Spirit with heightened sensitivity and attentiveness. It is, therefore, sometimes also called a 'conversation in the Spirit'.

In the early Church, some elements of the dynamics of Spiritual Conversation can be seen in the deliberations of the first disciples, such as in Luke's account of the Council of Jerusalem (Acts 15:6-21). Faced with the question of whether Gentile converts would need to be circumcised or not, the apostles and elders met to discern together. Luke highlights that in addition to discussing amongst themselves and reflecting on the faith tradition, the assembly also listened attentively to the first-hand experiences of Paul and Barnabas from the field, testifying to 'the signs and wonders God had done' (Acts 15:12). In reporting the outcome they wrote: 'It seemed good to the Holy Spirit and to us...' (Acts 15: 28).

1 Secretary General of the Synod of Bishops, *Vademecum for the Synod on Synodality* (Vatican City: Vatican Press, 2021), Appendix B, para. 8.

Thus it can be seen that their discernment involved listening deeply to a variety of perspectives and attuning to where the Holy Spirit was leading.

In more recent times, different kinds of group deliberations have been systematised by various schools of spirituality. For instance, in their 36th General Congregation in 2016, the Jesuits committed themselves to revitalising the Spiritual Conversation Method of communal discernment, tracing its roots to a key deliberation by their founder Ignatius of Loyola and his first companion.[2] Similar approaches were also gaining traction in the wider Church, such as in the continental and national ecclesial assemblies and councils occurring just before the Synod 2021–2024. In similar vein, at the Synod on Young People in 2018, Pope Francis introduced the practice of a three-minute silent pause in between several speeches because 'discernment needs space and time ... to allow everyone to recognise within their hearts the nuances of what they have heard, and to allow everyone to reflect deeply and seize upon what is most striking.'[3]

All these experiences indicated that the Spiritual Conversation Method would lend itself well to the process for the Synod 2021–2024. When the *Vademecum* was released in September 2021, it could be said that myriad creative videos and other training resources on the Spiritual Conversation produced spontaneously by people all over the world attested to its positive reception and broad-based traction.

The Steps of the Spiritual Conversation

In brief, the method comprises the following steps:

1. *Individual preparation*: Participants are provided with relevant information and some questions for discernment.[4] Each person prepares by reading, reflecting, and praying with the material, in order to get in touch with his or her experiences, viewpoints, and feelings, and to discern what the Holy Spirit might be revealing through these.
2. *Gathering:* In groups of ideally six to seven persons, participants gather at a conducive place and set aside at least an hour to carry out about three rounds of sharing.
3. *First round*: Every person is given equal time (usually three to five minutes) to share the fruits of his or her prayer and reflection. The

2 See Decree 1 in *Documents of General Congregation 36 of the Society of Jesus* (Rome: Society of Jesus, 2017).

3 Pope Francis, *Address at the Opening of the Synod of Bishops on Young People, The Faith and Vocational Discernment* (Vatican City: Vatican Press, 2018).

4 In the case of the Synod on Synodality, two main questions were suggested, dealing with the experiences and calls of walking together, and supplemented by ten topical questions on communion, participation, and mission.

others listen deeply without interrupting, paying attention to not only what is said but also to the feelings and inner movements in the speaker as well as in oneself and the group. Everyone gives the speaker full and undivided attention, setting aside preoccupations with what to say or how to respond. Listeners also refrain from giving advice, making comments, answering questions, or raising new enquiries.

4. *Silent pause*: A silent pause of about two to three minutes follows the first round so that group members can get in touch with what they heard in the first round, how it affected them, and what other significant movements they sensed. These might include deep joy, energy, enthusiasm, hope, gratitude, and inner peace, or anger, despondency, hopelessness, languor, and even tension or confusion.
5. *Second round*: Participants share what came up when they reflected on these points during the silence. As with the first round, everyone listens to each speaker attentively. This is not the time to share additional information that one would have liked to share in the first round but to reflect more deeply on the movements that were sparked by that round. After everyone has had a chance to speak, the group can engage in dialogue to explore particular convergences or tensions that seem to warrant closer attention. This is especially important when there is a decision to be made on the matter at hand.
6. *Silent pause*: Another time of silence follows, as above. Participants can try to sense what the Holy Spirit seems to be revealing to the group. This is usually resonant with what stirs them most deeply, what brings new insight or interior conversion, what invokes authentic commitment, what themes seem to recur frequently, what beckons further attention however subtly, or even new questions that arise.
7. *Third round*: Each one shares what emerged from this silent reflection, and the group notes the key points and interior movements that have come up.

Facilitating and Reporting the Spiritual Conversation

Due to its structured methodology, it is often best to have an assigned facilitator for the Spiritual Conversation. His or her role is to remind everyone of the process for each step, ensure that every group member has an equal time to speak, especially in the first round, hold the spaces for silence, encourage everyone to follow the dynamics of each round, and ensure that the group wraps up the conversation within the allotted time. The facilitator can be someone from within the group, as long as he/she is familiar with the rules and dynamics of the Spiritual Conversation. As a group member, the facilitator also has an equal turn to share the fruits of his or her prayer and reflection on the question at hand.

Usually the group is required to report the main points arising from its Spiritual Conversation. This report is not a mere collation of what was said by everyone nor even a summary of the majority viewpoint. Instead, it is a report of what the group discerns to be the main insights and movements that the Holy Spirit was leading them to become aware of in the conversation. This is usually quite evident by the third round if the group has followed the process faithfully. For this reason, rather than leaving it to just one or two persons, the group needs to take a few minutes after the conversation to note together what emerged in the conversation and to agree on what to report. This exercise is itself part of the communal discernment. Besides those points which gained greater resonance over the three rounds, there could also be some tensions, questions, or minority viewpoints that emerged and remain unresolved. These can also be highlighted if the group feels that they warrant further attention. Additionally, it is also helpful to report not only the conclusions but also the affective experiences of the group. These might include noteworthy moments of consolation or desolation, turning points in the group's energy level, or shifts in the sense of communion. All these affective experiences are integral to discerning the Spirit's movements.

Sometimes the groups are required to present their reports at a plenary assembly. The nature of such presentations can also be akin to a Spiritual Conversation. Representatives from each group are given an equal chance to speak, and everyone listens attentively and contemplatively, noting what is being said, what inner movements are aroused, and how the assembly seems to be responding. It is helpful to observe a brief moment of silence after each group or at least after several groups. If time allows, some people can share their observations or where they feel the Spirit is moving, and others can respond. Through this process, the assembly gradually begins to become aware of the resonant themes, the noteworthy points, significant tensions or questions emerging, and what the Holy Spirit might be revealing. Sometimes there is a Working Group to synthesise the group reports and plenary reactions, and circulate this synthesis back to the groups for further reaction and fine-tuning. Once again the process of Spiritual Conversation can be repeated. If there is a sustained good quality of listening and adequate opportunities for sharing, the whole assembly might eventually find itself in *singularis conspiratio*, which characterises the fruitful unity in diversity of the People of God, walking together in the Spirit.

The Value of the Spiritual Conversation

The basic process described above can be adapted to various contexts and communities. When carried out well, the Spiritual Conversation can be a helpful tool to actualise the communal nature of divine revelation. It enables a community to discern the voice of God's Spirit by contemplating the signs of the times, the concrete experiences of one another, and the developing faith tradition on the topic at hand. Moreover, its methodical structure helps a community to surface and deal with conflicting viewpoints in a fruitful and non-violent way, avoiding impulsive reactions or comments, and polarising debates. The methodical equality in participation also helps to counter power imbalances that might be present in a group. As mentioned above, sometimes tensions and questions are not resolved by the third round. This can underscore the pilgrim nature of communities, beckoning greater humility, patience, trust, and mutual commitment to walk further along together.

Spiritual Conversation works well when participants enter it with radical openness to the Holy Spirit, surrendering their attachments to certain preferred outcomes if any, and embracing a willingness to listen to and learn from others. Such interior freedom is itself a fruit of divine grace. Attentive listening is based upon a theological worldview which acknowledges God's Spirit present in all creation. In the Church, attentive listening has an added imperative from the principle of the *sensus fidei* of the baptised. For this reason, everyone's voice deserves an equal chance to be heard and to be assured of a welcoming, engaged, and respectful reception. In turn, those who speak must do so thoughtfully, honestly, and responsibly from a genuine basis of prayer and reflection. Spiritual Conversation highlights that discernment involves not just a rationalist stance but is something that engages the whole human person including the intellectual, social, affective, and spiritual dimensions.

Effectiveness in the Spiritual Conversation grows with practice over time. What is important is not so much an increase in the group's technical proficiency in the method but rather, its gradual growth in synodality through the underlying attitudes of communion, unconditional hospitality, inclusiveness, attentive listening, and thoughtful sharing. All these are engendered by the methodology of Spiritual Conversation. Not surprisingly, many people who have had a good experience in the Synod consultation said that they learned synodality by 'doing' synodality. Indeed, the method is the message!

SECRETARIA GENERALIS SYNODI

'ENLARGE THE SPACE OF YOUR TENT'

(*Is. 54:2*)

WORKING DOCUMENT FOR THE CONTINENTAL STAGE

Synod 2021 2024

Vatican City, 24 October 2022

Introduction

1. The Experience of the Synodal Journey
1.1 'The fruits, seeds and weeds of synodality'
1.2 Our common baptismal dignity

2. Listening to the Scriptures

3. Towards a Missionary Synodal Church
3.1 Listening that becomes welcoming
3.2 Sisters and brothers for mission
3.3 Communion, participation and co-responsibility
3.4 Synodality takes shape
3.5 Synodal life and liturgy

4. The Next Steps
4.1 A journey of conversion and reform
4.2 Methodology for the Continental Stage

INTRODUCTION

1. The Synod is on: one year after the opening of the synodal journey, we can enthusiastically affirm this! During this first part of the consultative phase, millions of people all over the world have been involved in the Synod's activities: some by participating in the meetings at the local level, some by collaborating in the animation and coordination of the activities at the different levels, and some by offering the support of their prayers: *'We also express our gratitude to the contemplative nuns who accompanied their people in prayer and continue to pray for the fruits of the Synod on Synodality'* (EC Peru). All of these people who got involved are the real protagonists of the Synod!

2. Participants were set in motion and urged on by a desire to respond to the basic question guiding the entire process: 'How does this "journeying together", which takes place today on different levels (from the local level to the universal one), allow the Church to proclaim the Gospel in accordance with the mission entrusted to Her; and what steps does the Spirit invite us to take in order to grow as a synodal Church?' (Preparatory Document, no.2).

3. Along the way participants experienced the joy of meeting as brothers and sisters in Christ, sharing what resonated within them from listening to the Word, and reflecting together on the future of the Church based on the impetus of the Preparatory Document (PD). This has nourished the desire for an increasingly synodal Church: synodality has ceased to be an abstract concept for them and has become a concrete experience; they have tasted its flavour and want to continue to do so. *'Through this process we have discovered that synodality is a way of being Church – in fact, it is* the *way of being Church'. 'The Holy Spirit is asking us to be more synodal'* (EC England and Wales).

4. Participants' experience has been translated into words, in the contributions that the different communities and groups have sent to the Dioceses. These submissions were synthesised and transmitted to the episcopal conferences, and in turn, from the outline contained in the PD, the episcopal conferences drafted a report that was sent to the General Secretariat of the Synod.

5. Globally, participation exceeded all expectations. In all, the Synod Secretariat received contributions from 112 out of 114 episcopal conferences and from all the 15 Oriental Catholic Churches, plus reflections from 17 out of 23 dicasteries of the Roman Curia, besides those from religious superiors (USG/UISG), from institutes of consecrated life and societies of apostolic life, and from associations and lay

movements of the faithful. In addition, over a thousand contributions arrived from individuals and groups, as well as insights gathered through social media thanks to the initiative of the 'Digital Synod'. These materials were distributed to a group of experts: bishops, priests, consecrated men and women, lay men and lay women, from all continents and with very diverse disciplinary expertise. After reading the reports, these experts met for almost two weeks together with the writing group, composed of the General Relator, the Secretary General of the Synod, the Undersecretaries and various officials of the Synod Secretariat, plus members of the Coordinating Committee. This group was finally joined by the members of the General Council. Together they worked in an atmosphere of prayer and discernment to share the fruits of their reading in preparation for the drafting of this Document for the Continental Stage (DCS).

6. The quotations that punctuate the DCS try to give an idea of the richness of the materials received, letting the voices of the People of God from all parts of the world speak as much as possible on their own terms and find resonance. They are not to be interpreted as endorsing the positions of any particular area of the globe, nor as simply representing geographical variety, although care has been taken to ensure a certain balance in terms of source provenance. Rather, these quotes were chosen because they express in a particularly powerful, beautiful or precise way sentiments expressed more generally in many reports. However, it is clear that no single document could condense the depth of faith, vitality of hope and energy of charity that overflows from the contributions received. Behind them one glimpses the power and richness of the experience that the different Churches have had by setting out and opening themselves to the diversity of voices that have taken the floor. Enabling this encounter and dialogue is the meaning of the synodal journey, whose ultimate purpose is not to produce documents but to open horizons of hope for the fulfilment of the Church's mission.

7. It is within this journey, which is far from reaching its conclusion, that this DCS is situated and finds its meaning. In view of the Continental Stage of the synodal journey, the Document organises around a small number of nuclei the hopes and concerns of the People of God from across the globe. In this way, it provides an opportunity for the local Churches to listen to each other's voices in view of the Continental Assemblies in 2023. Their task will be to draw up a list of priorities, upon which the First Session of the XVI Ordinary General Assembly of the Synod of Bishops, which will be held from 4 to 29 October 2023, will carry out their discernment.

8. Clarifying the DCS's function also allows us to focus on what it is not: it is not a conclusive document, because the process is far from being finished;

it is not a document of the Church's Magisterium, nor is it the report of a sociological survey; it does not offer the formulation of operational indications, goals and objectives, nor a full elaboration of a theological vision. Nonetheless it is theological in the sense that it is loaded with the exquisitely theological treasure contained in the experience of listening to the voice of the Spirit enacted by the People of God, allowing its *sensus fidei* to emerge. But it is also a theological document in the sense that it is orientated to the service of the Church's mission: to proclaim Christ who died and rose again for the salvation of the world.

9. To avoid misunderstandings in its reading, it is essential to keep in mind the particular nature of the DCS, as well as its structure. The Document opens with a chapter that offers more than a simple account of 'what happened', presenting a narrative of the synodality experienced so far, with the consultation of the People of God in the local Churches and the discernment of the Pastors in the episcopal conferences: it profiles the synodal experience, presents the difficulties encountered and the most significant fruits gathered, identifying the cornerstones of what constitutes an authentic collective experience of the Christian faith. In this way it does not provide a definition of synodality in the strict sense – for this you can refer to the PD or the materials listed on the Synod website (www.synod.va) – but expresses the shared sense of the experience of synodality lived by those who took part. What emerges is a profound re-appropriation of the common dignity of all the baptised. This is the authentic pillar of a synodal Church and the theological foundation of a unity which is capable of resisting the push toward homogenisation. This enables us to continue to promote and make good use of the variety of charisms that the Spirit with unpredictable abundance pours out on the faithful.

10. The second chapter presents a biblical icon, the image of the tent with which chapter 54 of the book of Isaiah opens. This image and narrative represents a key to an interpretation of the contents within the DCS in the light of the Word, placing them in the arc of God's promise that becomes a vocation for his People and his Church: *'Enlarge the space of your tent!'*

11. This tent is a space of *communion*, a place of *participation*, and a foundation for *mission*. In turn, the third chapter articulates the key words of the synodal journey connecting them with the fruits of listening to the People of God. It does so by gathering them around five generative tensions that are intertwined with one another:

1. listening as openness to welcome: this starts from a desire for radical inclusion – no one is excluded – to be understood in a perspective of

communion with sisters and brothers and with our common Father; listening appears here not as an instrumental action, but as the assumption of the basic attitude of a God who listens to his People, as the following of a Lord whom the Gospels constantly present to us in the act of listening to the people who come to him along the roads of the Holy Land; in this sense listening is already mission and proclamation;

2. our outgoing drive toward mission. This is a mission that Catholics recognise as needing to be carried out with brothers and sisters of other confessions and in dialogue with believers of other religions, transforming human actions of care into authentically spiritual experiences that proclaim the face of a God who cares to the point of giving his own life so that we may have it in abundance;
3. carrying out the mission requires assuming a style based on participation, this corresponds to the full assumption of co-responsibility of all the baptised for the one mission of the Church arising from the common baptismal dignity;
4. the construction of concrete possibilities for living communion, participation and mission through structures and institutions inhabited by people properly formed and sustained by a living spirituality;
5. the liturgy, especially the Eucharistic liturgy, the source and summit of Christian life, which brings the community together, making communion tangible, enables the exercise of participation, and nourishes the momentum toward mission with the Word and the Sacraments.

12. Finally, the fourth chapter offers a glimpse toward the future by appealing to two levels both of which are indispensable for proceeding along the path: the spiritual level that seeks to orientate us towards a horizon of missionary synodal conversion, and the methodological one that traces our next steps for the Continental Stage.

13. The DCS will be understandable and useful only if it is read with the eyes of the disciple, who recognises it as a testimony to the path of conversion toward a synodal Church. This means a Church that learns from listening how to renew its evangelising mission in the light of the signs of the times, to continue offering humanity a way of being and living in which all can feel included as protagonists. Along this path, the lamp to our steps is the Word of God, which offers the light with which to reread, interpret and express the experience that has been lived.

14. Together we pray:

Lord, you have gathered all your People in Synod.

We give you thanks for the joy
experienced by those who decided to set out
to listen to God and to their brothers and sisters during this year,
with an attitude of welcome, humility, hospitality and siblinghood.

Help us to enter these pages as on 'holy ground'.

Come Holy Spirit: may you be the guide of our journey together!

I
THE EXPERIENCE OF THE SYNODAL JOURNEY

15. The reports sent by Churches across the world give voice to the joys, hopes, sufferings and wounds of Christ's disciples. In their words we hear resonate what lies at the heart of all humanity. They express the desire for a Church that walks with Christ under the guidance of the Spirit to fulfil its mission of evangelisation. *'Our current 'synod' experience has awakened in the lay faithful the idea of, and a desire to, get involved in the life of the Church, in its engagement with the world today, and in its pastoral work on the ground'* (EC Canada).

1.1 'The Fruits, Seeds, and Weeds of Synodality'

16. The first part of the synodal journey has produced abundant fruit, new seeds that promise new growth, and above all, an experience of joy in challenging times: *'Largely, what emerges from the fruits, seeds and weeds of synodality are voices that have great love for the Church, voices that dream of a Church of credible witnesses, a Church that is inclusive, open and welcoming Family of God'* (EC Zimbabwe). Haiti speaks for many: *'Despite the continuous cases of kidnapping and violence recorded, the reports of the Dioceses express the joy of those who were able to actively participate in this first phase of the Synod'* (EC Haiti). This is a joy that many have asked be extended and shared with others. The Diocese of Ebibeyín (Equatorial Guinea) echoes this: *'this synodal experience has been one of the most rewarding that many have been able to experience in their Christian lives. From the first moment the work of the Synod began to the point where we are now, there is great enthusiasm among the People of God.'* Among the fruits of the synod experience, several summaries highlight the strengthened feeling of belonging to the Church and the realisation on a practical level that the Church is not just priests and bishops: *'While sharing the* *fundamental question: 'How is this journeying together happening today in your particular Church?' it was noted that people could realise the true nature of the Church and in that light, they were able to see the situation of their Particular Church'* (EC Bangladesh).

17. Widespread appreciation was given to the Spiritual Conversation Method which allowed many to look honestly at the reality of Church life and name the lights and shadows. This honest appraisal bore immediate missionary fruits. *'There is a strong mobilisation of the People of God, the joy of coming together, of walking together and of speaking freely. Some Christians who felt hurt and who had distanced themselves from the Church came back during this consultation phase'* (EC Central African Republic). Many emphasised that this was the first time the Church had asked for their opinion, and they wish to continue this journey: *'Meetings in the spirit of the synodal method, in which all members of the congregation or community can openly and honestly express their opinion, as well as meetings with various groups outside the Church, should continue. This kind of cooperation should become one of the 'unwritten laws' of the Church culture, so as to foster rapprochement between Church members and groups in society, thus creating a readiness of people for deeper dialogue'* (EC Latvia).

18. However, there has been no shortage of challenges, which the reports do not hide. Some are related to the coincidence of the consultative phase with the pandemic; others stem from the difficulty of understanding what synodality means, the need for a greater effort to translate and enculturate the materials, the failure to organise synodal gatherings in some local contexts, or resistance to the basic proposal. There is no shortage of very clear expressions of rejection: *'I distrust the Synod. I think it has been called to bring about further change to Christ's teachings and wound his Church further'* (individual submission from the UK). Quite frequently, the fear has been expressed that the emphasis on synodality could push the Church toward adopting mechanisms and procedures that depend on a democratic-type majority principle. Among the difficulties a scepticism about the real efficacy or intent of the synodal process should be noted: *'Some expressed doubts about the outcome of the synodal process due to their perception of the Church as a rigid institution unwilling to change and modernise itself, or due to a suspicion that the synodal outcome had been predetermined'* (EC Canada).

19. Numerous reports mention the fears and resistance on the part of the clergy, but also the passivity of the laity, their fear of expressing themselves freely, and the struggle to understand and articulate the priests' and bishops' role within the synodal dynamic: '*In this process there was also resistance, lack of participation, communities that did not join. This may have been partly due to the novelty of the challenge, since many communities are not accustomed to this way of living the Church. It was also due to the fact that some leaders and pastors did not assume the animating and guiding role that corresponded to them. Several diocesan reports complain about the lack or weak involvement of priests*' (EC Chile). In many cases, the synodal process and materials reveal that there is a widespread perception of a separation between priests and the rest of the People of God: '*Consultations in dioceses and at national level have shown that the relationship between priests and the faithful is difficult in many places. On the one hand, there is criticism of a perceived distance between clergy and laity; in some places priests are even experienced as an obstacle to a fruitful community. At the same time, the challenges for priests are named: the shortage of priests and also the increasing loss of volunteers lead to exhaustion; also, priests do not always feel heard, some see their ministry questioned. What makes a good priest? How can parish life be an enriching experience for everyone involved? Why do fewer and fewer men feel a vocation? These questions need to be discussed*' (EC Austria).

20. An obstacle of particular relevance on the path of walking together is the scandal of abuse by members of the clergy or by people holding ecclesial office: first and foremost, abuse of minors and vulnerable persons, but also abuse of other kinds (spiritual, sexual, economic, of authority, of conscience). This is an open wound that continues to inflict pain on victims and survivors, on their families, and on their communities: '*There was ongoing reference to the impact of the clergy sexual abuse crisis and the Church's response [...]. For many, the aftermath of this is still a powerful, unresolved issue. There was a strong urgency to acknowledge the horror and damage, and to strengthen efforts to safeguard the vulnerable, repair damage to the moral authority of the Church and rebuild trust. Some Dioceses reported that participants wished for them publicly to acknowledge and atone for past abuses*' (EC Australia). Careful and painful reflection on the legacy of abuse has led many synod groups to call for a cultural change in the Church with a view to greater transparency, accountability and co-responsibility.

21. Furthermore, in too many countries the synodal way has crossed paths with the wars that stain our world with blood, 'giving free reign to fanaticism of all kinds and to persecutions, even massacres. Sectarian and ethnic incitements were noted, which degenerated into armed and political conflicts, often bloody' (Maronite Church). Particularly painful are those situations in which Christians, including Catholics, live in countries at war with each other. Even in these fragile situations which intensify an encounter with the Cross and Resurrection, Christian communities have been able to take up the invitation addressed to them to build experiences of synodality, to reflect on what it means to walk together, and express a desire to continue to do so: '*Concerning the tragedy of the genocide against the Tutsi that has so divided the Rwandan people, one should better deepen the theme of communion with a view to an authentic healing of the collective memory. This Synod has given us a better understanding that the pastoral of unity and reconciliation must continue to be a priority*' (EC Rwanda).

1.2. Our Common Baptismal Dignity

22. Practices of lived synodality have constituted '*a pivotal and precious moment to realise how we all share a common dignity and vocation through our Baptism to participants in the life of the Church*' (EC Ethiopia). This foundational reference to baptism – not as an abstract concept but as a felt identity – immediately brings into focus the link between the synodal form of the Church and the possibility of fulfilling its mission: 'there was a growing understanding that it is important for all who have received the blessing of baptism to walk together, sharing and discerning the guidance of the Holy Spirit who calls them. There was a deep realisation that in the synodal Church walking together is the way to become a missionary Church' (EC Japan). Many local Churches within contexts that see the presence of numerous Christian denominations place particular stress on the baptismal dignity of all Christian sisters and brothers, and the common mission in service of the Gospel. A synodal process is incomplete without meeting brothers and sisters from other confessions, sharing and dialogue with them, and engaging in common actions. The reports express a desire for deeper ecumenical encounter, and the need for formation to support this work.

23. The reports present the synod process as an experience of novelty and freshness: '*People of God remarked on the uniqueness of speaking freely and being heard in organised conversations that were open-ended and attentive with guidance of the Holy Spirit. They spoke of how, after decades of church going, they had been asked to speak for first time*' (EC Pakistan). Another image refers to an experience of liberation and new life: the eggshell shattering as new life unfurls its wings.

24. Elsewhere, expressions emerge that evoke rather the idea of distance between family members and a desired return, the end of a collective alienation from one's identity as a synodal Church. To use a biblical image, one could say that the synodal journey marked the first steps of the return from an experience of collective exile, the consequences of which affect the entire People of God: if the Church is not synodal, no one can really feel fully at home.

II
LISTENING TO THE SCRIPTURES

25. It is to a people living the experience of exile that the prophet addresses words that help us today to focus on what the Lord is calling us to through the experience of lived synodality: '*Enlarge the space of your tent, spread out your tent cloths unsparingly, lengthen your ropes and make firm your pegs*' (Is. 54:2).

26. To the people in exile the prophet's words evokes the experience of the exodus, when they dwelt in tents, and announces the promise of the return to the land, a sign of joy and hope. To prepare, it is necessary to enlarge the tent, acting on the three elements of its structure. The first is the tent cloth, which protect from the sun, wind and rain, delineating a space of life and conviviality. They need to be spread out, so that they can also protect those who are still outside this space, but who feel called to enter it. The ropes that hold the cloths together are the second structural element of the tent. They must balance the tension needed to keep the tent from drooping with the softness that cushions movement caused by the wind. That is why if the tent expands, the ropes must be stretched to maintain the right tension. Finally, the pegs are the third element: they anchor the structure to the ground and ensure its solidity but remain capable of moving when the tent must be pitched elsewhere.

27. Listened to today, these words of Isaiah invite us to imagine the Church similarly as a tent, indeed as the tent of meeting, which accompanied the people on their journey through the desert: called to stretch out, therefore, but also to move. At its centre, stands the tabernacle, that is, the presence of the Lord. The tent's hold is ensured by the sturdiness of its pegs, that is, the fundamentals of faith that do not change but can be moved and planted in ever new ground, so that the tent can accompany the people as they walk through history. Finally, in order not to sag, the structure of the tent must keep in balance the different forces and tensions to which it is subjected: a metaphor that expresses the need for discernment. This is how many reports envision the Church: an expansive, but not homogeneous dwelling, capable of sheltering all, but open, letting in and out (cf. Jn. 10:9), and moving toward embracing the Father and all of humanity.

28. Enlarging the tent requires welcoming others into it, making room for their diversity. It thus entails a willingness to die to self out of love, finding oneself again in and through relationship with Christ and one's neighbor: '*Amen, amen,*

I say to you, unless a grain of wheat falls to the ground and dies, it remains just a grain of wheat; but if it dies, it produces much fruit' (Jn. 12:24). The fruitfulness of the Church depends on accepting this death, which is not, however, an annihilation, but an experience of emptying oneself in order to be filled by Christ through the Holy Spirit, and thus a process by which we receive richer relationships, deeper ties to God and each other. This is the place of grace, and of transfiguration. For this reason, the apostle Paul recommends, *'Have among yourselves the same attitude that is also yours in Christ Jesus, Who, though he was in the form of God, did not regard equality with God something to be grasped. Rather, he emptied himself, taking the form of a slave, coming in human likeness'* (Phil. 2:5-7). It is under this condition that the members of the Church, each and all together, will be able to cooperate with the Holy Spirit in fulfilling the mission assigned by Jesus Christ to his Church: it is a liturgical, Eucharistic act.

III
TOWARDS A MISSIONARY SYNODAL CHURCH

29. The biblical imagery of the tent relates to other images that appear in numerous reports: that of the family and that of home, the place to which people wish to belong, and to which they wish to return. *'The Church-home does not have doors that close, but a perimeter that continually widens'* (EC Italy). The dynamic of home and exile, of belonging and exclusion, is felt as a tension in the reports. One noted *'Those who feel at home in the Church feel the absence of those who don't'* (EC Ireland). Through these voices, we hear the dream of *'a global and synodal Church that lives unity in diversity. God is preparing something new, and we must collaborate'* (USG/UISG).

30. The submissions are encouraging because they avoid two of the main spiritual temptations facing the Church in responding to diversity and the tensions it generates. The first is to remain trapped in conflict, such that our horizons shrink and we lose our sense of the whole, and fracture into sub-identities. It is an experience of Babel and not Pentecost, well recognisable in many features of our world. The second is to become spiritually detached and disinterested in the tensions involved, continuing to go our own way without involving ourselves with those close to us on the journey. Instead, *'the call is to live better the tension of truth and mercy, as Jesus did [...]. The dream is of a Church that more fully lives a Christological paradox: boldly proclaiming its authentic teaching while at the same time offering a witness of radical inclusion and acceptance through its pastoral and discerning accompaniment'* (EC England and Wales).

31. The vision of a Church capable of radical inclusion, shared belonging, and deep hospitality according to the teachings of Jesus is at the heart of the synodal process: *'Instead of behaving like gatekeepers trying to exclude others from the table, we need to do more to make sure that people know that everyone can find a place and a home here'* (remark by a parish group from the USA). We are called to go to every place, especially outside the more familiar territories, *'leaving the comfortable position of those who give hospitality to allow ourselves to be welcomed into the existence of those who are our companions on the journey of humanity'* (EC Germany).

3.1 Listening that Becomes Welcoming

32. In this journey, the Churches have realised that the path to greater inclusion – the enlarged tent – is a gradual one. It begins with listening and requires a broader and deeper conversion of attitudes and structures, as well as new approaches to pastoral accompaniment; it begins in a readiness to recognise that the peripheries can be the place where a call to conversion resounds along with the call to put the Gospel more decisively into practice. Listening requires that we recognise others as subjects of their own journey. When we do this, others feel welcomed, not judged, free to share their own spiritual journey. This has been experienced in many contexts, and for some this has been the most transformative aspect of the whole process. The synodal experience can be read as a path of recognition for those who do not feel sufficiently recognised in the Church. This is especially true for those lay men and women, deacons, consecrated men and women who previously had the feeling that the institutional Church was not interested in their faith experience or their opinions.

33. The reports also reflect on the difficulty of listening deeply and accepting being transformed by it. They highlight the lack of communal processes of listening and discernment, and call for more training in this area. Furthermore, they point to the persistence of structural obstacles, including: hierarchical structures that foster autocratic tendencies; a clerical and individualistic culture that isolates individuals and fragments relationships between priests and laity; sociocultural and economic disparities that benefit the wealthy and educated; and the absence of 'in-between' spaces that foster encounters between members of mutually separated groups. Poland's report states *'Not listening leads to misunderstanding, exclusion, and marginalisation. As a further consequence, it creates closure, simplification, lack of trust and fears that destroys the community. When priests do not want to listen, making excuses, such as in the large number of activities, or when questions go unanswered, a sense of sadness and estrangement arises in the hearts of the lay faithful.*

Without listening, answers to the faithfuls' difficulties are taken out of context and do not address the essence of the problems they are experiencing, becoming empty moralism. The laity feel that the flight from sincere listening stems from the fear of having to engage pastorally. A similar feeling grows when bishops do not have time to speak and listen to the faithful.'

34. At the same time, the reports are sensitive to the loneliness and isolation of many members of the clergy, who do not feel listened to, supported and appreciated: perhaps one of the least evident voices in the reports is that of priests and bishops, speaking for themselves and of their experience of walking together. A particularly attentive listening must be offered to enable ordained ministers to negotiate the many dimensions of their emotional and sexual life. The need to ensure appropriate forms of welcome and protection for the women and eventual children of priests who have broken the vow of celibacy, who are otherwise at risk of suffering serious injustice and discrimination, is also noted.

An Option for Young People, People with Disabilities and the Defence of Life

35. There is universal concern regarding the meagre presence of the voice of young people in the synod process, as well as increasingly in the life of the Church. A renewed focus on young people, their formation and accompaniment, is an urgent need, including as a way to implement the conclusions of the previous Synod on 'Young People, the Faith and Vocational Discernment' (2018). On that occasion, it was precisely young people who brought out the need for a more synodal Church in view of the transmission of the faith today. The 'Digital Synod' initiative is a significant attempt to listen to young people and offers new insights for the proclamation of the Gospel. Antilles' report states, *'Since our young people experience a high degree of alienation, we need to make a preferential option for the young.'*

36. Numerous reports point to the lack of appropriate structures and ways of accompanying persons with disabilities, and call for new ways of welcoming their contribution and promoting their participation: in spite of its own teachings, the Church is in danger of imitating the way society casts them aside. *'The forms of discrimination listed – the lack of listening, the violation of the right to choose where and with whom to live, the denial of the sacraments, the accusation of witchcraft, abuse – and others, describe the culture of rejection towards persons with disabilities. They do not arise by chance, but have in common the same root: the idea that the lives of persons with disabilities are worth less than others'* (Report of the special synodal consultation of persons with disabilities by the Dicastery for Laity, Family and Life).

37. Equally prominent is the commitment of the People of God to the defence of fragile and threatened life at all its stages. For example, for the Ukrainian Greek Catholic Church, it is part of synodality to *'study the phenomenon of female migration and offer support to women of different age groups; to pay special attention to women who decide to have an abortion due to fear of material poverty and rejection by their families in Ukraine; to carry out educational work among women who are called upon to make a responsible choice when going through a difficult time in their lives, with the aim of preserving and protecting the lives of unborn children and preventing abortion; to care for women with post-abortion syndrome.'*

Listening to Those who Feel Neglected and Excluded

38. The reports clearly show that many communities have already understood synodality as an invitation to listen to those who feel exiled from the Church. The groups who feel a sense of exile are diverse, beginning with many women and young people who do not feel their gifts and abilities are recognised. Within these groups, that among themselves are highly heterogeneous, many feel denigrated, neglected, misunderstood. Longing for a home also characterises those who, following the liturgical developments of the Second Vatican Council, do not feel at ease. For many, the experience of being seriously listened to is transformative and a first step towards feeling included. On the other hand, it was a source of sadness that some felt that their participation in the synod process was unwelcome: this is a feeling that requires understanding and dialogue.

39. Among those who ask for a more meaningful dialogue and a more welcoming space we also find those who, for various reasons, feel a tension between belonging to the Church and their own loving relationships, such as: remarried divorcees, single parents, people living in a polygamous marriage, LGBTQI+ people, etc. Reports show how this demand for welcome challenges many local Churches: *'People ask that the Church be a refuge for the wounded and broken, not an institution for the perfect. They want the Church to meet people wherever they are, to walk with them rather than judge them, and to build real relationships through caring and authenticity, not a purpose of superiority'* (EC USA). They also reveal uncertainties about how to respond and express the need for discernment on the part of the universal Church: *'There is a new phenomenon in the Church that is absolutely new in Lesotho: same-sex relationships. [...] This novelty is disturbing for Catholics and for those who consider it a sin. Surprisingly, there are Catholics in Lesotho who have started practising this behaviour and expect the Church to accept them and their way of behaving. [...] This is a problematic challenge for the Church because these people feel excluded'* (EC Lesotho). Those who left ordained ministry and married, too, ask for a more welcoming Church, with greater willingness to dialogue.

40. Despite the cultural differences, there are remarkable similarities between the various continents regarding those who are perceived as excluded, in society and also in the Christian community. In many cases their voice has been absent from the synod process, and they appear in reports only because others speak about them, lamenting their exclusion: *'As the Bolivian Church, we are saddened that we have not been able to effectively reach out to the poor on the peripheries and in the most remote places'* (EC Bolivia). Among the most frequently mentioned excluded groups are: the poorest, the lonely elderly, indigenous peoples, migrants without any affiliation and who lead a precarious existence, street children, alcoholics and drug addicts, those who have fallen into the plots of criminality and those for whom prostitution seems their only chance of survival, victims of trafficking, survivors of abuse (in the Church and beyond), prisoners, groups who suffer discrimination and violence because of race, ethnicity, gender, culture and sexuality. In the reports, all of them appear as people with faces and names, calling for solidarity, dialogue, accompaniment and welcome.

3.2 Sisters and Brothers for Mission

41. The Church is the bearer of a proclamation of fullness of life: *'I came so that they might have life and have it more abundantly'* (Jn10:10). The Gospels present the fullness of life and the fullness of the Kingdom of God not as separate realities or spheres of action, but always as dynamically intertwined movements. The Church's mission is to make Christ present in the midst of His People through reading the Word, the celebration of the Sacraments and through all actions that care for the wounded and suffering. *'It is necessary for all of us in the Church to enter into a process of conversion in order to respond to this need, which would imply proposing the kerygma as the fundamental proclamation and listening to Christ crucified and risen for us. [...] Hence the importance of returning to the essence of Christian life and of our first love, and returning to our roots as the first communities; that is to say, where all things were held in common'* (EC Costa Rica).

42. Fulfilling our mission, we grow to the measure of our Christian vocation. 'Enlarging our tent' is at the heart of this missionary activity. Therefore, a Church that practises synodality offers a potent Gospel witness to the world: *'The Holy Spirit is pushing for the renewal of our strategies, commitments, dedication and motivation so that we can walk together and reach those who are farhest away: by spreading the Word of God with enthusiasm and joy, by putting our talents, gifts and skill to use, by accepting the new challenges* *and by producing cultural changes in the light of the Gospel and the life of the Church'* (EC Venezuela). Contained in the reports is the dream of such a Church: one deeply involved with the world's challenges, and capable of responding to these through concrete transformations. *'The world needs a "Church that goes forth", that rejects the division between believers and non-believers, that looks at humanity and offers it more than a doctrine or a strategy, an experience of salvation, a "coup of gift" that responds to the cry of humanity and nature'* (EC Portugal).

The Church's Mission in Today's World

43. Synodality is a call from God to walk together with the whole human family. In many places, Christians live in the midst of people of other faiths or non-believers and are engaged in a dialogue formed in the exchanges of everyday life and common living. *'A social climate of dialogue is cultivated with those who practice traditional African religion, too, and with every other person or community, whatever religious denomination they belong to'* (EC Senegal, Mauritania, Cape Verde and Guinea Bissau). However, the reports indicate that there is still a long way to go in terms of social, cultural, spiritual and intellectual exchange and collaboration.

44. The wounds of the Church are intimately connected to those of the world. The reports speak of the challenges of tribalism, sectarianism, racism, poverty, and gender inequality within the life of the Church, as well as the world. Uganda echoes many other countries in noting that in the structures of the Church *'the rich and the educated are listened to more than others'*. The Philippines report notes that *'many of the underprivileged and those who were marginalised in society felt that they are also left out in the Church'*. Other reports note the influence that ethnic discrimination and a culture based on tribalism has on the life of ecclesial communities. These realities form not just the background context of our mission but also define its focus and purpose: the message of the Gospel that the Church is charged to proclaim must also convert the structures of sin that hold humanity and creation captive.

45. The People of God express a deep desire to hear the cry of the poor and that of the earth. In particular, the reports invite us to recognise the interconnectedness of social and environmental challenges and to respond to them by collaborating and forming alliances with other Christian confessions, believers of other religions and all people of good will. This call for renewed ecumenism and interfaith engagement is particularly strong in regions marked by greater vulnerability to socio-environmental damage and more pronounced inequalities. For example, many African and Pacific Rim reports call on Churches around the world to recognise that addressing socio-environmental challenges is no longer optional: *'It is our desire to protect this part of God's creation, as the wellbeing of our people depends on the ocean in so many ways. In some of our countries the major threat is the ocean as changes in climate have drastic outcomes for the actual survival of these countries'* (EC Pacific).

46. Some reports also noted the importance of the role of the Church in the public sphere, particularly in relation to processes of peace-building and reconciliation. In heavily divided societies this is often seen as a crucial part of mission. Other reports called for the Church to be more confident in contributing to debate and action for justice in the public sphere. The desire was for greater formation in the Church's social teaching. *'[O]ur Church is not called to confrontation, but to dialogue and cooperation on all levels [...].Our dialogue cannot be an apologetic dialogue with useless arguments, but a dialogue of life and solidarity'* (Catholic Armenian Church).

47. A further theme common to many reports is the weakness of deep ecumenical engagement and the desire to learn how to breathe new life into the ecumenical journey, starting with concrete, daily collaboration on common concerns for social and environmental justice. A more united witness among Christians and between faith communities is expressed as an ardent desire.

Walking Together with All Christians

48. The call to ecumenism is not, however, merely aimed at common social engagement. Many reports emphasise that there is no complete synodality without unity among Christians. This begins with the call for closer communion between Churches of different rites. Since the Second Vatican Council, ecumenical dialogue has made progress: *'In the real life of the Central African Republic, 'living together' between Christians of different confessions is self-evident. Our neighbourhoods, our families, our mortuary places, our workplaces are real places of ecumenism'* (EC Republic of Central Africa). However, many ecumenical issues related to synodal structures and ministries in the Church are still not well-articulated. The reports also note that there is an 'ecumenism of martydom' where persecution continues to unite Christians. The reports request greater attention to divisive realities, for example the question of sharing the Eucharist.

49. The reports also point to the sensitive phenomenon of the growth in the number of inter-church and interfaith families, with their specific needs in terms of accompaniment. Revitalising the commitment to dialogue and accompaniment as a witness in a fragmented world requires targeted formation that increases confidence, capacity and motivation for ecumenical and interreligious dialogue among bishops, priests, consecrated women and men, lay men and women. *'Although the Catholic Church in India has attempted to foster ecumenical and inter-religious dialogue, there is a feeling that the mission in this realm is minimal. The dialogue efforts drew only a handful of elites and remained mostly as cerebral exercises limited to the realm of ideas and concepts rather than becoming a movement of the masses and becoming also a dialogue of life, love and action at the base, by getting people of various faiths and ideologies to discern, plan and work together for common causes'* (EC India).

Cultural Contexts

50. Numerous reports highlight the importance of recognising that the Church fulfills its mission of proclaiming the Gospel within specific cultural contexts, and is influenced by profound and rapid social changes. The factors vary, but create significant challenges for participation and shape the reality of the Church's mission. Legacies of sectarianism, tribalism, ethno-nationalisms – differently expressed and experienced in diverse places – share the same characteristic threat: to narrow the Church's expression of its catholicity.

51. Many local Churches express concern about the impact of a lack of trust and credibility resulting from the abuse crises. Others point to individualism and consumerism as critical cultural factors: *'Every day we can feel that even in our country the proclamation of the Gospel is challenged by growing secularisation, individualism and indifference to the institutional forms of religion'* (EC Hungary). Malta's report, like many others, underscores how historical entanglements between Church and political power continue to have an effect on the mission context. Many Churches feel they face all these cultural challenges simultaneously, but wish to grow more and more confident in proclaiming the Gospel in *'a consumerist society that has failed to ensure sustainability, equity or life satisfaction'* (EC Ireland). Others experience a pluralism of positions within themselves: *'Southern Africa is also impacted by the international trends of secularisation, individualisation, and relativism. Issues such as the Church's teaching on abortion, contraception, ordination of women, married clergy, celibacy, divorce and remarriage, Holy Communion, homosexuality, LGBTQ+ were raised up across the Dioceses both rural an urban. There were of course differing views on these and it is not possible to give a definitive community stance on any of these issues'* (EC South Africa). Many reports express particular regret and concern for the pressures experienced by families and the resulting impact on intergenerational relationships and faith transmission. Many As an reports ask for better accompaniment and formation for families, as they negotiate changing cultural conditions.

52. In some contexts, the witness of the faith is lived to the point of martyrdom. There are countries where Christians, especially young people, face the challenge of systematic forced conversion to other religions. There are many reports that emphasise the insecurity and violence with which persecuted Christian minorities must contend. In such cases, walking together with people of other faiths, instead of retreating behind the wall of separation, requires the courage of prophecy.

Cultures, Religions and Dialogue

53. An essential element of a synodal Church, one which still needs significant deepening and better understanding, is the call to a more meaningful inter-cultural approach. This approach begins by walking together with others, appreciating cultural differences, understanding those particularities as elements which help us to grow: *'The encounter between the Catholic Church in Cambodia and the Buddhist Monks and lay Cambodian Buddhists "creates a new culture". All our activities affect each other and affect the whole world. We may differ in religion, but we all seek the common good'* (EC Laos and Cambodia). It is the Churches that represent a small minority in the context in which they live that experience this most intensely: *'For example [there is] what we might call the "porosity" of our Churches, whose line of demarcation with civil society is paradoxically less marked than elsewhere [...]. There is no problem of doing things "inside" or "outside" the Church. We are an outgoing Church by definition, because we are always "in the home of others" and this has taught us listening, flexibility, and creativity in forms, language, and practices'* (EC North African Region – CERNA).

54. However, even when we come to acceptance or even appreciation of the other, the journey is still incomplete. The Church's intercultural approach aims at the horizon to which Christ calls us: the Kingdom of God. In the embrace of an enriching diversity, we can find our deeper unity and the opportunity to cooperate with God's grace: *'We should also take heed of the thoughts and ideas of the extended family and companions in the journey; non-Catholics, Politicians and non-believers. These are voices in our neighbourhood we cannot afford to avoid lest we miss out God's whispers through them!'* (EC Zimbabwe). This constitutes a witness within a world that struggles to see diversity in unity as a true vocation: *'The community [...] must take greater account of diversity, aspirations, needs and ways of living the faith. The universal Church must remain the guarantor of unity, but Dioceses can inculturate the faith locally: decentralisation is necessary'* (Archdiocese of Luxembourg).

55. In a good number of reports, there is a call to better recognise, engage, integrate, and respond to the richness of local cultures, many of which have

worldviews and styles of action that are synodal. People express a desire to promote (and in some cases recover and deepen) local culture, to integrate it with faith, and to incorporate it into the liturgy. *'In this context, Christians are called to offer their own contribution starting from their own vision of faith in order to enculturate it in the new cultural contexts [...]. This diversity of approaches should be seen as the implementation of a model of interculturality, where the different proposals complement and enrich each other, going beyond that of multiculturality, which consists in the simple juxtaposition of cultures, closed within their perimeters'* (Contribution of the Pontifical Council for Culture).

56. In many cases, the reports call especially for attention to the situation of indigenous peoples. Their spirituality, wisdom, and culture have much to teach. We need to reread history together with these peoples, to draw inspiration from those situations in which the Church's action has been at the service of their integral human development, and to ask forgiveness for the times when it has instead been complicit in their oppression. At the same time, some reports highlight the need to reconcile the apparent contradictions that exist between cultural practices or traditional beliefs and the teachings of the Church. On a more general level, the practice of synodality – communion, participation and mission – needs to be articulated within local cultures and contexts, in a tension that promotes discernment and generativity.

3.3 Communion, Participation, and Co-responsibility

57. The mission of the Church is realised through the lives of all the baptised. The reports express a deep desire to recognise and reaffirm this common dignity as the basis for the renewal of life and ministries in the Church. They affirm the value of all vocations in the Church, and above all, invite us to follow Jesus, returning to his style and way of exercising power and authority as a means of offering healing, reconciliation and liberation. *'It is important to build a synodal institutional model as an ecclesial paradigm of deconstructing pyramidal power that privileges unipersonal managements. The only legitimate authority in the Church must be that of love and service, following the example of the Lord'* (CE Argentina).

Beyond Clericalism

58. The tone of the reports is not anti-clerical (against priests or the ministerial priesthood). Many express deep appreciation and affection for faithful and dedicated priests, and concerns about the many demands that they face. They also voice the desire for better formed, better accompanied and less isolated priests. They signal the importance of ridding the Church of clericalism so that all its members, including priests and laity, can fulfil a common mission. Clericalism is seen as a form of spiritual impoverishment, a deprivation of the true goods of ordained ministry, and a culture that isolates clergy and harms the laity. This culture separates us from the living experience of God and damages the kinship relations of the baptised, producing rigidity, attachment to legalistic power and an exercise of authority that is power rather than service. Clericalism can be as much a temptation for lay people as clergy., as the report from the Central African Republic underlines: *'some parish priests behave like "order-givers", imposing their will without listening to anyone. Lay Christians do not feel they are members of the People of God. Initiatives that are too "clericalistic" should be deplored. Some pastoral workers, clerics and lay, sometimes prefer to surround themselves with those who share their opinions and stay away from those whose convictions are hostile and in disagreement with them.'*

59. Although frank in their diagnosis of the problem, the reports are not hopeless. They express a deep and energetic desire for renewed forms of leadership – priestly, episcopal, religious and lay – that are relational and collaborative, and forms of authority capable of generating solidarity and co-responsibility: *'The tasks of the authorities include encouraging, involving, leading and facilitating participation in the life of the Church [...] and delegating part of the responsibilities'* (EC Slovakia). Lay people, religious and clerics desire to put their talents and abilities at the disposal of the Church, and to do so they call for an exercise of leadership that enables them to be free. The reports express gratitude for those leaders who already exercise their role in these ways.

Rethinking Women's Participation

60. The call for a conversion of the Church's culture, for the salvation of the world, is linked in concrete terms to the possibility of establishing a new culture, with new practices and structures. A critical and urgent area in this regard concerns the role of women and their vocation, rooted in our common baptismal dignity, to participate fully in the life of the Church. A growing awareness and sensitivity towards this issue is registered all over the world.

61. From all continents comes an appeal for Catholic women to be valued first and foremost as baptised and equal members of the People of God. There is almost unanimous affirmation that women love the Church deeply, but many feel sadness because their lives are often not well understood, and their contributions and charisms not always valued. The Holy Land report notes: *'Those who were most committed to the synod process were women, who seem to have realised not only that they had more to gain, but also more to offer by being relegated to a prophetic edge, from which they observe what happens in* *the life of the Church;'* and continues: *'In a Church where almost all decision-makers are men, there are few spaces where women can make their voices heard. Yet they are the backbone of Church communities, both because they represent the majority of the practising members and because they are among the most active members of the Church.'* The Korean report confirms: *'Despite the great participation of women in various Church activities, they are often excluded from key decision-making processes. Therefore, the Church needs to improve its awareness and institutional aspects of their activities'* (EC Korea). The Church faces two related challenges: women remain the majority of those who attend liturgy and participate in activities, men a minority; yet most decision-making and governance roles are held by men. It is clear that the Church must find ways to attract men to a more active membership in the Church and to enable women to participate more fully at all levels of Church life.

62. In every area of their lives, women ask the Church to be their ally. This includes addressing the social realities of impoverishment, violence and diminishment faced by women across the globe. They call for a Church at their side, and greater understanding and support in combating these forces of destruction and exclusion. Women participating in the synodal processes desire both Church and society to be a place of flourishing, active participation and healthy belonging. Some reports note that the cultures of their countries have made progress in the inclusion and participation of women, progress that could serve as a model for the Church. *'This lack of equality for women within the Church is seen as a stumbling block for the Church in the modern world'* (EC New Zealand).

63. In different forms, the problem is present across cultural contexts and concerns the participation and recognition of laywomen as well as women religious. The report from Superiors of Institutes of Consecrated Life notes:

> *'Sexism in decision-making and Church language is prevalent in the Church. As a result, women are excluded from meaningful roles in the life of the Church, discriminated against by not receiving a fair wage for their ministries and services. Women religious are often regarded as cheap labour. There is a tendency – in some Churches – to exclude women and to entrust ecclesial functions to permanent deacons; and even to undervalue religious life without the habit, without regard for the fundamental equality and dignity of all baptised Christian faithful, women and men'* (USG/UISG).

64. Almost all reports raise the issue of full and equal participation of women: *'The growing recognition of the importance of women in the life of the Church opens up possibilities for greater, albeit limited, participation in Church structures* *and decision-making spheres'* (EC Brazil). However, the reports do not agree on a single or complete response to the question of the vocation, inclusion and flourishing of women in Church and society. After careful listening, many reports ask that the Church continue its discernment in relation to a range of specific questions: the active role of women in the governing structures of Church bodies, the possibility for women with adequate training to preach in parish settings, and a female diaconate. Much greater diversity of opinion was expressed on the subject of priestly ordination for women, which some reports call for, while others consider a closed issue.

65. A key element of this process concerns the recognition of the ways in which women, especially women religious, are already at the forefront of synodal practices in some of the most challenging social situations we face. The contribution submitted by the Union of Superiors General and the International Union of Superiors General notes: *'There are seeds of synodality where we break new ground in solidarity: securing a future of racial and ethnic justice and peace for black, brown, Asian and Native American brothers and sisters (United States); connecting in depth with indigenous and native sisters and brothers (Americas); opening new avenues of presence of religious sisters in diverse movements; alliance with like-minded groups to address key social issues (such as climate change, refugees and asylum seekers, homelessness), or issues of specific nations.'* In these contexts, women seek collaborators and can be teachers of synodality within wider Church processes.

Charisms, Vocations and Ministries

66. Responsibility for the synodal life of the Church cannot be delegated but must be shared by all in response to the gifts the Spirit bestows on the faithful. *'One group in Lae Diocese commented about the synodality in their parish: "In our parish pastoral council meeting, we see that we take the opinion/suggestion of all the people and also of woman before taking decision which will affect the life of all people in our parish." Another parish commented: "When we want to do anything in our parish, we meet together, take the suggestions of everyone in the community, decide together and carry out the decisions together"'* (EC Papua New Guinea and Solomon Islands). However, there is no shortage of expressions of difficulty in actually practicing co-responsibility: *'As bishops we recognise that the "baptismal theology" promoted by the Second Vatican Council, the basis of co-responsibility in mission, has not been sufficiently developed, and therefore the majority of the baptised do not feel a full identification with the Church and even less a missionary co-responsibility. Moreover, the leadership of current pastoral structures, as well as the mentality of many priests, do not foster this co-responsibility. Likewise, religious men and women, as well as lay* *apostolic movements, often remain subtly or openly on the margins of diocesan dynamics. Thus, the so-called "committed laity" in parishes (who are the least numerous) end up being overburdened with intra-ecclesial responsibilities that exceed their strength and exhaust their time'* (EC Mexico).

67. This desire for co-responsibility becomes grounded first of all in the key of service to the common mission, that is, with the language of ministeriality. As the Italian report says, *'The experience made [...] has helped to rediscover the co-responsibility that comes from baptismal dignity and has let emerge the possibility of overcoming a vision of Church built around ordained ministry in order to move toward a Church that is "all ministerial", which is a communion of different charisms and ministries.'* The theme of ministry as central to the life of the Church, and the need to articulate the unity of mission with the plurality of ministries, emerges from the consultation of the People of God. Recognising and promoting it *'is not here an end in itself, but an enhancement in the service of mission: different actors, equal in dignity, complementary to be a sign, to make credible a Church that is sacrament of the Kingdom'* (EC Belgium).

68. Many reports refer to practices for the recognition and promotion of ministries, which enable an effective entrustment by the community: *'The promotion of lay ministries and the assumption of responsibilities takes place through the election or appointment of the faithful who are considered to possess the requisites laid down'* (EC Mozambique). In this way, each ministry becomes a structural and structuring element of community life: *'The assumption of responsibility is guaranteed by the mandate received and the principle of subsidiarity. Catechists are instituted and have a special status in the Church Family of God. [...] Some of them are "instituted" as Community Leaders, especially in rural areas where the presence of priests is rare'* (EC RD Congo). There is no shortage of questions regarding spaces for the possible exercise of lay ministry: *'Many groups would like to see greater participation of the laity, but the margins for maneuver are unclear: what concrete tasks can the laity perform? How is the responsibility of the baptised articulated with that of the parish priest?'* (EC Belgium).

69. In some contexts, there is a need to consider the variety of charisms and ministries that emerge in an organised form within associations, lay movements and new religious communities. Attention is needed to their specificities, and also to safeguarding the harmony within each local Church. When it enters into the concrete life of the Church, the theme of ministeriality inevitably meets with the question of its institutionalisation. This raises the question of the structures through which the life of the Christian community unfolds.

70. In the Catholic Church, the charismatic gifts freely bestowed by the Holy Spirit, which help 'rejuvenate' the Church, are inseparable from the hierarchical gifts which are linked to the Sacrament of Orders in its various degrees. A great challenge of synodality that emerged during the first year is the harmonisation of these gifts, without pitting them against each other, under the guidance of the pastors, and thus without opposing the Church's charismatic and institutional dimensions.

3.4 Synodality Takes Shape

71. The synodal journey has brought out a number of tensions, made explicit in the preceding paragraphs. We should not be afraid of them, but articulate them in a process of constant communal discernment, so as to harness them as a source of energy without them becoming destructive: only in this way will it be possible to continue walking together, rather than each going their own way. This is why the Church also needs to give a synodal form and way of proceeding to its own institutions and structures, particularly with regard to governance. Canon law will need to accompany this process of structural renewal creating the necessary changes to the arrangements currently in place.

72. However, to function in a truly synodal way, structures will need to be inhabited by people who are well-formed, in terms of vision and skills: '*The entire synodal exercise was one of active participation at diverse levels. For this process to continue, a change of mindset and a renewal of existing structures are needed*' (EC India). This new vision will need to be supported by a spirituality that will sustain the practice of synodality, avoiding reducing this reality to technical-organisational issues. Living this vision, as a common mission, can only happen through encounter with the Lord and listening to the Spirit. For there to be synodality, the presence of the Spirit is necessary, and there is no Spirit without prayer.

Structures and Institutions

73. In terms of global-local tension– which in ecclesial language refers to the relationships of local Churches among themselves and with the universal Church – the dynamic of the synodal process places before us a novelty that is constituted precisely by the Continental Stage that we are currently living. Apart from a few regions characterised by a particular historical dynamic, so far the Church lacks established synodal practices at the continental level. The introduction of a specific Continental Stage in the process of the Synod does not constitute a mere organisational ploy, but corresponds to the dynamics of the incarnation of the Gospel which, taking root in areas characterised by a certain cultural cohesion and homogeneity, produces ecclesial communities with particular features, linked to the traits of each culture. In the context of a world that is both globalised and fragmented, each continent, because of its common historical roots, its tendency towards socio-cultural commonality and the fact that it presents the same challenges for the mission of evangelisation, constitutes a privileged sphere for stirring up a synodal dynamic that strengthens links between the Churches, encourages the sharing of experiences and the exchange of gifts, and helps to imagine new pastoral options.

74. Moreover, the dynamic of synodality challenges the Roman Curia itself: *'It is necessary to recall the collaboration with the other Dicasteries of the Roman Curia, with which we consult regularly [...]. It is felt, however, that in this area more means should be found to encourage the growth of a more synodal practice and spirit to be implemented in the Roman Curia, as desired by the Holy Father with the new Apostolic Constitution Praedicate Evangelium'* (Contribution of the Secretariat of State – Section for Relations with States and International Organisations).

75. Episcopal conferences are also questioning what synodality means for them: 'The bishops too have prayed and debated the question: *'How to make an episcopal conference more synodal? And how to live it in a more synodal way?'* (EC Paraguay). For example, *'While maintaining their collegiality and freedom of decision-making that is devoid of any kind of pressure, the episcopal conferences should include representatives of the clergy and laity of the various dioceses in their debates and meetings, in the name of synodality'* (Contribution of the Secretariat of State – Section for the Diplomatic Staff of the Holy See).

76. During the Continental Stage, episcopal conferences will be able to experience a new role, related not only to the promotion of communion within themselves, but also of dialogue between Churches linked by geographical and cultural proximity. In addition, the Continental Stage, through the proposed ecclesial and episcopal assemblies, will offer the opportunity to work out in grounded and practical terms how to articulate ecclesial synodality and episcopal collegiality. It will also offer the chance to reflect on ways to improve the harmony between the ordinary ways of exercising episcopal ministry and the assumption of a fully synodal style, a point on which some reports register a certain lack of energy. Revisiting the experience gained during the Continental Stage will help discern how to proceed more smoothly.

77. Far more than the Latin Church, the Oriental Churches offer a wealth of synodal structures, which are called to renewal today: *'The ancient synodal structures and ecclesial processes existing in the Syro-Malabar Church*

(Prathinidhiyogam, Palliyogam and Desayogam) express the synodal nature of the Church at the local, regional and universal levels, and are useful for forming us to synodality. They are at the service of the parishes and communities, which discover collaborative exercise of the pastoral ministries to move forward by listening to the Holy Spirit. Moreover, there are some new initiatives and attempts which try to empower the synodal structures of the Church' (Syro-Malabar Catholic Church).

78. The dynamic of co-responsibility, with a view to and in service of the common mission and not as an organisational way of allocating roles and powers, runs through all levels of Church life. At the local level, it calls into question the bodies of participation already envisaged at the various levels and with the specificities proper to the various rites, and those that may possibly be appropriate to set up in service to a strengthened synodal dynamic: *'it was discussed to have structure and organisation which sincerely reflects the spirit of synodality'* (EC Korea). These are first and foremost pastoral councils, called to be increasingly institutional places of inclusion, dialogue, transparency, discernment, evaluation and empowerment of all. In our time they are indispensable. Economic, diocesan and parish councils should then be added, taking note also of the episcopal and presbyteral councils around the bishop. Many reports show the need for these bodies to be not only consultative, but places where decisions are made on the basis of processes of communal discernment rather than on the majority principle used in democratic regimes.

79. In different parts of the world, transparency is seen as an essential practice for a Church growing into a more authentic synodality: *'The Catholic Church needs to become more open and transparent, everything is done in secret. Parish Council agendas and minutes are never published, financial committee decisions never discussed or balance sheets shared'* (individual observation from UK). Transparency will propel toward true accountability of all decision-making processes, including the criteria used for discernment. A style of leadership anchored in a synodal way of proceeding will produce trust and credibility: *'On some issues, the exercise of authority is effectively collegial, through consultation with the bodies embedded in the various structures of administration, management and pastoral animation [...]. But it is sometimes sad to note that in our Catholic Church there are bishops, priests, catechists, community leaders ..., who are very authoritarian. [...] Instead of serving the community, some serve themselves with unilateral decisions, and this hinders our synodal journey'* (EC Chad). In addition, many reports note the need to involve people with adequate professional competence in the management of economic and governance issues.

80. All Church institutions, as fully participatory bodies, are called to consider how they might integrate the call to synodality into the ways in which they exercise their functions and their mission, renewing their structures and procedures. A special case in point is represented by universities and academic institutions, which will be able to develop research addressing questions of synodality, helping to innovate in the design of educational and formation programmes. In particular, theological faculties will be able to deepen the ecclesiological, Christological and Pneumatological insights that synodal experiences and practices bring.

81. The adoption of an authentically synodal style also challenges consecrated life, beginning precisely with those practices that already emphasise the importance of the participation of all members in the life of the community to which they belong: '*Synodality in consecrated life affects discernment and decision-making. Although communal discernment has been practised in our Institutes, there is room for improvement. Membership in a body requires participation. [...] A shared desire is the establishment – both in the life of the Church and in the consecrated life – of a circular (participative) and less hierarchical and pyramidal style of governance*' (USG/UISG).

Formation

82. The overwhelming majority of reports indicate the need to provide for formation in synodality. Structures alone are not enough: there is a need for ongoing formation to support a widespread synodal culture. This formation must articulate itself in relationship to the local context so as to facilitate synodal conversion in the way participation, authority and leadership are exercised in view of more effectively fulfiling the common mission. It is not simply a matter of providing specific technical or methodological skills. Formation for synodality intersects all dimensions of Christian life and can only be '*an integral formation that includes personal, spiritual, theological, social and practical dimensions. For this, a community of reference is essential, because one principle of 'walking together' is the formation of the heart, which transcends concrete knowledge and embraces the whole of life. It is necessary to incorporate in the Christian life a continuous and permanent formation to put synodality into practice, to mature and grow in faith, to participate in public life, to increase the love and participation of the faithful in the Eucharist, to assume stable ministries, to exercise real co-responsibility in the governance of the Church, to dialogue with other Churches and with society in order to bring those who are far away closer in a spirit of fraternity*' (EC Spain). This training will have to be addressed to all members of the People of God: '*For the realisation of the said elements of synodality, there is an urgent need for the education and formation programmes* *for clergy and lay people for developing a shared understanding of synodality that is so vital for journeying together in the local Churches'* (EC Myanmar). In this way, the perspective of synodality will converge with catechesis and pastoral care, helping to keep them anchored in a mission perspective.

83. However, the need for more specific formation in listening and dialogue is also emphasised, for example through the establishment of synodality agents and teams. Many reports point to the need to ensure formation in synodality for those who will be called to assume leadership roles, especially priests: *'Though long, seminary formation is geared toward preparing the clergy for a priestly lifestyle and devoid of forming them for pastoral coordination. The formation and training on working together, listening to one another and participation in the mission together is essential in priestly formation'* (EC Sri Lanka).

Spirituality

84. A culture of synodality, which is indispensable for animating structures and institutions, requires adequate formation, and, above all, needs to be nurtured by familiarity with the Lord and the capacity to listen to the voice of the Spirit: *'spiritual discernment must accompany strategic planning and decision-making, so that each project is welcomed and accompanied by the Holy Spirit'* (Greek Melkite Catholic Church). For this we must grow in a synodal spirituality that is based on attention to interiority and conscience. *'In personal spirituality and in the message of the Church, the joy of the risen Christ must prevail and not the fear of a God who punishes'* (EC Czech Republic).

85. As has already been stressed many times, a synodal Church first of all needs to deal with the many tensions that emerge from encountering diversity. Therefore, a synodal spirituality can only be one that welcomes differences and promotes harmony, and draws from the tensions the energies to continue on the journey. To achieve this, it will have to move from accentuating the individual dimension to the collective dimension: a spirituality of 'we,' which can enhance the contributions of each person.

86. The first year of the synodal journey has already offered stimulating experiences in this direction, through the proposed method of Spiritual Conversation. This method has enabled the People of God to savor the flavor of an interpersonal encounter around the Word of God and the varied resonances it arouses in the heart of each person. In addition to making it an ordinary practice in the life of the Church, as is demanded by many, this method must evolve in the direction of communal discernment, particularly within the bodies of participation. This entails a greater effort to integrate the spiritual dimension within the ordinary life of ecclesial institutions and of their governance structures, articulating discernment within decision-making processes. Prayer and silence cannot remain extraneous to these processes, as if it were a preamble or an appendix.

87. Christian spirituality is expressed in different ways, related both to the multiplicity of traditions between East and West and to the variety of charisms in consecrated life and ecclesial movements. A synodal Church is built around diversity, and the encounter between different spiritual traditions can be a formative 'gymnasium' insofar as it is capable of promoting communion and harmony, contributing to overcoming the polarisations that many Churches experience.

3.5 Synodal Life and Liturgy

88. The reports emphasise in many ways the deep link between synodality and liturgy: *'In "walking together", prayer, devotion to Mary as a missionary disciple listening to the Word, lectio divina and liturgical celebration inspire the purpose of belonging'* (EC Colombia).

Roots that Reach Deep

89. The Eucharist is already, in itself, the 'source and summit' of the Church's synodal dynamism. *'Liturgical celebration and prayer are experienced as a force for uniting and mobilising human and spiritual energies. The prevailing opinion is that prayer fosters joy of life and a purpose of community, because it is seen as a point of reference, a place of strength and an oasis of peace. [...] the contributions underscore two modalities to be developed in view of a synodal journey: the unity of the community and the joy of life. This journey would pass through the great liturgical gatherings (pilgrimages...), to nourish popular piety, renew faith, nourish the feeling of belonging, and thus better accompany Christians so that they witness to the Gospel of charity in the face of communitarianism and "identity withdrawal" which are more and more visible and aggressive'* (EC Burkina Faso e Niger).

90. In countries in diverse areas of the world 'the bond of many baptised people with the Church passes above all through the phenomenon of popular religiosity. [...] Many people consider it a sign of belonging to the Church; for this reason, we must promote and evangelise [it], with a view to a more intense participation and a conscious incorporation into Christian life' (EC Panama).

Managing Tensions: Renewal and Reconciliation

91. Many reports strongly encourage the implementation of a synodal style of liturgical celebration that allows for the active participation of all the faithful in welcoming all differences, valuing all ministries, and recognising all charisms. The synodal listening of the Churches records many issues to be addressed in this direction: from rethinking a liturgy too concentrated on the celebrant, to the modalities of active participation of the laity, to the access of women to ministerial roles. '*While being faithful to the tradition, its originality, antiquity, and uniformity, let us try to make the liturgical celebration more alive and participatory of all the community of believers; priests, laity, youth and children, reading the signs of the time with sound discernment. The young people are trying to have a space in the liturgy with songs and it is positive*' (EC Ethiopia).

92. The current experience of the Churches, however, records knots of conflict which need to be addressed in a synodal manner, such as discerning the relationship to preconciliar rites: '*Division regarding the celebration of the liturgy was reflected in synodal consultations. "Sadly, celebration of the Eucharist is also experienced as an area of division within the Church. The most common issue regarding the liturgy is the celebration of the pre-Conciliar Mass." The limited access to the 1962 Missal was lamented; many felt that the differences over how to celebrate the liturgy 'sometimes reach the level of animosity. People on each side of the issue reported feeling judged by those who differ from them*' (EC USA). The Eucharist, sacrament of unity in love in Christ, cannot become a reason for confrontation, ideology, rift or division. Moreover, with direct impact on the life of many Churches, there are elements of tension specific to the ecumenical sphere, such as the sharing of the Eucharist. Finally, there are problems related to the modalities of faith inculturation and interreligious dialogue, which also affect the forms of celebration and prayer.

93. The reports do not fail to point out the main shortcomings of the actual celebratory praxis, which obscure its synodal effectiveness. In particular, the following are emphasised: the liturgical protagonism of the priest and the risk of the passivity of the wider liturgical community; poor preaching, including the distance between the content of the sermon, the beauty of faith and the concreteness of life; and the separation between the liturgical life of the assembly and the family network of the community. The quality of homilies is almost unanimously reported as a problem: there is a call for '*deeper homilies, centered on the Gospel and the readings of the day, and not on politics, making use of accessible and attractive language that refers to the lives of the faithful*' (Maronite Church).

94. A particular source of suffering are those situations in which access to the Eucharist and to the other Sacraments is hindered or prevented by a variety of causes: there is a strong demand to find solutions to these forms of sacramental deprivation. For example, communities living in very remote areas are cited, or the use of charging fees for access to celebrations, which discriminates against the poorest. Many summaries also give voice to the pain of not being able to access the Sacraments experienced by remarried divorcees and those who have entered into polygamous marriages. There is no unanimity on how to deal with these situations: *'Access to Holy Communion is denied to the divorced and remarried, and they expressed hurt at this exclusion. Some expressed the view that the Church should be more flexible, but others felt this practice should be upheld'* (EC Malaysia).

A Synodal Style of Celebrating

95. At the same time, the synod process represented an opportunity to experience anew the diversity in forms of prayer and celebration, increasing the desire to make it more accessible in the ordinary life of communities. The French report gives voice to three aspirations: *'the first [...] concerns the diversification of liturgies to the benefit of celebrations of the Word, that is, moments of prayer that place meditation on biblical texts at the centre. The second, less frequent, recalls the importance of pilgrimages and popular piety. The third calls for a renewed liturgical formation, to address a problem reported by many reports, namely the incomprehensibility of the language normally used by the Church'* (EC France). Some regions raise the question of the reform of the liturgy, even in the Oriental Churches where it is profoundly linked to the identity of the Church: *'In our Church, a liturgical reform is opportune, so as to re-read in the light of the Holy Spirit the action and participation of the People of God in God's work in our time'* (Greek-Melkite Church).

96. Many Churches also emphasise the importance of habitually linking liturgical celebration with the various forms of dialogical sharing and fraternal conviviality. *'Conviviality and fraternity were always part of the experience [of synod meetings]. In every meeting, from the initial one to the subsequent consultations in parishes and pastoral structures, there was salu-salo (sharing of food). Many pointed out how the [synodal] meetings positively influenced the celebration of the liturgies'* (EC Philippines).

97. The variety of ritual traditions of liturgical prayer, as well as the symbolic forms with which diverse cultures express themselves, is considered by all to be an asset. A renewed love for spirituality, a commitment to care for the beauty and the synodal style of celebration all support the radiance of a missionary Church: *'All the contributions received speak of celebrations as spaces that can offer inspiration and help to live the faith in personal, family, professional life, in the neighborhood and in the community itself'* (EC Uruguay).

IV
THE NEXT STEPS

98. Looking to the future of the synodal process requires considering two very different time horizons. The first is the long-term horizon, in which synodality takes the form of a perennial call to personal conversion and reform of the Church. The second, clearly at the service of the first, is the one that focuses our attention on the events of the Continental Stage that we experiencing.

4.1 A Journey of Conversion and Reform

99. In the reports, the People of God express a desire to be less a Church of maintenance and conservation and more a Church that goes out in mission. A connection emerges between deepening communion through synodality on the one hand and strengthening mission on the other: being synodal leads into renewed mission. As the Spanish report says: '*we believe that communion must lead us to a permanent state of mission: meeting and listening to each other, dialogue, reflection, discernment together are all actions with positive effects in themselves, but they are not understandable if they are not directed at pushing us to go beyond ourselves and our communities of reference in order to carry out the mission entrusted to us as Church.*'

100. The People of God have found joy in walking together and express the desire to continue doing so. How to do this as a truly global Catholic community is something that still needs to be fully discovered: '*To walk in a synodal way, by listening to one another, participating in mission, and engaging in dialogue, has possibly an 'already and not yet' dimension, it is there, but much more to be done. The laity are capable, talented and willing to contribute more and more, provided they are given opportunities. Further surveys and studies at the parish level can open up more avenues where the contributions of the laity can be immense and the result would be more vibrant and flourishing Church, which is the goal of synodality*' (EC Namibia). We are a learning Church, and to be so we need continuous discernment to help us read the Word of God and the signs of the times together, so as to move forward in the direction the Spirit is pointing us.

101. At the same time, walking together as the People of God requires us to recognise the need for continual conversion, individual and communal. On the institutional and pastoral level, this conversion translates into an equally continuous reform of the Church, its structures and style, in the wake of the drive for continuous 'aggiornamento,' the precious legacy of the Second Vatican Council to which we are called to look as we celebrate its 60th anniversary.

102. In the journey of conversion and reform, we are supported by the gifts we have received during the first year of the synodal journey, beginning with what Jesus shows us in the Gospels. The free and gratuitous attention to the other, which is the basis of listening, is not a limited resource to be jealously guarded, but an overflowing source that does not run out, but grows the more we draw from it. Listening and dialogue are the way to access the gifts that the Spirit offers us through the multifaceted variety of the one Church: of charisms, of vocations, of talents, of skills, of languages and cultures, of spiritual and theological traditions, of different forms of celebrating and giving thanks. The reports do not call for uniformity, but ask that we learn to grow in a sincere harmony that helps the baptised fulfil their mission in the world by creating the bonds necessary to walk together joyfully.

103. The message of our synodal way is simple: we are learning to walk together, and sit together to break the one bread, in such a way that each is able to find their place. Everyone is called to take part in this journey, no one is excluded. To this we feel called so that we can credibly proclaim the Gospel of Jesus to all people. This is the path we seek to continue on in our next Continental Stage.

4.2 Methodology for the Continental Stage

104. This Document for the Continental Stage (DCS) invites us to take a further step in this spiritual journey *'for a synodal Church: communion, participation and mission'* and constitutes its point of reference: *'Just as the experience of the disciples at Emmaus was only the beginning of their new mission, our synodal process is only a first step'* (EC Russian Federation). The continental level constitutes an opportunity to live synodality, which we are still learning to grasp and which we are now invited to practise concretely.

105. The DCS, which gathers and restores to the local Churches, what the People of God from around the world said in the first year of the Synod, is meant to guide us and enable us to deepen our discernment, keeping in mind the basic question that animates the entire process: *'How does this "journeying together", which takes place today on different levels (from the local level to the universal one), allow the Church to proclaim the Gospel in accordance with the mission entrusted to Her; and what steps does the Spirit invite us to take in order to grow as a synodal Church?'* (PD, no. 2).

106. The DCS is thus the privileged instrument through which the dialogue of the local Churches among themselves and with the universal Church can take place during the Continental Stage. To pursue this process of listening, dialogue and discernment, the reflection will focus on three questions:

- 'After having read and prayed with the DCS, which intuitions resonate most strongly with the lived experiences and realities of the Church in your continent? Which experiences are new, or illuminating to you?'
- 'After having read and prayed with the DCS, what substantial tensions or divergences emerge as particularly important in your continent's perspective? Consequently, what are the questions or issues that should be addressed and considered in the next steps of the process?'
- 'Looking at what emerges from the previous two questions, what are the priorities, recurring themes and calls to action that can be shared with other local Churches around the world and discussed during the First Session of the Synodal Assembly in October 2023?'

Key Stages in the Process

107. Each Continental Assembly is called to put in place a discernment process on the DCS that is appropriate to its local context, and draft a Final Document to account for it. The Final Documents of the seven Continental Assemblies will be used as the basis for drafting the *Instrumentum Laboris*, which will be completed by June 2023.

108. The vast majority of episcopal conferences that responded to the consultation sent by the General Secretariat of the Synod want representatives from the entire People of God to be involved in the Continental Stage. It is therefore asked that all Assemblies be ecclesial and not merely episcopal, ensuring that their composition adequately represents the variety of the People of God: bishops, presbyters, deacons, consecrated women and men, laymen and women. With respect to the participants in the Continental Assemblies, it is important to pay special attention to the presence of women and young people (laymen and laywomen, consecrated men and women in formation, seminarians); people living in conditions of poverty or marginalisation, and those who have direct contact with these groups and persons; fraternal delegates from other Christian denominations; representatives of other religions and faith traditions; and some people with no religious affiliation. Furthermore, bishops are invited to meet at the end of the Continental Assemblies to collegially reread the lived synodal experience from the perspective of their specific charism and role. In particular, they are asked to identify appropriate ways to carry out their task of validating and approving the Final Document, ensuring that it is the fruit of an authentically synodal journey, respectful of the process that has taken place and faithful to the diverse voices of the People of God in each continent.

109. The process leading from the publication of this DCS to the drafting of the *Instrumentum Laboris* will be marked by the following steps:

1. The DCS will be sent to all diocesan bishops; each of them, together with the diocesan synodal team that coordinated the first phase, will arrange an ecclesial process of discernment on the DCS, starting with the three questions indicated above in no. 106. Each local Church will thus have the opportunity to listen to the voice of the other Churches, gathered in the DCS, and to respond to it from its own experience.
2. With the involvement of its synodal team, each episcopal conference has the task of collecting and synthesising in the form most appropriate to its own context the reflections around the three questions coming from the individual Dioceses.
3. The reflection and discernment of each episcopal conference will then be shared within the Continental Assembly, according to the modalities identified by the Continental Task Force.
4. In planning the conduct of each specific Continental Assembly, it may be useful to reflect on how to use the widespread and much-appreciated Spiritual Conversation Method (see *Vademecum*, Appendix B, no. 8), which can facilitate the involvement of all in discernment. In particular, its three phases should be emphasised: the taking of the floor by each participant, the resonance of listening to others, and the discernment of the fruits by the group. As already highlighted in the Methodological Guidelines, it will be important to ensure the participation in the Continental Assemblies of bishops, priests, deacons, lay men and women, consecrated men and women, as well as people capable of expressing the views of those on the margins.
5. Each Continental Assembly will draft its own Final Document of a maximum of about twenty pages confronting the three questions from its own specific context. The Final Documents are to be submitted by each Continental Task Force to the Synod Secretariat by March 31, 2023. Based on the Final Documents of the Continental Assemblies, the *Instrumentum laboris* will be drafted by June 2023.

The People of God have Spoken

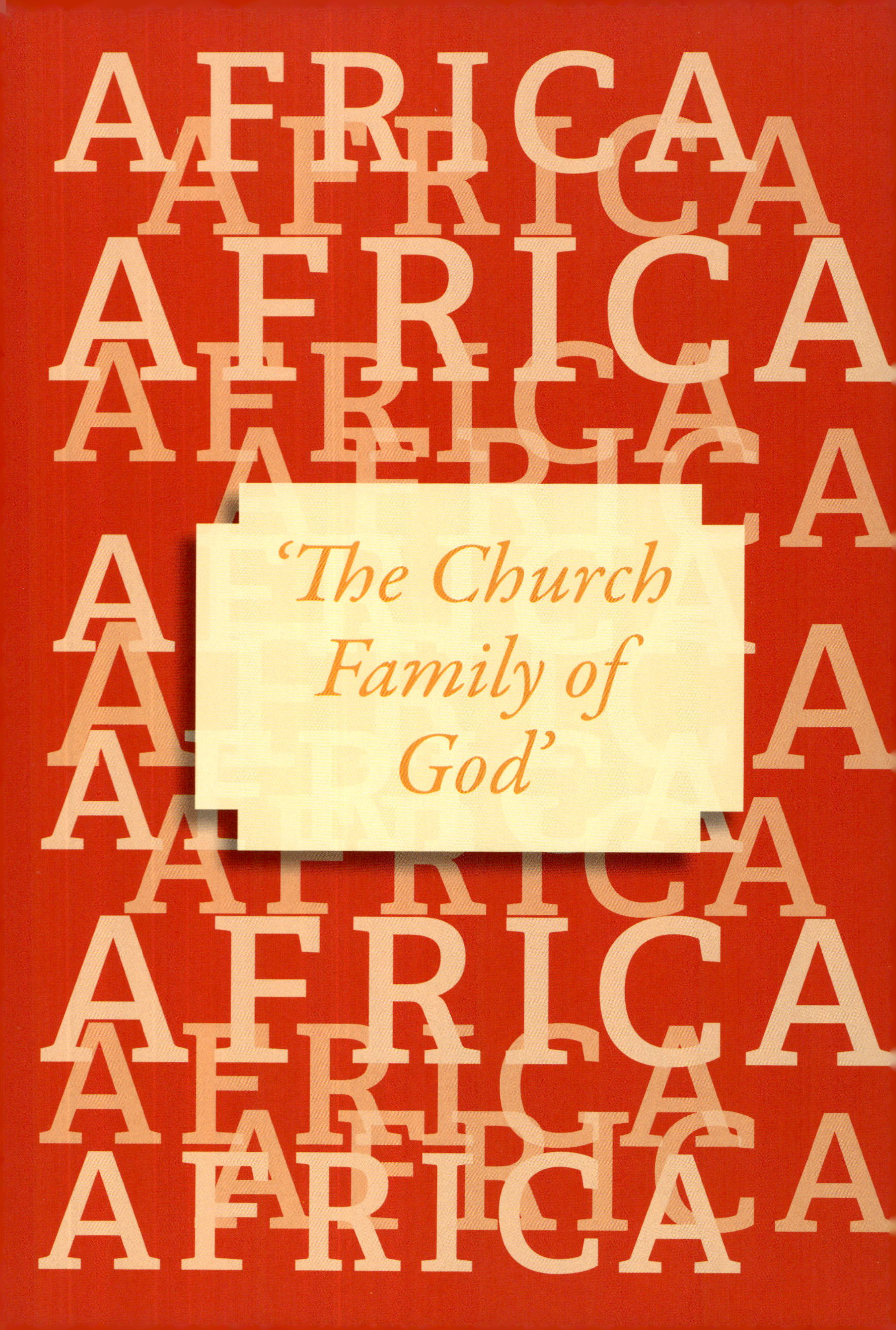
'The Church
Family of
God'

THE CHURCH FAMILY OF GOD: THE CONTINENTAL SYNODAL ASSEMBLY OF AFRICA

Marie-Laure Josée Abotcha-Boni

INTRODUCTION

In October 2021, Pope Francis convoked the Church to be in synod. The theme of the synod is: 'For a Synodal Church: Communion, Participation and Mission'. It is a time of listening, dialogue and communal discernment that calls for the involvement and participation of all the People of God to reflect on the life and mission of the Church.

The fundamental question guiding the whole process is: How does this 'journeying together', which takes place today on different levels (from the local level to the universal one), allow the Church to proclaim the Gospel in accordance with the mission entrusted to Her; and what steps does the Spirit invite us to take in order to grow as a synodal Church? (Preparatory Document, no. 2).

The first step in this synodal process is to listen to the People of God at the level of the local Church, and to send the respective national synthesis, elaborated from the outline contained in the Preparatory Document, to the General Secretariat of the Synod. This synthesis contains the contributions that the different communities and groups forward to the dioceses, summaries of which are then sent to the episcopal conferences. The listening phase expands thereafter from a local to a continental level.

This report gives an account of the African Continental Assembly, from the preparatory stages to the closing of this Assembly.

I
PREPARATORY PHASE

1. SECAM Plenary Assembly of August 2022

In preparation for the Continental Assembly, a coordinating committee was set up in August 2022, on the recommendation of the Bishops' Plenary Assembly of the Symposium of Episcopal Conferences of Africa and Madagascar (SECAM) in Accra, Ghana. This committee was composed of members of an independent structure called the African Synodal Initiative, which is a partnership between the Jesuit Conference of Africa and Madagascar (JCAM), the Symposium of Episcopal Conferences of Africa and Madagascar (SECAM) and the Association of Member Episcopal Conferences in Eastern Africa (AMECEA). It includes, among others, theologians and some lay people. It 'fulfills its goals by developing informative media productions, organising webinars that support the formation of the faithful, and convening various groups to reflect critically on synodality from an African perspective'.[1] The task of the coordinating committee was to prepare the continental assembly, which was to be held by the end of March, 2023.

This committee held its first meeting in Accra, during the same SECAM plenary assembly, with Andrew Nkea, archbishop of Bamenda in Cameroon, who serves on behalf of Africa on the Council of Bishops that guides the synod on synodality at the Vatican, and Mr Mauricio López Oropeza, a member of the Task Force for the continental meetings set up by the Secretariat of the Synod in the Vatican. The objective of this first meeting was to decide on the dates, location and composition of this continental assembly. The list of guests, the number and configuration of participants according to the regional conferences, were defined.

The results of this first meeting are as follows:

- Period of holding the continental assembly: March 1 until 6, 2023
- Location: Addis Ababa, Ethiopia
- Number of participants: approximately 162
- Members of African Synodal Initiative and Theological Commission: 30 people
- A total of ten guests which, besides six journalists, would include the following four guests from Rome: Mario Cardinal Grech, Jean-Claude Cardinal Hollerich SJ, Bishop Luis Marín de San Martin OSA, Sr Nathalie Becquart XMCJ

1 https://www.jesuits.africa/asi/ (access April 7, 2023).

NUMBER OF PARTICIPANTS PER REGIONAL CONFERENCE

Africa

No	Regional conference	Number of episcopal conferences	Number of participants
1	Association of Episcopal Conferences of Central Africa (ACEAC)	03	20
2	Association of Episcopal Conferences of Central Africa Region (ACERAC)	07	19
3	Regional Episcopal Conference of West Africa (RECOWA/CERAO)	16	20
4	Regional Episcopal Conference of North Africa (CERNA)	05	07
5	Association of Member Episcopal Conferences of Eastern Africa (AMECEA)	11	19
6	Inter-Regional Meeting of the Bishops of Southern Africa (IMBISA)	08	19
7	Episcopal Conferences of Indian Ocean (CEDOI)	05	19
8	Assembly of the Catholic Hierarchy of Egypt (AHCE)	01	00

At each regional conference, this committee communicated the configuration of delegates following the recommendations of the General Secretariat of the Synod. Overall, the pattern was similar to the following example:

The case of RECOWA/ CERAO

- 01 Cardinal
- 01 SECAM bishop, member of the regional conference
- the secretary of the regional conference
- 3 adult men
- 3 adult women
- 3 young men
- 3 young women
- 1 female religious
- 1 male religious
- 1 Seminarian
- 1 Novice
- 1 Protestant

The regional secretaries were responsible for distributing these requirements to the respective episcopal conferences.

It was then decided that each regional secretary should collect the contributions that each episcopal conference from his region had sent to Rome in the summer of 2022, and that from these reports a ten-page regional synthesis be written and submitted by the end of September, 2022.

2. Meeting in December 2022

In the first week of December 2022, again in Accra, Ghana, SECAM invited 28 people, members of the coordinating committee, to study together the summaries of the regional conferences in order to produce a report presenting Africa's contribution to this synod. This was considered in the light of the Document for the Continental Stage (DCS), which had been released in November 2022.

At this meeting, the method of Spiritual Conversation was introduced for the first time. After a training on the meaning and unfolding of this concept, each regional secretary was asked to train the delegates in his or her zone in this method.

3. Meeting in January 2023

A second meeting of the coordination committee took place in Nairobi, Kenya, in January 2023, with about 20 people. It should be noted that at this stage theologians were not invited. The same process and approach was observed, namely the study of the DCS and the reinforcement of the training in the method of Spiritual Conversation. Each person who took part was still responsible for spreading it around. It was at this stage that the programme for the continental assembly was developed.

4. After January 2023

After this meeting, each regional secretary contacted the General Secretaries of the episcopal conferences of each country to communicate the profile of their representative to the continental assembly and to collect his/her identity. Thus, at the level of the Regional Episcopal Conference of West Africa, the Catholic Episcopal Conference of Ivory Coast was asked to send a woman. The episcopal conference selected me, having been a member of the national contact team of the synod with a special responsibility for its Methodology Commission. On this basis, the list of participants by region was drawn up and a consolidated list of all delegates was finalised. Accordingly, the distribution of the delegates was as follows in charts on pages 74 and 75 overleaf:

This summary table of the list of participants reveals that all regions, apart from Egypt, participated in the African continental assembly. Out of a total of 55 episcopal conferences that are grouped in seven SECAM regions, twelve were not represented.

Some countries had more delegates than others. When we approached the organisers for some clarifications on this, they explained that approximately the same quota of participants was given to the seven regions of Africa. However, the different regions do not have the same number of countries. Country delegates from regions with fewer conferences were more numerous. When it was pointed out that countries like Ghana and Nigeria, which are part of the Regional Episcopal Conference of West Africa, had a larger number of representatives, the response was that many of them were not delegates from their countries, but were part of certain church institutions at the sub-regional or continental level and that it was in this capacity that they were participating in this meeting.

From the contacts of the designated participants, a WhatsApp group was created for our region. This platform allowed the participants to receive all information related to the continental synod. There were also two online conferences, the first of which introduced the Spiritual Conversation Method

Africa

N°	Regional Conference	N° Episcopal Conferences	N° Delegates Expected	Country	Delegates per Country
01	ACEAC	03	20	Congo	14
				Kinshasa	14
				Rwanda	11
				Burundi	5
TOTAL ACEAC		**03**	**20**		**30**
02	ACERAC	07	19	Chad	5
				Congo	5
				Brazzaville	5
				Cameroon	7
				Gabon	3
				Central African Republic	4
				Equatorial Guinea	2
				Sao Tome and Principe	2
TOTAL ACERAC		**07**	**19**		**28**
03	RECOWA/ CERAO	16	20	*Niger*	*0*
				Nigeria	9
				Benin	1
				Togo	2
				Ghana	13
				Ivory Coast	2
				Guinea	1
				Senegal	2
				Burkina Faso	2
				Mali	1
				Mauritania	0
				Liberia	1
				Sierra Leone	1
				Gambia	1
				Guinea Bissau	1
				Cape Verde	*0*
TOTAL CERAO/ RECOWA		**16**	**20**		**37**
04	CERNA	05	07	*Libya*	*0*
				Algeria	1
				Morocco	1
				Tunisia	2
				Western Sahara	*0*
TOTAL CERNA		**05**	**07**		**4**

Africa

Nº	Regional Conference	Nº Episcopal Conferences	Nº Delegates Expected	Country	Delegates per Country
05	AMECEA	11	19	*Sudan*	*0*
				Eritrea	1
				Djibouti	*0*
				Ethiopia	
				South Sudan	2
				Somalia	*0*
				Kenya	9
				Uganda	4
				Tanzania	6
				Malawi	4
				Zambia	3
TOTAL AMECEA		**11**	**19**		**29**
06	IMBISA	08	19	Angola	2
				Mozambique	6
				Namibia	3
				Zimbabwe	5
				Botswana	*0*
				Swaziland	1
				Lesotho	2
				South Africa	5
TOTAL IMBISA		**08**	**19**		**24**
07	CEDOI	05	19	Seychelles	1
				Comoros	*0*
				Madagascar	11
				Réunion	*0*
				Mauritius	6
TOTAL CEDOI		**05**	**19**		**18**
08	CHASE	01	00	Egypt	0
TOTAL HECA		**01**	**00**		**0**
09	OTHER			England	1
				Spain	2
				France	3
				Italy	4
				Luxembourg	1
				Mexico	1
TOTAL OTHER					12
All TOGETHER					**182**

and the DCS summary. The second one was to collect the concerns of the participants and to try to answer them. At each of these meetings, the importance of getting to grips with the Call to Action (CTA) was emphasised. Information and training were provided in both French and English.

One important point needs to be highlighted.

The provisions of section 109 of the DCS state: The process leading from the publication of this DCS to the drafting of the *Instrumentum Laboris* will be marked by the following steps:

1. The DCS will be sent to all diocesan bishops; each of them, together with the diocesan synodal team that coordinated the first phase, will arrange an ecclesial process of discernment on the DCS, starting with the three questions indicated in section106. Each local Church will thus have an opportunity to listen to the voices of the other Churches, gathered in the DCS, and to respond.
2. With the involvement of its synodal team, each episcopal conference has the task of collecting and synthesising, in the form most appropriate to its own context, the reflections around the three questions coming from the individual Dioceses.
3. The reflection and discernment of each episcopal conference will then be shared within the Continental Assembly, according to the modalities identified by the Continental Task Force.

This work was not done at the level of our local Church, so I went to the continental phase of the synod on synodality without the reflection and discernment document of my episcopal conference. Nobody seemed to be aware of this provision, even at the continental level.

II
THE CONTINENTAL SYNODAL ASSEMBLY

In union with the universal Church, the Church in Africa celebrated its Continental Synodal Assembly from March 1 to 6, 2023.

This Continental Assembly, initiated and organised by SECAM, was preceded by the work of the African Synodal Initiative group which worked independently.

The proceedings of the Assembly on each day are given in summary form as follows:

1. Wednesday March 1, 2023

On March 1, 2023, 182 people from 49 countries on the African continent convened in Addis Ababa, the capital of Ethiopia, to join the Ethiopian hosts and guests from other continents, in particular from the Secretariat of the Synod of the Holy See.

Our meeting was an ecclesial assembly, which took into account the configuration of the list mentioned in section 108 of the DCS. A total of 206 participants gathered to walk, pray and celebrate together, under the guidance of the Holy Spirit. Among us were 9 cardinals, 29 bishops (38 bishops altogether), 41 priests and consecrated persons. But the majority of the assembly was made up of lay people, women and men, including young people, representative of the continent's Catholics. It also welcomed some guests from the continent's major religious traditions: Muslims, members of traditional African religions and sister churches. This assembly is the first of its kind, as previous continental assemblies convened by SECAM, known as 'plenary assemblies', have so far gathered only bishops.

2. Thursday March 2, 2023

The assembly took place at the Liepold Hotel. At the beginning of the day, bags containing notepads, pens, the DCS in the official language, a booklet containing the program and the texts of the Mass in each of the three languages, were distributed to each participant. The African Synodality Initiative group also designed a small document entitled: 'A Pocket Companion for Synodality: Voices from Africa'. This pocket booklet, translated into French, English and Portuguese, was distributed free of charge to participants according to their language. In order to enable us to follow the meeting correctly and to participate fully, translators were present and, with the help of headphones, we followed all the stages in our respective languages. The constitution of the working teams also respected this configuration.

It should be pointed out that the speed of the interpretation, and sometimes its poor quality, did not allow us to participate fully in this meeting, which took place mainly in English (approximately 70%).

The Assembly opened on Thursday, March 2 with the celebration of the Eucharist presided over by Cardinal Mario Grech, with the homily given by Cardinal Jean-Claude Hollerich SJ, respectively Secretary General of the Synod and General Relator of the Synod on Synodality.

Rafael Simbine, Secretary General of SECAM and Bishop Lucio Muandela, the first vice-president of SECAM, led a prayer consisting of a meditation on Acts 8, 1b-40, showing how Philip and the Ethiopian man listened to the Spirit. It was a reminder of the very ancient origin of Ethiopian Christianity.

Father Giacomo Costa SJ, Consultor of the Synod and member of the Steering Committee of the Synod on Synodality in Rome, subsequently offered a presentation on the Spiritual Conversation, its meaning, method and implementation, and guided a time of personal meditation on the theme 'What has been my personal experience of synodality during these two years of synod?'

The participants were then invited to meet in 15 small groups to answer two questions: 'What is the intuition that resonates most with us and can help us to grow as a synodal missionary church?', and 'What question/tension do we think should be addressed next October by the bishops in the universal phase of the synod?'

It should be noted that of these 15 groups, three groups were made up solely of bishops and cardinals, two of which were English-speaking and one French-speaking. Each of the small groups had a coordinator and a rapporteur, appointed from among the members of the coordination committee. There were a few women among them.

After an hour of sharing, the assembly gathered to listen to the groups' reports.

In the afternoon the official opening ceremony of the continental assembly took place. March 2 is a bank holiday in Ethiopia, in remembrance of the Battle of Adoua in 1896 where Ethiopians saved their independence by defeating an attempt at colonisation. Because of this commemoration, a number of personalities could not be available in the morning and the official opening ceremony was postponed to the afternoon.

After a word of welcome addressed to the whole Assembly by the Secretary General of the Ethiopian Catholic Bishops' Conference, Fr Teshome Fikre, Fr Rafael Simbine presented the delegations present, that of the Holy See, the Standing Committee of SECAM, the General Secretariat of SECAM (Frs Rafael and Fr Germain Rajoelison) and their valiant team, the various regions of Africa (North, East, West, Southern, Indian Ocean and the two regions of Central Africa) and the African Synodality Initiative group. He then detailed the composition of the assembly with a majority of 109 lay people, including 32 young people and 50 women, as well as 41 priests and 38 bishops (nine of them cardinals). Finally, he welcomed the guests from other religious traditions and sister churches.

The President of the Conference of Catholic Bishops of Ethiopia Berhaneyesus Demerew Cardinal Souraphiel, the Apostolic Nuncio to Ethiopia Mgr Antoine Camilleri, the Secretary General of the Synod of Bishops Mario Cardinal Grech, and the Vice President of the African Union Commission, Dr Monique Nsanzabaganwa, were then invited to speak. The President of SECAM, Fridolin Cardinal Ambongo, Archbishop of Kinshasa, spoke last. The speeches were interspersed with Ethiopian songs presented by the Catholic Secretariat Choir.

The speakers underlined the judicious choice of Ethiopia for holding this assembly, as a land considered to be the cradle of Christianity and humanity, the land of Lucy, the land of the Bible, the land of conviviality and synodical practice, the country that takes pride in having received the first companions persecuted by the prophet of Islam, the country that has succeeded in preserving its independence and dignity, and is today the seat of the African Union.

The Secretary General of the SECAM explained the absence of the Hierarchical Catholic Assembly of Egypt (AHCE) because it was participating in the 'continental' assembly of the Arabic-speaking Middle East.

Cardinal Grech underlined the importance for us to listen and discern whether what is proposed comes from the Holy Spirit. He reiterated the objectives of the assemblies in relation to the preparation of the Assembly of Bishops in October 2023. He pointed out that we will always be learners in the area of synodal functioning, but with more experience and renewed vigilance.

The Deputy Chairperson of the African Union Commission stressed the need to reflect on the theme of synodality, highlighting the importance of consultation processes in rendering a decision, especially with regard to the challenges facing the continent today (inequality, poverty, climate change, conflicts) where great collaborative efforts are needed. The African Union and the African Union Commission have the task of promoting peace, security and sustainable development. Synodality could be added in the sense of inclusiveness, participation and dialogue. Mrs Nsanzabaganwa reiterated the commitment of the African Union Commission to support values and initiatives such as these and expressed her wish for a positive impact of this Synod on the African continent.

Speaking last, the President of SECAM, Cardinal Ambongo warmly thanked all the participants for their commitment and our hosts for their presence. He also underlined the relevance of the choice of Ethiopia and Addis Ababa as the venue for the continental assembly. He expressed his gratitude to Pope Francis for his initiative to rediscover the value of synodality, pointing out how this is rooted in African principles such as the *palaver* or *Ubuntu*, where the family is valued. The Cardinal expressed the hope that our synodal journey will lead to concrete transformations and insisted on the capacity of all of us, pastors and other faithful, to enter into the listening world of the other and to hear the voice of the Spirit. He then presented the three questions on which our assembly would be called to work the following day.

The day ended with an official photo opportunity, refreshments and dinner.

3. Friday March 3, 2023

The Assembly entered its second working session. Prayer, reflection, Spiritual Conversation and sharing on the DCS remained the key points of our program today.

The first item on the agenda was the Eucharist, presided over by Cardinal

Antoine Kambanda, Archbishop of Kigali in Rwanda. The Cardinal opened the day by reminding us of the need to encourage listening.

He expressed regret saying, 'We do not listen to each other despite the many means of communication we have.' He stated that 'the most precious gift God has given to humanity is the Word, and the Word fulfils its purpose and has meaning when it is listened to. We must listen to this Word of God in order to live and receive His divine life'. The Eucharist, celebrated today in French, ended with this strong appeal.

At the beginning of the work, after the recapitulation of the experience and the process of the previous day, the major part of the morning of this second day was devoted to the practice of Spiritual Conversation: this method, presented at the beginning of the Assembly, aims to encourage listening to the Holy Spirit and mutual listening between the participants.

In this context, Rev. Fr Agbonkhianmeghe Orobator SJ, President of JCAM, introduced the morning's work by providing a guide to reading the DCS, based on a projected PowerPoint document. He first invited the participants to recognise their common baptismal dignity. Baptism, the Jesuit recalled, 'is our founding identity, which qualifies us to participate in the life and mission of the Church, in communion, sharing and dialogue with people of all faiths'. He then recalled that the heart of the Spiritual Conversation 'is prayer and silence' which allows all participants to express their opinions openly and honestly.

Referring then to the invitation to 'enlarge the space of the tent', he recalled how the image of the tent from the book of the prophet Isaiah can be compared to the African *Tukul*, a house *par excellence* consisting of a roof, walls and a central pole. Whether it is a tent or a Tukul, 'the house-church has no doors that close, but a perimeter that expands continuously'. Finally, the Jesuit recalled several times how this moment 'is a time to thank God who has brought us together, guided by the Spirit of God. It is a time to rejoice: let's not let the weeds get in the way, let's let the Spirit move us forward'. He ended his remarks by asking all the men present to stand and applaud the women for the great role they play in the life of the Church. Then we gathered again for group work.

During the afternoon session, having used the method of Spiritual Conversation the 15 groups reported their findings in their respective groups.

Various groups proposed some areas of priority on which the Synod Fathers should focus during the Assembly in October 2023: unity, the fight against poverty, the fight against social inequality, neo-colonialism.

Others focused on the Church as the family of God, called to evangelise through formation. A well-formed family will enable society to be good and to develop according to African values. The groups vouched for the synodal church as a family of God with well-defined roles and responsibilities that promote African values and improve the structural governance of the Church of God family by empowering the laity through formation.

Synodality invites to walk together and not to walk alone through the diversity of African cultures. Africa is called to examine all the mechanisms in place to make the journey together into a lived reality. Synodality invites to a profound conversion. This can be done through a respect for African values in which the family can play a major role. African voices must be taken into consideration in the decision-making process of the Church. The groups stressed the need for a family-centered understanding of synodality and the promotion of African values and a holistic catechism for all.

The day ended with the closing prayer.

4. Saturday March 4, 2023

The last working day of the Synodal Continental Assembly for Africa began with a Mass celebrated in the Ethiopian rite at the Cathedral of the Nativity of the Blessed Virgin Mary in Addis Ababa. In the homily of the Divine Liturgy, the Bishop of the Eparchy of Emdeber in Ethiopia stressed the importance of protecting and preserving African values.

After this Mass, which was very rich in rites – incomprehensible and new for most of us – the morning was devoted to the practice of Spiritual Conversation in Working Groups, on the draft Final Document which had to be submitted to the General Secretariat of the Synod by March 31, 2023. The aim was to define the eight priorities that the Church of Africa could present to the Assembly to be held in October 2023.

In the early afternoon, all met in plenary to share the fruits of the morning's work, before returning to group work and then to plenary again for feedback.

Much of the late afternoon was spent refining the Final Document, with corrections and amendments. It was hard but genuine collegial work during which everyone could express their opinion. The Assembly succeeded in approving a set of priorities, which it intends to offer as the document of the African Synodal Assembly to the universal Church for the work of the 16th General Assembly of the Synod of Bishops. The *ad hoc* group of experts, which has been working on the Addis Ababa Synodal Assembly document since the Accra and Nairobi seminars, was mandated to further refine the document according to the indications received from the Assembly before sending it to the General Secretariat of the Synod.

This drafting team was made up of five people including Rev. Vitalis Chinedu Anaehobi (theologian; Secretary General of RECOWA/CERAO), Rev. Father Edouard Ade (theologian; rector of the Catholic University of West Africa; UCAO in Benin), Rev. Agbonkhianmeghe Orobator SJ, President of the Jesuit Conference of Africa and Madagascar (JCAM), Rev. Ester Lucas Jose Maria

(Professor of Grand Seminary) and Rev. Rafael Simbine (Secretary General of SECAM). These persons volunteered to write the Final Document.

In the early evening, the Assembly participated in the closing of the continental stage of the synod at the level of the African continent. The speakers were Cardinal Berhaneyesus Souraphiel, who hosted the meeting, Archbishop Lucio Muandula, First Vice-President of SECAM, Cardinal Jean-Claude Hollerich, General Relator of the 16th Ordinary General Assembly of the Synod of Bishops, and finally the President of SECAM, Cardinal Ambongo, who officially closed the meeting.

The evening was devoted to a festive meal combined with cultural activities.

5. Sunday March 5, 2023

There was a beautiful closing Mass in the cathedral, presided over by the President of SECAM, Cardinal Ambongo. In the afternoon, the group visited the African Union headquarters and the city, while the Cardinals and Bishops met, as recommended by Rome: 'Furthermore, bishops are invited to meet at the end of the Continental Assemblies to collegially reread the lived synodal experience from the perspective of their specific charism and role. In particular, they are asked to identify appropriate ways to carry out their task of validating and approving the Final Document, ensuring that it is the fruit of an authentically synodal journey, respectful of the process that has taken place and faithful to the diverse voices of the People of God in each continent' (DCS 108). They therefore studied the document again to validate it. There were no major changes in the substance. Then the different delegations returned to their countries according to their departure date.

The media were invited to participate in the meetings.

6. Conclusion

The days experienced during the continental stage of the Synod on Synodality from March 1 to 6 in Addis Ababa were days of abundant graces and blessings from God.

In addition to the group work and the plenary sessions, the breaks and meal times were great moments for us when synodality was fully and concretely lived. We spontaneously approached each other, exchanging information about our nations, our local churches, our traditions, etc. and I personally learned a lot. I was even surprised to learn in Addis Ababa about the extent of the terrorist drama that the Church of Jesus Christ in Burkina Faso, a neighbouring country of mine, is experiencing.

As the Synodal Family of God in Africa, we have found immense joy in walking together and we want to continue to do so. Our journey is one of conversion, reform and growth at the personal, community and institutional levels of the Church.

As the Synodal Family of God in Africa, we wish to thank God for bringing us together and guiding us through the Spirit of the Risen Christ. We also express our deep gratitude to the Holy Father for this pastoral initiative to call the whole Catholic Church to rediscover the precious value of synodality. This synodal process, placed under the sign of communion, participation and mission, constitutes a time of grace and a favourable moment of true ecclesial communion.

On the one hand, this synodal process confirms the Church's way of doing things in Africa. Indeed, rooted in African anthropological principles, which emphasise community spirit, a sense of family, teamwork, solidarity and conviviality, the Catholic Church in Africa has grown as the Family of God.

In this sense, the Fathers of the Special Assembly for Africa of the Synod of Bishops in 1994 recommended the image of the Church as the Family of God, insofar as this image emphasises 'attention to others, solidarity, warmth in human relations, mutual acceptance, dialogue and trust' (Ecclesia in Africa, n.63). They wanted to highlight the African family as a model for living the Church and living in the Church.

Furthermore, the papal initiative to convene this Synod is timely. It is an invitation to all members of the Church-Family of God in Africa and the Islands to pause and evaluate their journey as a Family.

Indeed, despite the remarkable growth of the Church-Family of God in Africa and the Islands, there are visible situations of weakness, including bitter and painful experiences of conflict and war, racial tensions and tribalism, xenophobia, political instability, 'injustice, selfish political actions, looting of the national wealth [...] and quick enrichment by illegal [...]means.'[2]

In view of the above, we hope that this synodal journey will give us the courage to evaluate our faith and to speak with freedom, courage and charity about the challenges we face in Africa, both at the level of the Church and society, and to engage deeply with these challenges in order to respond to them through concrete transformations.

The Holy Spirit has enabled us, through this time of listening, to identify the priorities that the Church, God's family in Africa, will present to Rome. May the Lord lead this whole synodal process.

2 Symposium of Episcopal Conferences of Africa and Madagascar, *Pastoral Exhortation of the Symposium of Episcopal Conferences of Africa and Madagascar (SECAM): 'Kampala Document'* (Kampala: SECAM / SCEAM, 2019), nr. 156.

DOCUMENT OF THE AFRICAN SYNODAL CONTINENTAL ASSEMBLY

Addis Ababa, Ethiopia

I
INTRODUCTION

1. From 9 to 10 October, 2021, the Holy Father Pope Francis officially launched the Synod on Synodality and on 17 of the same month the initiative was launched in all the Dioceses of the world. This first phase of the Synod was experienced in the local Churches. This involved consultations, seminars and sensitisation activities at the various levels of the Dioceses. Different religious bodies and groups in the local Churches were organised to express their views on the new initiative. The results of these consultations were brought together by each Diocese and were, further, collected at the national levels. The National Episcopal Conferences, finally, produced the national syntheses of the lived experience of Synodality which contains the expectations of the People of God concerning the Synodality initiative. These syntheses were sent to the General Secretariat of the Synod in Rome.

2. In September 2022, the Secretaries General of the Regional Episcopal Conferences in Africa submitted the syntheses of the contributions of the National Episcopal Conferences of their regions to the Symposium of Episcopal Conferences of Africa and Madagascar (SECAM). From these, SECAM produced a document that recapitulates the expectations of all the regions in Africa.

3. Having gone through the syntheses of the episcopal conferences from all the countries of the world, the General Secretariat of the Synod on Synodality produced a universal synthesis from what was received

from the local Churches called 'Working Document for the Continental Stage' (DCS). From 5 to 9 December 2022, and from 22 to 26 January, 2023, SECAM brought together the members of the Continental Team for the Synod on Synodality, namely: General Secretaries of the Regional Episcopal Conferences, members of the African Synodality Initiative, theologians, religious and some lay faithful, numbering 28 and 20 persons respectively, to receive the Working Document for the Continental Stage and to familiarise themselves with the practice of the Spiritual Conversation Method towards the Continental Assembly.

4. The final phase of the continental celebration of the Synod on Synodality took place in Addis Ababa in Ethiopia from 1 to 6 March, 2023. This event brought together about 209 people made up of cardinals, archbishops, bishops, priests, religious men and women, and lay faithful, with the lay faithful being in greater number. It was an occasion for an inclusive listening where, using the Spiritual Conversation Method, everyone was given the opportunity to express his/her views about Synodality, guided by the Document for the Continental Stage. For five days, the Church Family of God in Africa through the continental representatives prayed, listened and reflected on the new way of being a Church today, i.e. the Synodal way. It was a spiritual Synodal journey of the Church Family of God in Africa, an opportunity to practise Synodality in reality. At the end of the session, the assembly went through the Final Document and officially adopted it as the Document for the African Church.

5. In the spirit of collegiality, all the cardinals and bishops sat together in another meeting on the last day of the Assembly to evaluate the whole Synodal process. They expressed satisfaction about the process, especially about the family spirit that prevailed throughout the Assembly. They, equally, went through the Final Document and unanimously adopted it as the Final Document for the African Continental Synodal Assembly.

6. These meetings became the basis for the elaboration of the present document which took into consideration all the main ideas raised during the discussions.

7. At the opening of the first working session in Accra, the purpose of the session was given as follows:

- To come to know one another better, a way of living the Synodality in a concrete manner.
- To enter into communion with the universal Church in the process of

deeper prayer, listening and discernment to hear what the Holy Spirit is saying to the Church.
- To listen to what the people of Africa said during the first year of the Synod.
- To reread the Document for the Continental Stage in the context of the Church in Africa.

8. The method used in the work is the Spiritual Conversation Method. The method was not familiar to most of the participants. It was, therefore, taught to the group.

9. Having learnt the method, the group practised it for the remaining days of the working session starting from the first day. The evening session of the first day was devoted to the practical aspects of the method. Five groups were constituted and asked to give their 'personal impressions from the regional summaries and synthesis: What have the People of God from the Church in Africa said in the first year of the synod?' The session ended with the reports of the various groups on the outcome of their reflection on the question.

10. The second day of the session was devoted to the study of the Document for the Continental Stage. This was done with two presentations on the major outlines and logic of the document. After the exposé, the participants were given time to pray, reflect and study the document individually. The evening session was, then, devoted to group study of the documents focusing on:
- Intuitions that resonate most strongly with the lived experiences and realities of the Church on the African continent.
- Questions or issues that should be addressed and considered in the next step of the process.
- Priorities, recurrent themes and calls to action that can be shared with other local Churches around the world and discussed during the first session of the Synodal Assembly in October 2023.

11. At the end of the first working session in December 2022, each participant was asked to practise what was learnt, especially the use of the Spiritual Conversation Method, with the people of his or her faith community, or Regional Conference, as the case may be. This was meant to be a way of renewed listening to the people at the grassroot levels and a way of mastering the method which would be used in facilitating the continental event in March 2023.

12. The working session in Accra was followed by another in Nairobi, Kenya, from 22 to 26 January, 2023. The aim was to continue deepening the knowledge of the Document for the Continental Stage and training members of the working team to help them in facilitating the planned Continental Assembly to be held in Addis Ababa from 1 to 6 March, 2023.

13. The working session of Nairobi was an opportunity for members of the team to share their experiences with regard to the use of the Spiritual Conversation Method in the study of the Document for the Continental Stage with their various communities after the Accra session. The sharing of the experiences exposed some difficulties that occurred while listening to others in the spirit of Synodality. These difficulties include:

- Listening to the other was not easy, as most people wanted their positions to be taken into account.
- Some people were not happy that they were not consulted at the initial phase of the consultation only to be invited at the continental phase.
- There was a sort of reticence from some people who felt that having worked at the Diocesan phase, they should not start the same work all over again.
- The time was too short to reach out to the right persons to deepen the understanding of the document and obtain the desired result.
- It was difficult to apply the Spiritual Conversation Method to a big text like the Document for the Continental Stage.
- There was difficulty in meeting people physically and the alternative means which was that of telecommunications also met with the problem of insufficient resources.
- Those who were not in an official position in the Church found it difficult to bring people together to study the Document for the Continental Stage using the Spiritual Conversation Method because people listen more to those in authority in the Church.

14. The general experience of the participants was that people were eager to be involved in the life of the Church and that the Synod on Synodality has awakened a new desire for a Church that takes into account the thoughts, concerns and feelings of every member. They were ready to make contributions and wanted to be sure that their expectations would bear durable fruit by bringing lasting changes in the life of the Church and her institutions.

15. The two previous experiences of Accra and Nairobi formed the basis for the Addis Ababa event which involved representatives from all the countries of Africa and the Islands. The group used the same method of

prayer, silence and Spiritual Conversation. They worked in plenaries and in small groups and were able to discern the Synodal Priorities for the Church in Africa.

16. The choice of Addis Ababa as the venue for the Continental Assembly was conditioned by a number of factors: it is the seat of the African Union (AU), a body that unites all the countries of Africa; it is a country that has the three monotheistic religions: Judaism, Christianity and Islam; it is a country marked with a welcoming culture.

II
THE SYNODAL EXPERIENCE AT THE CONTINENTAL STAGE

17. The encounter as a concrete experience by Africans of Synodality, by working and journeying together for five days, helped us to become aware of some intuitions that generally resonate from one country to the other and raised some pertinent questions concerning Synodality.

2.1 Intuitions

18. Our prayer and reflection on the Document for the Continental Stage gave rise to the following intuitions from our African background:

1. **The Church in Africa has lived out Synodality from the time of the Second Vatican Council. The fruit of this is seen in the formation of SECAM and other Regional Episcopal Conferences during and immediately after the Council.**
   Some important documents on and from the African Church are also fruits of Synodality. They include *Ecclesia in Africa* (1995), *Africae Munus* (2011) and the *Kampala Document* (2019).
   The Small Christian Communities are the fruits of Synodality at the grassroot levels where people live and act together with common faith concerns.
2. **The image of the tent as the principal image for Synodality 'enlarge the space of your tent' (Is. 54:2) was heavily contested by many, who associate the image with warfare, displacement and refugee situations.**
   The assembly preferred the image of the Family of God where everyone has his or her place and responsibilities according to 'family values' (though there is no homogeneity on what the latter includes in all countries).
3. **Listening is an attitude of the Synod and the Church must be a listening Church if it is to remain Synodal. However, the realities listened to are**

not always the same: family, church, national issues, social problems, spiritual problems, etc., often vary in interpretation or social importance. Listening helps to bring healing to those who are wounded. Listening invites us to another way of celebrating our liturgy in a culturally authentic manner. Applying the culture of listening to the liturgical celebration will help to put the people at the forefront, enhance their active participation and make them more actors than spectators.

The Church listens to all, but the listening disturbs in such a way that the Church is, sometimes, so overwhelmed that some persons feel that the Church does not listen, or at least is selective in whose voices matter. Many would want the Church to listen to all and bring solutions to all problems of the society, thus confusing the role of the Church with that of the State and government.

Listening is not only listening to people. It involves listening to the local culture with the dynamics of co-responsibility and with the consciousness that culture is dynamic and evolving. The Church in Africa is a fruit of the endeavours of Western missionaries. The Church came with a culture into another culture. Synodality should help to listen to the cultural practices that have been either ignored, condemned or suppressed by the Western culture through which the Gospel was preached to Africans. These cultural practices, some deeply influenced and changed by Western and Christian cultural influences, continue to affect the way Christians live out the Gospel. They should, therefore, be listened to in view of either integrating, purifying or collectively rejecting them based on a clear understanding of the exigencies of the Gospel.

4. **The need for the participation of women, youth and physically challenged persons in the life of the Church is another intuition that comes out strongly in the Document.**
Women form a greater percentage of active members of the Church. They make meaningful contributions to the life and mission of the Church. Many of them feel that they are not given a sufficient place in the decision-making structures of the Church. There is a call to create more opportunities and structures for women to do more in the Church.

The youth also complained that they would like to be more visible in the life of the Church. An idea that was strongly felt was that of a preferential option for the youth. There is a call to adapt the activities and celebrations of the Church to styles that will attract and maintain the youth in the Church.

The need to enhance the participation of persons with disability in the life and mission of the Church also came out clearly in the Document. The Church should guard against the way the society tends to cast them aside. They are often considered as not having much to offer based on the false idea that their lives are worth less than others. If the appropriate opportunity is created, they can feel at home in the Church and can contribute towards the progress and growth of the Church. This calls for special initiatives, formations and structures that will help them to have a prominent place in the Church.

5. **It is evident that there are mundane forces that are opposed to the mission of the Church.**
   Such forces include ideologies and economic or political policies that are prejudicial to the doctrines of the faith. Some of these forces influence Church leaders and put pressure on theologians with the intention of diluting the content of the faith. There is a call for the Synodal Church to be awake to such influences and remain focused on the Word of God and the firm tradition of the Church.
6. **Synodality draws everyone's attention to the need for co-responsibility – making it relevant to learn to walk together through listening, discernment and dialogue.**
   Many expressed the view that decisions in the Church are sometimes taken without sufficient dialogue, but Synodality requires taking everyone as important and responsible. The recognition of the value of everyone in a Christian community imposes the necessity of taking their opinions into consideration for proper discernment and decision-making.
7. **The Synodal Church should seek to balance her efforts in addressing the concrete issues in people's lives with the spiritual aspects.**
   This idea comes from the experience of some people who believe that the Church seems to concentrate more on their spiritual needs than on concrete material needs. Just as Jesus fed the hungry, the Synodal Church should learn to balance her care for spiritual issues with her care for material problems.
8. **A sensitisation on Synodality as tied to evangelisation:** from the image of the Church as a Family of God, where efforts should be made to accommodate everyone who so desires and even those who are deliberately outside, comes the intuition that inclusivity should be harmonised with conversion, since walking together in communion, participation and mission cannot be divorced from evangelisation. The mission of the Church to spread the Gospel of Christ to the ends of the earth should be based on the need to help people abandon their old ways that are not in conformity with the Word of God and embrace the truth of the Gospel.
9. **There is the need for openness of all Catholics to continuous formation.**
   The understanding of the Synodal Church as one that walks together

with everyone calls for the formation of the clergy and the laity on this new consciousness. Pastors who lead the People of God should be the first to imbibe the Synodal mentality and apply it in their life and ministry. There is an urgent need for educational and formational programmes for the clergy and the lay faithful to initiate the necessary conversion to imbibe the new culture of walking together as a Synodal Church, especially at the local Church level. This formation should touch on the formation received in the seminaries, so that future pastors are prepared to embrace the new culture of walking together and acquire the capacity for listening to the Spirit of God and to the people.

10. **Some feel that the Synodal Church should be less conservative and have the courage to do a self-examination on how she has accepted new ideas.**
The new culture of the Synodal Church would demand a lot of openness and a learning attitude from the Church, in order to remain relevant in the world. However, some feel that the Church must not be too open to every new idea since some ideas are perceived as not for the betterment of the world. In such cases, the Church should even have courage to go against certain currents of thought. Much depends on Christians' perception of new social forces – some well-informed, others less so – and the degree to which such ideas that challenge the Church's official positions might have valid points should be discerned more openly and thoroughly.

11. **The care and protection of children and vulnerable persons was also invoked as an integral aspect of the mission of the Synodal Church.**

12. **To open the family means accommodating those who feel marginalised, for example, people in polygamous marriages, divorced and remarried, and single parents.** Many people expressed the desire to revisit the position of the Church on those that considered themselves officially marginalised due to irregular family situations. How does the openness of the family apply to such people in the spirit of Synodality that encourages the Church to walk together with all believers? And what domestic arrangements have we overlooked?

13. **About clericalism, there is a new awareness that clericalism is even present among lay people who give credence to or accept without question what the priest says.** Inasmuch as some priests could be accused of being closed and authoritative, the internalised clericalism of laity is also seen as promoting such a culture by not playing its proper role in the Church and by deferring to priests to carry all the burden of leading, teaching and making all the decisions. This deference is seen as another form of clericalism.

14. **There is the need to deepen reflections on no.35 of the Document for the Continental Stage about the youth, with regards to real accompaniment and the need to help the youth and be close to them in their crucial moment to help them rediscover the value of marriage.** Give more attention to the youth in the Church by providing more formative programmes to deepen their faith, give them a voice, and create opportunities (through structural changes) that allow the youth to bring innovative ideas to the Church today. Without attending to the issues faced by the youth, we cannot walk together. The issues of the youth go beyond religion. We need to reflect on contemporary political and economic systems like new capitalism that will not only lead to unemployment but also to redundancy (caused by lack of jobs through technological advancement).
15. **There is the need to keep alive the Synodal spirit in the Church beyond the Continental Assembly in Addis Ababa.** Many issues that are local to Africa came up in the discussions and such problems can only be treated locally. Based on this, there is a call for each local Church to continue deepening the experience of Synodality in order to evolve a more dynamic Synodal Church that goes beyond the Continental Synodal Assembly.
16. **Give and make deliberate efforts to overcome cultural marginalisation of minority groups, especially the indigenous peoples. Pay more attention to cultural issues as in nos. 55 and 56 of the Document for the Continental Stage.** There is the need to reread the history of the indigenous people and then recover, promote and integrate their cultural practices into the liturgy. This is a proper inculturation which enhances diversity, moving from multi-culturality to inter-culturality where different practices complement and enrich one another.
17. **To deepen the study of no.88ff of the Document for the Continental Stage on Liturgy which seems more theoretical.** This process could help to make it more practical and sensitive to cultural differences. The emphasis here should be on getting people to participate more actively in liturgical and community prayer gatherings. This will require getting in deep contact with the people's cultural ways of worship. There is the call to make liturgy more contextual.
18. **Liturgically, the Church should find a way of doing things differently, so that those who come to liturgical celebrations should feel that they are actually being considered and given an opportunity to express themselves and participate actively.**
19. **African Unity.** To be able to ask questions and try to resolve problems without removing our capacity to reflect and achieve what we need

by ourselves. Undertaking a deep evaluation of all the documents, for example, the *Kampala Document*, so that we do not look for answers outside us. At the level of Solidarity, we are weak: a problem in Uganda should be of concern to Algeria. A Synodal African Church should be able to unite Africans.

20. **The need for Church authorities to engage the political leadership of the society in advocacy for Good Governance and Justice.** This is to be seen as part of the missionary mandate of making Christ known to the world. A Synodal Church should, therefore, be a Church in continuous mission in all the dimensions of human existence.

2.2 Questions or Issues

19. A careful study of the Document for the Continental Stage raises a number of questions and issues that need to be clarified. They include:

1. What mechanism do we put in place to cater for the respect for diverse cultures?
2. How is the Synodal Church more empathetic and what are her means of promoting concrete Solidarity?
3. There is a tension between a strong understanding of truth and the principle of mercy (particularly the accommodation with difference, minority views and dissent), between belonging to the Church and not living as a full member of the Church, between autonomy and co-responsibility. How do we deal with it?
4. Where is Synodality taking us as we listen to the voices of diverse people? Is this not leading us to democracy? Thus, there is only a thin line between dialogue, listening and decision making and the rule of the majority.
5. Everything we have raised is important. How would the local Church make use of all the points that are being raised in our discussions?
6. In listening to others, to the Holy Spirit and to the Word of God, what are the criteria for discernment and judgement?

2.3. Conclusion

20. Having listened to other Churches and to the experience of Africans, we consider the following eight points to be recurrent and urgent priorities on which it is important to continue discernment at the level of the universal Church. These points are directly related to a manner of living out the Synodal spirit of Communion, Participation and Mission:

1. **To deepen Catholic Synodality according to the values of the Church as Family of God, nurture life from conception to natural death, based on co-responsibility, biblical hospitality (Eph. 2:19), dignity**

of children, women and men, and reaching out to the entire human family and all creation, from the Small Christian Communities to the Vatican level.

The Church is built on the Word of God, Tradition and the Magisterium. The Synodal Church style should be founded on the traditions and teachings of the Church through which the Church has engendered values that have stood the test of time. Synodality should stand on such values to be able to have a firm foundation that could lead the Church to the desired renewal, even as we draw on reason and the lived experience of all the faithful.

2. **African voices and values should be taken into consideration when elaborating the doctrines and teachings of the church, values such as family, solidarity, communitarian life, reverential dialogue, hospitality and co-responsibility.**

   Africans have equal responsibility for the doctrines and teachings of the Church in collaboration with other local Churches (Eph. 2:19). Accordingly, it is paramount that their experiences and ever-evolving cultural values be taken into consideration and their problems be always equally considered. This will help them to own the teachings and to be committed to living them out.

3. **The commitment of the Church, Family of God (Africae Munus, 1) to conflict resolution, to fight against economic colonialism and illegal exploitation of resources in Africa, and the promotion of Good Governance, Justice and Peace.**

   Peace has become so fragile in our time that sometimes, securing an end to conflict is difficult because of the vested interests of the intervening powers. In such situations, it has become necessary for the Synodal Church to get involved in advocacy and concrete negotiations for peace, especially among warring nations and communities. The Synodal Church should make more effort to devise effective mechanisms for active engagement in peace making at the international and local levels in the manner of Christ, the Prince of Peace (Is. 9:6).

   Religion is, equally, a cause of conflict in Africa. The desire to promote peace should also lead the Church to promote ecumenism and inter-religious dialogue. There is need for the Synodal Church to work together with other faith communities in the promotion of peace and conflict resolution in building the kingdom of God on earth.

   It is clear that one of the major causes of conflict in Africa is the manipulative attitude of the exploiters of natural resources. The Church should stand with the people and ensure that there is no exploitation without free, prior and informed consent of the population.

The Church should equally foster good governance in African countries, including the pastoral accompaniment of the faithful engaged in social, economic and political life.

4. **The process of synodality must also involve inculturation and liturgical renewal in order to respond to the aspiration, participation and overall growth of the African faithful.**
   Inculturation helps the faith to be rooted in the life and practice of the people. Worship in Africa is an integral experience involving the whole person: mind, spirit and body. The current ways of celebrating the liturgy sometimes leave many Africans unfulfilled. A synodal Church should take into consideration the nature of Africans to have a more participatory liturgy, in line with authentic liturgical theology and doctrine.
5. **Synodality is the way of being Church and hence the necessity of formation as a means of making the synodal model a pastoral model of the Church's life and practice.**
   The new understanding about the synodal Church would lead to a new way of understanding and exercising authority in the Church like Jesus (Lk. 22:27). This new understanding will necessarily demand the formation of the clergy, consecrated persons and the laity in the practice of synodal leadership. An African proverb says 'crops are to be cultivated whereas weeds grow on their own.' The synodal model needs to be planted in the life of the People of God. Each group must be open to ongoing formation in the synodal way of being Church, including bishops, clergy, lay women and men, young people and consecrated persons.
6. **Synodality should strengthen subsidiarity on all levels of the Church's life so as to promote the inclusion, participation and communion of all the members, especially women, the youth and persons living with disability.**
   The principle of subsidiarity helps each group to autonomously contribute its quota in the development of society and to deal with local pastoral challenges. This should apply to the activities of the synodal Church in all its dimensions.

   Women form the greater percentage of active members of the Church. They continue to make enormous contributions to the Church in Africa. However, there are not enough structures to encourage and enhance their participation, especially in the decision-making processes and platforms of the Church. The Church in Africa wishes that, following the principle of subsidiarity, formal forums for women participation in the Church be enhanced.

   The above is also true of young people who form the greater percentage of the African population. They have creative ideas and desire to take initiatives in the Church and in society. Often they do not find enough space to exercise their initiatives in the Church. In Africa most young people are faced with the difficult decision of remaining Christians in the face of many competing options.

For persons living with disability, there is need to offer them opportunities to feel at home in the Church. This will demand putting in place structures that should be concerned with them at the highest level of the Church. The Church should not only listen to the challenges of the people but also, based on the principle of subsidiarity, find ways of creating opportunities for them to contribute to the life of the Church.

7. **The family is an important structure in the promotion of the synodal Church and demands pastoral care that focuses on marriage and family, and their challenges in the present-day Africa, especially situations of polygamy, divorced and remarried people, single parenthood and child protection.**
   In Africa we are faced with the challenges of broken marriages based on traditional practices that have been difficult to transform through Christian values and other socio-economic factors, including polygamy which is still imposed by some social conditions in African societies. Divorce is also becoming a common occurrence. There is equally the situation of elective and circumstantial single parenthood, widowhood and cohabitation. We equally note the necessity of protecting children from abuse. People involved in these still want to remain practising Catholics. There is a need to develop an evangelising family pastoral care and catechesis that will make it possible to help them to live their faith with confidence and joy.
8. **Ecological justice and stewardship should become a way of life of the synodal Church.**
   Climate change is an existential threat to the whole world and the Church is not separated from the world. Africa bears the brunt of the current climate crisis, although it contributes the least to it. The Church ought to continue to do more in finding solutions and developing innovative strategies to respond to this urgent crisis as an integral part of her mission.

21. To conclude, synodality, founded on love, inclusion and respect for all, particularly those who are marginalised, has engendered a new dynamism through the Synod on Synodality. This dynamism should be sustained so that synodality becomes a Christian identity (Jn. 13:35), a way of being Church from the grassroots to the highest level. This can

only happen if everyone sincerely opens up to the gospel and to the Holy Spirit who has enkindled this synodality as a new way of Christianity in our time.

Adopted Unanimously by the African Continental Synodal Assembly
Addis Ababa, Ethiopia
05 March 2023

Adopted Unanimously by the Bishop Delegates
to the African Synodal Continental Assembly
Addis Ababa, Ethiopia
05 March 2023

'Tapping the Voice of the Holy Spirit'

TAPPING THE VOICE OF THE HOLY SPIRIT IN A MULTI-RELIGIOUS AND MULTI-CULTURAL CONTEXT: THE CONTINENTAL SYNODAL ASSEMBLY IN ASIA

Vimal Tirimanna CSsR and Jessica Joy Candelario

The FABC and the Asian Continental Ecclesial Assembly

In holding the first ever Asian Continental Ecclesial Assembly the structure of the Federation of Asian Bishops' Conferences (FABC) was of immense help. This 'federation' of the Asian Catholic Episcopal Conferences was founded in 1970 during the end of the visit of Pope Paul VI to Manila, the Philippines. During that visit, when the Pope addressed some 180 Asian bishops gathered in Manila, they expressed the need to set up a continental episcopal organisation to experience their continental episcopal collegiality and help coordinate their work of evangelisation and social development in the ancient continent. A couple of years later, with the explicit blessing of the Pope, the FABC came into being. Today, the FABC comprises of 17 episcopal conferences, 2 Synods of Oriental Churches and 3 Associate Members covering 29 Asian countries.

Since 1970, this Asian episcopal network has been successful in keeping the episcopal fraternal links and a sense of solidarity among the Churches in Asia. It has also been able to coordinate and promote common pastoral endeavours across Asia since the 1970s. In the multi-cultural, multi-religious Asian continent, where Christianity still is a tiny minority (except in the Philippines and East Timor), the primary mode of evangelisation mooted by the FABC has been through a triple-dialogue: dialogue with the great Asian religions (inter-religious dialogue), dialogue with the ancient Asian cultures (inculturation) and dialogue with the teeming millions of the Asian poor (option for the poor). Asia, which is not only the largest continent geographically, but has more than half of the world population, is also the arena of scenes of violence, terrorism, wars, ethnic and religious tensions, political instability, corruption, injustice and natural disasters as its typical characteristics.

The Asian Continental Ecclesial Assembly (ACEA) was held at the sprawling edifice of *Baan Phu Waan Pastoral Training Centre* of the Archdiocese of

Bangkok (which is situated in Sampran, some 60 kilometers away from Bangkok), a frequent host to FABC gatherings. In a sense, it was providential that the ACEA of the current synodal process in the universal Church was held from February 24 to 26, 2023 at the same venue, just three months after the 'FABC 50 Conference' which was held to mark the Golden Jubilee of the FABC.[1] The latter was a sort of a forerunner, in the sense that it paid its main attention to the contemporary context and challenges which the peoples of Asia were encountering. Thus, it tried to reflect on the signs of the times, to understand and respond to the emerging realities in Asia and to discern where and how the churches in Asia could share the Good News with their fellow pilgrims. Moreover, as the 'FABC 50 Conference' was coming to an end in late October 2022, the Document for the Continental Stage (entitled 'Enlarge the Space of your Tent') of the current synodal process was released in Rome. Copies of this document (DCS) were distributed among all the participants of this FABC Conference. In addition, during this Conference, a special Asian Task Force was formed by the Central Committee of the FABC in order to facilitate and coordinate the Asian continental phase of the synodal process. It consisted of some selected Executive Secretaries of the FABC offices and sub-regional representatives nominated by the FABC Central Committee.

The Organisation of the Asian Continental Ecclesial Assembly

Within a week after the FABC 50 Conference, the Asian Task Force met via Zoom on November 7, 2022. Having seriously studied and reflected on the guidelines (especially on the methodology to be followed during the continental synodal process) sent to them by the Secretariat for Synods in Rome, the members of the Asian Task Force set February 24 to 26, 2023 as the dates for the ACEA. All the 22 FABC members were requested to go through the DCS carefully and submit their responses to it (in 10 pages) on or before January 15, 2023.

In the meantime, the FABC Central Committee decided that the Asian Task Force could also serve as the Discerning and Drafting Team (DDT), to which some members were added. Its main task was to draw up a 'draft framework' for the ACEA. In this Team, there were seven men and two women (six priests, one consecrated woman, one lay man and one lay woman). They were Frs William La Rousse (Assistant Secretary General, FABC), Clarence Devadass (Malaysia), Enrico Emmanuel A. Ayo (Philippines), Joseph Philip Gonsalves (India), Anthony Corcoram SJ (Kyrgyzstan), Hai-Tinh Nguyen SJ (Vietnam), Ms Momoko Nishimura SEMD (Japan), Ms. Estella Padilla (Philippines) and Mr Pablito A. Baybado Jr (Philippines). Coordinated by Fr La Rousse, the DDT met at the Camillian Pastoral Centre, Bangkok, Thailand, from January

1 This celebration was delayed by two years due to the Covid-19 pandemic.

30 to February 4, 2023 to read, reflect and discern on the responses to the DCS sent by the member Asian Episcopal Conferences, Synods and Associate members. Altogether there were 21 responses received, and the DDT was divided into three sub-groups with each of them being assigned with seven response reports. Thus, the responses were read individually, as a sub-group and also as one team. The DDT followed the process of Spiritual Conversation, with spaces of silence and prayer in between their discussions and reflections. Thus, having been together for five days to read, reflect and discern prayerfully the 21 reports, the DDT produced 'a draft framework'[2] of the would-be Asian Continental Document (ACD) which consisted of responses to the three questions as posed by the DCS, under the three sub-headings: Asian Resonances, Asian Tensions, and Asian Realities and Divergences. In addition, the draft framework of the would-be ACD had a fourth sub-heading entitled 'Priorities from the Asian Responses' that presented six specific priorities deemed important for the continent of Asia, based on the issues that emerged at the FABC 50 Conference hardly three months before. In introducing this last sub-heading, the DDT had written:

> *'The Asian responses were varied and diverse, encapsulating a variety of issues and challenges, each peculiar to one's region. However, there are some commonalities that we see in the responses. The following are some key priorities that have been identified through a process of prayer and discernment with the hope that they reflect the Asian heart's desires'.*

Prior to their arrival in Thailand (i.e., on February 15) this draft framework of the would-be ACD was sent to all the member episcopal conferences, the two Synods and the three Associate members of the FABC, and also, to all the participants, so that the delegates could read and reflect on it as a remote preparation for the ACEA.

The Participants at the ACEA

The FABC Central Secretariat, as per approval from the FABC's Central Committee, invited each and every member episcopal conference/Synod to send three delegates, and the Associate members two delegates, for the ACEA – preferably, a bishop, a woman (religious or lay) and a man (priest, religious or lay), who were involved in the local synodal consultations and thus could speak out of their personal experiences of the synodal process in their particular contexts. While most of the episcopal conferences did their best to abide by this important criterion stipulated by the organisers (based on DCS 108-109), a couple of them sent only bishops and priests. The two Asian members of

2 The DDT preferred to call it a 'draft framework' rather than a 'draft document' in order to avoid any doubt that the document was pre-planned.

the Theological Commission[3] for the synodal process in the universal Church appointed by the Secretariat of the Synod in Rome were also invited. In the official list of the names of the participants, the following were categorised as 'Guests', most of them being members of the Secretariat of the Synod in the Vatican: Cardinal Mario Grech (Secretary General of the Synod), Cardinal Jean-Claude Hollerich SJ (general relator of the Synod for Synodality), Sr Nathalie Becquart XMCJ (Undersecretary of the General Secretariat of the Synod), Fr Giacomo Costa SJ (Italy), the lay man Thierry Bonaventura, Media Office of the Secretariat of the Synod – Vatican, the married lay woman Susan Pascoe (Australia), Sr Bernadette Mary Reis FSP (USA – Media Office, Vatican) and Mr Jan Zupan (Germany). Altogether, there were some 80 Asian participants from the 22 members that constitute the FABC. See chart on next page.

They consisted of all strata of the People of God in Asia – 6 cardinals, 5 archbishops, 18 bishops (hence 29 bishops in total), 28 priests, 4 religious sisters and 19 lay persons (7 men and 12 women), thus, making this ACEA more a real 'ecclesial' than a mere 'episcopal' Assembly, though the clergy far outnumbered the laity at this Asian Continental Ecclesial Assembly. Although these delegates may have represented various voices of the Church in Asia, this disproportionate participation of the non-clerical members in Asia (such as the religious and lay persons) at the ACEA surely is not in line with the synodal spirit, as so emphatically promoted not only by the official documents of the Secretariat of the Synod with regard to the current synodal process in the universal Church, but also by the Pope himself and by the responses of the People of God to the questionnaire (Cf. DCS 108).

Listening to the Holy Spirit through Prayer and Spiritual Conversation

As is well-known, one of the key elements of the current synodal process is to listen carefully and prayerfully to the voice of the Holy Spirit who speaks through the members of the Church, i.e., through all the baptised. Thus, at this ACEA, too, a special effort was made to listen to the Holy Spirit's voice expressed through the voices of all the participants. The special prayer of the Synod, *Adsumus Sancte Spiritus* ('We stand before you, O Holy Spirit') was prayed at the beginning of each and every Plenary Assembly Session. This was to invoke the Holy Spirit (as had been traditionally done from ancient times in various ecclesial councils, synods and other important Church gatherings) to guide and inspire all the participants so that they could truly reflect the voice of the People of God in Asia. One ought to notice here a clear effort to harness

3 The two members are the Professor of Patristics and Eastern Theology, Thomas Kollamparambil CMI and the Professor of Moral Theology, Vimal Tirimanna CSsR. The official list of the delegates for the ACEA listed them as members of the delegations from India and Sri Lanka respectively, but they had not been appointed by their National Episcopal Conferences. Rather, they had been invited as members of the Theological Commission of the Synod on Synodality.

Asia

Country	No. Participants	Ecclesial Status[1]
Bangladesh	3	1 Bishop, 1 Layman, I Laywoman
Cambodia	1	1 Layman
Hong Kong	2	1 Bishop and 1 Laywoman
India	14	6 Bishops, 5 Priests, 1 Religious Sister, 1 Layman, 1 Laywoman
Indonesia	4	2 Bishops, 1 Priest, 1 Layman
Japan	4	1 Bishop, 1 Priest, 2 Laywomen
Kazakhstan	1	1 Bishop
Kyrgyzstan	1	1 Priest
Korea	4	2 Bishops, 1 Priest, 1 Religious Sister
Laos	2	1 Bishop, 1 Layman
Macau	1	1 Priest
Malaysia	5	2 Bishops, 2 Priests, 1 Laywoman
Mongolia	1	1 Laywoman
Myanmar	3	1 Bishop, 1 Priest, 1 Laywoman
Nepal	2	1 Bishop, 1 Priest
Pakistan	4	2 Bishops, 1 Priest, 1 Layman
Philippines	8	2 Bishops, 3 Priests, 1 Layman, 2 Laywomen
Sri Lanka	3	2 Bishops, 1 Priest
Singapore	1	1 Laywoman
Taiwan	3	1 Bishop, 1 Priest, 1 Laywoman
Thailand	5	1 Bishop, 3 Priests 1 Religious Sister
Timor (East)	3	1 Bishop, 2 Priests
Vietnam	3	1 Bishop, 1 Priest, 1 Religious Sister
Asian members of Theological Commission for Synod on Synodality[2]	2	2 Priests
Guests	8	2 Bishops, 1 Priest, 2 Religious Sisters, 2 Laymen, 1 Laywoman

Chart Footnotes

1 All the cardinals, archbishops and bishops are categorised here as 'Bishops'.

2 The third Asian member of this Theological Commission, Ms Estella Padilla of the Philippines, was already a member of the Discerning and Drafting Team, and hence, she was *ipso facto* a participant of the Assembly. She was counted as a member of the Filippino delegation.

as much as possible the *sensus fidei fidelium* as taught in *Lumen Gentium* 12.

On the first two days, the participants were invited to journey through the synodal process listening to the Holy Spirit's voice by using the three-step method called the 'Spiritual Conversion'. The first step ('Taking the floor') involved each participant of the group speaking for two minutes about their experience of the Synodal process, with no discussion or intervention, followed by two minutes of silence to internalise the sharing. The second step ('Making room for others') involved each member of the group speaking for two minutes on what resonated most from what the other/s had said, with no discussion or intervention and followed again by two minutes of silence to digest the sharing. The third step ('Building together') involved interaction among the members to identify the fruit of the conversation, recognising convergences, common questions, disagreements and prophetic voices. As is obvious, this method allowed space for moments of grace to take effect, which helped the participants (in both the Plenary and small groups) to address one fundamental question: 'where is the Holy Spirit leading us in Asia?'

It's worth mentioning here how in the specific set-up of the venue of this gathering, the Assembly Hall and the Chapel were facing each other. This configuration was conducive to prayer and discernment, making it easier for the participants to move from prayer to deliberations and discernment and *vice-versa* during the whole Assembly.

Orientations and Inputs

In order to further enhance the openness to the Holy Spirit's voice for Asia, each day was highlighted by short presentations on synodality which were to last less than ten minutes. Many of these presentations only reiterated what has been already presented in the various documents on synodality, and the speakers did not appear as 'experts' but as companions walking together with the rest of the participants of the Plenary Assembly. They were meant to be orientations for the Assembly, as was indicated in the programme itself.

On the first day, Cardinal Mario Grech reminded the Assembly that no one is ahead in the synodal journey and that we are all learners in the synodal process. Stressing the importance of the roles of every baptised person – both clergy and the laity – in the synodal journey, the cardinal reminded that the main task of the Assembly should be to listen to the Holy Spirit speaking through each and every participant. As such, invoking the image of 'removing sandals', the Cardinal pointed out the importance of getting rid of our own agendas and listening to the Spirit's voice during the Assembly.

The lay theologian, Christina Kheng from Singapore (one of the Asian representatives in the Methodology Commission for the Synod on Synodality in Rome who had been part of the group in Frascati that had drafted the DCS) spoke next, enabling the participants to understand how the DCS had come about, and how the draft framework for Asia was drawn up; she also reminded the Assembly on the key elements of discernment.

On behalf of the DDT, Fr Clarence Devadass, a priest from the diocese of Kuala Lumpur (Malaysia) also complemented the previous speakers by giving a resume as to how the draft framework of the would-be ACD was formed, insisting that it was meant only as an orientation. On the second day, Sr Nathalie Becquart XMCJ observed that though tensions were mentioned in the draft framework for the would-be ACD, the Assembly had courageously and truthfully taken them up, and in the process, there were no visible tensions as such in the Assembly hall.

On the last day, when the Assembly was to discuss and discern about ecclesial structures in view of making synodality a way of ecclesial living, Cardinal Jean-Claude Hollerich SJ picked up on the word 'symphony' mentioned by one of the small groups, and remarked how a symphony includes repetition and discipline and requires that every musician takes care of the instrument assigned to him/her. He noted how a piano that is not tuned creates not symphony but cacophony. Similarly, he said: 'Synodal conversion is the way in which we have to tune our instruments. Conversion is always conversion to Christ.' He also pointed out how synodality requires humility, because it is only in humility that we can work and walk together on this synodal journey. As he himself was in Asia for many years (when he was working in Japan as a Jesuit missionary), he concluded with the challenging reminder to every participant that the Church in Asia has a lot to offer to the universal Church.

The Proceedings of the Assembly

The DDT was also entrusted by the FABC leadership to plan the programme for the ACEA. So, with their own enriching first-hand experience with the discernment process (thanks mainly to the Spiritual Conversation Method), the DDT proposed the same discernment process also during the Asian Assembly, and this was eventually approved by the FABC leadership as the procedure to be followed.

Prior to their arrival in Thailand for the ACEA, all the delegates were provided with three documents: the draft framework of the would-be ACD, the Working Document for the Continental Stage and an article entitled 'Francis the Discerning Pope' by Nicholas Austin SJ.[4] The FABC Secretariat also sent a presentation on the Perspectives and Method for the Continental Stage which highlighted the Method of Spiritual Conversation.

4 Cf. https://www.thinkingfaith.org/articles/francis-discerning-pope (access: 01.04.2023). On their arrival at the venue of the Assembly, at their registration, all the delegates were provided with the same three documents in printed form.

To facilitate each day's Plenary Sessions, there was a team of three moderators consisting of a bishop and two lay women, which further enhanced the spirit of synodality as process and experience during the Assembly itself.

It's worth stressing that throughout the proceedings of the Assembly, the moderators as well as the organisers of the Assembly kept on emphasising the value of Spiritual Conversation as the method to follow during the entire Assembly.

The three-day ACEA (from February 24 to 26, 2023) was structured around the reading, reflection and discernment of the contents under the four main sub-headings of the draft framework of the would-be ACD. As mentioned above, each day provided short inputs on synodality from Vatican representatives[5] or from the Asian DDT, which was followed by Spiritual Conversation Method in small groups.

The celebration of the daily Eucharist, as well as the time spent in silent prayer in the chapel (which was just facing the Assembly Hall within the same building at *Baan Phu Waan*) in between some of the Plenary Sessions, further enabled the participants to get imbued in a spirit of respect for and inclusion of the other's views. Each small group discussion session ended with the secretary of the respective small group reporting to the Plenary what had emerged in the discussion in the Group, in a very succinct and inclusive form. Such reportings were taken note of by the members of the DDT. As a rule, after the presentation of six reports in the Plenary, the moderators invited the whole Plenary to a two-minute silence, before the rest of the six reports were presented. The same method of Spiritual Conversation with silence, prayer, reflection and discernment was also followed in dealing with each of the four sections of the draft framework of the would-be ACD. The meal times, as well as private friendly conversations in-between the Assembly sessions, provided further opportunities for the participants to build relationships/friendships and to deepen their own synodal experience. The two special festive dinners on the first and third days of the Assembly likewise facilitated the furtherance of such a spirit.[6]

The first session of the first day opened with the celebration of the Mass of the Holy Spirit. In the second session that followed, the draft framework of the would-be ACD was presented to the Assembly by Fr Clarence Devadass on behalf of the DDT. During the four sessions that followed, each of the main sub-headings of this document – Asian Resonances, Asian Tensions, and Priorities from the Asian Responses – were taken up for reflection and discernment in the small groups. At the two afternoon sessions on the second day, the small

5 On the first day, the main input was from Cardinal Mario Grech, while Sr Nathalie Becquart and Cardinal Jean-Claude Hollerich gave the main inputs on the second and third days, respectively.
6 At the special festive dinner on the last day, there was a sing-song and a few cultural presentations from some delegates representing various countries.

groups were to formulate their amendments to the document (again using the Spiritual Conversation Method) and submit them to the drafters through their respective Group Secretaries.

In the middle of the second day, the organisers felt it best to provide time for the small groups to evaluate their experience of the process followed in the Assembly up to that point. It was a helpful interlude that facilitated these Groups towards becoming more open to learning from one another, and more importantly, to be honest about how they felt about the entire process.

On the third and final day, the first two sessions in the morning were dedicated to discussing the Plenary amended draft which the DDT had prepared so painstakingly the previous night and that had taken into consideration what has been submitted by the small groups. In order to collate the summary of all the reports sent via Google by the small groups with their amendments, the DDT revealed to the Assembly that they made use of the modern technique of Artificial Intelligence (AI) in producing the amended draft. Not a few felt uncomfortable about this revelation, i.e., that the overall collated summary was created from an AI portal. However, as mentioned by many, given the short amount of time that was at the disposal of the DDT, this was the most practical way to achieve the task. The amended draft was sent via email to all the participants on the last day of the Assembly. For those who did not have an electronic device with them, printed copies were provided.

The last two sessions in the afternoon were devoted to sharing in small groups the amendments that would facilitate the necessary ecclesial structural renewal in order to promote a culture of synodality in the Church. Towards the end of the final session, the entire Assembly endorsed the amended draft by consensus expressed through acclamation in each and every small group. This last collective act made all the participants of the Assembly own the amended draft. The Assembly also approved the entrusting to the DDT the task of finalising the Final Document of the ACEA.

Listening and Discerning in Small Groups

The participants of the Asian Assembly were divided into 12 small groups with 6-7 members in each Group. The organisers had intentionally composed these Groups in such a way that each Group would consist of participants from various countries and various states of ecclesial life, i.e., clergy, consecrated persons and lay persons. However, since the vast majority of the Assembly participants were bishops and priests, each Group had only 1-2 lay women or men. There was a moderator and a secretary for each Group nominated by the organisers of the Assembly.

The Spiritual Conversations that took place in these small groups were quite inspiring in the sense that even though opposing views were expressed, they were not contested or debated. A spirit of respect for and inclusion of everyone's opinion prevailed, thanks mainly to the Spiritual Conversation Method which paved the way for an atmosphere of silence and prayer that was called for after a certain number of interventions within the small group.

However, given the limited time that was allotted for each discussion, some small groups found it difficult to follow meticulously the Method of Spiritual Conversation. Consequently, they noted that often there was no time for silence in between each round as they had to finish the discussion within the allotted time, and so, the Group conversation proceeded more like a normal discussion in regular meetings. Of course, part of the difficulty could be attributed also to the lack of prior preparation of the assigned moderators and secretaries to follow the Method of Spiritual Conversation. In a very few cases, added to this was the lack of competence to communicate in English, which was the only medium used in all the proceedings of the entire Assembly.

In each session, the secretaries of the small groups had the task to input the responses of their respective Groups in a Google link provided. Though initially seen as time-consuming and overwhelming for secretaries, the delegates soon discovered how the method was helpful to collect immediately all the interventions, and to send them to the DDT. During the Plenary reporting, each small group secretary was given two minutes to present the highlights of the conversations in the respective Group. Although the allotted time to each secretary to present the respective Group report appeared theoretically to be sufficient, many groups seemed to have reported the summary of the discussions and not the result of the discernment process. Given the newness of the Method of Spiritual Dialogue, this may be understandable at this stage of the synodal process.

Daily Eucharistic Celebration

The daily Eucharistic celebrations were handled by the host country, Thailand. The main celebrants and concelebrants were assigned from the synod participants by the organisers. The Thai seminarians from the nearby *Lux Mundi* Major Seminary shouldered most of the liturgical organising, especially with regard to the singing of hymns at Mass. The Assembly opened with the Mass of the Holy Spirit which was presided over by the Archbishop of Tokyo, Tarcisio Isao Kikuchi, SVD, who is also the general secretary of the FABC. This Eucharistic celebration was highlighted by the blessing of the candles which were to be used during the small group meetings throughout the entire Assembly. At the end of the Eucharist, these candles were given to the twelve moderators of the small groups, and they brought their candles to their respective tables in the Plenary Assembly hall, creating an impressive and meaningful connection between the Eucharist and the synodal encounter of dialogue and discernment. These candles, which were to symbolise the Light of Christ that inspires and prompts sharing, discussions and discernment in the Groups (thus, reflecting the synodal journey) were lighted at the start of each small group encounter.

During the closing Mass, which was presided over by the Archbishop of Yangon, Cardinal Charles Bo, SDB, who is also the president of the FABC, the same candles in floral holders were offered by the secretaries of small groups by placing them in front of the altar, and they were blessed by the main celebrant. At the end of the Mass, as the secretaries stood in front of the altar with the lit candles facing the entire congregation, the main celebrant sent them off symbolically to be a light in the synodal journey to the various local Churches in Asia. The provisional draft of the Final Document was also handed over to the president of the FABC, Cardinal Bo, at this Eucharist by the representatives of the twelve small groups. The second day's Mass, which was the Mass for Asia was presided over by the Archbishop Emeritus of Karachi, Cardinal Joseph Coutts who is also a member of the Council of Bishops for the current synodal process.

Participation of Those Belonging to Other Faiths and Those in the Peripheries

Only those representatives nominated by the episcopal conferences, bishop members of the FABC offices, the three Asian members of the Theological Commission for the Synod on Synodality and the members of the DDT and the invited guests (mostly from the Secretariat for the Synod in Rome) participated at the Assembly. Given the fact that almost all the Churches in Asia are diffused among multitudes of fellow Asians who are not members of the Catholic Church, this surely was a serious *lacuna* for the synodal process which basically is understood as a 'walking together', especially in view of the repeated recommendations in the documents issued by the Secretariat of the Synod in Rome (for example, DCS 53-56). Moreover, the fact that the FABC ever since its foundation has been insisting on the indispensability of the 'triple-dialogue' in evangelising multi-cultural and multi-religious Asia, makes the absence of those outside the institutional Church even more surprising if not confusing. Another group of conspicuous absentees were those from the peripheries of Asian societies and of ecclesial life itself, in spite of the general guidelines of the Secretariat to be inclusive especially with regard to the persons concerned.[7] The absence of the above-mentioned groups in the Assembly hall was obviously a set-back for the synodal journey in Asia.

7 All the documents emanating from Rome ever since the current synodal process began, especially, the Continental Stage Document 'Enlarge the Space of your Tent' (which reflected in succinct form what the People of God from all over the Catholic world had expressed) had been insisting on the need to be inclusive in a given contextual reality when one is on the synodal journey. See for example DCS 38-40.

The Media and the Assembly

Perhaps due to the tight schedule, there was no media/press conferences as such before, during or after the Assembly. Instead, there was a press release of the proceedings of the Assembly daily, thanks to the two media groups present throughout the assembly. The Thai Catholic Media Office was involved in covering all the proceedings from arrival of the delegates to the closing of the Assembly. Daily newsletters in both English and Thai were made available for those interested in following the Assembly proceedings through their website https://bangkok.synod2023.org/asia/. Likewise, the Media Unit of the Vatican's Secretariat for the Synod communicated information about the ACEA. This Media Unit further enhanced the synodality process with special interviews with some of the participants which were communicated through the Vatican News that was available at https://www.vaticannews.va

Approval of the Final Draft of the Asian Continental Document

Through the process of Spiritual Conversation, prayer and communal discernment, all the participants of the ACEA were involved in revising and amending the draft framework of the would-be ACD which eventually became the final amended draft. At the last session of the Assembly, they approved it through consensus expressed in and through each small group. As mentioned above, the insights of the participants on each of the four main sections of the draft framework of the would-be ACD were taken into consideration by the DDT in producing the final version of the final amended draft, which admittedly was not an easy task. This provisional final draft of the ACD was then submitted to the FABC Central Committee (consisting of the bishop-presidents of the Asian Episcopal Conferences) for its final approval.[8] Eventually, the final approved ACD was sent to Rome on March 16, 2023. It was published on the website soon after.[9]

8 The same Central Committee meeting which was due in the first week of March was also to approve the Final Document of the FABC 50 General Conference. Unfortunately, in the popular mass media these two Documents were often considered as one Document, and consequently, there arose an unwarranted confusion with regard to the Asian Continental Document (synodal) and the synodal process itself.

9 https://www.synod.va/en/synodal-process/the-continental-stage/final_document.html (access: 01.04.2023).

FINAL DOCUMENT OF THE ASIAN CONTINENTAL ASSEMBLY ON SYNODALITY

Bangkok, Thailand

I
THE ASIAN CONTEXT

1. Asia, blessed with diverse cultures, religions, languages, and ethnicities, is the world's largest continent in terms of both geographical area and population. It has a landmass of 44.6 million square kilometres, about 30% of the total earth's surface. Asia is home to approximately 4.6 billion people with over 2,300 languages spoken across Asia. It is also considered the birthplace and cradle of major world religions like Hinduism, Islam, Christianity, Buddhism, Jainism, Sikhism, Taoism, Confucianism and several others. Islam is the most prominent religion and is practised by 1.2 billion people, followed by Hinduism with 900 million people.

Asia

Population	Catholic Population	%	Priests	Consecrated men & women	Lay missionaries & catechists
4.6 billion*	150 million*	3.31%	70,254	187,021	432,035

Source: Catholic Church Statistics 2021 released by Agenzia Fides on World Mission Sunday 2022
* Rounded up to the nearest whole number.

2. Though the systems of beliefs, values, and symbols vary from place to place, the interconnectedness of the human community draws the

Asian peoples together. The Asian value of being relational (with God, self, other human beings, and the cosmos) brings with it the unity of the human family and the unity of the peoples of Asia.

3. Asia holds the dubious distinction of having the most billionaires in the world on one hand, while on the other, it has 320 million people that are extremely poor, living below the poverty line, according to the World Bank Report. The recent pandemic has further exasperated the inequality and economic divide between the haves and the have-nots.

4. Politically too, we see diverse systems of governance that include parliamentary democracies, military dictatorial regimes, communist rulers, constitutional monarchies, and presidential forms of government.

5. Despite the benefits that unity and diversity bring to Asia, it is also entrenched with many challenges that directly affect the Church and the lives of the people of Asia. Some of the challenges are the widespread poverty across Asia, the ecological threat that has brought disequilibrium in the lives of people, the challenges of systemic corruption, the waves of economic migration in search of better lives, the political instability that causes internal disruption to peace and harmony, and much more. All of these have a direct impact on the Church as she seeks to reach out to all peoples.

6. While Christianity remains a very small minority in most parts of Asia, the vibrancy and richness of the individual cultures bring joy to the life of the Church. The Asian continent is vast and is divided into four recognisable regions, namely Central, East, South and Southeast Asia.

7. Founded on our common baptismal dignity, this synodal journey is indeed an expression of the universal Church and the local Churches walking together as one. The positive effects of bringing people from all walks of life, both within and outside the Church, into a process of praying with one another, listening to one another, and discerning the voice of the Holy Spirit bring forth in them a new experience of vitality and dynamism to the life of the Church.

8. Among the 4 billion people living in Asia, the Catholic Church comprises only 3.31% of the total population, yet it contributes greatly to the fields of education, healthcare, social welfare and reaching out to the poor and marginalised groups in society.

9. In a pluralistic Asian society, the Catholic Church continues to spread the message of love by empowering those on the margins through quality education and integrating them into the mainstream of society.

10. Thousands of priests, consecrated men and women, along with lay missionaries and catechists are involved in faith formation and catering to the spiritual and pastoral needs of the Catholic community across Asia.

II
THE SYNOD PROCESS

2.1 Pre-Synodal Phase: FABC 50 General Conference

11. Pope Francis' call for the XVI Ordinary General Assembly of the Synod of Bishops came while the Federation of Asian Bishops' Conferences (FABC) was preparing for a General Conference – patterned after those of the Consejo Episcopal Latinoamericano y Caribeño (CELAM) – to highlight the contribution of the Church in Asia to the wider Church. With the approach of the 50th anniversary of the Asian Bishops' meeting that was held during Pope St Paul VI's visit to Manila in 1970, the General Conference was first set for November 2020. The coronavirus disease pandemic, however, forced the FABC to postpone the General Conference to October 2022.

12. The coincidence of both movements was considered providential: the General Conference process was bringing to the fore the current situation and challenges of the peoples of Asia as well as the contemporary mission of the Churches in Asia, while the synodal process was providing the methodology and sometimes even creating the listening mechanisms for conducting the General Conference consultations.

13. The fruits of the General Conference will be most evident in the section on 'Gaps' below. These represent the concerns and priorities that were recognised during the General Conference but were not extensively covered in the Asian responses to the Document for the Continental Stage.

14. As Pope Francis remarked at the beginning of the FABC General Conference, Paul VI encountered in Asia a Church of the poor, a Church of the young and a Church in dialogue. Fifty years later, the Church of the poor is a Church that cares for our common home, the Church of the young is now navigating and evangelising the digital continent, and the

Church in dialogue is called to build bridges between cultures, religions and peoples.

2.2 First Phase: Churches of Asia in the FABC

15. The Federation of Asian Bishops' Conferences (FABC) comprises 17 episcopal conferences,[1] two Synods of Oriental Churches[2], and three Associate Members.[3] There are 29 territories included in the FABC membership.[4] There is the hope to welcome the Church in mainland China in the FABC membership.

16. As the General Conference was ending the Document for the Continental Stage (DCS) was released. Copies were printed and ready on 28 October and distributed to all the participants on 29 October 2022. The Asian Task Force was formed and approved by the Central Committee at a meeting during the General Conference. The Task Force was to coordinate the entire Asian Synodal process.

17. The Task Force met via Zoom on 7 November, 2022. A letter was sent describing the process, along with the DCS and other information from the Synod Secretariat on the methodology for the Continental Stage including the FAQ. The dates for the Asian Continental Assembly on Synodality were set for 24 to 26 February, 2023.

18. All 22 FABC members were requested to respond in 10 pages to the DCS on or before 15 January, 2023. The Task Force would then send to the members a draft framework of the Asian Final Document on or before 15 February, 2023. Twenty-one out of 22 responses were received. The draft framework was sent out as scheduled on 15 February.

19. Most found that there was very little time to do this, as it overlapped with Advent and Christmas. It took time for the needed translations, given the diversity of languages in Asia. Each conference chose its manner of

1 Catholic Bishops' Conference of Bangladesh (CBCB), Catholic Bishops' Conference of Central Asia [Conferenza Episcopale Cattolica dell'Asia Centrale] (CECAC), Conference of Catholic Bishops of India (CCBI), Catholic Bishops' Conference of India (CBCI), Catholic Bishops' Conference of Indonesia [Konferensi Waligereja Indonesia] (KWI), Catholic Bishops' Conference of Japan (CBCJ), Catholic Bishops' Conference of Korea (CBCK), Catholic Bishops' Conference of Laos and Cambodia [Conférence Episcopale du Laos et du Cambodge] (CELAC), Catholic Bishops' Conference of Malaysia-Singapore-Brunei (CBCMSB), Catholic Bishops' Conference of Myanmar (CBCM), Pakistan Catholic Bishops' Conference (PCBC), Catholic Bishops' Conference of the Philippines (CBCP), Catholic Bishops' Conference of Sri Lanka (CBCSL), Chinese Regional Catholic Bishops' Conference (CRBC) [Taiwan], Catholic Bishops' Conference of Thailand (CBCT), Conferencia Episcopal Timorense (CET), Catholic Bishops' Conference of Vietnam (CBCV).

2 Syro-Malabar Bishops' Synod (India), Syro-Malankara Catholic Church (India).

3 Diocese of Hong Kong, Diocese of Macau, Apostolic Vicariate of Nepal.

4 Afghanistan, Bangladesh, Brunei, Cambodia, Hong Kong, India, Indonesia, Japan, Kazakhstan, Korea, Kyrgyzstan, Laos, Macau, Malaysia, Mongolia, Myanmar, Nepal, Pakistan, Philippines, Singapore, Sri Lanka, Taiwan, Tajikistan, Thailand, Thailand, Timor Leste, Turkmenistan, Uzbekistan, Vietnam.

responding to the DCS. This included using the existing synodal teams at the deanery, diocesan and national levels. In some places, online meetings were held. Small group meetings were utilised, focus groups, assemblies where possible and bishops' and priests' councils.

2.3 Second Phase: Discernment and Writing Team

20. The second phase is the writing of the draft framework of the summary of the episcopal conferences' reports. It was held at the Camillian Pastoral Care Centre, Bangkok, Thailand from 31 January to February 2023. The FABC Central Committee appointed the Asian Task Force to be the Discernment and Writing Team and to accomplish the task of drawing up a draft framework. The team was expanded and was composed of 9 individuals: 2 lay people (1 female and 1 male), 1 consecrated female, and 6 priests, with the FABC General Secretary overseeing the process, representing the four FABC regions, namely South Asia, Southeast Asia, East Asia, and Central Asia.

21. For four days, the team devoted themselves to praying, sharing and conversations, listening, discerning, and writing the draft framework in the atmosphere and spirit of synodality. The team was divided into three groups reading seven country reports. Each team discerned the common themes, context, and peculiarities in answering the three questions from the DCS, namely Resonances, Tensions and Priorities, using the Spiritual Conversation methodology.

22. The team came into a plenary to further reflect and discuss their insights, and wrote the draft framework. They would again pray, reflect, and discern as they continued to revise, improve, and develop the draft framework. The draft framework document was sent to all the episcopal conferences and Associate Members on 15 February, 2023.

23. The team also planned the programme for the Asian Continental Assembly. The four days' experience enriched them so much that they proposed the same discernment process in the Asian assembly. The programme was submitted to the FABC Central Leadership for their comments and approval.

2.4 Third Phase: Asian Continental Assembly

24. By the procedure outlined during the FABC 50 General Conference, each episcopal conference was asked to send three delegates and each Associate Member could send two delegates to the Asian Continental

Assembly on Synodality, which was held from 24 to 26 February 2023. It was further determined that these delegations should consist of the bishop president or his delegate, and two others chosen based on the DCS 108 and 109. Delegates were sent information about the meeting in advance along with instructions for preparation for this event.

25. On 23 February, participants arrived at Baan Phu Waan Pastoral Training Center in Bangkok, Thailand. Delegates from 17 episcopal conferences, 2 Synods of Oriental Rites, and 3 Associate Members of the FABC were joined by members of the General Secretariat for Synod, the Relator General for the XVI Ordinary General Assembly of the Synod of Bishops and several other guests. The number of Asian participants at the Assembly was: 6 Cardinals, 5 Archbishops, 18 Bishops, 28 priests, 5 consecrated women, 7 laymen and 11 women.

26. Before the beginning of the sessions, the participants were provided with the following materials as a resource for discernment and discussion: The Continental Stage Document (DCS), a copy of the Draft Framework for the Final Document (FD) prepared by the Discernment and Writing Team, and a compilation of Pope Francis' Catechesis on Discernment.

27. In our endeavour to compose a draft of the Final Document that is to be submitted to the FABC Central Committee after 'validation and approval' from this body, which will then be forwarded to the General Secretariat, the Asian Continental Assembly included the following elements: Spiritual Conversation; input from brief presentations; common and individual prayer periods; general as well as small group discussion, review and reworking of versions of the draft (which was created using a framework text proposed by the Discernment and Writing Team); and a forum during plenary sessions for interventions from participants.

28. Groups were intentionally designed to consist of a mix of people from various conferences and different states of life (i.e., clergy, consecrated persons, lay, etc.). Artificial Intelligence (AI) technology assisted in the process of compilation of input derived from the group work.

29. The responses of the groups to the discernment sessions that looked more deeply into the different parts of the draft document were slowly integrated day by day into the working draft as the Team met at the end of each day. Moreover, it added two more steps for participants to contribute to the writing of the draft: firstly, bringing back the edited draft to all in the small groups, the Team asked what they would want to amend, and what would they want to add. Secondly, after the Team integrated amendments and additions from the small groups, it again asked all the participants to read the whole text and reflect as a group on what the Team missed significantly.

30. The working sessions concluded with an expression of unanimous affirmation of the draft document by the various groups of participants. Following this, the assembly members discussed the following two questions: (1) Which ecclesial structures need to be changed or created to enhance the synodality of the Church in Asia? (2) What do you wish to see happen between the October 2023 session and the October 2024 session of the Synod on Synodality?

31. Cardinal Charles Bo, president of the FABC, presided at the closing Liturgy of the Assembly, during which representatives from the Assembly presented a 'provisional draft' of the Final Document from the Asian Continental Assembly of Synodality.

2.5 Fourth Phase: Discernment and Writing Team

32. The Discernment and Writing Team was entrusted with finalising the final document. They met from 27 to 28 February 2023 to incorporate the amendments as suggested by the delegates of the Asian Assembly. The Team also participated actively in the assembly by joining in with the groups in the discussions, Spiritual Conversations, and communal discernment. Listening to all and feeling the pulse of the participants aided the discernment process in the writing of the Final Document.

33. The final editing of the document was done in a spirit of communal writing, warm companionship, and prayerful discernment. The Team then forwarded its work to the FABC Central Committee for 'validation and approval'.

2.6 Fifth Phase: FABC Central Committee

34. The Final Document of the Asian Continental Assembly on Synodality was presented to the FABC Central Committee at their online meeting on 3 March 2023. This was for the Bishop-Presidents of the episcopal conferences to validate and approve the Final Document of the Asian Continental Assembly, ensuring that it was the fruit of an authentically synodal journey, guarding the unity of the Church that can never degenerate into uniformity or polarisation.

35. After having deliberated on the draft final document, the FABC Central Committee, on 3 March 2023 'approved and validated' the final document with some very minor changes to be incorporated, indicating that it should be further edited and then be sent to the Synod Secretariat as the Final Document for the Asian Continental Assembly on the Synod.

III
GENERAL SENTIMENTS TO THE PROCESS

36. Despite the challenges, the synodal journey is not a democratic process but is a 'moment of grace and healing' for the Church. The image of the Church as 'tent' projects it to be a place of refuge that can be expanded to all in a spirit of inclusivity. It also expresses that God can pitch His tent wherever the Spirit of God blows, including in places where there is violence, unrest, and suffering.

37. Most importantly, in the tent, there is room for everyone, with no one being excluded because it is a home to everyone. In this process, those who in the past felt 'left out' now realised that they have a home in this tent, a sacred and safe space. Most of the respondents responded positively to the image of the tent.

38. The image of the tent also reminds us that Jesus pitched His tent among us through the incarnation and therefore the tent is also a place of encounter with God and one another. The tent, now seen as the common home, has also rekindled a sense of belonging and sharing in the common baptism. The synodal process has brought about a greater awareness of the importance of walking together in the Church as a communion of communities for the organic growth of the Church.

39. The continental consultation in the respective countries took varied forms. Some countries were able to involve many people from different walks of life while others were only able to gather smaller groups of people. As mentioned earlier, the challenges of time and language became an obstacle for some countries. Nevertheless, those who took part in this process of reflecting on the DCS contributed constructively through a spirit of prayer and discernment for the betterment of the Church.

40. The involvement of such a vast number of people in the synodal process has revealed a profound love for the Church despite the shortcomings and weaknesses of the Church as an institution.

41. The inability to translate the DCS into the many vernacular languages was another limitation experienced by the Churches in Asia. However, the FABC 50 General Conference that was held in October 2022 was indeed a blessing in preparing for this stage of the synodal process.

42. Many of the conversations that were held before and during the FABC General Conference already provided indications regarding the context of the Church and Asia. In 'listening' to the reports, it has been noted that on the horizon, there remains a sense of hope and joy for the Church to move forward because of the love of God for His people. We are convinced that the Holy Spirit neither stops nor fails in inspiring the People of God to move in the direction of personal, communal, and structural conversion.

43. We also acknowledge that the process of having the synodal conversations as requested has sometimes been painful and unsettling, while at the same time, making us vulnerable to each other.

44. The DCS in a succinct way has been able to capture the hopes, aspirations, desolations, and challenges of the people in a way that opens the door for a greater renewal in the life of the Church. The invitation to listen to people from all walks of life demonstrates openness to one another and the spirit of dialogue facilitates moving together as one unit: 'Enabling this encounter and dialogue is the meaning of the synodal journey' (DCS, 6).

45. What the DCS has been able to do is be the catalyst for more profound Spiritual Conversations. In many places, it was indeed experienced as a moment of living synodality in the Church through a process of shared identity and shared responsibility.

46. The general sense of concern for the Church as demonstrated in the participation of all in this process reflects a natural or organic inclination to authentic synodality. In some countries, the 'process of listening' itself was not new because there were already mechanisms to implement pastoral plans of local Churches and communities at a variety of levels which brought about synergy and convergence with the spirit of synodality.

47. The FABC itself has been playing a vital role in living synodality between episcopal conferences. This indeed captures the sense of walking together as members of the Body of Christ towards the reign of God and in that process, being able to widen our experiences and enlarge the tent.

48. Considering these general observations that have provided not only the *locus* for the Church in Asia to reflect on the DCS, we also acknowledge the vast diversity of views and experiences across Asia has made it challenging to synthesise every single opportunity and challenge raised by the different countries. Guided by the Holy Spirit, the following paragraphs provide insights into the resonances, tensions, and priorities as articulated by the Churches in Asia.

49. The Discernment and Writing Team has also taken the liberty to identify some of the gaps (*lacuna*) that we felt were either absent or not sufficiently treated in the reports sent by the episcopal conferences but were key points of discussion at the FABC 50 General Conference. It is our prayer and hope that the following insights are faithful to the mind and heart of the respective processes undertaken by the countries in Asia.

IV
ASIAN RESONANCES

After having read and prayed with the DCS, which intuitions resonate most strongly with the lived experiences and realities of the Church in your continent? Which experiences are new, or illuminating to you?

50. The resonances that the Churches in Asia sensed while reflecting on the DCS are underlined by the fact, as already mentioned earlier, that there is a deep love for the Church. In that deep love for the Church resides varied emotions like joy, sadness, vulnerability, and woundedness.

51. Despite this potpourri of emotions and the diversity of Asia which encompasses ethnicity, race, culture, language, and religion, the spirit of synodality as called for by the Church, challenges us (Church) to have the courage to 'walk together' despite some resistance within the Church, the lack of appreciation for the rich spirituality in Asia, and also the loss of a sense of sin.

52. Although the process has been well received and facilitated throughout the countries in Asia, a few reports mentioned that the process of consultation and listening brought about by the synodal journey could cause some disenchantment and disappointment due to an absence of clear explanation and acceptance of the goal of gathering and listening. The temptation to engage in this process could be described as a more political or, even, ideological (i.e., as resembling more a forum for

'parliamentary-type' discussion) rather than as a truly synodal endeavour from a Catholic-Christian perspective. Some faithful are sceptical regarding the purpose and the prospective outcome of such a synodal process.

53. Some dioceses maintain this lingering doubt if the voices of those living in minority settings and traditional Christian communities would have equal influence on the synodal process and even its outcomes. It was also mentioned that listening is a difficult task because many people would prefer to be praised rather than be criticised or commented on. Those who dared to speak up were sometimes considered to be antagonists by certain sections of the community because their comments and opinions were seen to be not of mainstream thought or could negatively impact the Church as a whole.

4.1 The Experience of Joy

54. It must be noted that the synodal process called for by the universal Church is both a spiritual experience and a spiritual journey. For this reason, it is necessary to put our egos aside, empty ourselves, and listen to God so that we can constantly be renewed under the guidance of the Holy Spirit and go deeper in the spirit of synodality.

55. The dynamics of listening as widely as possible which is entrenched in the synodal process, have indeed motivated the Church to listen more intently and discern wisely where the Holy Spirit is leading us toward embracing and becoming a more synodal Church.

56. This journey that we have initiated helps us realise the true nature of the Church and the ability to see the situation of the Church. The experience of joy is heightened because the synod process is certainly a place of grace, encounter, and transfiguration.

4.2 The Experience of Walking Together

57. The process of walking together brings forth to the local Churches a greater awareness of their unique contexts and rich cultures across Asia, including that of the indigenous communities that are often neglected and forgotten. This wealth needs to be nurtured through communion and dialogue as an experience of walking together.

58. As Catholics in Asia living in diversity, we seek to enhance the quality of our friendship with one another by listening to, respecting, and caring

for each other, so that we can be a good mother and an example to bring peace and unity to the world. Faith formation that is founded on the living word of God, is foundational to synodal spirituality.

59. In walking together, the synodal journey has gathered us at the table of the Lord, so that through Him, in Him and with Him, we have realised our natural and organic inclination to synodality and are inspired and strengthened to traverse and discover new pathways for the Church in Asia.

60. It is heartening to read repeatedly of the profound love for the Church from so many local Churches across the world. This love and commitment to the faith resounds throughout the DCS and certainly reflects the almost universal sense expressed by Catholics throughout the world.

61. The experience of walking together is also marred by external threats that make living the faith challenging. It has been noted that in several countries across Asia, there are still many Christians who suffer from various threats because of keeping their faith.

62. Despite these new forms of 'martyrdom' many still are faithful to the faith and are even willing to give up their life for it. In some areas, threats and violence against Christians have been noted while in other areas there are other ways in which Christians are discriminated against for their beliefs.

4.3 The Experience of Wounds

63. The reports also resonated with the vulnerabilities and wounds of the Churches in Asia emphasising the need for healing. Among the many wounds of the Church are abuses related to finance, jurisdiction, conscience, authority, and sex. These would have certainly portrayed the Church negatively, which has led to some leaving the Church because of the lack of credibility. At the level of governance too, the lack of transparency and accountability has led to a crisis of credibility in the Church.

64. The reports also point to the fact that due to these abuses, there is growing intolerance, resentment, and negativism against the Church. These are expressed through social and print media, and other public domains. Responsibility for the Church must belong to all and therefore everyone should be allowed to participate actively in the process of making decisions through communal discernment.

65. There is also a deep concern on the lack of sufficient inclusion of women in governance and decision-making processes in the Church. Women in consecrated life, despite being committed to the various ministries of the Church, experience a sense of alienation and whose voices are not often heard sufficiently in the policy decisions of the Church. They are actively involved, and their committed services are very much evident.

66. The synodal conversations have called for a rethinking of women's participation in the life of the Church given that women played an important role in the Bible. There is a need in the Church for a renewal of governance structures that will allow the meaningful participation of women in all aspects of the Church.

67. The reports acknowledge the Church's lack of understanding and failure in providing sufficient pastoral care to some groups of people who are part of the Church but are often struggling to feel welcomed. Among them are single parents, people in irregular marriage situations, mixed marriages, people who identify themselves as LGBTQI+, as well as migrants and others.

68. Several reports raised grave concerns about the absence of the youth in many Churches and especially in the decision-making process. At the same time, the young people continue to inspire and challenge the whole Church to have the courage to take risks and make changes.

69. Very sporadically some reports make a passing mention of the plight of the indigenous peoples. It has also been noted that many of their aspirations and voices were not sufficiently highlighted in the DCS.

70. At the same time, listening to the cry of the poor and the earth were issues that were not treated adequately given that these are grave concerns for the peoples of Asia. It must be the role of the Church to listen to vulnerable communities and work towards protecting them and their environment, rights, and privileges.

71. Some of the wounds experienced in the Churches were brought about by the infiltration of ideologies such as individualism, consumerism, and materialism, that is caused by the rapid economic growth and freedom of access to social media. Though much of these may have brought about development in many parts of Asia, the Church is also influenced by its various side effects.

72. The voice of the Church has been silenced by oppressive regimes to an extent that it has not been possible for the Church to play its prophetic role. The silence has also led to passive complacency, compounded by fear and sometimes even apathy. There is a need for Churches across Asia to support Churches under oppressive regimes in ways that do not threaten or jeopardise their existence.

4.4 The Call to Embrace New Pathways

73. The experience of joys and wounds across Asia can only be seen as opportunities to explore new pathways toward a synodal Church. Standing together as a united Body of Christ calls for a new vision in the pastoral mission of a 'new Church', a synodal Church.

74. The Church must begin in a spirit of inclusion where everyone feels both welcomed and a sense of belonging inside the tent. As a People of God, no one should be excluded; even if they are frail and weak, inclusivism within the Church is a must for the synodal Church.

75. The diversity of religions in Asia makes it almost compelling to engage in ecumenical and interreligious dialogue as a way of building peace, reconciliation, and harmony. Many reports speak of fruitful engagement with other Christians and persons of other religions. Despite the diversity of religions and cultures across Asia, there are still limitations in matters concerning ecumenical and interreligious dialogue.

76. In some places, this push for dialogue has been the initiative only of the Catholic Church and there are times when reciprocity is not forthcoming. It has also been seen as the 'work' of the clergy rather than of the laity.

77. Some expressed reservations about these dialogues for various reasons, including mistrust and suspicion regarding the motives for such dialogues. The Church plays a significant role in building bridges for peace, reconciliation, justice, and freedom.

78. Though very little is mentioned about safeguarding (minors and the vulnerable) in the Asian reports, there is a need to develop and nurture the environment of a culture of safeguarding in the Church, at all levels.

79. The synodal process has called for widespread listening to one another to bring about transformation at all levels of the Church. Together with the laity, and consecrated women and men who have been saying that

they have not been heard or given a voice in the Church, some priests felt that they were not sufficiently heard, even to a point of feeling neglected.

80. Reading the reports, there is a strong sense of an inward-looking Church that must cast its nets further and wider. The mission *ad-extra* must be at the core of the Churches in Asia. We have the task of transforming an inward-looking, individualised and polarised approach to spiritual life towards a more missionary, communitarian and integrated approach.

81. The tent needs to be expanded in ways best known to the respective Churches in Asia so that we can move in promising ways that fulfil our mission as a Church.

82. The Churches in Asia have been able to relate and resonate with much of what has been said in the DCS. This only indicates that there are many similarities with the Churches in other countries and continents, for which we give thanks to God that we are all on this journey together.

83. We also recognise that some of these issues may be peculiar to certain regions, but we take consolation that as we walk together, there can be a renewal in the Church and the expansion of the reign of God.

V
ASIAN TENSIONS

After having read and prayed with the DCS, what substantial tensions or divergences emerge as particularly important in your continent's perspective? Consequently, what are the questions or issues that should be addressed and considered in the next steps of the process?

84. Having prayed, studied, and read the different reports, we are filled with hope that this synodal journey will bear fruit in not only extending the tent but also recognising the work of the Holy Spirit in Churches throughout Asia.

85. In reading the DCS, the Churches in Asia also recognised some universal tensions and some that are particular to the context of Asia. Keeping in mind that some of these tensions are far more intricate than they seem, our task is not to seek solutions at this time, but rather to acknowledge these tensions and divergences and to further reflect on what the Holy Spirit is saying to the Church in Asia.

5.1 Tensions in Living Synodality

86. The Church is composed of people from all states of life (clergy, consecrated, and laity); yet there seems to be a kind of 'divide' within the Church – between the clergy and laity, bishops and priests/ religious congregations, ecclesial groups and movements, dioceses, and conferences and even outside –between the Church and political authorities and even between religions, as indicated in many of the reports. In the spirit of a participatory Church, the experience of leadership in the 'servant model' needs greater attention for living synodality

87. The challenge to become more participatory is often hindered by leadership styles that prevent (sometimes even exclude) others from living out their baptismal call to be authentic disciples. The servant model of leadership is hindered and sometimes counter-witnessing when priests tend to dominate and even come across as imposing, domineering, and authoritative over the laity. Reconfiguring the role of the laity includes expanding spaces for possible lay ministry through a variety of charisms, including counselling and employment guidance for the youth, care for the sick, education, and protection of children.

88. We recognise, too, the work of catechists in Asia who are not only teachers of faith but also leaders of the community in their own right. For centuries, they have been preparing the faithful for the sacraments and accompanying them in living the faith. We affirm, therefore, Pope Francis' directive that episcopal conferences... render effective the ministry of Catechist (cf. *Antiquum Ministerium*, n.9).

89. Acknowledging the tensions between clergy, religious men and women, and the laity, the theme of co-responsibility of all in the life and mission of the Church has been raised time and again in the reports. Many problems arise when the exercise of power is divorced from accountability and transparency.

5.2 Tensions in Decision-Making

90. It was noted that in some places, collaborative responsibility in the discernment and decision-making process was lacking; often left to only priests or bishops. The voices of the minority and even the laity are not considered in this process. At times, there is superficial dialogue and lack of consultation even in those structures recommended or prescribed by the Canon Law like the pastoral council and the finance council. Some Churches consider this a form of clericalism because it is dominated by the clergy.

91. The lack of accountability and transparency in decision-making and financial matters in the Church has led to a further divide in walking together in the spirit of a synodal Church. Those who question these matters are sometimes excluded from the Church. The authoritative and domineering styles of leadership do not only exist among the clergy but there are also leaders among the laity that exhibit such traits. This tension continues to hinder the journey towards being a participatory Church in a synodal way.

92. In the Asian context where respect for leaders is an inherent value, there are times when the laity are overly deferential to the clergy and there is a high possibility that this respect can be abused, and power and control become the *modus operandi*. This further undermines the 'non-clergy' in being co-responsible in the mission of the Church, as well as with its governance.

5.3 Tensions in Priestly Vocations

93. It was also noted that the excessive critical view of the clergy has contributed to the decrease in vocations to the priesthood in some parts of Asia. There are areas in Asia where there is a growing need for priests to serve and for the faith to continually grow. The need for priests is real and for the spread of the Gospel. Scandals by priests and the unhealthy attitudes and behaviour displayed by the priests are also causing the decrease in vocations.

94. Together with this, some reports also acknowledged the influence of a secular and materialist culture on priests and even lay leaders. This often challenges the witnessing of Gospel values in the mission of the Church.

5.4 Tensions in Women's Involvement

95. In many of the Churches of Asia, the participation of women in the everyday life of the Church is significant. However, there is a lack of the presence of women in leadership roles. In some societies, their voices are hardly heard.

96. Some attribute this to the cultural differences and the traditional patriarchal structures of Asian societies. In some places, women in leadership roles are not very welcome due to their cultural mindset. It would seem that men make decisions or lead the group and the women simply implement the decisions or work under the guidance of men. The role of women is considered secondary or simply discarded as being an assistant to men, this includes women in consecrated life.

97. However, some countries report that the men are not in the Church, and in these circumstances, it is the women who take on leadership roles effectively.

5.5 Tensions About the Youth

98. A common phenomenon noted in the reports is the absence of youth in our Churches. Given that they form a significant number in our population (approx. 65%), they are relatively absent in the life of the Church. Though some are present in the life of the Church, there is a need for faith formation, accompaniment and greater inclusion in leadership roles and decision-making processes.

99. Amid the generational gap between the old and the young, the Church as a 'mother'needs to extend her loving embrace around the youth and reach out to those who are lost, confused, and have disconnected themselves from the Church. Though the reports state the youth are missing in the Church, perhaps a point to ponder is that the youth are possibly saying that the Church is missing in their lives.

100. While the youth are more tech-savvy in parts of Asia where digital access is more easily accessible, the reports also call for greater investment in the fields of media and social communications to be able to reach out to them for evangelisation and proclaiming the good news of Jesus Christ. Nevertheless, there remains the challenge of engaging with the youth in the dialogue between the virtual world and the real world.

101. Gifted with a large population of young people, the Church in Asia could envision herself as a 'digital tent' to be where the youth are, and minister to them effectively. Synodality with the youth also means experiencing the tensions they are bearing in the fast-changing world today.

102. Notwithstanding the benefits of the digital world, the negative impact of social media was also highlighted – people spending more time with gadgets than with people; how it is used to spread hatred, prejudice, and fear in society; some say social media is swaying people away from the faith.

5.6 Tensions of the Poor

103. Like a mother in a poor Asian family with many children who struggles and at times is not adequately cared for, the Church in Asia also struggles and painfully embraces a great number of poor and marginalised people who need special accompaniment in this process of synodality.

104. Various are the faces of the poor in Asia: the materially poor such as the minority ethnics, the migrant workers, urban slum dwellers, fleeing refugees, etc.; the socially poor, those often neglected by the Church and society, such as the uneducated, the indifferent youth, the persons with disabilities, persons deprived of liberty, those from lower castes, divorced and remarried, single mothers, elderly and infirmed, HIV positive persons, substance dependents, persons who identify as LGBTQI+, etc.

105. We recognise however that the term poverty is relative, one can be materially poor but rich in culture, spirituality, and hospitality.

106. Despite some cultural barriers that may exist, the Church in Asia must desire to courageously direct her eyes on the faces of the poor, to lovingly recognise, acknowledge, and welcome everyone as God's children who now deserve our attention. We recognise the tensions to be inclusive and yet be faithful to the Gospel values and the moral faithfulness to the ways of the Church – perhaps even a scandal if they are welcomed in the Church.

107. The Church must strive to find ways to incorporate the poor into her life and mission, so that, being healed, nurtured, and formed in *sensus fidelium* within the framework of our apostolic tradition and Catholic identity, they could be equal partners and respected companions with everyone else in the Church. As mentioned by several of the reports, some of these changes will require canonical revisions that would facilitate the inclusiveness of the Church towards the poor.

108. The Church must also be the voice of the poor. There are times when the Church remains silent about the plight and cry of the Dalits, tribals, indigenous people, and the poor. Due to the tension of not wanting to cause trouble with the authorities or worry of being silenced, the Church may have alienated these people and turned a deaf ear to the 'cry of the poor'. The voice of the Church must defend the voiceless and powerless.

5.7 Tensions of Religious Conflicts

109. Even though there is a diversity of religions across Asia, there are also growing religious conflicts and even persecution (subtle and direct) in some areas. The worsening of the culture of violence across Asia, partly due to the lack of recourse to a functioning justice system, is also unsettling. The politicisation of religions has made it difficult to practise the faith of minorities. Among the challenges include political oppression, dictatorial governments, corruption, and unjust laws.

110. The Churches in Asia are always having to walk this tightrope of balancing between being faithful to the Gospel and yet not putting the Christians in a position of being threatened. Even what is taken for granted in many places, like giving a child a Christian name, is sometimes an obstacle in another place.

111. There are times in situations such as these, what is required is patience, and hope that things will change. The Church in Asia constantly deals with such tensions and there is a need for mutual support in walking together with courage and love.

5.8 Tensions of Clericalism

112. Clericalism, like in many parts of the world, is also a concern in Asia. Many of the responses indicate clericalism as a tension in their regions and some also state it as one of the causes of a lack of synodality in the Church in Asia.

113. However, it has been noted that clericalism means different things to different people. The word clericalism seems to cover a wide range of issues, while at the same time, some regions are more specific. Among the expressions of clericalism are the lack of consultation in administrative matters, domineering attitudes and sense of entitlement shown by those in authority especially priests, overexertion of power on the people, etc.

114. Some root causes of clericalism were identified, e.g., the individual character or psychological immaturity, some hint at more systemic causes, and others point out the subculture of silence and impunity. Proper formation of bishops, clergy, and laity for a synodal Church may thus be among the primary responses to such abuses.

115. On the other hand, the clergy feel overly criticised by the laity, so much so that some feel lonely, isolated, and scrutinised all the time. This further leads to demotivation among the priests and apprehension among young men who might be considering and discerning a vocation to the priesthood. Some attribute the lack of vocation due to the unreasonable demands that are being made by the people

VI
ASIAN REALITIES AND DIVERGENCES

116. Being aware that Christianity is a minority in Asia (it is estimated that Catholics are approximately 3.31% of the Asian population and in several places less than 1%), there is a great sense of love for Jesus and His Church. The joy of journeying together in this synodal renewal is palpable. Our faith energises our relationships not only among Christians but also with peoples of neighbouring faiths in our quest for harmonious living through a process of bridge-building. In places where discrimination and violence are more pronounced than in other places, faith in the Risen Jesus keeps us strong and hopeful amidst these adversities.

117. Asian spirituality, characterised by contemplation and respect for nature, is interwoven with a deep sense of piety and popular devotion. These devotions at times animate the faith and draw people to the Church, Catholics and non-Catholics alike.

118. Our embodied expressions of worship and prayer – encompassing the human senses, dance, art, poetry, and silence – sometimes find tension in the formal manner of celebrating the sacraments. Several reports pointed out the need to creatively rediscover the essence of the liturgy, that is, to draw people to God with Asian expressions of worship.

119. It was also noted that in some places, Catholics were more engaged in popular devotions rather than reflecting on the Word of God, spiritual discernment, or personal prayer. Overall, the need for liturgies to be more alive and relatable – text they can understand, the music they can sing, and rituals they can relate to, were expressed in a variety of ways in the reports.

120. We recognise that the Asian *ethos* that has long been part of its peoples (for example, reliance on God, communal interaction, relationality with God, self, other human beings, and the cosmos, etc.) is now being eroded by the globalised cultures of individualism, secularism, and relativism.

121. We are aware that tension exists between Asian cultures and our faith expressions in terms of languages, images and even concepts about authority and power.

122. There is a growing tension between traditional (spiritual) values and modernity even among the clergy, the religious, and the families. Some of the effects seen due to this global invasion are that faith is relativised, priests are drawn to a materialistic and individualistic way of living, and a lack of credible witnessing, which is among the reasons for the erosion of the spiritual life. In the end, the number of people not practising any religion will increase due to modernism, materialism, and secularism.

123. Family (nuclear and extended) is very important in many Asian societies. Filial allegiance extends to the point where many will make generous sacrifices for the sake of family unity and peace. The role of families in the synodal renewal of the Church and its witness to societies is therefore very important. They will be the first formation space for the synodal renewal that we are envisioning.

124. Several reports cite their concern for marriages and family life today domestic violence, unwed mothers, single parents, delayed marriages due to the dowry system, divorce and nullity, etc. Christian families break up due to a lack of awareness about the faith and anxieties brought about by poverty and economic conditions.

125. The contemporary tendency to excessive individualism further exacerbates this crisis in vocation, along with various economic trends that render embracing family life as undesirable for many. There are also tensions about belonging to the Church and their family relationships.

126. Amid such a vast array of challenges, the Church in Asia needs, more now than ever, to hear the voices of families, especially of interreligious-intercultural families that are becoming more of a norm than the exception in many places across Asia.

127. Coming from our communal *ethos*, the common life in Asian communities and neighbourhoods is the *locus* where the joys and struggles are lived. The common spaces are opportunities for informal dialogues and convivial living (dialogue of life). Fraught with socio-political, economic, and ecological challenges, we not only survive but there are situations where we thrive in the strength of this relationality at the grassroots.

128. In recent times, we also see a growing division among the peoples of Asia – people divided based on caste, language, ethnicity, and socio-economic status, and a growing intolerance within this divide.

129. Even if we are community-oriented people, the rapid economic growth resulting from material abundance has also resulted in more people suffering from emotional, spiritual, and mental impoverishment. In some Asian societies, the secular appearance and lifestyle in Church leadership also cause tension as it is opposed to *evangelical poverty* and a mission to be the Church of the poor in Asia.

130. In a continent as diverse as Asia, interreligious dialogue remains an integral characteristic of the Church in Asia. Despite bridge-building efforts, we noted that religious and social intolerance was on the increase, which leads ultimately to persecution and the worsening conditions of the lives of the people, especially religious minorities. In extreme situations, false blasphemy accusations and terror are the main issues faced by Christians.

131. The breakdown in democratic structures, including militarisation and political oppression, challenges the lives of many people in certain countries.

VII
GAPS IDENTIFIED IN THE ASIAN RESPONSES

132. The FABC 50 General Conference in its Guide Document and Final Message had identified some concerns that were either not captured in the country's responses to the DCS or not given sufficient consideration. Studying all these documents side-by-side, we have taken the liberty to include the gaps that were identified and have included them in this report in the sure hope that these will be considered the 2023/24 Synod Assemblies.

7.1 Care for our Common Home

133. Ecological crisis always has an impact on vulnerable communities and the Asian continent is one of the places where the impact of climate change is alarming. Despite the possibility that Asia could lead the way in advocating care for the common home, the Asian responses did not sufficiently capture the intensity of the ecological crisis in this region.

134. There is a great need to listen more intently and profoundly to the cry of our land and our people, especially among the poorest who are most affected and to preserve the environment.

7.2 Sharing of Resources

135. Many countries in our continent with poor resources mostly depend on international financial assistance from donors and financial institutes. This surely encourages the socio-economic uplift of the poor segment of society. However, the Asian Churches also need to be aware of the need to share our resources (even if it is limited) with sister Churches/ countries in the region.

136. By sharing our resources, not only do we share our material gifts but also the spiritual gifts that we receive from one another which enrich us, e.g., the animation of Basic Ecclesial Communities and the charisms of ecclesial movements. We stand together, as a synodal Church, with one another as peoples of Asia.

7.3 Youth for the Present

137. The youth are often spoken of as the future, but the youth are also the present. Our *preferential option* for the young should include personal experience of God's love within the Church, holistic formation, vocation discernment, and accompaniment. The youth look for authentic and credible witnesses within the Church – they need a synodal community to walk together.

138. By knowing who they are in front of God through their hopes, dreams, realities, struggles, and limitations that they face in life, they experience that they are supported and not alone in their path and can also encourage others to walk together in the journey of life.

139. The problems faced by the youth such as drug, gambling, and online addictions, breakdown of families, and mental health issues, were not sufficiently addressed. The 'broken youth' are not able to contribute to this synodal journey. For this reason, a synodal Church must learn how to accompany these youth for their healing, growth, and discernment of vocation.

7.4 Family and Marriage

140. The family is the domestic Church that nurtures the life of society, and the family is also the 'school of synodality' because it is here that the

character is formed. However, the new challenges facing families include the breakdown of families, a lack of commitment to promoting life, fear of marriage and decreasing birth rates due to economic difficulties and ideological conditioning, and much more is shaping the family units today in Asia.

141. In some countries, abortion is masquerading as a 'women's rights issue'. In others, abortion is promoted as a means of population control and eugenics. There is also a disastrous culture of silence in cases of domestic violence, incest, honour killing etc. A need to promote the spirituality of family life to reflect its call as a holy sanctuary.

142. In some parts of Asia where communities are ageing, the care for the elderly must also be given consideration.

143. The rising number of marriages in Asia that are interfaith and intercultural calls for greater pastoral attention as this can be both challenging and also an opportunity to grow in respect for other religions and cultures. Interfaith families can be the first school of interreligious dialogue.

7.5 Poverty, Corruption, and Conflict

144. Poverty across Asia is a major problem (World Bank estimates more than 320 million people in Asia live in extreme poverty). The Church has been at the forefront of working tirelessly among the poor and for their upliftment. Yet there is little mention of the growing poverty across Asia and how that impacts being a synodal Church.

145. We also recognise that unsustainable urbanisation and systemic corruption are major problems in Asia and are somewhat connected to the poverty of the Asian people. This systemic corruption at all levels of society affects the lives of ordinary citizens. The responses to the DCS have not given this 'problem' much consideration.

146. The Church in Asia is a demographic, socioeconomic, cultural, and political minority and therefore, we are becoming more vulnerable to progressively oppressive or fundamentalist regimes as well as to political conflicts. In such situations, what does it mean to be a synodal Church?

147. The disconnect between religiosity and morality is indeed concerning. Despite the connectedness of Asian people with a form of religiosity or spirituality, moral lives are sometimes not transformed by religious experiences. For example, one may be religious but corrupt at the same time.

7.6 Indigenous Peoples

148. Nearly 60% of the world's indigenous peoples, call Asia their home. Bearers of traditions that are rooted for thousands of years, the indigenous peoples manifest how humanity can live in harmony with creation. We acknowledge that many indigenous peoples have embraced the Christian faith, yet even in the Church – wounded by tribalism and prejudice – they struggle to be respected as fellow agents of evangelisation. Despite the large populations of indigenous peoples in Asia, very little is spoken about them in the responses.

7.7 Church in the World

149. The Church exists in the world and for the world. Yet many of the responses have been very insular – looking within the Church only. A level of comfort that has left the Church to be only comfortable in addressing her affairs may have led to a lack of reference to how the Church transforms the world (Asia) so that all people will enjoy the fruits of the kingdom of God. The Church in Asia must constantly keep asking how can the *missio ad gentes* be recognised and lived in a synodal manner as one way of enlarging the space of our tent.

150. The Church cannot be self-referential and therefore must seek to engage in renewing the world. One of the ways is the building of Basic Ecclesial Communities (BEC) to bring about social transformation – care for the common home, and interreligious dialogue. The culture of dialogue with religions and encounter with cultures must be integrated into the life of the Church. The Church must move towards greater networking with others (organisations and institutions) for the common good of all.

7.8 Migrants, Refugees, and Displaced Peoples

151. The issues related to migrants, refugees, displaced people as well as human trafficking, etc. are fast growing in the Asian regions. The primary drivers for the movement of such large numbers of people include conflict, the desire for better economic opportunities, environmental destruction, victims of exploitation, etc.

152. The political instability in some parts of Asia has made people become refugees and asylum seekers. How does the Church become a 'welcoming tent' to these people who seek peace, security, and harmony? In many of these places, they become missionaries of the gospel as they bring not only their lived experiences but also their faith. The migrants, refugees, and displaced people also give vibrancy to the life of the local Churches through their presence. The Church must seek to integrate and accompany them on this journey as the new evangelisers.

7.9 Peacebuilding

153. In countries where there are internal conflicts due to oppressive and dictatorial regimes, the Church must play an integral role in the work of peacebuilding and conflict resolution. Among the many other roles of the Church, the peace and harmony of all citizens must be among its pastoral priorities.

154. Working towards peace and reconciliation could be among the new forms of evangelisation. Apart from seeing the Church as a 'tent' of inclusivity, the Church must also be a 'bridge builder' in the work of peace and reconciliation.

7.10 Safeguarding

155. The protection of minors and the vulnerable is a concern for the Church in Asia. Despite the low rate in the number of cases being reported (partly due to cultural reasons), it is a major concern. There is very little mention in the responses to the DCS on this matter. However, this must be prioritised in terms of training all Church personnel.

156. The Church in Asia must hear, watch over, protect, and care for the abused, exploited and forgotten children, wherever they are by creating safe environments and implementing protective procedures.

7.11 Role of Bishops

157. For obvious reasons, Bishops play an irreplaceable role in animating the synodal process in the local Church. As the primary pastor of the People of God, the level of zeal and sincerity in which he embraces the synodal approach in his manner of leadership to a large extent sets the tone of the endeavour to rediscover this vital Christian practice among the clergy and laity whom he is called to serve.

158. His responsibility to affirm the authentic tradition of the Christian community is inspired by a willingness to witness a radical trust in the Spirit's life-giving activity in the life of this community: 'Doing synod is doing evangelisation' (Pope Francis). Imitating the Good Shepherd in encouraging the flock to continual growth and conversion through desiring and knowing the Way and the Truth alone leads to life – true life, life in abundance, life eternal.

159. In this manner, he remains faithful to his role and calling in the context of sustaining and strengthening Catholic identity, while charging others to engage in three of the essential aspects of Christian reality: *communion, participation, and mission.*

160. In joyfully accepting the authority of the leaders of the community, clergy, consecrated, and laity are strengthened in their vocations to know God, to love and serve Him in others. *Listening* to God in His Word, through His Church, and in dialogue with others, all members of the community share the responsibility of serving according to their baptismal character.

161. Bishops today can attest to the words of the early Christian pastor, St. John Chrysostom, who claimed that 'Church and Synod are synonymous'. These bishops lead God's people and are in turn encouraged, accompanied, and informed by the promptings of the Holy Spirit as expressed in the lives of all in the community.

162. No one is exempt or excluded from the responsibility to discern and embrace this common, baptismal call and it is Christ's will that no one is left unaided by that grace through which life is made more abundant and the world in which we live reconciled and sanctified.

163. In all the above gaps, the synodal way must permeate when addressing these gaps and the synodal journey must be at the heart of the life and mission of the Church.

VIII
PRIORITIES FROM THE ASIAN RESPONSES

164. The Asian responses were varied and diverse, encapsulating a variety of issues and challenges, each peculiar to one's region. However, there are some commonalities that we see in the responses, all of which point to a need for authentic prophetic servant-leadership that is dependent

upon and leads to continuous conversion. It is evident that, to a large extent, the synodal journey is made more possible with the awareness and willingness of the People of God to embrace this reality.

165. The following are 6 priorities that have been identified through a process of prayer and discernment with the hope that they reflect the desires of Asian hearts.

8.1 Formation

166. For a synodal Church, there needs to be an initial and ongoing formation at all levels, for all people, beginning with the families and Basic Ecclesial Communities (BECs).

167. Seminarians, priests, bishops, and consecrated men and women must be formed to live synodal leadership styles, communal discernment, and decision-making – the promotion of a culture of synodality that entails renewal of training of seminary formators, professors of theology, and the present seminary programme needs to be more life-ministry oriented.

168. The laity needs to be formed to take active roles, according to their baptismal call, to serve with generosity to God and a love for the Church and its people. Formation for a synodal spirituality must be at the heart of the Church's mission and vision.

8.2 Inclusivity & Hospitality

169. The women, youth, and those marginalised or excluded, with special attention to the abandoned (e.g., street children and elderly), also significant pastoral care should be provided to divorced, remarried, single parents, broken families, persons with disabilities (PWDs), prisoners, persons who identify as LGBTQI+, the elderly, substance dependents, commercial sex workers, etc.) the wounded and victimised, fractured families and those struggling with gender identity, the displaced and the persecuted, and a whole spectrum of many others must find their place in this 'tent' (Church).

170. Structures may need to be revisited so that everyone feels a sense of belonging in the Church and each person becomes an ambassador of Christ, an ambassador of inclusivity and hospitality.

8.3 Missionary Disciples

171. In the context of Asia, we must learn how to prophetically witness and 'whisper' the Gospel to one another, which, first and foremost, entails actively living out one's faith founded on personal encounters and personal experiences with Jesus and contributing to the community of the Church as a communion of communities.

172. While recognising that Christians are a minority in Asia, the incomparable witness of Asian martyrs provides a challenge and source of encouragement.

173. We must also learn to grow in dialogue, consultation, and communal discernment. At the same time, respecting the sensitivities of other Asian peoples must also be at the heart of the Church. Interfaith families are becoming a common sight and therefore how do we bring Christ to others? We need to embrace a culture of encounter and bridge-building to bring Christ to the world.

174. In this post-pandemic era, the hybridisation of the Church life (onsite and online) is a reality that we must embrace and maximise opportunities to evangelise, including the wider and more discerning use of technology in this endeavour, as our Christian mandate.

8.4 Accountability and Transparency

175. The call to be accountable and transparent not only in financial matters but also in decision-making processes and governance. This may necessitate the revision of some provisions of Canon Law. Those in leadership roles – whether clergy or lay, are also accountable for the formation of the laity and the youth.

176. A spirit of collaboration and co-responsibility must be promoted with each embracing the other's vocation and state of life and the manifold charisms in the Church.

8.5 Prayer and Worship

177. Our prayer and worship must reflect and touch the hearts of the Asian people. Liturgical celebrations must be more 'synodal' (participatory, inculturated, relatable, and convivial) so that everyone can find a sacred and safe space to worship God. The integration of culture in the life and worship of the Church must also animate the lives of the faithful.

8.6 Environment

178. In the care for the common home, the Church must be at the forefront in not only protecting Mother Earth but also healing her. As Jesus came to redeem and reconcile all things, the Church must seek to renew the face of the earth.

179. As members of the one Body of Christ, we are called to become a green Church and live in solidarity and respect, protect, defend, and nurture the oneness of all of God's Creation. Environmental concern is not merely ecological but also has a spiritual and social dimension as it affects everyone, the poor the most.

IX
'TAKING OFF OUR SHOES': THE ASIAN SYNODAL JOURNEY

180. It is a common practice among Asians to take off our shoes when we enter houses or temples. It is a beautiful sign of respect; of how we are conscious of the others whose lives we are entering into. Moreover, it is also an expression of our deep awareness of the holy.

181. It reminds us of what God told Moses (Exodus 3:5): 'Remove the sandals from your feet, for the place where you stand is holy ground'. More importantly, 'taking off our shoes' makes us aware of the earth we are all called to protect and care for.

182. 'Taking off our shoes' is also a beautiful symbol of our synodal journey as the Church in Asia. Characterised by diversity in cultures and religions, it reminds us to respect all as we listen and converse, discern and decide. It also means in authentic listening; we leave behind our prejudices and biases to welcome the other.

183. Shoes could be a symbol of status and by taking them off, we recognise that we are equal as human beings. Barefoot, we become aware and also identify ourselves with the poorest among us.

184. 'Taking off our shoes' makes us also very conscious of the soil, the ground we are stepping on. The socio-political context of Asia is very challenging and how the Church moves in this context is of paramount importance in journeying with humanity. It makes us feel closer to the ground realities of the people of Asia.

185. 'Taking off our shoes' as a synodal ecclesial image articulates our experience of the Church as relational, contextual and missional, journeying together in humility and hope.

X
CONCLUSION

186. The synodal journey that began in October 2021 is not a process that was new to the Churches in Asia. In many countries, there were already opportunities for listening and discernment to develop pastoral plans. However, these were only at the parish, diocesan or national levels. There have been both successes and challenges at these levels.

187. The synodal journey gave Catholics who participated in this process a better regional and universal understanding of the consolations and concerns of the different Churches. There was an acknowledgement that the consolations and challenges were not only unique to the different regions but also complex in their ways.

188. The process of discernment to a large extent invigorated the life of the Church through the active participation of many Catholics whose experience before this may have been on the periphery. For many people, seeds of hope were sown through this process while at the same time, we acknowledge that some were sceptical for various reasons.

189. This is a process that needs to filter into every level of the life of the Church. The process of synodality, that is, discernment and Spiritual Conversations, must be part of the life and ministry of the Church henceforth. Some Churches across Asia have already started implementing the fruits of having listened during the earlier phase of the synodal process.

190. While the change of structures is important to implementing the synodal changes, the aspects of relationality must not be forgotten on this journey as an integral part of being a synodal Church.

191. At the Asian Continental Assembly (24-26 Feb 2023), it was suggested that the *relatio finalis* from the Synod in October 2023 be released the soonest as possible so that conferences, dioceses, and parishes can begin to work on suggestions that may arise at the XVI Ordinary General Assembly of the Synod of Bishops.

192. Given the diversity of languages across Asia, it will be beneficial that a summarised form of the *relatio finalis* be published too so that countries could work on the various translations, and this is disseminated to as many people as possible.

193. There should be sub-regional synodal conversations after the Synod gathering in October 2023. These gatherings can be a means for ongoing listening and discernment for the Churches in Asia and perhaps even an Ecclesial Synod in 2024.

As we offer this Final Document, the fruit of our listening and discerning, we implore the maternal protection and intercession of Mary, the Mother of Asia, in this synodal pilgrimage together with the rest of humanity.

'A Profound Spiritual Experience of Listening'

A PROFOUND SPIRITUAL EXPERIENCE OF LISTENING: THE CONTINENTAL SYNODAL ASSEMBLY OF EUROPE

Myriam Wijlens and Arnaud Join-Lambert

The European Continental Assembly for the world wide 2021-2024 Synod entitled *For a Synodal Church: Communion – Participation – Mission* took place in Prague from 5 to 12 February 2023. Here the Church of Europe, living in very different contexts, met to listen to what the Spirit has to say to the Church in this continent. The Church of Europe finds itself in rather different contexts: some faithful live in countries that are mainly Catholic, others in predominantly Protestant or Orthodox countries. Secularisation is a theme for all: some embrace it, others see is as a danger and threat.[1]

The Final Remarks of the Prague Assembly express gratitude to the Spirit who guided the process for the gifts received during the meeting.[2] It reports that insights were gained through the synodal process, and tensions and questions were faced. The Assembly once again 'felt the pain of the wounds that mark our recent history, starting with those that the Church has inflicted through the abuses perpetrated by people who were performing an ecclesial ministry or office.' Europe met while the continent is suffering from violence of the aggression war disfiguring Ukraine. Solidarity was expressed with victims of an earthquake in Syria and Turkey.

The gathering was experienced as rich and exciting, though not without its problems and difficulties, captured in the Final Remarks. The Assembly communicates:

> We went through a spiritual experience that tells us it is possible to meet, listen to each other and dialogue starting from our differences and to reach beyond the many obstacles, walls and barriers that our history puts in our way. We need to love the variety within our Church and support each other in mutual esteem, strengthened by

1 This contribution contains some passages from the article: Arnaud Join-Lambert, 'Une nouvelle étape pour l'Église catholique: L'assemblée continentale de Prague', Études nr. 4305 (2023) 79-90 ; id., 'Un kairos per la Chiesa cattolica. Uno sguardo all'Assemblea continentale di Praga', *La Rivista del Clero Italiano* nr. 6 (2023) 421-434.

2 The CCEE has a special website on which all documentscan be found in one dossier. https://prague.synod2023.org/en/final-document/ (access 15.06.2023). The Dossier is published in Italian and English. The English text is in the second part of the dossier. The Final Remarks are in English on pp. 37-39.

> our faith in the Lord and the power of his Spirit. This is why we wish to continue walking in a synodal style: more than a methodology we consider it a way of life of our Church, of communal discernment and of discernment of the signs of the times. Concretely, we want this Continental Assembly not to remain an isolated experience, but to become a periodic appointment, based on the general adoption of the synodal method that permeates all our structures and procedures on all levels. In this style, it will be possible to address the issues on which our efforts need to mature and intensify: the accompaniment of the wounded, the 'protagonism' of young people and women, the learning from marginalised people, etc.
>
> The synodal style also allows us to address tensions from a missionary perspective, without being paralysed by fear, but drawing from them the energy to continue along the way. Two in particular have emerged in our work. The first encourages unity in diversity, escaping the temptation of uniformity. The second links the readiness to welcome as a witness to the Father's unconditional love for his children with the courage to proclaim the truth of the Gospel in its entirety: it is God who promises 'Love and truth will meet' (Ps 85:11).
>
> We know that all this is possible because we have experienced it during this Assembly, but even more because the life of the Churches from which we come bears witness to it. We are thinking here in particular of ecumenical dialogue, which has echoed strongly in our work, and also of interreligious dialogue. But above all, we believe that it is possible because grace is involved: building an increasingly synodal Church is a way to concretely implement equality in dignity of all the members of the Church, founded in baptism. It configures us as children of God and members of the body of Christ, co-responsible for the unique mission of evangelisation entrusted by the Lord to his Church.[3]

As the statement reveals: the gathering in Prague of the People of God of Europe was an astonishing, unique, and unprecedented event. It deserves to be recounted and contemplated upon, because many lessons can be learned from it. This study does not reflect about the content of the document that the European Continental Assembly presented to the Secretariat for the Synod. Rather the focus lies on the organisational and methodological dimension of the meeting.

3 Idem

An Unprecedented Event: A European Continental Ecclesial Assembly

The European continental meeting in Prague is really unprecedented. Unlike Latin America, the Catholic Church of Europe knows no tradition of an ecclesial assembly at the continental level. There have been a few synodal processes at a national level since the Second Vatican Council, such as in The Netherlands (1966-1970), in Germany (1971-1975 in Würzburg for West Germany, 1973-1975 in Dresden-Meissen for East Germany, and 2019-2023 for the reunited whole country), Switzerland (1969-1975), Austria (1973-1974), as well as England and Wales (1980). The continent witnessed two plenary councils, one in Poland (1991-1997) and the other in the Czech Republic (1997-2005). Italy celebrated five National Ecclesial Assemblies (1976, 1985, 1995, 2006 and 2015). Furthermore, the continent has celebrated three ecumenical assemblies in Basel (1989), Graz (2004) and Sibiu (2007). Nevertheless, none of these processes compare to the current Roman Synod as a whole, nor to this particular Assembly in Prague.

The General Secretariat of the Synod in Rome entrusted the entire organisation of the continental meetings to continental institutions in which episcopal conferences already cooperate. Hence the Council of Bishops' Conferences of Europe (CCEE, *Consilium Conferentiarum Episcoporum Europae*)[4] based in St Gallen, Switzerland organised the European Continental Assembly. The CCEE Presidency[5], inspired by the suggestions of the General Secretariat of the Synod and the Methodological Note on the Continental Assemblies, decided on the rules of participation and the working method. There were two meetings: from 5-9 February 2023 the Continental Ecclesial Assembly of Europe took place. Subsequently, from 10-12 February, the CCEE held a meeting in which the presidents of the episcopal conferences of Europe that make up the CCEE met among themselves. The study focuses in particular on the first meeting.

The Location and Accommodation

Prague as location was in itself already symbolically strong. Located in the former communist occupied territory, the capital of the Czech Republic lies not only in the centre of Europe, where it somewhat bridges Eastern and Western Europe, but the city also holds a major place in European religious history. It is of

4 Created in 1971, the CCEE 'is made up of thirty-nine members, of which thirty-three are Bishops' Conferences, the Archbishops of Luxembourg, the Principality of Monaco, the Maronite Archbishop of Cyprus and the Bishops of Chişinău (Moldova) of the Mukachevo Eparchy and the Apostolic Administration of Estonia; all together they represent the Catholic Church in forty-five countries in the European continent.' Cf. https://www.ccee.eu/ccee/?lang=en

5 The president of the CCEE is Archbishop Gintaras Grusas (Episcopal Conference of Lithuania) and the Vice-presidents: Cardinal Jean-Claude Hollerich (Luxembourg) and Archbishop Ladislav Nemet SVD of Belgrade, Conference of SS. Cyril and Methodius.

relevance for Judaism, for the Reformation and for Catholic renewal. Currently, the Czech Church finds herself in a strong secularised society.

The logo serving the European Continental Meeting captures the event: It holds the official logo of the Synod, which shows God's people in their diversity walking through the world with the Holy Spirit hovering over them, and contextualises this with the Charles Bridge and the Old Town Bridge Tower, the symbol of Prague. The explanation offered is that the gate protected the bridge, and was a kind of triumphal arch through which the Czech king passed on his coronation journey. The logo 'reinforces the idea of synodality by showing that the People of God do not walk together in some imaginary setting, but in the concrete conditions of this world. Walking on a bridge that connects shores and divided worlds, synodality thus contributes to overcoming obstacles, building bridges and establishing relationships between people with each other and between man and God. The wandering People of God are directed to the tower-gate through which they enter the city. This depiction may evoke the eschatological dimension of the wandering of God's people as they head for the heavenly Jerusalem where the Lamb is the light (cf. Rev. 21).'[6]

The European Continental Assembly gathered in a hotel which, in conformity with its shape, is named: 'Pyramida'. However, as many participants commented, Pope Francis' call for understanding the Church as an inverted pyramid, in which the top is located beneath the base, was fully realised. *Within* the hotel the People of God not only gathered on the main floor, but were also given the opportunity to encounter each other in such a way that all felt respected and equal in dignity while respecting the diversity of charisms present. A number of factors might have been conducive to this: all were praying, listening, working, eating and relaxing together. Food was served in a buffet style thus inviting people to get up, join the end of the line, meet others and sit down with those not known yet.

The conference hall had a classroom seating style, all facing the leadership or moderators of the sessions, who were seated on a podium. Of the many plenary sessions, only one was moderated by a woman.[7] Comments were made about the need to change this in the future. In the hall, there was no seat assignment, but in practice – in particular due to daily celebrations of the Eucharist in the same hall – many bishops were sitting up front and the other participants to a large extend behind them. The delegates of a number of episcopal conferences sat beside each other, and others were dispersed over the hall.

6 https://www.ccee.eu/continental-assembly-of-the-synod/?lang=en. The explanation of the logo adds to the above mentioned quotation the remarkable sentence: 'After all, the emperor and Czech king Charles IV (1316-1378), builder of the Charles Bridge, conceived of Prague as the New Jerusalem, the centre of Christianity.' The logo can be found on p. 161.

7 The lay women Dr Beate Gilles, the secretary general of the episcopal conference of Germany.

Participants in a Hybrid Meeting

The European Ecclesial Continental Assembly had a unique feature: the meeting was hybrid, implying that some participated on site, others remote. Each of the thirty-nine members of CCEE could send four delegates to participate on site and ten persons to participate online. It was left to each member to decide who should participate. The number of persons was irrespective of factors that may greatly differ from one episcopal conference to another such as the number of dioceses, faithful or financial strength. Hence, for the example, the church of Luxembourg or Monaco composed of one diocese and not belonging to any episcopal conference were invited to send the same number as did e.g. the episcopal conference of the predominantly Catholic country Poland, the economically well situated German episcopal conference or the with over 200 dioceses established Italian episcopal conference. The intention was to listen to each and everyone. This decision might reflect a biblical value. In the end, in a synodal process the 'least among you' is as much worthy to be listened to as the stronger ones, because in a synodal process each one has something to contribute. Hence, the voices carry an equal weight. This is in line with and implements the exhortation of the *Preparatory Document* (2021)[8] on the place to be given to all, especially to those who are marginalised, are not given the floor or who do not dare to take it.

This 'equality' was also put into practice for the Working Groups in Prague, where while being in the listening phase of the Synod everyone's voice was of equal relevance, whether they were bishops, priests, deacons, lay people or consecrated persons. Also guests such as the prefect from the Dicastery for Bishops, Cardinal Marc Ouellet and the Secretary General of the Synod Office in Rome, Cardinal Mario Grech were given the floor and attentively listened to. That being said, it would seem that people who are marginalised, in great precariousness or in a situation of disability did not seem to be personally present. At some point a group of persons stood outside a Church building in which the Ecclesial Assembly was celebrating the Eucharist. They asked that attention be paid to those who are sexually abused within the ecclesial context.

With regard to the on-site meeting in Prague itself, the delegation was usually composed of the president of the conference – hence a bishop – and three other delegates. However, as it turned out, not all members succeeded in sending four persons. Some, it was said, were absent for health reasons such as COVID-19, other members had not nominated four persons. Hence, instead of the possible 156 only 140 delegates were present. In addition, there were 42 invited participants from movements, associations organisations as well as

8 Synod of Bishops, *Preparatory Document*, Vatican : 2021 https://www.synod.va/en/news/the-preparatory-document.html

other churches and ecclesial communities and non-Christians.[9] Together with the guests, the redaction committee, support staff and translators a total of 200 persons met in Prague. The number of women who participated was 73 and they did in different capacities: 49 as delegates, 11 as guests, 2 as a member of the Redaction Committee, 2 belonging to the media team, 4 worked as staff and 7 provided translations. The number of 73 women contrast with the 52 bishops who were there: 42 bishops participated as delegates and 10 as guests. It shows that the number of women as delegates (49) was larger than the number of bishops (42), and that the number of women as guests (11) was just outnumbering the number of bishops (10).

Considering that each member could have sent ten delegates to participate online, the total number of the online participants could have been 390, but in the end only 269 persons joined the Assembly, 115 of them being women. The final report of the Prague meeting lists the names of all delegates and other persons who were somehow involved. Unique for Europe was the invitation by the CCEE and the Union of European Conferences of Major Superiors to the communities of contemplative life from all over Europe to join the meeting, in a special way, with continuous silent Adoration.

In order for as many people to be part of the synodal process, and for the process to be transparent, the organisers saw to it that all plenary sessions and liturgies were live streamed with translations in five languages available. Furthermore, accredited journalists were invited to stay in the same hotel, where they could be seen conducting interviews during breaks as well as eating together with the participants.

The Preparation and Task

The *Document for the Continental Stage 'Enlarge the Space of your Tent'* (DCS)[10] was not only available in the five languages used in the Assembly, it had been translated into local languages of many if not most European countries. All participants had been asked to read it before the meeting. The DCS (nr. 106) suggested three questions to be addressed in the continental meeting:

1. Which intuitions expressed in the DCS resonate most strongly with the lived experiences and realities of the Church in your continent? Which experiences are new, or illuminating to you?
2. Which substantial tensions or divergences emerge as particularly important in your continent's perspective?

9 For example: Focolare, Schönstatt, Neocatechumenal Way, Justitia et Pax, Caritas Europe, Renovabis, International Federation of Catholic Universities, Council of European Churches (CEC), Observatory on Intolerance and Discrimination against Christians in Europe (OIDACE) etc. All are listed in the final document (cf. European Continental Assembly, Concluding Dossier, pp. 73-75).

10 https://www.synod.va/content/dam/synod/common/phases/continental-stage/dcs/20221025-ENG-DTC-FINAL-OK.pdf

3. What are therefore the questions or issues that should be addressed and considered in the Synodal Assembly of October 2023?

The episcopal conferences had not been invited to submit a written response to the three questions before the meeting. Europe chose to have an oral presentation by each delegation of six minutes with a maximum of two persons speaking. Generally, the president of the conference and one other delegate – often a woman – spoke. The sequence of speaking occurred according to alphabetic order of the Italian name of the episcopal conference. This procedure meant that the redaction team of the final document could begin its work only after the opening of the Assembly.

There is a lack of data on how this DCS was used in all the local churches and episcopal conferences belonging to the CCEE while preparing for the Prague Assembly. Based on the information provided by spokespersons, agencies and church media as well as personal contact of the authors, it seems that some delegations had written their response after a consultation in their respective entity either with the local churches, the bishops of these local churches, or with the episcopal conference. Others seemed to express the view of the delegation as such or of individual members of the delegation. Indeed some delegations had prepared one intervention that was read out by two persons, whereas others submitted two separate papers that did not necessarily connect. The vast majority of the contributions deepened the reports that the respective episcopal conference had submitted after the first phase of listening in the local churches in the summer of 2022.

The Opening of the Assembly

On Sunday evening, the Assembly opened with a celebration of the liturgy of the hours followed by the Eucharist. The next morning the first plenary session opened with the prayer of the synod, the *Adsumus*, followed by words of welcome by the president of CCEE, archbishop Gintaras Grusas. He recalled that in 1968 Prague experienced a Spring which had been brutally ended and now the Centre of Europe once again suffered from a war. Yet, the president said there is hope for Europe, especially for those who have faith. He underscored that the continental meeting is not to stress one's own point, but required is to be synodal and thus to listen to each other in the presence of the Holy Spirit. This was followed by an address of the Secretary General of the Synod, Cardinal Mario Grech, who underscored the need to listen, the awareness that each and everyone has something to say, that all feel that they are heard, and that the Holy Spirit guides the process. He stressed that the topic of the synod is to focus on what it means to be a synodal church.[11]

11 All addresses and interventions can be found on the website: https://prague.synod2023.org/en/files/

The Assembly then attentively listened to a spiritual input by Tomáš Halík, the Czech theologian and professor of sociology at Charles University in Prague, who during the communist time had been secretly ordained to the priesthood. He gave a very remarkable and inspiring lecture on the specific secularised context in which the Church of Europe finds herself.[12] In summary, he said: 'The Church as a communion of pilgrims is a living organism. This means that the Church must always be open, transforming and evolving! He suggested that the task of the Church is to keep ever-present in human hearts the desire for this goal and, at the same time, to resist the temptation to consider any form of knowledge, from the Church, society, religion, philosophy or science, as being final and perfect. Finally he warned that we must not approach others with the pride and arrogance of those who claim to possess the truth. The Truth is a book that none of us has yet read all the way through. We are not owners of the truth, but lovers of the truth and lovers of the One who can say, I am the Truth. We must not be afraid. This was his closing appeal to all those attending and probably to the whole Church.'[13]

Plenary Sessions and Working Groups

The organisors consciously decided not to adopt the method used so far in Roman Synods of Bishops in which each participant can address the whole assembly for a few minutes. Such a method would have implied that not only each of the 156 delegates would have spoken for three minutes amounting at least eight hours within three days. Moreover time would have been needed for guests to speak as well. Sure, it would have meant that each person could have spoken in plenary, but there would not have been time to deeply listen together to what the Spirit is saying to the Church in Europe. There would have been no time to move to a next level together.

Hence, it was decided to work according to the method of Spiritual Conversation which implied working in small groups. Thus, the program foresaw a number of plenary sessions as well as three sessions of one and a half hours each to work in language groups.

Each member of the CCEE – thus basically each episcopal conference – could address the plenary through two delegates for a total of six minutes in which they would share their response to the three questions identified by the DCS. There were three plenary sessions in which thirteen members presented their response through maximum two delegates. Hence in one plenary session a maximum of twenty-six people spoke. After four presentations there was a

12 The address is available in English, French, German, Italian, Polish and German: https://prague.synod2023.org/en/6-february/#226-232-press-kits-1674732308

13 A summary of the lecture found at : https://www.ofmconv.net/en/cechia-sulla-strada-di-una-chiesa-sinodale/

three minute prayer sessions: different episcopal conferences shared a prayer or showed a short meditative video. After one set of thirteen presentations, the Working Groups met to share what they had heard and deepen their understanding of what was said. Each of the three sessions of the Working Groups focused on one of the DCS questions at a time. Following the Working Groups sessions, all met in plenary to listen to what had come to the fore. All reports were submitted electronically to the drafting team in one of the five languages.[14]

The Languages and Spiritual Conversation

An important characteristic of the European meeting was that with the help of translators it simultaneously worked in five languages: English, French, German, Italian, and Polish. Despite this service, nevertheless for the majority of the people present this still meant that they did not participate and engage in their mother tongue, but in another language. The numerous languages reflect the diversity and richness in culture as well as the challenge to really understand each other and find a way of expressing faithfully what concerns all.

Before the Assembly began, the participants had indicated in which of the five working languages they could work. The organisors mixed them in such a way that participants from different countries and with different ecclesial status could meet in different language groups. Thirteen of them were in Prague: three Italian, five English, two German, two in French and one multilingual. There were eleven online groups: two Italian, three French, four English, one Polish, one German. Hence in total there were twenty-four groups. Each group had about 12-14 participants.

The Working Groups were invited to use the method of Spiritual Conversation which the Secretariat for the Synod had proposed. At the beginning of the meeting Mauricio Lopez,[15] a member of the Methodological Commission and of the *Task Force* for the continental meetings in the Secretariat for the Synod in Rome, explained the method. This method in combination with the composition by way of language in different Working Groups was important for one reason and decisive for another. On the one hand, the contributions of the groups to the collective work of discernment were considered on a par with the reports drawn up beforehand. The plenary sessions thus were not just a place of taking note of what was said; rather these sessions implied a deep listening and discernment. On the other hand, these groups were fixed for the duration of the Assembly, which allowed them to open up the possibility of development, progression and common deepening, beyond the sometimes-obvious differences. For

14 The reports are all online : https://prague.synod2023.org/en/files/
15 Director of CELAM's network and pastoral action programs and Executive Secretary of the Amazon Ecclesial Conference.

example, after the first session, one person in a German-speaking group considered to leave the meeting, but all tried to continue together. Towards the end of the Assembly they noted how beneficial and fruitful it had been to have gone through the moment of near incomprehension to later arrive at a source of common learning in what it means to live unity in diversity. During the final meeting, almost all the groups emphasised how the method of Spiritual Conversation had been an important discovery and a spiritually enrichment. The wish was expressed to deepen and continue this in the future.

Remote Participation

The possibility of remote participation while others were on-site, was another unique feature of the European Assembly. A precedent had been set during the pre-synod meeting of young people and the 2018 Roman Synod of Bishops on Young People: at that time, all young people who wanted to participate had been invited to join Facebook groups. The online participants of the Prague meeting were mostly isolated and connected to others only in their virtual language Working Group. The liturgical and fraternal aspects of the meeting were missing.

Exceptional, and possibly exemplary, were the gatherings of the online delegates of France and Switzerland. The ten delegates gathered in one place together: The Swiss met in Wislikofen and the French met in the Abbey of Saint Wandrille. They stayed and prayed together for the duration of the whole meeting. The (one-sided) participation was ensured by the live transmission of everything that was common, i.e. both the liturgical services and the plenary meetings. Each person in these two groups belonged to different online Working Groups. They had a daily meeting with the delegates of their respective episcopal conference, who were physically present in Prague. Towards the end, they wrote a report with their group which was presented in plenary. According to a French and a Swiss participant, the dominant feeling at the closing of the Assembly was that of an intense spiritual experience in the conference hall in Prague and a real participation in the discernment process, despite the obvious frustrations such as being deprived of all the informality of such a meeting. The strongest regret was about the telecasting itself, because the cameras were mostly focused on the podium.

Liturgy and Prayer

The European Assembly was embedded in liturgical celebrations with different forms of prayer. The Eucharistic celebrations were at times in different nearby churches and at other times in the Assembly hall in the hotel. The Assembly opened with Vespers and a celebration of the Eucharist on Sunday afternoon in the Premonstratensian Church of the so-called Norbertine Fathers. The archbishop of Prague, Jan Graubner, preached. On the Monday morning the Assembly celebrated the Eucharist in the Assembly hall with Cardinal Jean-Claude Hollerich SJ, Vice President of the CCEE and general Rapporteur for the Synod, presiding and preaching. It commenced its session by praying the *Adsumus* prayer of the Synod. On Monday evening the prayer service was led by the Brothers of Taizé. On Tuesday morning Cardinal Marc Ouellet, prefect of the Dicastery for Bishops, presided over the Eucharistic celebration. The omission of an enthronement of the Gospel at the beginning, the synodal rite par excellence since the Council of Ephesus in 431,[16] was made up during this celebration. The Tuesday closed with a prayer service guided by the Ukrainian Greek Catholic Church. On Wednesday morning, the session opened with an ecumenical prayer service guided by the representatives of the Conference of European Churches. In the evening the Assembly walked or went by coach to St Vitus Cathedral of Prague to celebrate the Eucharist together with many other faithful including those who had participated in the national synodal phase in the Czech Republic. Cardinal Mario Grech, Secretary General of the Synod, presided over the celebration. On Thursday morning, the Assembly gathered again in the hotel to celebrate the Eucharist with the apostolic Nuncio to the Czech Republic, Archbishop Jude Thaddesu Okolo presiding.

As mentioned above, the different presentation in the Assembly Hall were interrupted for meditative moments of prayer which were mostly supported by video clips allowing all to get a glimpse of the rich diversity of liturgical expressions, songs and spirituality present in the many local churches in Europe. This diversity contrasted beautifully with the Eucharistic celebrations, which were in Latin with mostly Gregorian chant: the People of God experienced in the different liturgies both unity and diversity in a unique way. One room in the hotel was transformed into a meditative room with a possibility for adoration of the Blessed Sacrament.

Transparency

Another totally innovative and unprecedented point is that of transparency. The CCEE Presidium had decided on online broadcasting to facilitate the participation of as many people as possible in Europe. This was achieved by the aforementioned broadcasting of all plenary sessions, speeches and liturgies on the CCEE *YouTube* channel live. These videos are still available online[17] and

16 A. Join-Lambert, 'Lévangéliaire pour une mystagogie de la présidence du Christ dans l'assemblée', in: M. Klöckener (e.a.), *Présence et rôle de la Bible dans la liturgie*, Fribourg, 2006, pp. 345-365, www.academia.edu/4278087.
17 https://www.youtube.com/@CCEEMediaoffice/streams (accessed 31/3/2023).

should remain so. Furthermore, the text of all submissions, speeches, and group reports are online accessible.[18] This transparency should contribute to trusting the synodal process and reinforcing the legitimacy of this Prague document. As mentioned before, accredited journalists were invited to stay in the same hotel. Many interviewed participants during the breaks, thus allowing people back home to hear or read first hand and in their own language what was happening in Prague. Furthermore, there was a team of five persons responsible for the media.

The Redaction Committee

The Redaction Committee was composed of six persons: two lay women, two lay men and two priests. The lay women and one laymen are university professors at faculties of theology, the other lay man is a journalist. One of the lay women is also Consultor to the Synod and a member of the Coordinating Team of the Synod on Synodality in Rome. The Jesuit Giacomo Costa, also a Consultor to the Synod and member of the Coordinating Team in Rome, coordinated the editorial work in Prague. The other priest had been teaching theology for a number of years. By way of nationality, place of study and country of residence the drafting committee holds ties to at least nine European countries dispersed all over Europe.[19] The Committee worked in English, but each of the five working languages could be understood by at least one member.

After the meeting had started, the Redaction Committee realised that the number of reports that would come in over the course of three days, the five working languages in which they arrived and the very short time to prepare a draft would require assistance. The Committee felt relieved when the presidency of the CCEE gave green light to the two female university professors to invite two women working at their respective chair to support the Redaction Committee. These two women provided invaluable work around the clock for three days. Since the Committee worked in English, the two women saw to translations with the help of computer programs and prepared the different files and reports into workable formats.[20]

The Redaction Committee were neither delegates nor invited guests and were, therefore, completely free to listen. They attended the general sessions, but did not participate in the Working Groups. Its task was to see to it that the Assembly had a good draft of the report to be submitted to the General Secretariat in Rome by March 31, 2023.

18 https://prague.synod2023.org (accessed 31/3/2023).

19 The members of the Redaction Committee are the Italian Giacomo Costa SJ (Milan-Italy), the Romanian Klara Csiszár (Linz / Austria), the French-Swiss Arnaud Join-Lambert (Louvain la Neuve / Belgium), the Italian Andrea Gagliarducci (Rome), the Polish Miroslow Tykfer (Poznan-Poland), the Dutch Myriam Wijlens (Erfurt / Germany).

20 The Czech theologian Adaela Muchova (Linz) and the Mexikan canon lawyer Yeshica Marianne Umaña Calderón (Erfurt).

The Committee began its work with an empty sheet of paper. In a preparatory session it recalled that its task was to be at the service of the Assembly and articulate faithfully but in a synthetic way what had come from the floor. Since it was not the task of the Assembly to address specific issues or even solve them, it was therefore neither the task of the Redaction Committee to do so.

The Drafting and Presentation of the Report

The Redaction Committee followed the principle of transparency by faithfully synthesising what had come from the floor. Considering that there were 39 reports of the members, as well as 50 reports from all the Working Group sessions presented in one of the five languages and which were submitted as the meeting was taking place, this was no mean task. Each day the focus of the Working Groups was on one of the three questions, which implied that some order was already provided for the structure of the final document. By listening to the reports and interventions, the Committee members could sense first hand the emotions, vibrations, tensions and relief of and in the meetings. This helped when reading and discerning the reports with regard to identifying common points, tensions and differences expressed in relation to the three questions.

The Committee prepared an outline as to how the different aspects could be best honoured. Subsequently, the reports were read again also to identify expressions and phrases that 'represent the richness, breath and lifelines of the exchange. The quotations were chosen because they express in a concise, powerful and precise way sentiments expressed in a number of contributions. They are not to endorse a specific position' (European Prague Document, nr. 8).

Soon a particular challenge came to the fore: the submissions had been translated into English. A number of submissions had themselves already been a translation of a native language into one of the five working languages of the meeting. There was a danger that an original text had been translated twice, thus increasing the possibility of inaccuracy. How to make sure that the report of Prague was faithful to what had been submitted? It was a blessing that due to the composition of the Redaction Committee it was possible to read a fair number of European languages and thus check the translations. Yet, another challenge was that none of the drafters had English as a mother tongue. At times, the Committee would contact a delegate at a coffee break to verify whether what had been submitted in writing was understood correctly.

The drafting of the twenty or so pages is based solely on all the work delivered or done in Prague. Nothing was prepared before the meeting. After working three days and a whole night, the Committee was able to present a draft to the Assembly. It was read out loudly by a native speaker from the United Kingdom, while the translators did their amazing work. All were listening attentively. Of course, it was a pity that the draft could not be presented in printed format in the five languages to all present locally or online. Nevertheless, due to the life-streamingg the whole world could listen. It was a great relief when after the final paragraph had been read, the Assembly welcomed the document as an applause was given. There was no voting.

After a coffee break, the program foresaw the possibility to make comments in the plenary or in writing. These comments were mostly requests to reconsider sentences or assessments, because it was felt that they would be too generic, over-generalise or simplify very complex situations, e.g. emphasising some divisions between East and West or between supposedly conservatives and liberals. Some suggestions seem to reveal a possible misunderstanding of the synodal process. For example, by asking to juxtapose certain statements made during the Assembly with magisterial teaching, or by demanding that terminology be clarified in such a way that tensions would be resolved. Some submissions tried to advocate a certain position and shut down the common search, thus neglecting the intention to seek a common path and a new synthesis while listening to each other. The Redaction Committee attended very carefully to each one of them as a team, thus discerning in a synodal way. It pondered the question: what is really proposed and what action can or must be taken while remaining faithful to the whole process?

Final Remarks and the Publication of the Report

Following the presentation of the report, the Assembly agreed on a two page text entitled 'Final Remarks', which would present some reflections on the experience and narrates some insights. The Final Remarks also lists the issues that the Assembly identified as priorities, which the first session of the Synod of Bishops would need to address.

The twenty page European / Prague Document had been drafted within three days (and one night). The Redaction Committee had not even had time to read the complete document from the beginning to the end before it was presented in the Assembly hall. Anyone aware of drafting documents knows that editing is necessary. Above all the remarks received from the Assembly in relation to the draft needed careful consideration. The numerus quotations (the draft had 138!) originating from all reports in five different languages needed to be checked to make sure they were not taken out of context and to see if the translation was correct. Moreover, there was a need to attend to a slightly better balance of quotations of all episcopal conferences. It must be stated very clearly: the text was ready by the end of the meeting, but checks and translation took more time than anticipated. On April 7, 2023 the text was finalised for publication in its two 'original' languages: Italian and English. The publication of the European Continental Assembly includes the report as well as the program and the names of all who were engaged in the process.[21] Soon after its publication the report itself was translated into a number of languages (e.g. Dutch, French, German, Polish, Russian) and they appeared on different websites.

The Endorsing Meeting by the Bishops

When in the summer of 2022 the Secretariat of the Synod in Rome asked the episcopal conferences whether they wanted to meet in continental meetings as an exclusive group of bishops or rather with a participation of some other members of the People of God, the vast majority of episcopal conferences that responded to the request, replied that they would favor a meeting that would involve a representation of the entire People of God. Consequently, the continental structures such as the CCEE were asked to organise an ecclesial Assembly. At the same time, it was suggested that the bishops meet after the Continental Assembly 'to collegially reread the lived synodal experience from the perspective of their specific charism and role' (DCS 108). They were invited to validate and approve the document, 'ensuring that it is the fruit of an authentically synodal journey, respectful of the process that has taken place and faithful to the diverse voices of the People of God in that continent' (DCS 108). The CCEE opted for such a gathering, bringing together the bishops that represent the members of the CCEE.

A two day session from February 10 till 12, 2023 was scheduled to be held in Prague in the same hotel. The bishops gathered had participated in the Continental Ecclesial Assembly. They met in the same hall, in which meanwhile the seating had been reordered into a boardroom style set up for the thirty-nine members of CCEE. They welcomed the Secretary General of the Synod Cardinal Mario Grech in their midst. These sessions were behind closed doors, so the authors of this study cannot report on what happened in that meeting.

Rather soon it became clear though that the bishops had decided not to write a long commentary to the Prague document, but to issue a one page statement in which they expressed above all deep gratitude for the meeting which had been a 'profoundly spiritual and truly synodal experience'. They wrote that all that they had heard converged into the final document presented at the Assembly and they thanked the Redaction Committee for its work. The bishops expressed a commitment to keep the synodal process in their dioceses alive and foster it. They voiced the desire to journey together with the whole People of God in Europe, including brothers and sisters from other

21 https://prague.synod2023.org/en/final-document/

Christian denominations. Alluding to the title and content of the DCS, their final sentence reads: 'We shall work tirelessly to enlarge the space of our tents so that our ecclesial communities become even more places where everyone feels welcome.'[22]

22 The 'Concluding Note from the Bishops' is published in English in the *Final Dcoument*, p. 67. https://prague.synod2023.org/en/final-document/

CONCLUDING DOSSIER SYNOD 2021-2024 EUROPEAN CONTINENTAL ASSEMBLY

Prague, Czech Republic

1. Final Remarks

Final remarks approved by the European Continental Assembly in the final session of its work (9 February) and immediately circulated. They constitute a kind of *executive summary* of the more extensive Final Document.

2. Final Document

Final document approved in draft form by the European Continental Assembly at the final session on 9 February and subsequently supplemented by the Redactional Committee with amendments gathered in written form following the assembly exchange.

3. Concluding Note

Concluding note from the Bishops, approved at the Closing Session of the Meeting of the Presidents of the Bishops' Conferences (11 February) and immediately circulated.

All documents, together with other materials related to the European Continental Assembly, are available on the dedicated website
https://prague.synod2023.org
and on the CCEE website
www.ccee.eu

FINAL REMARKS

We have experienced four days of listening and dialogue based on the resonances aroused by the *Working Document for the Continental Stage* within the Churches from which we come. As the European Continental Assembly, we realise that we have had a profoundly spiritual experience through the synodal method.

We give thanks to the Spirit who guided us and for the gift we received, and here we wish to share it. We deepened the insights that the ecclesial communities of our continent have gained through the synodal process, as well as the tensions and questions that the European Churches are facing.[1]

Above all, we once again felt the pain of the wounds that mark our recent history, starting with those that the Church has inflicted through the abuses perpetrated by people who were performing an ecclesial ministry or office. We have mentioned several times the ruthless violence of the aggression war disfiguring Ukraine. We thought about the victims of the earthquake that devastated Turkey and Syria.

Our work has been rich and exciting, though not without its problems and difficulties. It has allowed us to look into the eyes of the Church in Europe, with all the treasures of the two great Latin and Eastern traditions that make it up. With an awareness that has grown over the course of the Assembly, we feel today that we can affirm that our Church is beautiful, showing a variety that is also our wealth. We feel that we love her even more deeply, in spite of the wounds she has inflicted, for which she needs to ask forgiveness in order to be able to move on to reconciliation, the healing of memory and the welcoming of the wounded. We are convinced that these sentiments also fill the hearts of all the people who have been involved in the journey of Synod 2021-2024 since September 2021.

Throughout the days of the Assembly, we went through a spiritual experience that it is possible to meet, listen to each other and dialogue starting from our differences and move beyond the many obstacles, walls and barriers that our history puts in our way. We need to love the variety within our Church and support each other in mutual esteem, strengthened by our faith in the Lord and the power of his Spirit.

1 This work will give rise to a more articulated document that will be sent to the General Secretariat of the Synod as a contribution to the next steps of the Synod process, and mainly the drafting of the Instrumentum laboris of the Synodal Assembly taking place in October. Together with a lot of information on our work and video recordings of all the plenary sessions, this document will be available on the website of the Prague Continental Assembly, https://prague.synod2023.org, and on the websites of the Bishops' Conferences that wish to make it public in the different national languages.

This is why we wish to continue walking in a synodal style: more than a methodology, we consider it a way of life of our Church, of communal discernment and of discernment of the signs of the times. Concretely, we want this Continental Assembly not to remain an isolated experience, but to become a periodic appointment, based on the general adoption of the synodal method that permeates all our structures and procedures on all levels. In this style, it will be possible to address the issues on which our efforts need to mature and intensify: the accompaniment of the wounded, the 'protagonism' of young people and women, the learning from marginalised people, etc.

The synodal style also allows us to address tensions from a missionary perspective, without being paralysed by fear, but drawing from them the energy to continue along the way. Two in particular have emerged in our work. The first encourages unity in diversity, escaping the temptation of uniformity. The second links the readiness to welcome as a witness to the Father's unconditional love for his children with the courage to proclaim the truth of the Gospel in its entirety: it is God who promises 'Love and truth will meet' (Ps 85:11).

We know that all this is possible because we have experienced it during this Assembly, but even more because the life of the Churches from which we come bears witness to it. We are thinking here in particular of ecumenical dialogue, which have echoed strongly in our work, and also of inter-religious dialogue. But above all, we believe that it is possible because grace is involved: building an increasingly synodal Church is a way to concretely implement the equality in dignity of all the members of the Church, founded in baptism. It configures us as children of God and members of the body of Christ, co-responsible for the unique mission of evangelisation entrusted by the Lord to his Church.

We are confident that the continuation of Synod 2021-2024 can support and accompany us, in particular by addressing at the level of the Synodal Assembly some priorities:

- deepen the practice, theology and hermeneutics of synodality. We have to rediscover something that is ancient, belongs to the nature of the Church, and is always new. This is a task for us. We are taking the first steps on a path that opens up as we go along it;
- address the question of an all ministerial Church, as the horizon of a reflection on charisms and ministries (ordained and non-ordained) and the relationships between them;
- explore the forms of a synodal exercise of authority, i.e. the service of accompanying the community and safeguarding unity;
- clarify criteria for discernment on the synodal process and which decisions belong on which level, from the local to the universal;
- take concrete and courageous decisions on the role of women within the Church and on their greater involvement at all levels, also

in decision-making and decision-taking processes;

- consider the tensions around the liturgy, so as to synodally re-understand Eucharist as the source of communion;
- foster the formation to synodality of the whole People of God, with particular regard to the discernment of the signs of the times with a view to carrying out the common mission;
- renew a lively sense of mission, bridging the gap between faith and culture to bring the Gospel back to people's feelings, finding a language capable of articulating tradition and aggiornamento, but above all, walking with people rather than talking about them or to them. The Spirit asks us to listen to the cry of the poor and the earth in Europe, and in particular the desperate cry of the victims of war who demand a just peace.

Loving the Church, the richness of its diversity, is not a form of sentimentalism for its own sake. The Church is beautiful because the Lord wants her to be so in view of the task he has entrusted to her: to proclaim the Gospel and invite all women and men to enter into the dynamic of communion, participation and mission that constitutes her raison d'être, animated by the perennial vitality of the Spirit. To build our European Church means then to renew our commitment to carry out this mission, even on our continent, in a culture marked by the many diversities we know.

We entrust the continuation of our Synodal journey to the Patron Saints and martyrs of Europe!

Adsumus Sancte Spiritus!

FINAL DOCUMENT

I
INTRODUCTION: THE EXPERIENCE OF THE EUROPEAN CONTINENTAL ASSEMBLY

1. The European Continental Assembly met in Prague within the framework of a journey initiated in 2021: the Synod 2021-2024 entitled *For a Synodal Church: Communion, Participation, Mission*. The fruits of the first phase of the Synod, dedicated to the consultation of the People of God, which involved millions of people, have been summarised in the *Working Document for the Continental Stage* (DCS). This was in turn submitted to our local Churches – as well as those of each of the other continents – with the aim of gathering their resonances and facilitating a dialogue among the local Churches in Europe.

2. It was the first time in Europe that the People of God – bishops, priests, deacons, consecrated men and women, lay men and women – gathered to listen to one another and dialogue in an atmosphere of prayer and listening to the Word of God.[2] It was a new and unexpected experience. The joy of being part of the Church, which we had previously experienced in the diocesan stage, flourished and multiplied. Everyone had the opportunity of getting to know realities different from the one in which they live. Together we discovered our common adhesion to Christ. Sometimes we experience tensions and uncertainties, but we realise that trusting the Lord, we can go on walking together. After four days of listening and dialogue based on the resonances aroused by the *Working Document for the Continental Stage* (DCS) within the local Churches from which we come, as the European Ecclesial Assembly, we realise that we have had a profoundly spiritual experience through the synodal method. We give thanks to the Spirit who guided us for the gift we received and here we wish to share it.

3. We deepened the insights that the ecclesial communities of our continent have gained through the synodal process, as well as the tensions and questions that the European Churches are facing. Our work has been rich and exciting, though not without its problems and difficulties. It has allowed us to look into the eyes of the Church in Europe, with all its treasures, starting with those of the great Latin and

2 CCEE and UCESM (Union of European Conferences of Major Superiors) we invited communities of contemplative life from all over Europe to support the European Continental Assembly through prayer, in a special way with continuous silent Adoration.

Eastern traditions that make it up. In this journey of mutual listening, we realised that we can be united in diversity: *Diversity, which is not lacking – in history, culture, traditions, socio-religious contexts – is a great wealth. We have experienced the beauty of dialogue at 360 degrees, not only East and West, but also North and South, let us not forget: from Cyprus and Malta to the Nordic countries. We are exchanging precious gifts that generate fraternity and dispose us for mission* (Free intervention by an invited guest).

4. With an awareness that has grown as the Assembly unfolded, we feel today that we can confess that our Church is beautiful, a bearer of a vital diversity that is also our wealth. We feel that we love the Church even more deeply, in spite of the wounds it has inflicted, for which it must beg forgiveness in order to be able to pursue the path of reconciliation, heal memories and welcome the wounded. We are convinced that these sentiments also fill the hearts of all the people who have been involved in the journey of Synod 2021-2024 since September 2021.

1.1 The Composition of the Assembly and the Organisation of its Work

5. The Churches in Europe are characterised by a great variety of languages, cultures and rites. In all, the Assembly was composed of 200 people: 140 delegates from the 39 members of the CCEE[3] (each one could nominate up to a maximum of four), to which were added 42 guests from the General Secretariat of the Synod, the CCEE Commissions, and a number of institutions, networks, associations and movements of the Catholic Church active on the continental level. In addition, each member of CCEE was invited to name up to ten delegates (numbering 269 persons) who participated online and contributed to the online Working Groups. In order to serve the work of the Assembly, members of the CCEE Secretariat and the General Secretariat of the Episcopal Conference of the Czech Republic, as well as the Redactional Committee of this Document and the Media Team attended the meeting.[4]

6. After the publication of the DCS, each local Church had been invited to work with the document and provide feedback. In plenary the delegation of each member of the CCEE shared the feedback to the DCS gathered from the Churches within their territory. These reports were inspired by the guiding questions formulated in n.106 of the DCS. Each local Church

3 As far as CCEE members are concerned, the name of the country is simply indicated, except: the eparchy of Mukachevo, Ukraine (with the distinction between Greek-Catholic and Latin Church), and the two multi-national episcopal conferences: Nordic countries (Sweden, Denmark, Norway, Finland, Iceland) and the International Bishops' Conference of Saints Cyril and Methodius (Serbia, North Macedonia, Montenegro and Kosovo). Working Groups are indicated through the language they used.

4 The complete list of participants is available on our website : [Cf fn. 1 above].

as well as the episcopal conferences organised the collecting process of reactions to the DCS and its presentation in the manner most suitable and appropriate to their context and circumstances.

7. The European Continental Assembly in Prague worked in five languages (English, French, German, Italian, and Polish). Following the opening session, the work[5] was divided into three units, each of which was structured as a broad Spiritual Conversation: delegations taking the floor in the plenary assembly; sharing resonances in Working Groups; collecting and expressing reactions on the shared points in the plenary (group reports and free interventions). Delegates participating online were divided into groups that worked on a platform. They provided their contribution to the Assembly in a special session (online group reports).

8. Out of a deliberate option for transparency and with the aim to allow as many people as possible to participate in the journey, all the plenary sessions of the European Continental Assembly in Prague were live streamed. The recordings remain available on the YouTube channel of the CCEE Press Office.[6] The presentations of the delegations, other interventions, speeches and homilies, as well as the reports of the Working Groups, are available on the official Website[7] of the European Ecclesial Assembly in Prague. In order to hear the voices of the participants as much as possible on their own terms, the current Document provides quotations from the contributions shared. They aim to represent the richness, breath and lifelines of the exchange. The quotations were chosen because they express in a concise, powerful or precise way sentiments expressed in a number of contributions. They are not inserted to endorse a specific position.[8]

9. The presidency of the CCEE entrusted a Redactional Committee specifically with the task of crafting this Document. The work began by listening to all the contributions, reports and interventions presented during the Assembly and was based on the outline suggested by the General Secretariat of the Synod. An initial draft was read out during one of the sessions on the last day of the proceedings in Prague, and was approved by the Assembly. Reactions and proposals for modifications of this text were collected, both during the plenary session and in written

5 The detailed programme of work can be found on our website.
6 https://www.youtube.com/@CCEEMediaoffice/streams
7 https://prague.synod2023.org/en/
8 It should be noted that the reports submitted to the Assembly are oftentimes themselves already a translation of one language into one of the five working languages. This posed a specific challenge when using quotations.

submissions, were examined by the Redactional Committee and after necessary editorial work the document was completed.

10. The purpose of this Document is solely to provide a concise account of the work of the European Continental Assembly. It offers the contribution of the Churches in Europe to the dialogue of the Church worldwide and to the drafting of the *Instrumentum laboris* of the Synodal Assembly to be held in October 2023. It, therefore, voices the main intuitions and consonances recorded, as well as the divergences and tensions that did not fail to emerge, ahead of identifying the priorities to be submitted to the discernment of the Synodal Assembly which is currently being prepared. The European Continental Assembly acknowledged this report to be faithful to the work carried out. The Document does not offer solutions or theological interpretations, but rather intends to hold the tensions brought forward by the local Churches. It is not therefore to be interpreted as the expression of a final position nor as the indication of operational strategies of the European Churches concerning issues upon which discernment will take place in the subsequent phases of the synodal process.

11. After briefly outlining some basic elements of the context in which the local Churches in Europe live and work, in which, therefore, the Prague Continental Assembly should also be placed, the text will go on to identify seven intuitions that may underpin the path towards a synodal Church in a European perspective, and therefore seven tensions which the local Churches feel challenged by in order to continue their journey; it will then conclude with the formulation of what the Churches in Europe considers to be the priorities for the work of the Synodal Assembly in October 2023.

1.2 Some Features of the Context in which the European Churches Operate

12. During the working sessions of the Assembly, we heard the news of the dramatic earthquake that hit southern Turkey and northern Syria on 6 February 2023. Tens of thousands of people lost their lives. The Assembly prayed for and expressed its solidarity with those particularly affected by the earthquake.

13. Europe is deeply affected by the pain and suffering of the war of aggression unleashed against Ukraine a year ago. The Assembly was deeply touched by the presence of people from the affected regions. The situation raised new questions: *We would do well, together with the whole Church, to reflect on how to show Christ in war and post-conflict*

conditions. How to reach people affected by violence and rape with the Good News? (Ukraine, Latin Church).

14. The local Churches in Europe acknowledge the wounds caused by sexual and other kinds of abuse in its own midst. The report of Ireland echoed others when is stresses that the courageous voice of the victims *went to the heart of what is necesary for our Church: conversion* (Ireland). As the trustworthiness and credibility of the Church are at stake, there is a need to address both the cases of abuse and the wounds they cause, as well as the issue of their management by the Church authorities.

15. The synodal experience takes place within the peculiar context that characterises the Church in Europe, starting from the diversities that run through it, which at times create tensions between its parts: between Eastern and Western Europe – a legacy of the division of the continent into opposing blocs at the end of the Second World War – as well as between North and South, between countries that have a strong Catholic tradition and others where Catholics or even Christians have been a minority for centuries. Nevertheless, the work of the Assembly reveals a picture of Europe and the European Churches that is much more diverse than the traditional stereotypes of large homogeneous opposing blocs. The confessional pluralism that has characterised Europe for centuries is today the ground on which ecumenical initiatives of many kinds flourish, starting with ecumenism of praxis.

16. The religious context of contemporary Europe is marked above all by the phenomenon of secularisation: *our rich European Christian tradition also entails knowledge, which we carry in a very secularised context. Within this context, we need to pave new paths towards the desire to 'meet everyone with the burning lamp of the Gospel* (Malta). *A negative attitude that condemns the world and society is sterile. We have much to offer the world but we also have much to receive from it. Openness to the world can help us to better understand the Gospel. [...] The whole synodal process invites us to understand the signs of our time, also the signs of contemporary secularised society* (Belgium). Current challenges include the need to engage in a *dialogue with contemporary culture and thought, on issues such as artificial intelligence, robotics or gender identity issues (LGBTQI+)* (Portugal). Despite difficulties, the synodal process is considered to be a chance within a secularised culture: *By enlarging our tent, we must be able to accompany as many people as possible on the path of the Christian experience* (Monaco).

17. Churches in Europe also have to deal with the problem of migration. It is caused by wars or disastrous economic situations. It removes members from Christian communities, impoverishing them and making them almost irrelevant. Moldova remarks that there are communities *which are in danger for various reasons, first and foremost poverty and the phenomenon of migration, of disappearing and seeing the transmission of the faith tradition interrupted.* Elsewhere, communities struggle in coping with a sudden influx of migrants, who may soon constitute a large majority: *The new reality of the Catholic Church in Greece: [...] Some parishes have a foreign majority (95% in the three parishes in the centre of Athens, in Rhodes, in Mykonos), with a small presence of Greeks. [...] Other parishes show a multinational makeup. Only on islands with a century-old Catholic presence are all Greeks. The problem is worsened by the fact that thousands of immigrants live in towns, villages and islands without the presence of a Catholic parish priest, and therefore without a Catholic Church life* (Greece).

18. On several occasions it was emphasised that the Churches in Europe are Churches of martyrdom. Some suggested to draw up a common European martyrology *to spread the memory of the martyrs of our continent and let ourselves be guided by their witness in order to grow in faith and fidelity to our Christian and Catholic identity* (Free intervention of an invited guest).

19. Amidst such complex challenges, there is a need to revitalise listening to the Word of God: *It is essential that the Church gives the Word of God all the space it deserves, reintegrating the spiritual dimension into its ordinary life, in all its pastoral and also its governing activities* (France).

II
FOR A SYNODAL CHURCH IN A EUROPEAN PERSPECTIVE

20. The discussion and exchange starting from the DCS have led to the identification of seven points of reference for the path of building a synodal Church in a European perspective. These are shared intuitions from which we can all draw inspiration and ideas for implementation in specific local contexts: 1) the spiritual dimension of synodality, in a perspective of a continuous conversion to Christ; 2) the rediscovery of the common baptismal dignity and its implications; 3) the essential

between synodality and mission; 4) dialogue as a way of life of the Church; 5) the commitment to overcome prejudices and reconcile memory; 6) preferential attention to families, women and young people; 7) the adoption of the synodal method for all ecclesial processes.

2.1 Journeying with Christ, Filled with His Spirit

21. The lifestyle of Jesus Christ, his kenotic existence in the service of humanity, is a path that every Christian and every Christian community is invited to undertake: *Conversion, understood as interior and exterior conformation to Christ the servant, should be the first and last criterion of the synodal journey, which shapes the style of the Church of the future (Turkey). The term 'synod' itself refers to the person of Jesus Christ: In our synodal journey, the image of the Church as a community of all the faithful of Christ was emphasised. The faithful who are with Christ, who said of himself: I am 'hodos' = the way (also: the truth and the life). [...]. Christians are 'synodoi' (Ignatius of Antioch). Thus, synodality is first and foremost 'con-Christianity'. And the 'synodoi' are all 'con-Christians'. That is, precisely because with Christ, and only on this Christological basis, all the baptised are 'synodoi' in the time of salvation, in the following of Christ and in service to their brothers and sisters, in their pilgrimage towards the risen Christ* (Bosnia and Herzegovina).

22. In a complementary manner, numerous interventions in the plenary and group works pointed to the Holy Spirit as the main protagonist and driving force of the synodal journey. This was emphasised by the Czech theologian Tomáš Halík in his spiritual introduction: *Above all, it is through spirituality – the spiritual experience of individual believers and of the whole Church – that the Spirit gradually introduces us to the wholeness of the truth.* We experienced this directly during the Assembly in Prague, when we meditated with a Pentecost icon shared by the Slovakian Delegation: all those in attendance are united, even if the colours of their clothes are different. The image reflects what has been experienced: the diversity of opinions expressed is not an obstacle to the declared desire of all to be faithful to Christ and participate together in building a single Church of unity in diversity guided by the Holy Spirit, *cum Petro et sub Petro*.

23. Proceeding along the synodal journey requires *maintaining a spirit of continual discernment so that the Church can always be a place of personal and communal encounter with Jesus and his Gospel, and a starting point for mission* (Portugal). If Christ is our model and the Spirit is the source of power that inspires us, an attitude of conversion and the care of the spiritual dimension are indispensable to remain attentive to their voice. At the heart of a synodal Church can therefore only be a personal relationship with God: *Only when we have a personal experience of God the Father can we be brothers and sisters in Christ to one another, going into the world with the content of the Gospel and revealing the richness of faith* (Slovenia). Nurturing this relationship requires engaging in a journey of conversion that also involves the communities as a whole and beyond: *We believe that the foundation of all our actions, desires and proposals must be a personal and communal conversion and communion with Christ, with each other and with our brothers and sisters* (Spain).

24. Fidelity to Christ must also be lived as a spiritual union with those who have given their lives for the Gospel: *The martyrdom of men and women, consecrated or not, teaches us that communion is possible despite hard trials; that being faithful to God is the most beautiful witness that can be offered to humanity of all times (Albania). Indeed, Christian martyrs did not give their lives for a custom, but for Truth: for Christ* (Hungary).

2.2 Rediscovering the Common Baptismal Dignity

25. *In baptism we are grafted into Christ* (Slovenia). Numerous reactions to the DCS emphasise the link with Christ through baptism and the consequences deriving from it: *We are all called to holiness and share responsibility for building up the Church, the Body of Christ* (English language Working Group). Therefore: *We must recognise and reaffirm our common baptismal dignity as the basis for renewal of life and ministries in the Church. Every baptised person must become more aware of their identity, dignity and vocation in Christ. [...] Each vocation must be better understood and more widely appreciated if we are to cultivate the collegial nature of the Church* (Scotland). Many found the synodal process a very useful opportunity for a lived reappropriation of that notion: *The intuition that emerged strongly in this synodal journey was the rediscovery of the baptismal dignity and the common responsibility derived from it for the edification and mission of the Church* (Italy).

26. The equal dignity rooted in our common baptism has been pointed out several times. This theological affirmation takes on a more concrete and urgent dimension when it prompts us to reflect on the place and role of women in the Church: *The present synodal experience is an important sign of hope for many and encourages them in the common search for new credible paths. This includes the recognition of the dignity and vocation of all baptised people, especially women* (Switzerland). In other words, *the involvement of women is not a substitution for male scarcity, but a responsible implementation of the theology of the common priesthood of the faithful* (Czech Republic) The challenge is even more crucial with regard to young people.

2.3 Synodality Serving and Enhancing Mission

27. Synodality has a constitutive missionary dimension. Discovering the dynamism of evangelisation and renewing themselves, our local Churches grasp that synodality and mission are interdependent and a permanent task for the Church. Synodality entails journeying together at different levels; it is a way and style of being a missionary Church and constitutes the framework of our participation in the divine mission: *If we take seriously the principle of synodality, then mission cannot be understood as a one-sided process, but rather as accompaniment in a spirit of dialogue, a quest for mutual understanding. Synodality is a process of learning in which we not only teach but also learn* (Tomáš Halík, Spiritual Introduction).

28. Walking as a missionary synodal Church we meet companions whom we learn to love and appreciate because together we are called to bear witness to the love of God in a wounded world. The expectations of the people towards the Church are immense. The faithful want to shape this missionary Church and they want their opinion, their life experiences, their concerns, their suffering to be heard.

29. Being a missionary Church means at the same time to listen as followers of Christ, to see the existential wounds of people, humanity and creation, and to act to redress them: *A synodal Church can help to redress and bind these wounds. It can help us to be reconciled with ourselves, with God, with one another, and with creation* (Ireland). The DCS's emphasis on the diaconal character of a missionary synodal Church was warmly welcomed. To express its importance, the image of the Church as a field hospital often recurs.

30. Currently, there are many wounds in Europe and around the world: the war in Ukraine, people's existential crises, the degradation of the environment, the pandemic, and the wounds caused to people by the Church through abuse and any kind of violence, exclusion, or humiliation. *Many voices express gratitude for the document's focus on the pressing crises of the present. We think in particular of the existential crises of the protection of creation, climate justice, wars, poverty and disease. As the Church in Switzerland, we can credibly engage in these crises if we also work on our own internal problems and solve them* (Switzerland).

31. Synodality supports the Church in the process of becoming increasingly missionary, but it also quickly reveals obstacles and tensions that must be overcome or endured along the way. A synodal Church adopts different criteria for evaluation; it does not avoid dialogue, but seeks it; it does not devalue, but strives to come out of its own security and question itself; it opens up spaces for experimentation and seeks subsidiary solutions, if necessary.

2.4 Growing as a Church in Dialogue

32. For the Church, dialogue is a way of life, with solid trinitarian and ecclesiological foundations, which must shape our relationships at all levels. This affects the relationships within and among our local Churches and concerns ecumenical, interreligious, and social relationships as well as interactions with all marginalised and wounded people.

33. Our local Churches are marked by a rich diversity, which is not always simple to live: people of different nationalities and ethnic groups live together, as well as faithful belonging to both Eastern and Western traditions. The Churches of Moldova, Romania and Ukraine express the challenges: *In a minority context, an additional difficulty is represented by the difference of cultures among Catholics belonging to the same ecclesial community, who experience the separation of traditions, languages and closure in the sense of belonging that generates division* (Moldova). Nevertheless, *diversity must not be seen only as a problem, but as a resource (the rites of the different Churches, the liturgy, the history and traditions of the national Churches in Europe, etc.). All these realities call for a transformation of our hearts, of the language we use in relation to today's culture. We all feel involved in the journey of encounter, which begins with our metanoia* (Italian language Working Group).

34. With respect to relations with other Christian denominations and religious faiths, it has been pointed out that in many parts of Europe, Catholics are a small minority and have a rich experience of what it means to think and live ecumenically, alongside Protestant or Orthodox Churches. Many local Churches are involved in dialogue with Judaism and in interreligious dialogue, especially with Islam (e.g.: Turkey, Bosnia and Herzegovina, Albania): *The ecumenical effort of the Catholic community in relation to Orthodox Christians (there are very few other Christians in the country) and the work on dialogue with Muslims as well as with the Jewish community are part of the life of the Church in a religiously and ethnically mixed society* (Bosnia and Herzegovina).

35. The Churches in the countries of Eastern and South-Eastern Europe are aware that they find themselves on the border with the Orthodox world or live together with the faithful of the Orthodox Church, who count for the majority of the country's population. Living together has not always been easy and there are still wounds to heal. The local Churches want to face this task: *The synodal path has rekindled ecumenical awareness. The Greek Catholic Church has the ecumenical vocation in its DNA and painfully feels the lack of Christian unity. We are not simply at the geographical border with Orthodoxy, but above all with our Orthodox brothers and sisters with whom we share the same ritual and cultural heritage. Naturally, we want to intensify our involvement in ecumenism with all confessions, but especially with our sister Church, showing a spirit of initiative and creativity, overcoming the wounds and injustices of the past through a genuine healing of memory* (Romania).

36. The Churches of Western and Northern Europe benefit from their good ecumenical relations with the Protestant Churches. It was emphasised that praying as well as journeying together, should not be limited to the annual celebration of the Week of Prayer for Christian Unity, but should go further, identifying new possibilities. The Latvian delegation, for example, told us about the tradition of an ecumenical Way of the Cross, which has been held in Riga on Good Friday for 18 years now and was also organised during the pandemic with the participation of the Lutheran and Baptist communities.

37. The style of dialogue also concerns relations with the secularised society: *In Europe [the] change takes a specific form due to the confrontation with an increasingly secularised society. In reality, homogeneous Christian societies no longer exist. It is not good just to observe this situation or to experience it as a threat and as something to be opposed to. As a Church, we live in the world, but not necessarily in a Christian world. This requires a change of mentality and a true conversion on our part* (Belgium). At the same time, in the face of secularism and pluralism, some express concerns that the teachings of the Church will be diluted and for example that the traditional understanding of marriage and family will change. These voices plead for the Church not to be worldly, even if it remains in dialogue with the world.

38. The local Churches in Europe are aware that it is necessary to enter and remain in dialogue with society. Dialogue with the world helps the Church to be missionary, to know and understand the sufferings and wounds of people and creation, and to act accordingly, first of all inside our communities: a tension has been detected *between the socio-ecological changes we demand from society in order to live together peacefully in justice, and the lack of our own capacity for conversion towards more justice, such as practicing a second-class status of women* (English language online Working Group). For the commitment to justice, peace and reconciliation, time is running out. It is insufficient to only name issues; there is an urgent need for discernment to be followed up with action.

2.5 Facing Open Wounds, Overcoming Prejudices, Reconciling Memories

39. The Church has inflicted deep wounds and at the same time has been deeply wounded. Many reports pay tribute to *women and men who have courageously come forward to speak out about sexual, institutional, emotional, psychological, physical and spiritual abuse by members of the Church* (Ireland). They also bring to the fore how the wounds caused by abuse have eroded the very credibility of the Church. Expressing disappointment for the dismissive and non-empathetic treatment of these people by the Church authorities, some ask: *'To what extent is a distinction still made between the members of the institution and the institution itself?'* (Nordic countries). Others see the responsibility for the cover-up of abuse cases as both individual and systemic: There are *serious individual faults; too many clergy members abused their power and those responsible, not least the bishops, covered up the atrocities. But there are also systemic causes of the abuse of power. We cannot deny them. We are determined to draw the spiritual and structural consequences* (Germany). Some call for more decisive steps to address the problem in a more transparent way: *abuse is an open wound and will remain a barrier to communion, participation and mission until it is fully addressed* (Ireland).

40. *Only when we listen to the voices that are often not heard, can we grow and discern. We wish especially to hear the voices of specific groups within the Church: the poor people, the marginalised people, those who feel left out or not welcome, the LGBTQI+ community, divorced and remarried people, migrants, and people whose lives did not turn out as they hoped for* (The Netherlands). The link between synodal reform and concern for victims and marginalised people in the Church must be maintained: *In the struggles for the future of the Church, we want to put concrete people and their suffering first* (Multilingual Working Group).

The sick and people with disabilities are often mentioned too. A number of delegations express an urgency to take steps, because many people and groups *feel rejected, degraded and discriminated against in our Church, often unfortunately rightly so. They want safe encounters and honest dialogue at eye level. Time is pressing: We see the need for a real conversion!* (Switzerland)

41. During the Assembly, not only differences of opinion emerged, but also mutual accusations. Nevertheless, for the Churches of Europe, the path of encountering and mutual trusting is still open: *We underline the joy of being on the same path, between countries and Churches of Europe, of being able to discover that we are all living different sufferings and experiences but common in the love of Christ* (French language Working Group). The Prague Assembly is not the end of this journey, but just a step beyond the beginning: we all need time for a deeper understanding of what others are saying, which is sometimes difficult for some to accept, and which requires further reflection, study, discernment, and listening to the voice of the Holy Spirit who wants to lead us to a common future: *Let us walk together in the way the Spirit of God leads our Church: in many places, with many people, in many forms. It is a kairos of the Church to discover and shape its own synodality* (Germany).

42. The meeting and sharing among the delegates, particularly during the group work, made it clear that the differences in worldviews do not only run between East and West, North and South. Despite real differences between local Churches, it is not possible to draw a simplistic picture of a Europe anchored in old divisions. The report from Luxembourg mentions *the great gap between those who seek reform or even transformation and others who are afraid of change to the point of rejecting it. May these gaps make us curious to discover each other's arguments, may they make us vigilant to respect each other in order to build the future of our communities together, and not against each other, seeing in diversity a wealth.*

43. The call to conversion has resounded in the context of mutual prejudices on the part of individuals or even entire communities, including local Churches. We all need to *recognise the diversity of living environments and historical experiences* (Croatia) to cleanse ourselves of the historical memory that prevents us from approaching one another with an attitude of openness and trust. *Reading the DCS we are fascinated by the global diversity of the realities of our common faith in Christ. The listening-*

expressing relationship has become more balanced, and we have all become more aware of the value of each one's specific way of expressing ourselves (Romania).

44. Some delegates openly expressed the need for all of us to convert, purify and heal our memories in order to reconcile our local Churches and become more credible for secularised societies. We all need to confront our hard theological and pastoral positions to better respond to contemporary challenges. *The process of secularisation has not caused the disappearance of Christianity, as some expected, but its transformation* (Tomáš Halík, Spiritual Introduction). There is a need for a kenotic ecclesiology, so as not to be afraid of the death of certain forms of Church: *Mission overcomes many problems, because it means going out of oneself. In the danger of losing, there is a greater possibility of receiving* (Italian language Working Group).

2.6 Attending to Families, Women and Young People

45. Many contributions underscored the need to support families. They are responsible for transmitting, strengthening, celebrating and living, the faith. Furthermore, they are also agents of evangelisation: *The most important place of formation is the family, which is in crisis for various reasons: pastoral efforts towards families must be emphasised* (Slovakia). *The family is the fundamental unit of society, in which we learn tolerance and mutual acceptance, and to which we can return to in times of crises. We are all called, therefore, to work for marriage and the family* (Hungary). This commitment also has an ecumenical and interreligious dimension as Albania underlines: *The five religious denominations (Islam, Bektashi, Orthodox, Evangelicals, Catholics) officially recognised by the State have together formed an Interreligious Council. Beyond the monotheism that characterises us, what unites us most, and for which we think we can offer something to the people of today, are the human values we feel we share* (Albania). A special reference to families is made here.

46. The contributions of practically all the delegations devoted space to the topic of the participation of women and their role in the Church. *Many women communicated their pain at the denial of their participation in the life of the Church and spoke of feelings of exclusion and discrimination. Women play a crucial role in the life of the Church, but many men and women spoke of a Church that 'excludes' the fullness of women's gifts* (Ireland). This is one of the most frequently recurring points in all reports and finds expression in similar words. Belarus emphasises *the greater*

attention given to the role of women in the life of the Church. On the basis of the sacrament of Baptism, as members of the People of God with equal dignity, they must take their rightful place in the implementation of the Church's mission and activities. (Belarus) Luxembourg calls for *strengthening the role of women and their participation at all levels of Church life, finally taking into account their charisms and talents.*

47. Delegations call for being more attentive to young people, which are the present and not only the future of our Churches. *More than ever, young people are looking for belonging, authenticity and autonomy. Many suffer from depression and loneliness and no one really cares about them and listens to them. Young people are already in our Church now, not only in the future* (The Netherlands). Slovakia laments the *absence of young people in the life of the Church*, because they can teach the Church how to be a missionary Church. The Church needs *young people who accept this mission of Christ, who give witness, who conduct a dialogue, who present to other communities and nations all these values that we bring into our lives as young Catholics* (International Bishops' Conference of Saints Cyril and Methodius).

2.7 Building the Synodal Method into Church Structures and Processes

48. As the European Continental Assembly progressed, the awareness of the depth and fruitfulness of the method of Spiritual Conversation, also called by some the synodal method, came to the fore: *The synodal process is a gift of the Holy Spirit, who calls us to active listening, deep dialogue and community discernment through the methodology of Spiritual Conversation* (Spain). As the direct experience of the work of the Prague Assembly also testifies, Spiritual Conversation triggers a profound dynamic in the people involved: it allows people to be listened to and asks from them to learn to listen by leaving their prejudices behind, accepting different ways of expressing oneself, which at times may hurt. Above all, it stimulates deep personal and communal listening to the Word of God, community prayer and conversion. People realise that they listen to their 'brothers and sisters in Christ', but even more so, that they listen to the Spirit, who is the true protagonist. People are invited to be driven by the Lord's style, and not their own ideology, in order to identify together the steps to be taken. This is what the term discernment refers to, though for some it still needs clarification. With appropriate adaptation, the synodal method can also be applied to other areas of togetherness, especially in the social, interreligious or ecumenical context.

49. Synodality should not remain an abstract and formal idea. Hence, the synodal method *needs deepening, formation and institutionalisation* (Austria). On the one hand, a more thorough elaboration of a theology of synodality is needed; on the other hand, many emphasise the importance of *'formation in synodality, for clergy and laity together'* (England and Wales), especially through learning-by-doing processes. We can grow in a synodal style through practice, under the guidance of the Spirit and with the accompaniment of skilled people. Thus, the Maltese delegation asks: *Given the clear difference we observed between processes in which the 'Spiritual Conversation' was central and those that seemed to replicate normal surveys, what skills and what spirituality are needed for synodality not to remain just a concept, but to become an inspiration for our structures, so that they really become spaces of community discernment in which God's will is truly at the centre?* (Malta)

50. The use of the synodal method is, therefore, called to become structural, entering into the ordinary life of the communities *as the correct approach to each ecclesial meeting and to the implementation of local pastoral plans* (Moldova) to the point of shaping a new style of being Church. According to the Slovak delegation, it is a priority to *bring the synodal spirit into the life of local communities – to introducing active listening and spiritual discernment in decision-making/taking processes*. For this reason, there is a strong call to attend to canon law reforming the structures and processes that promote and protect the synodal method. One of the priorities is to make *parishes a place of true 'synodal culture' where all are invited to participate, to manifest themselves, to make their contribution to pastoral action, in councils or assemblies, assuming an effective co-responsibility* (Portugal). It is also a way to make the Church less clerical, cold and bureaucratic, as some, especially the young, are asking for.

51. It is a matter of continuing to learn how to be a synodal Church, building on previous experience, but not without being satisfied with the steps already taken, however beautiful they may be, by bearing concrete witness that it is possible to live tensions without seeing them as irresolvable oppositions that crush us. That is why *formation in the concrete practice of synodality and authentic listening to the other and to the Holy Spirit is necessary* (The Netherlands).

III
THE EUROPEAN CHURCHES FACING SYNODALITY: QUESTIONS AND TENSIONS

52. At the heart of the synodal process is the identification of the tensions that run through the Churches in Europe. As suggested by an Austrian delegate, tensions can be opportunities, but it depends on how one deals with them: they can be swept under the carpet, turned into a conflict with losers and winners, or become the road to synodality, which then requires opening up spaces for experimentation. *Europe has a history of religious conflict, but tensions are reduced when we listen to each other, so let us thank God for this process of synodal listening* (English language online Working Group).

53. Multiple tensions of various kinds are often a source of great concern. The image of the tent proposed by the DCS, however, makes it clear that they are not necessarily negative: without tension, the tent collapses, while too much tension damages it. Tensions risk turning into polarisations, but *polarisation is wounding the Church, the body of Christ* (English language online Working Group). Yet, *Tensions can be overcome if the tent is a safe space where everyone feels they can speak and be heard. Spiritual conversation has been a useful practice in this regard* (English language online Working Group). There is, therefore, an important challenge: *to inhabit tensions* (French and Italian language Working Groups). *Tensions allow us to have an opportunity for change in a more creative way, and together we can look for ways to succeed in doing this* (English language Working Group). Along these lines, some prefer to speak of complementarity or the ability to maintain a balance between polarities. This is how the seven tensions brought to the fore by the Prague Assembly should be grasped: 1) the relationship between proclaiming the truth of the Gospel and witnessing to God's infinite mercy; 2) the articulation between fidelity to tradition and aggiornamento; 3) the liturgy in the life of the Church; 4) the pluralism of understanding mission; 5) the ability to exercise the co-responsibility of all in the light of the diversity of charisms and ministries; 6) the forms of exercising authority in a synodal Church; 7) the articulation and unfolding of diversity and unity and the local-global dynamic.

3.1 Truth and Mercy

54. To express the tension between truth and mercy, some delegations resort to the DCS (nr. 30): *The dream is of a Church that more fully lives* *a Christological paradox: boldly proclaiming its authentic teaching while at the same time offering a witness of radical inclusion and acceptance*. Others, using a different language, speak of a tension between pastoral care and doctrine, to be addressed through an intensive dialogue involving the whole People of God.

55. In any case, the attitude of openness and welcome suggested by the image of the widening of the tent is considered a fundamental characteristic of a Church that is truly synodal and knows no boundaries: it is a token of its coherence. There is recognition of the urgency of a real closeness to all those who are poor, excluded, victims of injustice and prejudice, whose dignity is trampled upon: *It is not enough to proclaim that they are welcome, but we must discover with them their place in the Church* (Czech Republic). At the same time, the risk is perceived that this may lead to a watering down of the demands of the Gospel, whereas *the Church needs to communicate Christian truth authentically and clearly* (Hungary). Furthermore, fear is expressed that *considering pastoral solutions related to these issues could be a prelude to 'doctrinal changes'* (Poland).

56. Slovenia expresses two requirements highlighted often: *Young people want a Church close to people, including those on the margins, open to the issues of separated and remarried persons, LGBTQI+ people. But they also want the Church to make it clear that not everything is acceptable! So the Church should listen, but also tell the whole truth with great love!* (Slovenia).

57. Both emphases are a way of responding to the need for authenticity of the disciples who wish to follow in the Lord's footsteps: *The convergence between the DCS and the discernment of the local Churches reinforces the concern for a Church open to all because its eyes are fixed on Christ: young people, the poor and excluded, people with disabilities, homosexuals, the divorced and remarried, everyone must feel that they are expected in the Church and that they have a place in it because they are members of the same body, that of Christ (cf. 1 Cor 12)* (France).

58. Welcoming all as a sign of God's unconditional love and the proclamation of the truth of the Gospel are both demands rooted in the Church's unique mission: *God is the Truth, therefore he wants every person to be able to know this Truth and live it. [...] Jesus Christ alone is the only Lord and Saviour of the world. And the model of all interpersonal relationships is God in the Trinity of Persons* (Ukraine, Latin Church).

59. This tension cannot be resolved once and for all, but must be inhabited responsibly, resisting the temptations of ideological approaches and instead taking a step in the direction of greater spiritual depth: *The tension between pastoral and doctrine [...] can correspond to that between love and truth. Rather than opposing them, should we not rather articulate their complementarity in the sense of Psalm 85,10 'Steadfast love and faithfulness will meet'?* (French language Working Group). The path is that of a contemplative gaze that allows us to get to know the Lord Jesus better and the way in which he was able to articulate the two drives: *the fundamental truth of Jesus Christ is a moment of grace and mercy because mercy leads to truth* (English language online Working Group). This contemplative attitude is the basis for necessary discernment: *Unconditional acceptance does not prevent discernment in order to articulate mercy and truth in specific situations* (France).

60. Hence the need for a formation in truth and mercy: a *formation that holds in tension the authority of Scripture, Tradition, Magisterium and personal experience* (England and Wales). But even more fundamentally, we encounter here a call to personal and communal conversion: *While striving to enlarge the space of its tent and to be more inclusive, in what way should the Church modify itself, its doctrine, or its praxis? And to which extent should it ask its members to modify their heart and mindset, calling everyone for conversion? A shared journey of conversion becomes one of the first forms of inclusion* (Malta).

3.2 Tradition and Aggiornamento

61. *Perhaps the most pervasive tension in Europe is the growing divide between the Church and secular culture. To bridge this gap, the language of the Church must be accessible to all, without diluting the Gospel message* (Scotland). We must realise that *the language of faith as used in the Church is often very different to what people understand and use in everyday life in today's society* (Netherlands). As a consequence, the question *What does Jesus Christ want from his Church today?*, formulated by the Portuguese delegation, was repeated several times and in different forms.

62. The fear of breaking away from tradition particularly emerged when dealing with differences among theological sensitivities on the relationship between reference to tradition and reading the signs of the times. *The gap [...] between tradition and modernity is becoming increasingly wide and more and more aggressive. This is particularly painful in the area*

of liturgy (Nordic countries). Indeed, for liturgy – and not only liturgy – it is important to use a language that adheres to tradition while being significant for the people of our time.

63. Many delegates called for quick and radical changes following the meeting between theology and contemporary culture: *We must become a Church of presence, a Church that listens and is listened to. Transforming the Church without just turning around ourselves, having a view for the world. [...keeping] a double dynamic: a process of internal reform and a response to the challenges of today's world while renewing and maintaining our Christian identity* (Luxembourg).

64. Others expressed the concern that adopting changes would risk the integrity of the Church's teaching. For example, the Romanian delegation *hopes that the Church will be open to dialogue with the world without becoming of the world. That Church members speak boldly and uncompromisingly on matters of faith and morals*. Some remarks voiced the fear of inappropriate reforms of the Church, which may dilute the message of the Gospel: *We believe it is not right for the Church to conform to the world just so as not to feel persecuted, or considered unfashionable* (Albania).

65. Living the tension between tradition and aggiornamento without being crushed requires the ability to articulate the dynamic between the two poles: *We all would like to develop and implement new ideas, but we need to find a balance between Church traditions and new thoughts* (Estonia). *The pressing problem seems to be finding a wise consensus among the divergences and pastoral solutions that, without compromising doctrinal consistency, will allow a more adequate response to contemporary pastoral challenges* (Poland). In order to succeed, it has been stated that *serious attention must be paid to the theology of the living Tradition (DV 8) which includes, yes, a historical memory, but also an accurate discernment and judgement aimed at the new challenges of our society. The starting point, therefore, is found in listening to the Holy Spirit and discerning the signs of the times (GS 4), which courageously proceeds beyond historical experience* (Czech Republic). Synodality cannot be manipulated and bent to support ideological stances, nor does it consecrate all opinions expressed during the consultations. Rather, it is a dynamic way of listening to one another, humbly and opening our hearts to what the Holy Spirit suggests.

3.3 Liturgy as a Focal Point to Observe Tensions in the Church

66. The centrality of the liturgy, which gathers and fosters all the life of the Church, makes it a mirror in which the community – including its tensions – is reflected. Significantly and challengingly for discernment in Europe, liturgy is very often mentioned in connection with complex tensions or with pastoral difficulties. Instead, the joy of the liturgy in general and of the Eucharist in particular is rarely expressed. Perhaps this is so obvious that it goes without saying, but it is worth questioning.

67. From a fundamental point of view, it is possible to detect the link between Church and liturgy, between ecclesiology and the theology of liturgy: *The liturgical dimension in the Church is a place of strong tensions. These tensions are part of a deeper tension of an ecclesiological nature. Ecclesiological tension often arises from a vision of the Church based on one's own expectations* (Italian language Working Group). In this context, the tensions and sufferings concerning the ancient form of the Roman liturgy should be understood, with explicit references by France, England and Wales, and Nordic countries to the pre-conciliar liturgy according to the Missal of 1962.

68. Several times the liturgy is mentioned in relation to the sacraments of Christian initiation, and in particular with Confirmation, which poses a great challenge in those contexts where it does not correspond to a deeper insertion into the life and mission of the Church, but to a distancing. In several countries, there are calls for reflection and action for a renewed liturgical language, and more profoundly for a renewal that articulates the mystery of faith and liturgy, on the one hand, and the relationship between liturgy and life, on the other. *Some of the faithful note that in general in Bulgaria, priests and the Church do not use contemporary language, while times have changed and the churches are half empty* (Bulgaria). Elsewhere, there is also a tension between the desire for spirituality and an overly formal liturgy. A particular problem concerns the homily. *This is linked to the need to pay attention to the formation and support of priests, who must be close to the People of God, also expressing the closeness of the whole Church through the simplicity of preaching, which must be there everywhere* (Mukachevo).

69. In conclusion, *liturgy is the space where we let God call us as one people and empower us by His Spirit to join in Jesus' mission. We need to deepen our understanding on how the way we celebrate our liturgies can further form us as a synodal Church* (Malta).

3.4 Understanding the Mission

70. At a deeper level, the above tensions are linked to the understanding of mission: *We are being convoked for what? Some might mix belonging to the Church with retreating into a comfortable cocoon. Others can imagine it more of a space where everyone can mix and match without any sense of commitment or conversion. For some of us, it's not clear what mission entails. And if it's all ministerial, how are we to understand the specific gifts of the ordained within the one holy People of God?* (Malta). A process of maturation is needed concerning the implications of these tensions: *Generally speaking, it seems that there is a need for a more complete appropriation and assimilation of concepts such as ´missionary nature´ and the ´missionary dimension´ of the activity of the Church* (Ukraine, Greek Catholic Church). In the tension around the understanding of mission, different interpretations become visible: some local Churches consider that the task of a missionary Church is the strengthening of catechesis and the growth of religious practice; others understand mission as going out into the world to make God's love tangible for all people, especially for marginalised and those who were hurt by the Church; others again add that the Church should be a home for all people, especially the young. In short, one perceives a tension *between being locked in one's own community (elitism) and the need to go out on mission* (Slovakia).

71. A tension in the understanding of mission is also evident in the contributions from local Churches that are severely affected by cases of sexual abuse. How can the Church be missionary when it has inflicted severe suffering on many people? It touches on the credibility of the Church. Acknowledging the pain of the victims, the serious tensions are recognised and voiced. Finally, also among the mission-related tensions, *the fear is expressed that the synod process will remain without concrete structural consequences, which are seen as a prerequisite for a credible mission* (Austria).

3.5 Co-Responsibility of All, in the Diversity of Charisms and Ministries

72. *The synodality of the Church also requires recognition of the gifts and charisms of each member of the faithful, the equal dignity of each, seeking the symphonic articulation of the different vocations within the Church. It is necessary to recognise the authority of the pastors and the mission they have received. It is equally necessary to recognise the sensus fidei of each believer, whether cleric or lay. Rather, the ordained ministers can be understood as serving the baptismal life, granting* *each baptised and confirmed believer full participation in the life and mission of the Church* (France).

73. One of the most visible manifestations of common priesthood and synodality is the exercise of specific ministries and leadership, as well as participation in the governance of the Church at all levels. It is a way of realising the co-responsibility of all the baptised for the mission of the Church, based on their common baptismal dignity. This is why we speak of a ministerial Church as a concrete challenge, first of all for our ability to imagine concrete forms for its realisation. The synodal process leads to the desire of a *fraternal Church with an exercise of authority that is adapted to it and excludes every form of abuse of power, a synodal Church without clerical deviations* (Belgium) in the exercise of all ministries, ordained and non ordained: *In an 'all ministerial' Church, rethink the task and identity of priests* (Italy); or, with a different emphasis: *The involvement of the laity is an opportunity to complement, but not replace, the mission of ordained persons* (Hungary).

74. In this perspective, the Prague Assembly reaffirms that *the priestly ministry is a great gift from God for the Church* (France) and in various ways expresses a deep concern for priests. It voices their wish for *a positive image of priests* (Austria) and the faithful's concern for the wellbeing and loneliness of priests. *Young people observe that priests for the most part are poorly trained to work with persons, but are also often alone and without the right interlocutors* (Slovenia). On the other hand, there is a lack of reflection on the ordained diaconate, except in those cases where its opening to women is envisaged.

75. Some contributions also point to the existence of questions concerning the limits of access to ordained ministry: *The historical variability of the figure of the priest must be open to debate about the ordination of married men* (Czech Republic). Another concern is the ordination of women to the diaconate, even though this is not a simple topic. *There are also tensions concerning so-called divisive issues, such as women's access to the sacrament of Orders, ordination of married men* (Portugal). In particular, *opinions are divided on the ordination of women to the diaconate/priesthood* (English-language Working Group). According to Luxembourg, *The question of women's access to ordained ministries must be studied in depth.*

76. More broadly, the question of the place of women in the exercise of authority came up in many delegations. *The question of women's priesthood is not a hot topic, but we have had many discussions about women's participation in decision-making* (Lithuania). For several groups it is even a condition for a more fruitful Church in Europe. *Without doubt: the participation of lay people and especially women at all levels in the Church is felt as a priority [...] the Church needs the voice and specific leadership and community building qualities of women* (The Netherlands).

77. In any case, a great convergence appears: *Promote the real and effective co-responsibility of the People of God, overcoming clericalism. It is important to promote lay ministries* (Spain). This is not just a question of the place of women in the Church, but an understanding of the diversity of ministries as an expression of the synodal nature of the Church.

78. This calls for a deepening of the issue of collaboration between priests and laity in the mission of the Church: What is *still missing is not only the experience of a community of life, but also a healthy collaboration between priests and laity* (Lithuania). Many interventions identify it as a place of tension or frustration, even going so far as to see it as a tension between institutions and charisms. Therefore, *it seems important to model cooperation and the assumption of ministries on the basis of capacities* (Nordic countries).

79. For this collaboration to be fruitful, there is an insistence on the need for specific formation, for seminarians (initial formation), for priests (ongoing formation), and not only: *The formation of all the baptised is indispensable to help them rediscover the meaning of their vocation and their task in the Church, in a logic of co-responsibility and not of substitution* (Italian language Working Group). This formation must be permanent and involve priests and laity together, which requires the creation of spaces and opportunities for experimentation. Lastly, the Turkish delegation was the only one to mention the training of priests from abroad, a phenomenon that affects almost all European countries, who *must learn the language and culture very well in order to be able to incarnate and embody the Good News in the local culture* (Turkey).

3.6 The Exercise of Authority within a Synodal Church

80. The contributions addressed various aspects of the exercise of authority in the Church. They express that a true ecclesial and missionary renewal

aimed at by the current synodal process is rooted in two principles: all specific authority in the Church proceeds from Christ, and is guided by the Holy Spirit. *Any real renewal and strengthening of synodality of and in the Church must start from the fundamental principles of the Church itself, from the foundations on which the Church was founded by Jesus Christ our Lord* (Nordic countries). The consequences touch the very nature of the Church, in which the Holy Spirit is still at work today. *The Church is essentially synodal and essentially hierarchical. The tasks and challenges involved can be described as 'decision-making' and 'decision-taking'. There must be no winners or losers. [...] The Holy Spirit is often the third option* (Austria).

81. *There are rigidities to be overcome: excessively top-down ways of understanding the exercise of authority, forms of clericalism at various levels (and not only among priests), forgetting that when something concerns everyone, it should be discussed with everyone. Those who have a responsibility in the community have the task of involving and valuing everyone's contribution, because we all have something to learn from each other* (Italy). Moreover, *the common priesthood of all does not contradict the ministerial priesthood, and vice versa. We already experience joint deliberation in the synodal process. How do we also take decisions together?* (Germany).

82. This must result in profound changes: *A synodal institutional model should be built for the exercise of the ecclesial power and authority, with structures and bodies that reflect the spirit of synodality [....] and that do not have only consultative functions* (Mukachevo). *Synodality seems to require a profound change of mentality in the Church and especially in all those who exercise a responsibility in it* (Belgium). At the same time, *the faithful must be more aware that they are part of the Church and that they are needed for the work of the Church, remembering that the diversity of charisms without a hierarchical order becomes anarchy, just as the strictness of the hierarchy without a living charism becomes dictatorship* (Mukachevo).

83. This change must be reflected in concrete decisions, which the Church shall have to discern. *This will demand the courage and wisdom of the Spirit to review and inspire any necessary doctrinal, structural, canonical, and pastoral changes, without destroying communion or losing sight of the person and teaching of Jesus Christ* (Ireland). Surely the bishops are key players in this change towards a renewed and synodal exercise of authority. *We believe in the value of episcopal ministry* (Italy).

84. Authority must be deployed in a more fraternal and participative governance: *In order to experience better governance in the Church, many are calling for a rethink of a more participative governance, which gives room for listening and discernment, conceiving authority as an act of love and service* (France), but *a tension between authority and ministry is also pointed out* (Multilingual Working Group). European societies also have some specific needs: *to be a trustworthy and credible partner in the public arena and with the people, the European Church must meet the standards of functioning and governance acquired in society (DCS 62). Hence the need for transparency, accountability and participative leadership (DCS 79)* (Belgium). For this, *mechanisms of regular consultation between clergy, laity and religious should be established or renewed, ensuring transparency, better communication and co-responsibility* (Scotland).

85. The most essential feature noted by many contributions is the link between authority and listening. The theological tradition refers to it with the notion of *sensus fidei fidelium* (the sense of the faith of the faithful). The Synod 2021-2024 places renewed emphasis on it and this *a cause of great joy, encouragement, and hope for all who love the Church as the People of God* (Ireland).

3.7 Unity in Diversity: Between Local and Universal

86. In Prague, the Churches of Europe had the privilege of experiencing unity in diversity. *The diversity in the Catholic Church is a richness, as we know there are two lungs, the Eastern Catholic Lung and the Western Catholic lung, each has its own way of thinking, its own way of speaking, even of governing* (Cyprus). The synodal journey provided an opportunity to realise and appreciate this diversity: *Although coming together and engaging in dialogue has not always been easy, many Russian Catholics have perceived the synodal process as enriching and helpful. It has enabled them to discover that the Church, in Christ, is one family and that being multi-ethnic, multi-cultural and multi-institutional is a wealth* (Russia). There is thus a call to *take more account of the diversity of ways of living in the faith, which, in our opinion, is expressed well in the appreciation of traditions, both ritual and theological, that are at the same time united on the foundation of the one faith of the universal Church* (Mukachevo). The Eastern Churches have preserved institutions that give expression to synodality: *They can bring a lot of positive elements to the understanding and unfolding of the Church's synodality, especially through the adaptation of already existing provisions of the governing* *of the Church sui iuris* (Ukrainian Greek Catholic Church). However, the Eastern Churches too are invited to renew existing institutions and recover institutions that have disappeared or fallen into disuse. *Required is not only the desired synodal conversion in the communion of the Church, but also the possible revision of some canonical norms so as to better reflect the identity of this Church and facilitate and support its mission both in its canonical territories and in the diaspora* (Romania).

87. The call to live unity in diversity also arises when the Churches face topics that concern a specific context at a specific time and which might, therefore, demand a contextual response: this is the question of decentralisation in a Church that is both local and universal. There is a need for clarity and transparency on who can decide which issue should be handled locally, regionally or universally. On each level the discernment should occur in a synodal way. Numerous contributions ask for appropriate institutions and canonical structures to assist the Church in putting synodality into practice.

88. In light also of the positive experience of the Prague Assembly a specific proposal was made to establish an Ecclesial Assembly for Europe: *It could take place in 2025. Sixty years after the Ecumenical Council proclaimed the Pastoral constitution Gaudium et Spes, this Ecclesial Assembly could gather to share 'the joys and hopes, the grief and anguish of the people of our time'. We could listen to the cry of the poor and the Earth in Europe and the world, we could pray and work together for Justice and Peace* (Invited guest).

IV
PERSPECTIVES AND PRIORITIES

89. Throughout the days of the Assembly, we went through a spiritual experience that led us to realise, for the first time in our Church in Europe, that it is possible to meet, listen to one another and dialogue starting from our differences and overcoming the many obstacles, walls and barriers that history has placed across our way. We need to love the diversity within our Church and support one another in mutual esteem, strengthened by our faith in the Lord and the power of his Spirit.

90. This is why we wish to continue journeying in a synodal style: rather than a methodology, we consider it a way of life of our Church, of community discernment and discernment of the signs of the times. Concretely, we want this European Continental Assembly not to remain an isolated experience, but to become a regular event, based on the general adoption of the synodal method that permeates all our structures and procedures at all levels. Doing so will allow us to address the issues on which our efforts need to mature and intensify: the accompaniment of wounded people, the protagonism of young people and women, openness to learning from marginalised.

91. The synodal style also makes it possible to deal with tensions from a missionary perspective, without being paralysed by fear, but drawing energy from them to continue along the path. Two in particular emerged in our work. The first encourages unity in diversity, escaping the temptation of uniformity. The second associates readiness to welcome others (as proof of the Father's unconditional love for his children) with the courage of proclaiming the truth of the Gospel in its entirety. It is God who promises 'Steadfast love and faithfulness will meet' (Ps 85:10).

92. We know that all this is possible because we have experienced it during this Assembly, but even more so because the life of the Churches from which we come bears witness to it. We are thinking, here in particular, of ecumenical and interreligious dialogue, the echoes of which resonated strongly in our work. But above all, we believe that it is possible because grace is involved: indeed, building an increasingly synodal Church is a way to give concrete expression to the equality in dignity of all the members of the Church, founded in baptism, which makes us as children of God and members of the body of Christ, co-responsible for the unique mission of evangelisation entrusted by the Lord to his Church.

93. We are confident that the continuation of the Synod 2021-2024 can support and accompany us, particularly by addressing some specific priorities at the October 2023 Synodal Assembly:

- deepen the practice, theology and hermeneutics of synodality. We need to rediscover something that is ancient and belongs to the nature of the Church, while always being new. This is a task for us. We are taking the first steps along a path that opens up as we walk it;
- address the meaning of an all-ministerial Church, as a horizon in which to place the reflexion on charisms and ministries (ordained and non-ordained) and the relations between them;
- explore forms for a synodal exercise of authority, namely the service of accompanying the community and preserving unity;
- clarify the discernment criteria for the synodal process and at what

level, from local to universal, decisions are to be made.

- take concrete and courageous decisions on the role of women within the Church and on their greater involvement at all levels, including in decision-making and taking processes.
- consider the tensions around the liturgy, so as to consider, from a synodal perspective, the Eucharist as the source of communion;
- care for a synodal related formation of the entire People of God, with specific attention to discerning the signs of the times, with a view to carrying out the common mission;
- renew the living sense of mission, overcoming the rift between faith and culture in order to once again bringing the gospel to people's heart, finding a language that can articulate tradition and renewal, but above all that can walk with people instead of talking about them or to them. The Spirit asks us to listen to the cry of the poor and the earth in our Europe. In particular the desperate cry of the victims of war call for a just peace.

94. Loving the Church and her rich diversity is not a form of sentimentalism for its own sake. The Church is beautiful because the Lord wants her to be so, in view of the task he has entrusted to her: to proclaim the Gospel and to invite all women and men to enter into the dynamic of communion, participation and mission that constitutes her raison d'être, animated by the perennial vitality of the Spirit. Loving our Church in Europe, therefore, means renewing our commitment to carry out this mission, also on our continent, in a culture marked by the many differences of which we are well aware.

95. Let us entrust the continuation of our synodal journey to the Patron Saints and Martyrs of Europe!

Adsumus Sancte Spiritus!

CONCLUDING NOTE FROM THE BISHOPS

We thank the Lord for the experience of synodality which has seen us all – bishops, priests, consecrated and lay men and women – side by side for the first time on a continental level. We rejoice because during these days in Prague we found that the moments of prayer lived together and even more the work of the Assembly have been a profoundly spiritual and a truly synodal experience. Mutual listening, fruitful dialogue, and the story of how our ecclesial communities lived out the first phase of the synodal process and prepared for this continental meeting are an unmistakable sign of our unique belonging to Christ.

The national reports, the group work, and the many interventions that we have heard converged into the final document presented to the Assembly. It will be the contribution of the Churches in Europe to the drafting the *Instrumentum laboris* of the Synod. We thank those who have shared their experiences frankly and with respect for different sensitivities. We are also grateful to the Redactional Committee for the great work done in drafting the document.

As a fruit of this synodal experience, we bishops are committed to keep living and promoting the synodal process in our diocesan structures and life. This experience of care for the whole Church in Europe heartened us in our commitment to faithfully live out our universal mission. We are engaged in supporting the indications of the successor of Peter, our Holy Father, to become a synodal Church nourished by the experience of communion, participation, and mission in Christ.

We want to walk together, as holy People of God, both lay persons and pastors, pilgrims along the roads of Europe to proclaim the joy of the Gospel which springs from the encounter with Christ. We want to do it together with our brothers and sisters from other Christian denominations.

We shall work tirelessly to enlarge the space of our tents so that our ecclesial communities become even more places where everyone feels welcome.

Prague, February 11, 2023
Memory of the Blessed Our Lady of Lourdes

LATIN AMERICA AND THE CARIBBEAN

The Call to 'Enlarge your Tent'

(cf. Is. 54:2)

THE CALL TO 'ENLARGE OUR TENT' (CF. Is. 54:2): THE CONTINENTAL ASSEMBLY OF LATIN AMERICA AND THE CARIBBEAN

Birgit Weiler MMS and Ricardo González

1. Context of the Synodal Process in Latin America and the Caribbean

The region of Latin America and the Caribbean is extraordinarily rich in biodiversity and cultural diversity. Five hundred years ago, the arrival of Europeans, mainly from Spain and Portugal, and the consequential colonial era had a strong impact on the whole region politically, socially and culturally. The multiple consequences are experienced until today. One of them is the fact that in the majority of Latin America, Spanish is the predominant language, although Portuguese is spoken in Brazil, and in some countries of the Caribbean, English and French. For a long time, the indigenous cultures were not appreciated throughout the region. They were rather marginalised and the State did not foster learning indigenous languages. In recent times, this has begun to change.

In the 19th and 20th century, the whole region was also influenced by waves of immigrants from European and Asian countries (Japan, China etc.). At present, in Latin America and the Caribbean deep cultural changes are taking place rapidly. Members of the majority of families come from different cultures, leading to a weaving together of different cultural strands and patterns, and thus something new is emerging. At the same time, there is an important presence of indigenous and Afro-descendant communities that maintain their languages and forms of organisation, enriching other cultures and faith manifestations.

Latin America is considered a Catholic continent, as the majority of Christians still belongs to the Catholic Church, although during recent times the Evangelical and Pentecostal communities and Churches have been growing steadily. In Brazil and Guatemala their number is already quite high. Should the present rhythm of growth continue, soon most Christians in both countries will belong to one of these communities. At the same time statistics reveal a reality which until now has not received the attention it needs, namely that the group which is growing most in numbers is young people who do not identify themselves with any Christian Church, and/or with the Christian religion, but consider themselves as being on a spiritual search in a broad sense. There is yet another transformation taking place in the region: the change from a social and cultural reality in which the Christian religion was absolutely dominant and members of other religions were only a tiny minority, to a new reality of increasing religious pluralism.

The colonial past of Latin America marked its social and political forms of government as well as the relations between the different groups of population. Thus racism and other forms of discrimination are continuously a strong obstacle for building relationships based on equality and respect for human and social rights. Today's democracies in the region are incipient, fragile and in several countries they are at a significant risk due to political polarisation, as well as increasing social and economic gaps. There are multiple social problems like growing violence, drug trafficking, migration due to social, economic and cultural injustices, as well as a strong violence in different forms against women and persons belonging to the group of LGBTQI+. The environmental deterioration is alarming, and the negative impacts of climate change and the climate crisis are affecting mostly the health and living conditions of the poorest.

Ecclesiastically, Latin America and the Caribbean are composed of 22 episcopal conferences. The Bishops Council of Latin America and the Caribbean (*Consejo Episcopal de Latinoamérica y El Caribe* – CELAM) was born at the General Conference of the Episcopate in Rio de Janeiro in 1955, in order to unite the pastoral efforts of the local Churches of the region. It was the first Episcopal Council of this kind worldwide. Then followed the Conferences of Medellín (1968), Puebla (1979), Santo Domingo (1992) and Aparecida (2007), each one with specific accents and concrete options for ecclesial work on the basis of the preferential option for the poor. In Medellín, the Church in Latin America and the Caribbean assumed this option, and the subsequent General Conferences reaffirmed as a fundamental option.

Latin America and the Caribbean has a history of synodal experiences; even though the general conferences which were already mentioned, were mostly episcopal, they included local elements of community work such as 'Basic Christian Communities' (*comunidades eclesiales de base*), with popular movements of workers, biblical groups and others contributing their insights, observations and proposals. Their contributions originated from their practice to analyse reality, illuminate it with the Word of God and propose pastoral perspectives to bring about necessary changes in society and Church. Usually, before the General Episcopal Conferences would meet, CELAM presented a Preparatory Document on which all the faithful could comment. However, it depended on the bishop of each place how dialogical and transparent the process would be.

2. A Landmark: The Amazon Synod

In 2013/2014 the Catholic Church founded the Pan-Amazonian Ecclesial Network (*Red Ecclesial Panamazónica*, REPAM). It works ecumenically and promotes alliances and close cooperation among Church as well as civil organisations like the Confederation of Indigenous Organisations of the Amazon Basin (COICA).[1] REPAM plays a vital role in facilitating a broad participation of the different population groups in Amazonia, among them about 390 Indigenous and Tribal peoples as well as Afro-descendant communities. In accordance with the preferential option for the poor, special attention was paid to assure the active participation of representatives of those men and women who are mainly marginalised in Latin American societies within the Amazonia territory, and are suffering from racial, cultural and gender discrimination. The high participation of those groups through their representatives in the process of listening to each other, consultation and discernment in the preparatory phase of the Amazon Synod (2019) and in the actual celebration of the Amazon Synod itself (2019) surely constituted a historical moment in the Catholic Church of Amazonia, as well as in the Catholic Church worldwide. This is especially true with regard to the indigenous peoples who, in a very lively way, contributed in both moments.

The overall theme of the Amazon Synod was: 'New ways for the Church and an integral ecology'.[2] Already the Final Document of the Amazon Synod (hereafter: FDAS) speaks of 'the missionary synodality of the entire People of God under the guidance of the Spirit' (Chapter V a) and stresses that 'in order to walk together, the Church today needs a conversion to the synodal experience. It needs to strengthen a culture of dialogue, reciprocal listening, spiritual discernment, consensus and communion in order to find areas and ways of joint decision-making and to respond to pastoral challenges. In this way, co-responsibility in the life of the Church will be fostered in a spirit of service' (FDAS 88).

It also talks about the urgency to generate more spaces for active participation of women in the processes of discernment, decision making and decision taking, the creation of 'an instituted ministry of *women community leadership*' (FDAS 102). It mentions that in a large number of consultations carried out in the Amazon territory, 'the permanent diaconate for women was requested' (FDAS 103).

Out of a synodal spirit, the Amazon Synod gave the impulse for the creation of a new ecclesial body in the worldwide Church, the 'Ecclesial Conference of the Amazon' (CEAMA). As an 'Ecclesial Conference', it is a leadership body not

1 For more information: http://secretariat.synod.va/content/sinodoamazonico/en/the-pan-amazonian-region/repam.html, visited April 30, 2023.
2 See: https://www.vatican.va/roman_curia/synod/documents/rc_synod_doc_20191026_sinodo-amazzonia_en.html, visited April 30, 2023.

only with bishops but also with other faithful. It is the first ecclesial body of this kind in the history of the Catholic Church[3] and was canonically erected by Pope Francis in 2021. At present its statutes are approved *ad experimentum*.

The Amazon Synod inspired also further synodal processes in the Church of Latin America and the Caribbean; some are named below:

> The example of REPAM together with the Amazon Synod was a strong impulse to strengthen further networking in different regions of the Church in Latin America and the Caribbean. Thus, with time, two more wide ranging ecclesial networks were formed: In 2019 the Mesoamerican Ecological Ecclesial Network (REMAM) was established and in 2021, the Ecclesial Network of the Gran Chaco and the Guarani Aquifer (REDCHAG)[4] was built. All these networks have in common that they were created to address the environmental and social challenges in their respective regions, inspired by an integral ecology (LS 137) and in a global perspective.

In 2021, the CELAM initiated a process of renovation and restructuring with two main dimensions which are intertwined: 'a synodal Church which goes forth' and 'human development and integral ecology'.[5]

The Amazon Synod was also an inspiration for the First Ecclesial Assembly in Latin America and the Caribbean.

3. The Significance of the Ecclesial Assembly (2021)

When in 2019 the Latin American bishops expressed to Pope Francis the idea of a sixth general conference of the episcopate of the whole region, he responded by inviting them to something different and new, which would be even more synodal: a 'General Assembly of the Latin American and Caribbean Church'. This concretely meant an Assembly not exclusively for bishops; all the People of God were invited to participate in different ways. It was an unprecedented and valuable experience: despite the pandemic and the restrictions imposed by COVID-19, more than 70,000 people were involved in the phase of listening to each other and discerning the signs of the present time in this region, seeking the will of God regarding the mission of the Church in the given reality. Due to the pandemic, the listening to each other on a large scale occurred through internet platforms. This was a new practice with many advantages but also disadvantages. The internet and virtual media made it possible to reach out to many people across the subcontinent. At the same time, the lack of accessibility

3 https://www.catholicnewsagency.com/news/249341/pope-francis-officially-recognises-amazon-region-ecclesial-conference, visited on April 30, 2023.
4 See for further information: https://www.ncronline.org/earthbeat/justice/south-american-church-network-forms-gran-chaco-zone-guarani-aquifer, visited on April 30, 2023.
5 For further information: https://celam.org/wp-content/uploads/2022/02/documento-de-trabajo-ingles.pdf, visited on April 30, 2023.

to the internet limited very much the possibilities to participate for many who are living in conditions of poverty.

The contributions received revealed that there was a convergence of the many voices with regard to the following points: The Church in Latin America and the Caribbean is called to an ongoing conversion to really become a synodal Church in which the common dignity of all the baptised, and the common vocation to be together the People of God, are fully recognised, and the charisms, gifts and skills as well as the testimony of faith of all members of the People of God are appreciated for the good of the Church and its mission. This requires among other aspects: to strengthen the commitment to a more social and ecological justice and to surpass manifestations of discrimination and violence; to care more deeply prophetically for the Earth, our common Home, in the face of climate crisis, to become a more inclusive Church in which people from different ethnicities and cultures, different sexual orientations and persons with physical and/or mental disabilities feel at home; to include effectively much more women in the processes of decision making and taking at the different levels of the Church, and to give room for a stronger protagonism of young people in our Church. The insights and pastoral priorities which were discerned in the First Ecclesial Assembly (2021) are presented in the Document *Toward a Synodal Chruch Going Forth into the Periphery*.[6]

4. A Synodal Process: from Regional to Continental

At the level of the National Episcopal Conferences, as well as at the level of the dioceses, a commission was established to motivate and accompany the consultations on the Working Document for the Continental Stage. Both commissions were asked to work in close coordination in order to accompany the process.

Given the organisational structure of CELAM, it was decided to meet in the already established four regions as this would work best to assure a broad participation. The meetings took place in: San Salvador (El Salvador) for the Central American region and Mexico; Santo Domingo (Dominican Republic) for the Caribbean region; Quito (Ecuador) for the Bolivarian region (Bolivia, Colombia, Ecuador, Peru and Venezuela) and Brasilia (Brazil) for the Southern Cone region. A total of 415 people participated: 96 in Central America and Mexico; 41 in Caribbean countries; 92 in the Bolivarian region and 177 in the Southern Cone. There were 65 bishops, 70 priests, 61 men and women religious, 16 deacons and 194 lay men and women.

The activities for the continental phase of the Synod in Latin America and the Caribbean were prepared and carried out in dialogue and close

6 See: https://asambleaeclesial.lat/wp-content/uploads/2022/10/ingles.pdf, visited on April 30, 2023.

coordination among the presidency and the general secretariat of CELAM, the general secretary of the Confederation of Latin American Religious (CLAR), the executive secretary of Caritas Latin America, the director of CELAM's Center for Pastoral Action Programs and Networks (*Centro de Programas y Redes Pastorales* – CEPRAP) and the director of CELAM's Center for Communication. The persons in institutional leadership mentioned above divided among themselves the task to accompany the four regional meetings. In each region it was decided in dialogue between the episcopal conferences and CELAM how many bishops, priests, religious men and women and deacons would be invited to take part in the respective regional meeting. The episcopal conference of each country then chose a number of representatives (lay people, priests, religious men and women) to participate in the meeting of the region; the number was proportional to the total population.

There was the request for integrating especially those people who are part of groups that had not been sufficiently listened to during the diocesan phase, for example: representatives of sectors at the social and existential peripheries who had not been convoked or people who are working with groups at the peripheries, such as those who engage in prison ministry or in pastoral work with migrant communities.

It is important to mention the Digital Synod as well in which influencers and digital communicators, mainly young people, from all over the continent participated. It was the initiative of Father Juan José Montalvo, better known as 'Father Borre', from the diocese of Monterrey, Mexico. He had prepared a questionnaire to be filled out online which invited young people to express their perceptions of the Church, what they appreciate, what they criticise and what their expectations are, etc.; He found different ways of interacting with young people by making use of digital communication, inviting them to make their voices heard.

A weak point in the regional meetings was the fact that there was almost no participation by non-believers or members of other Christian communities and religions. Nevertheless, several persons who are not linked with the Church, but willing to collaborate with it in projects for the common good, participated in the meeting of the so called '*países bolivarianos*.' In several regional meetings some representatives of the indigenous peoples and Afro-descendant communities took part. There is still the challenge of developing a more intercultural way of carrying out meetings.

In the regional meetings the participants presented their insights and conclusions of the discernment on the Working Document for the Continental Stage. They understood themselves as representatives of the People of God in their respective places and brought the work, insights and knowledge of these people to the reginal meeting for a sharing with all present. It is also worth considering that many of the participants in the regional meetings had already been active directly or indirectly in the Ecclesial Assembly; thus, they were familiar with the instruments of listening and discernment, which was of great help. Most of the meetings were held in Spanish, the documents were also translated into Portuguese (Brazil), English and French (for some Caribbean communities). Nevertheless, during the meeting the communication was mainly in Spanish, because most participants were able to understand it.

5. Organisation and Spirituality of the Regional Meetings

Each regional meeting was opened with a spiritual retreat of one day. It was a moment of profound encounter with the Spirit of God; here the physical space in which the retreat took place, was significant: For the region of Central America and Mexico (CAMEX) the retreat took place in the martyrial chapel of St Oscar Romero (El Salvador) and for the Caribbean region the retreat was held in the First Cathedral of America in Santo Domingo. After the retreat, while initiating the work to be done, there was first a reflection on the synodal process in relation to the Ecclesial Assembly, because for some people these seemed to be parallel processes, separated from each other. Therefore, it was important to clarify that both processes have a particular dynamic but are not to be understood in opposition to each other nor as being in contradiction. Rather, there was to be a continuity between both processes.

Then the methodology of Spiritual Conversation was explained to all the participants. Afterwards the so called 'communities of life' were formed with the assistance of members of the coordinating team. It was a great joy and a surprise for many to be able to converse openly and freely with bishops on a level of horizontal fraternity. For many this was a completely new experience and the first time this had happened. Those present expressed that being invited to speak, being listened to and their voices being taken into consideration was a deep and significant experience of synodality.

Spiritual moments strongly marked each day of the regional meetings. They facilitated a common discernment and a working together in a climate of encounter with God, which enabled a sense of fraternal community beyond the diversity in states of life, language, social and cultural background of the participants. At the beginning of each day, the team for spirituality offered a symbol or sign that would help to get acquainted with the dynamics of the day. In the Eucharist, cultural elements of the respective region were presented, such as processions with the offerings accompanied by native dances and songs. In addition, the local organisers offered moments of recreation or cultural exchange, which strengthened the bonds of belonging to each region.

The biblical call 'Enlarge the space of your tent' (Is 54,2) accompanied the reflections and sharing of each day like a spiritual refrain. A song, inspired by the biblical text, which had been composed previously, was sung continuously during the meeting.[7]

6. A Method for Listening

In order to create the conditions for a deep listening to each other, participants met in groups of six to eight persons. Attention was paid to ensure that the composition of the group would represent the different vocations and ministries: a bishop, one or two priests, one or two religious, and lay people. It was stressed that all were invited to fully participate on equal terms, because all share as baptised people the same dignity and are called to co-responsibility for the life and mission of the Church. The groups assembled around a candle put in the centre, which helped to recall the active presence of the Spirit among all. In the first round, each person spoke for two or three minutes, sharing the fruits of their personal discernment, including their inspirations and insights related to the topic discussed. In the CAMEX region the members of the group held an image of Bishop Romero in their hands while sharing. The others listened in silence. Then there was a moment of silence and prayer to let the voices of the others resound in one's heart.

In a second round, all were invited to share how the words of others resonated in their own heart. This truly helped to open oneself in heart and mind to what the others expressed and to perceive how one was touched by their reflections. Again, each participant spoke for two or three minutes. This was followed by another moment of prayer in silence.

Finally, a community discernment was carried out, trying to welcome the insights that the Spirit had helped to emerge during listening and dialogue. Some consensus was reached and evidenced to be welcomed by all. This was shared in the plenary at the end of the day.

The discernment material used for the small groups and plenary sessions, was the same for everyone. The Document for the Continental Stage had listed three questions which guided the gatherings. They were:

- After having read and prayed with the DCS, which intuitions resonate most strongly with the lived experiences and realities of the Church in your continent? Which experiences are new, or illuminating to you?
- After having read and prayed with the DCS, what substantial tensions or divergences emerge as particularly important in your continent's perspective? Consequently, what are the questions or

7 The song in spanish version: https://youtu.be/OWLiUrP4vDE, visited on April 30, 2023.

issues that should be addressed and considered in the next steps of the process?
- Looking at what emerges from the previous two questions, what are the priorities, recurring themes and calls to action that can be shared with other local Churches around the world and discussed during the First Session of the Synodal Assembly in October 2023?

At the end of each day, a plenary session with all communities was held as another moment for community discernment.

The Spiritual Conversation Method turned out to be very helpful and fruitful. At the same time, it was noted that some aspects require improvement. In several cases, the moderators would have needed more training which would have enabled them to effectively keep pace with the participants. In several cases, the moments of communal prayer could have been better prepared. In some groups, the moderator did not hold well to the different times for listening, dialogue and discernment. It was not always possible to reach consensus. At times the results of communal discernment seemed more like a list of topics which had been treated or just like a sum of individual discernment points. Among the different moderators were men and women, representing the different vocations in the Church, clergy, laity and religious.

Comments expressed that a communal discernment requires a previous personal discernment. This would be of great help at the time of sharing insights and identifying what the different contributions have in common. The personal discernment already done would then help to recognise the voice of God in the voice of others, to enrich one's perspective and agenda by attentively listening to others, and to become aware of the areas of light and deeper insight which the Spirit helps to perceive in the dialogue.

A team set up by CELAM registered and systematised the contributions by identifying common themes, while at the same time respecting the multiplicity of voices heard. On the last day of the regional meetings the participants met in small groups related to their different vocations; they were asked to reread the experience of those days and to identify contributions for the next stage.

In the time between the end of the four regional meetings and the beginning of the meeting to prepare the Continental Document, a team of CELAM assembled the synthesis elaborated by each region at the end of its meeting. They added to them written reflections that some pastoral organisations and leadership bodies such as the Ecclesial Conference of the Amazon (CEAMA), the Pan-Amazonian Ecclesial Network (REPAM) and the Network of Pastoral work with Afro-descendants had submitted as their responses to the Working Document for the Continental Stage. Altogether, it was very rich material containing the fruits of Spiritual Conversation and communal discernment in which many people had been involved. All these materials were sent to the members of the Working Group that was to draft the Continental Document of Latin America and the Caribbean before they met.

7. Drafting Team and the Way of Proceeding

From 17 to 20 March, 2023 the team that was to draft the Continental Document met at the CELAM headquarters in Bogotá (Colombia). It was a group of men and women, lay people and priests from different countries with different theological and pastoral expertise, among them were several members of CELAM's theological and pastoral reflection group. All members of this Working Group had been appointed by CELAM. Many of them had participated in the regional meetings. They came from Argentina, Brazil, Mexico, Peru and Venezuela thus representing the different regions established by CELAM. Furthermore, the group had a team of facilitators who were responsible for applying the methodology of Spiritual Conversation and communal discernment in each session. From the beginning, the members of the coordinating team for the continental phase joined them. The Working Group of sixteen persons was accompanied by Father Giacomo Costa SJ from the General Secretariat of the Synod who assisted in orienting the process.

The writing of the document required a discernment in light of the Spirit. Therefore, the first morning was dedicated to read personally the materials received in a prayerful and discerning attitude. Then there was a sharing in small groups according to the method of Spiritual Conversation. Soon it became clear that there were strong points of convergence among the syntheses received from the regions and the other parts, which allowed for easy identification of the main topics. In a plenary session, the fruits of the Spiritual Conversation in the small groups were shared and the work of elaborating a structure for the Document began. The whole group discerned, as a group, the different topics and elements of content which had been proposed, to decide what needed to be included in the Document and how it be best structured. There was general agreement. Subsequently, small groups were formed which saw to drafting sections on specific topics. All were encouraged to insert literal quotations from the materials received into the Document. These quotations where selected because in most cases they are 'pearls' as they express in an excellent way the different voices heard in the regional meetings.

In the plenary, the draft of the complete text was discerned, then observations and suggestions were made and considered for inclusion. Finally, the draft was approved unanimously by the drafting team. It also found the full support of CELAMS's president and general secretary, both of whom had participated in the entire meeting. A small team was tasked to do the editorial work to prepare the document for presentation to the bishops.

8. The Role of Bishops in Validating the Document

On 21 March, 2023, in a context of a face-to-face meeting in the headquarters of the CELAM in Bogotá, the General Secretaries of the National Episcopal Conferences in Latin America and the Caribbean with the participation – either through physical presence or virtually – of many presidents of the episcopal conferences, reviewed the Draft of the Document in a synodal spirit. After a due process of discernment, which led to some editorial suggestions, they approved the Continental Document. It was then sent to the General Secretariat of the Synod in Rome.

Certainly, the common reflections and dialogue were enriched by the presence of Cardinal Jean-Claude Hollerich SJ, rapporteur of the Synod, Bishop Luis Marín de San Martín, undersecretary of the General Secretariat of the Synod and Father Giacomo Costa SJ, coordinator of the Preparatory Commission for the Synod.

Several members of the Group commissioned to draft the Document emphasised in their reflections during the meeting that it is very important that after its publication, the Continental Document will be returned to the People of God in this region for further reflection and for keeping alive the shared commitment for a synodal Church that goes forth to the social and existential peripheries and cares in alliance with others for our Common Home.

EA	Ecclesial Assembly of Latin America and the Caribbean. 'Towards a synodal Church going forth into the peripheries. Reflections and pastoral proposals from the first Ecclesial Assembly of Latin America and the Caribbean' (2022)
BOLIVARIANA	Meeting of the Bolivarian Region (February 27 - March 3)
CAMEX	Central America and Mexico Regional Assembly (February 13 to 17, 2023)
CARIBE	Caribbean Regional Assembly (February 20 to 25, 2023)
CEAMA-REPAM	Contribution of the Ecclesial Conference of the Amazon and the Pan-Amazonian Ecclesial Network
CELAM	Latin American Episcopal Council
CONO SUR	Southern Cone Region Assembly (March 6 to 9, 2023)
DA	Conclusive Document of the Fifth General Conference of the Latin American and Caribbean Bishops in Aparecida (2007)
DCS	Document for the Continental Stage. Synod on Synodality (2022): 'Enlarge the Space of your Tent'.
DOC. PREP.	Synod on Synodality (2021-2024): Preparatory Document. For a Synodal Church: Communion, Participation, Mission.
EG	*Evangelii Gaudium*, Apostolic Exhortation by Pope Francis
EN	*Evangelii Nuntiandi* Apostolic Exhortation by Pope Paul VI
Hch	Bible: Book of Acts of the Apostles
Is	Bible: Book of the Prophet Isaiah
ITC Synodality	International Theological Commission, Document: Synodality in the Life and Mission of the Church (2018).
LG	*Lumen gentium*: The Dogmatic Constitution on the Church, document of the Second Vatican Council
LGBTQI+	Lesbian, gay, bisexual, transgender, queer, intersex, and others
QA	*Querida Amazonia*, post-synodal Apostolic Exhortation by Pope Francis (2020)
REDCHAG	The Gran Chaco and Guarani Aquifer Ecclesial Network
REMAM	Mesoamerican Ecological Ecclesial Network
REPAM	Pan-Amazonian Ecclesial Network
Rev.	Bible: The Book of Revelation
SD	Fourth General Conference of the Latin America and the Caribbean Bishops (1992)
UR	*Unitatis redintegratio*, Decree on Ecumenism, document of the Second Vatican Council

ASAMBLEA ECLESIAL
DE AMÉRICA LATINA Y EL CARIBE

CELAM

SYNTHESIS OF THE CONTINENTAL STAGE OF THE LATIN AMERICA AND THE CARIBBEAN SYNOD

Bogotá, Columbia

NARRATIVE

1. 'It is possible to walk with Christ at the centre, allowing ourselves to be led by the Spirit of God. We have a growing hope that we are already living a new time for the Church.' This expression, by one of the participants in the continental phase of the Synod, reflects the enthusiasm aroused by the process in Latin America and the Caribbean, which had as its central moment of discernment the four regional meetings held in El Salvador, Santo Domingo, Quito and Brasilia in February and March.

2. The preparation for the continental phase began a year earlier with the creation of a commission to accompany the national teams responsible for animating the diocesan phase and, at the same time, to define, in dialogue with the General Secretariat of the Synod, the modalities of the continental assembly. A working team was established after a few months consisting of the following members: Miguel Cabrejos (President of CELAM), Msgr. Jorge Lozano (General Secretary of CELAM), Fr Pedro Brassesco (Assistant Secretary of CELAM), Sr Daniela Cannavina (Secretary General of CLAR), Fr Francisco Hernández (Executive Secretary of Caritas Latin America), Mauricio López (Director of Ceprap of CELAM and liaison with the General Secretariat of the Synod) and Oscar Elizalde (Director of the Communication Centre of CELAM).

3. The Latin American and Caribbean Church has a long history of participatory experiences marked by the five General Conferences of

the Latin American Episcopate, the Synod of the Amazon, the Ecclesial Assembly and the ecclesial structures of communion in the continent.

4. Our Church is nourished by the social and cultural diversity of each region, which is an aspect to be cared for and strengthened to consolidate the common identity and a renewed inculturation of the Gospel among the peoples. For this reason, it was decided that the continental phase would have, as its central moment, the realisation of regional meetings. These would allow for greater participation, discernment, and listening to contribute to the richness and the particular way of being of the Church.

5. Out of a total of 400 participants, each country was assigned a number of representatives (taking into account its total population), as well as an estimated number of bishops, priests, religious, deacons, and lay people. Among the latter, a special request was made for the inclusion of people from areas that had not been sufficiently heard in the diocesan phase. Finally, CELAM invited representatives from peripheral sectors that had not been invited.

6. The regional meetings were held in San Salvador, El Salvador, from 13 to 17 February for the Central America and Mexico Region. In Santo Domingo (Dominican Republic) for the Caribbean Region, from 20 to 24 February; in Quito (Ecuador) for the Bolivarian Region, from 27 February to 3 March; and in Brasilia (Brazil) for the Southern Cone Region, from 6 to 10 March.

7. A total of 415 people participated: 96 from Central America and Mexico; 41 from the Caribbean; 92 from the Bolivarian region and 177 from the Southern Cone. There were 65 bishops, 70 priests, 61 men and women religious, 16 deacons and 194 lay people.

8. Each Assembly began with a retreat on Monday morning, a moment of deep encounter with the Spirit. The physical environment in which they were held was significant: in El Salvador, the Martyr Chapel of St Oscar Romero, and in Santo Domingo, the Cathedral of the Primate of the Americas. The afternoon was dedicated to the presentation of the synodal process in relation to the Ecclesial Assembly as well as to the explanation of the methodology of the Spiritual Conversation and to the formation of the communities of life. It was a first meeting to facilitate mutual acquaintance.

9. The following days were dedicated to reflecting on the Document for the Continental Phase and the three questions it poses. The third chapter was divided into three parts, with each day devoted to one of them in three group sessions, one for each question. At the end of each day, all the communities were brought together in a new moment of common discernment. A total of 423 syntheses were collected with intuitions, tensions and themes to be deepened on the basis of what was developed in the DEC. A CELAM team recorded and systematised these proposals, identifying common themes and respecting the diversity of voices and proposals.

10. On the last day, the assemblies were divided into vocation groups to re-read the experience and make new contributions to the horizons for the next stage, which made it possible to receive another 30 documents with contributions.

11. In addition to the contribution of the regions, there has been the process of some pastoral organisations, such as the Ecclesial Conference of the Amazon (CEAMA), the Amazonian Ecclesial Network (REPAM) and the Afro-pastoral, which have made their own way in the light of the DEC in various meetings and assemblies.

12. Moments of spirituality marked each day, creating a climate of encounter with God and a sense of fraternal communion that transcended the diversity of life situations, languages, positions, or places of origin of each participant. The local organisers also offered moments of recreation or cultural exchange that helped to strengthen the bonds of belonging to each region. Each meeting culminated in the celebration of the Eucharist.

13. From 17 to 20 March, a meeting was held at the CELAM headquarters in Bogota, Colombia. The purpose of the meeting was to draft the continental synthesis based on the contributions of all the assemblies. Members of the CELAM Pastoral Theological Reflection Team (many of whom participated in the assemblies), the facilitators who carried out the methodology in each assembly and the members of the continental phase coordination team were invited. A team of sixteen people, accompanied by members of the General Secretariat of the Synod, guided the process.

14. The process of drafting the document involved individual and then group discernment of the main themes in the light of the Spirit and lived experience. The outline was agreed upon during the assembly, and the

themes were drafted in groups with the contributions of all, taking care to include quotations that reflected the voices heard. The drafting team consolidated the final text from the common reading, corrections and suggestions.

15. In the framework of the face-to-face meeting of the General Secretaries of the episcopal conferences, and with the online participation of their Presidents, the day of 21 March was dedicated to a collegial re-reading of the lived Synodal experience on the basis of their specific charisms and responsibilities. The bishops were presented with the developed process and the proposed text of the synthesis. Then, gathered in pastoral regions, they read the document and, finally, in plenary, they made their contributions and evaluations. The dialogue was enriched by the presence of Cardinal Jean-Claude Hollerich, SJ, Rapporteur of the Synod, Bishop Luis Marín de San Martín, Undersecretary of the General Secretariat of the Synod, and Father Giacomo Costa, Coordinator of the Preparatory Commission for the Synod.

16. Thus, the experience lived during this continental phase has consolidated the participatory and communitarian character of the Church on pilgrimage in Latin America and the Caribbean, and has brought new notes from the methodology used, the strong spiritual imprint sought, and the openness to listening to new voices.

INTRODUCTION: A CHURCH IN SYNODALITY

17. The Church of Latin America and the Caribbean has completed the continental phase of the synodal process called by Pope Francis with the theme: *For a Synodal Church: Communion, Participation and Mission.* The preceding narrative explained the process of listening, dialoguing and discerning carried out in the four regional assemblies involving the twenty-two episcopal conferences. In this journey together, we have learned to develop more fully the sense of 'we' as an ecclesial community, and we are reaping the fruits of it, in various ways.

18. Conciliar, synodal and collegial life has a long history in our Church. In the path taken by the great missionaries of the first evangelisation, we find St Mary of Guadalupe with her dark face, her message of *'God for whom we live'*, her inculturated pedagogy through conversation in the indigenous language and the search for a land without evil. She is the first missionary disciple of the continent. In the Church on pilgrimage in Latin America and the Caribbean, the Spirit has distributed a rich diversity of gifts among its peoples, endowing them with spiritual and communitarian values such as respect for Sister Mother Earth. For five centuries the Church, with light and shadow, with holiness and sin, has evangelised the continent, bearing witness to the faith and struggling for justice, especially through its saints and martyrs, thus helping to form communities of children, brothers and sisters.

19. In recent times we have welcomed the power of the Holy Spirit, who always rejuvenates his face through significant synodal processes. This common journey has been intensified since 1955 with the celebration of the First General Conference of the Latin American Episcopate in Rio de Janeiro and the creation of the Latin American Episcopal Council (CELAM), an organism of communion and coordination at the service of the bishops and episcopal conferences. Also noteworthy are the meetings of the General Conferences of the Episcopate: Medellin (1968), Puebla (1979), Santo Domingo (1992) and Aparecida (2007), in the Marian Shrine of Brazil, with the invitation to be disciples and missionaries of Jesus Christ, so that our peoples may have life in Him.

20. In 2019, Pope Francis proposed the preparation of a first Ecclesial Assembly of Latin America and the Caribbean, insisting that it would not be a meeting solely of bishops, but of all the holy and faithful People of God who walk, pray, speak, think, discuss and seek His will. The celebration of this Assembly in 2021 was received with great joy. This unprecedented experience, fruit of the outpouring of the Spirit, took place in the midst of the pandemic crisis and was, in times of suffering and death, the prophetic sign of a Church alive and close to her people, to sow hope and build the future. It is a true milestone that unites the participation of many members of the People of God with the exercise of the pastoral ministry of the Bishops and Episcopates. With all that has been shared, the text *Toward a Synodal Church Going Forth to the Peripheries. Reflections and Pastoral Proposals from the First Ecclesial Assembly of Latin America and the Caribbean* was elaborated.

21. In addition, other synodal processes of different dimensions and scope have taken place that teach us to walk together: the renewal and restructuring of CELAM with a more synodal style; the Assembly of the Synod for the Amazon Region; the creation of the Ecclesial Conference of the Amazon – CEAMA; and the creation of several ecclesial networks:

Pan-Amazonian Ecclesial Network – REPAM; Mesoamerican Ecological Ecclesial Network – REMAM; Ecclesial Network of the Gran Chaco and the Guarani Aquifer – REDCHAG. These networks pay special attention to the inculturation of the Gospel and the Church, to the specific problems of indigenous and Afro-American communities, to the values of interculturality and to the care of the common home.

22. In the context of these ecclesial processes and in the midst of the complex realities of our countries and our region, the Churches of Latin America and the Caribbean received the convocation of Pope Francis to the Synod on the Synodal Church. We wanted to integrate this new process into the regional experience and at the same time contribute to the synodality of the whole Church from recent history, knowing that the Spirit weaves harmony. The People of God are experiencing the call to be active subjects of the Church. In the Assembly of the Region of Central America and Mexico (CAMEX), a lay person expressed: '*This is already a synod*'. All these processes have been interwoven and have generated rich contributions of experiences, concerns and proposals.

23. The Synod Secretariat has formulated the main question that will guide the journey in the following way '*How is this "journeying together" that enables the Church to proclaim the Gospel in accordance with the mission entrusted to her being carried out today at different levels (from the local to the universal)? What steps does the Spirit invite us to take to grow as a synodal Church?*' (Preparatory Document 2, 26, Document for the Continental Stage 2, 105). During the regional meeting people were invited to respond to the question: '*What do we mean when we say "synodal church"*'? These great questions invite us to deepen a theological, pastoral and spiritual reflection that helps us to live ecclesiality, synodality, ministeriality and collegiality.

24. Here we summarise the main contributions of the itinerary carried out during the continental phase in Latin America and the Caribbean around eight main themes. They include and refer to other important questions for the spirit and practice of synodality, bringing together concerns, tensions and priorities. Each will be considered from the perspective of synodality.

1. The Protagonism of the Spirit in a Synodal Church.
2. The Synodality of the People of God.
3. Synodality: The Way of Being and Doing in the Church.
4. The Synodal Missionary Church.

5. Synodality: Socio-ecological Commitment in a Fragmented World.
6. Synodal Conversion and Restructuring Reform.
7. Vocations, Charisms and Ministries from a Synodal Perspective.
8. Contributions of the Latin American and Caribbean Synodal Itinerary.

I
THE PROTAGONISM OF THE SPIRIT IN A SYNODAL CHURCH

25. The Church is seen as '*a people made one in the unity of the Father, Son and Holy Spirit*' (LG 4). The journey we have been on has allowed us to see how God is truly leading the Churches of Latin America and the Caribbean towards an increasingly synodal way of being. This is inherent to the Church, but it is becoming increasingly important in the face of the challenges that changes in society pose to its life of communion and mission. This implies an awareness of the experience of our smallness and fragility, intensified by the pandemic crisis. It is necessary to 'trust and affirm that the Holy Spirit is the protagonist of this process and that he illuminates the changes that can take place in the Church of Jesus' (CAMEX).

26. At Pentecost the Spirit is at the origin of the Church and is the constant source of its vitality. It is He who moves it to flow and to go through history with relevance and meaning, and who leads it along paths of renewal and into the future. He shapes the face of the Church and the relational fabric that makes unity in diversity possible. Without him, there is no authentic following of Jesus, no new life, no ecclesial kairos. The Spirit encourages his Church to an authentic conversion that requires listening, dialogue, discernment, a refined attention to reality and the ability to understand the cry of God in the constant cries that resound in history. '*This is the moment to recognise the kairos in which we live, with trust in the Spirit and the certainty that everything is God's work*' (Cono Sur).

27. The experience of knowing that we are inhabited by the Spirit has taken us beyond our own analysis and reflections, inviting us to overcome the temptation of intimism, fundamentalisms and ideologies that make us pretend to want God when they are the pursuit of particular interests. He asked us to place ourselves in the context and to root the ecclesial journey in the depths of history, until we allow ourselves to be permeated by reality, recognising that in it, God manifests himself and acts, calling us to commitment, to work with Him, passionate for His Kingdom. We have understood the synodal journey *'as a personal and communitarian process of radical openness to the action of the Holy Spirit, who alone is capable of creating a new Pentecost in the Church and overcoming the constant temptation to fragment ourselves'* (Bolivariana).

28. The action of the Spirit, like everything in the dynamism of the Kingdom of God, needs to be discerned, its voice heard and welcomed, listening to *'what the Spirit says to the churches'* (Rev 2:11). His promptings require the docility of our hearts. Hence the need for a constant attitude of discernment, seeking not to do our own will but, like Jesus, to do the will of the Father of Mercy. This creates a great tension when we live in a time in which individuality and voluntarism have been so exalted and the 'I' has been made the measure of all things. When we are tempted to impose on others our own intentions and ideologies, which are partial visions of reality. To discern is to distinguish, among so many voices and movements, what comes from the Spirit, what the Lord tells us and expects of us. This is what we have been doing in this process, trying to overcome our own temptations. This discernment must become ever more communitarian, like the experience of faith itself, and attentive to the *'sensus fidei'* of the People of God on the journey.

29. We are summoned to a profound reform of the Church, that which arises from God's action in the heart of history. *'Behold, I am doing a new thing; now it springs forth, do you not perceive it? I will make a way in the wilderness and rivers in the desert'* (Isaiah 43:19 RSV). We are called to live a conversion that has its origin in faithful listening to God and to reality, a listening that is the condition for the transformation of the heart. We must listen to one another and discern the signs of the times to seek together the Will of God in the light of Sacred Scripture.

30. During this Synodal journey, we have felt the call to listen to the melody of the present, convinced that the quality of listening determines the quality of the response and opens up ways of missionary commitment. We note, that today more than ever, the Church is committed to a new style of relationship, one more contextualised, incarnated in reality, capable of listening and of making the different voices resonate and of positioning itself to generate the necessary dialogue that favors encounter. We feel called to generate an authentic dynamic of listening, participation, communion, shared mission and co-responsibility.

31. In those who have participated in the synodal process, one fruit of the Spirit is the renewal of their hope and the humble and confident recognition of how the synodal conversion is being led by the Spirit. We have moved from an attitude centred on the synodal assembly and the final document as the desired response, to a recognition of the need for patience, perseverance, determination, creative courage and boldness, virtues linked to hope. We have moved on to the conviction that synodal conversion begins on the stage of our own daily lives and from there, like leaven in the dough, projects itself towards the transformation of the whole world. *'In the synodal journey we must not run, we must follow the rhythm of the Spirit so that the experience allows us to give time to each moment'* (CAMEX). *'The synodal journey is an invitation to be farmers of faith; this requires us to learn new verbs: to wait without despairing, to water what is necessary for each type of plant, to persevere without tiring, certain that we are being led by the Spirit'* (Bolivariana).

32. The People of God walked in the hope of the Saviour's coming. Today they walk in the joyful hope of his return, which encourages our service to the kingdom and longs for the fullness of life for all.

II
THE SYNODALITY OF THE PEOPLE OF GOD

33. Voices heard in the four regional assemblies remind us that synodal renewal implies *'recovering the conciliar proposal expressed in the concept of the People of God, which emphasises equality and common dignity before differences of ministries and charisms'* (Bolivariana).

34. The Church is the community of those who follow 'the way of the Lord' (Acts 18:25), the People of God on pilgrimage in the world. Synodality is the expression of the social and historical dimensions of the Church. It is rooted in the pilgrim state of the human person, who journeys through life in search of happiness. The People of God is called to walk with the whole human family as a sacrament of salvation and hope. Here is the twofold dimension of synodality, in that it expresses the common journey in the life of the Church and the accompaniment of the history of Peoples towards the fullness of the Kingdom of God.

35. In the common journey of the churches of Latin America and the Caribbean, we are developing a sense of 'we' through the experience and dynamics of old and new synodal processes. In this process, we give life to our conviction that the *path* along which *the People of God* walk together is the subject of Synodal communion. The assemblies have reaffirmed what the Second Vatican Council expressed about the common dignity and fundamental equality of all the baptised, women and men. The gift of faith and the sacrament of Baptism make us followers of Jesus and give us all, membership in the one People of God, from the least of the baptised to the Successor of Peter.

36. In our journey we feel and affirm that synodality helps us to be a more participatory and co-responsible Church. A synodal Church is challenged to promote the participation of all, according to the vocation of each one, with the authority given by Christ to the College of Bishops, presided over in charity by the Bishop of Rome. Participation is based on the fact that all the faithful are called and enabled to place the gifts they have received from the Holy Spirit at the service of others. The authority of the Pastors is a gift of the same Spirit from Christ, the Head, for the edification of the whole Body. In synodal communion, Bishops exercise their apostolic mission by accompanying and guiding their brothers and sisters to follow Jesus, the Way, the Truth and the Life.

37. Synodality expresses the condition of subject that belongs to the entire Church and everybody in the Church. We believers are brothers and sisters on the same journey, called to be active subjects by participating in the one priesthood of Christ. The Holy Spirit is the source of a great diversity of vocations, identities, talents, skills and ministries which enrich unity in communion. There is a constant challenge here for the synodal way of fostering diversity so that it does not become division, and of building unity so that it does not become homogeneity. The vast majority of the Christian faithful are lay men and women who receive the faith and learn to live the communion of love within their families and communities.

38. Synodal life bears witness to a Church made up of persons and communities who are free and diverse subjects, called to relate to one another fraternally in bonds of mutual respect and affection. Many voices questioned how we relate to one another in the Church, especially between pastors and lay people, and between women and men. In all the assemblies, we heard a deep cry that called out to be treated well, to

be respected as an equal, and to be valued in one's own identity and in one's specific contribution. The shared discernment shows that we still have a long way to go in relating to one another in a more evangelical, humanising and synodal way. '*We need a structural change that uninstalls us. It requires flexibility, dialogue, tolerance, acceptance and respect. Not putting new wine in old wineskins*' (Caribbean).

39. One of the challenges is to open up spaces, provide means and create ways for the effective participation of women in the discernment and decision-making processes. The Synodal Assembly of October should deepen these themes: the leadership of women and their contribution in theological reflection, in pastoral councils, in the accompaniment of communities, in the areas of elaboration and decision-making. '*The participation of women is a prophecy; it is a factor of hope*' (Cono Sur).

40. Synodality is founded and expressed in the celebration of Baptism and the Eucharist, the source and summit of Christian life. In the Eucharistic assembly the baptismal communion is actualised and a dynamic of participation is generated. There is a tension between different ways of appreciating and living these sacraments. There are those who point to '*a tension between a ritual liturgy and an open and inculturated liturgy*' (Cono Sur). '*It is necessary to construct new languages and liturgical expressions that keep the Eucharist as the source and summit of the journey together*' (Bolivariana).

41. Synodality encourages the ecumenical commitment of all Christians because it is an invitation to walk together toward full unity in Christ. Without minimising differences, synodality opens us to recognise legitimate differences in a mutual exchange of gifts and guides our steps toward '*reconciled harmony*'. At the same time, a synodal Church desires to continue to promote interreligious dialogue and universal fraternity on all continents.

42. The Church expresses her authentic catholicity and shows the beauty of this plural face in the different peoples who experience the gift of God according to their own culture '*to advance in the formation of Churches with their own face and to respond to the specific challenges of their context, the Amazon region feels the need for greater autonomy and diversification of the local Churches, as well as of their representative bodies, such as the Episcopal Conferences*' (Ceama – Repam).

III
SYNODALITY: THE WAY OF BEING AND DOING IN THE CHURCH

43. Synodality is the dynamic dimension of ecclesial communion, called to incarnate a way of being and acting founded on union with the Holy Trinity, animated by the Spirit, and centred in Jesus Christ. The encounter with the person of the Lord is the fundamental criterion of all discernment and what sustains the evangelising mission of the Church. We are convinced that *'the great horizon is the discernment of a new way of being Church, starting from the encounter with Christ as a path to communion, participation, and mission, with a clear pastoral conversion that reflects the desire to live in synodality in all its areas, until synodality becomes a way of life* [...]' (Bolivariana).

44. Missionary disciples find their source of life and inspiration in the celebration of the Eucharist and in the personal and communal prayerful reading of the Word of God, which allows them to live in a continuous process of pastoral conversion, to strengthen the sense of belonging to the ecclesial community and to enliven a co-responsible participation in the synodal journey.

45. The missionary Church of disciples, attentive to the signs of the times, feels invited to cultivate an incarnated and Marian synodal spirituality because *'Mary reminds us that Christ is the centre of our life and model of the synodal journey'* (Bolivariana). It rescues the richness of faith and popular piety *'to strengthen the inner experience of our people as a complement to the liturgical life'* (Bolivariana), which should be inculturated, and should express the *'wisdom, joy and teachings of our peoples [...] They contribute, celebrate, listen, welcome, accompany, give and receive in the various dimensions of existence'* (Afro-Garifuna Contribution).

46. The synodal way of being and acting in the Church requires a style of communal discernment based on mutual listening to the Spirit and on truthful and trusting dialogue. It is *'the Spirit who impels us to this openness, to this search for the newness of God, with all the risks that this entails'* (Caribbean). We must *'overcome our fears in the face of listening, knowing that it obliges us to act and to respond to the brother who has been listened to'* (Cono Sur).

47. For this discerning listening, the Church must consider and practice Spiritual Conversation. As a method and practice, it helps to learn to listen, to dialogue, to be formed in itineraries, dynamics and processes that support personal, ecclesial and structural conversion. In the light of this style, the necessary reciprocity is generated, which leads us to the complementarity of the vocation and gifts of each one. The dynamic will be '*to learn to listen, to listen to each other and above all to listen to each other deeply, because when we listen to the other person with depth (full attention) it touches, stirs our being and requires us to transform attitudes, change ways of relating and move on to dialogue*' (Indigenous Peoples contribution). This way of being helps to recreate bonds and invites us to have a new way of relating, open to the action of the Spirit, who always surprises and opens new paths. Synodality supposes a '*spirituality that consists in loving and listening, with responsibility, with commitment and without fear*' (Cono Sur); it moves us to embrace the '*path of forgiveness and reconciliation, recognising our faults and omissions, to rebuild from our own vulnerability, the synodal Church*' (CAMEX-Sur).

48. Reflecting on the Spiritual Conversation Method, which is particularly suited to this time, intuitions, tensions and priorities emerge that can help in this process. Spiritual Conversation allows us to speak freely about uncomfortable and painful topics in a horizontal relational experience. Far from canceling one's own identity and life story, it helps to put oneself in the other person's place, to tune into his or her feelings, and from there to refine one's own convictions. This experience is a formative journey: open to learning, to the combination of feelings and ideas, which leads to changes, makes possible improbable encounters, favors dialogue and creates channels of communication.

49. The animation and action of the Spirit is perceived throughout the process. It is necessary to live this experience from an inner freedom and with an open heart, avoiding polemics, imposing ideas, 'agendas' and everything that prevents the Holy Spirit from being the protagonist.

50. The method is like an ascending spiral cycle that goes from the 'I' (1st moment – feelings: personal) to letting myself be touched by the other, the 'you' (2nd moment – echoes: relational), to finally arrive at the 'we' (3rd moment – choosing the will of God: the common). The method should not be the sum of individual discernment, but the means and expression of a communitarian process.

51. It is important to seek how to integrate the hermeneutic method of 'See – Judge – Act', adopted by the Church in Latin America and the Caribbean, with the process of Spiritual Conversation, in such a way that a profound analysis of reality, linked to discernment, is maintained and that it always leads to the search for consensus in to achieve a transforming action. Certainly, there are already advances in our region that come from the experience of the continental synodal work: combining seeing with listening, contemplating; judging with discerning, interpreting; and acting with projecting, responding.

52. To facilitate the process of synodal discernment its times and steps, in fidelity to what is shared and to what the Spirit wants to say, it is considered important to train and introduce the moderators and secretaries of the groups. The moderator should be trained so that he/she can animate the process as such and not become a mere group of opinions; and the secretary should be trained so that he/she can help to elaborate a synthesis of the community and not remain a mere brainstorming.

IV
THE SYNODAL MISSIONARY CHURCH

53. A synodal Church, according to the motto of the Synod, is a Church in communion and participation – '*the Church that is synodal has the challenge and the mission to be missionary*' (Caribbean). Therefore, '*structures are urgently needed to ensure a missionary synodality that includes all the members of the periphery*' (CAMEX). Rather than closing the Church in on itself, synodality leads to a missionary Church at the service of the universal fraternity. Like synodality, missionary is constitutive of the Church, because every baptised person is a missionary disciple of Jesus Christ in his Church. Discipleship is the following of Jesus, a journey with him to collaborate in his work and to extend it in history. In turn, the work of Jesus is to evangelise, and therefore this is also the mission of the Church. As Paul VI said, 'the Church exists to evangelise' (EN 14). What is needed is a '*revision of the structures and of the ecclesial institution as a whole, in the function of service and evangelisation*' (Cono Sur).

54. Jesus, in his person, his life, his work and his Passover, makes present the Kingdom of God. The Kingdom is an absolute to which everything becomes relative. The evangelising mission of the Church is none other

than to give continuity to the mission of Jesus and to contribute to the growth of the Kingdom in the world, especially in the peripheries, which must be its centre. It is necessary *'to take the Good News to the peripheries, recognising that there it is incarnated and is life, that it is lived and builds synodality'* (Bolivariana).

55. The mission, from the Synodal perspective, is not proselytism. This leads to a self-referential Church that eclipses the Kingdom of God of which it is a sacrament. It is necessary *'to be a credible Church, the sacrament of the Kingdom'* (Caribbean). The mission consists of the joyful and gratuitous proclamation of Jesus Christ and his paschal mystery to all humanity, in an intercultural relationship, since it is situated in a plural and diverse world. It is pointed out that *'the clearest horizon that opens up is the challenge of evangelisation in diversity. How to be missionary disciples amid the diversity of contexts, situations and the complexity of the world'* (Caribbean). It is urgent to *'attend to the subjects of evangelisation, respecting their culture, inviting them to participate, approaching their way of life and understanding their vision of the world'* (Southern Cone). The mission consists in incarnating the Gospel in the cultures, contributing to the formation of autochthonous local Churches with the face of the peoples that integrate them. An incarnated Church corresponds to an inculturation of the evangelisation of the Church as an institution, in its organisation and structures.

56. Synodality helps all the baptised to be active subjects of the evangelising mission and helps the People of God to journey with a humanity that is all on a pilgrimage, in an attitude of dialogue and service to the world, in view of a universal fraternity. It is pointed out that: *'the world needs the Church to go forth, a Church that rejects division, which turns its gaze to humanity and offers it, more than a doctrine or a strategy, an experience of salvation, an 'overflowing gift' which responds to the cry of humanity and nature'* (CAMEX). In the evangelising mission, others are not only recipients but also interlocutors, because the missionary disciples are placed in a horizontal relationship of communion with all people of goodwill in whom the Spirit of God is at work. Synodality leads to open missionary activity, to participation and exchange without limits.

57. However, the evangelising identity of the Church does not always seem to be present in all communities, because sometimes they are more concerned with solving their internal problems than with proclaiming the Good News. There is a tension *'between a self-centreed Church and a* *missionary Church*' (Cono Sur). This can lead to the temptation '*to believe that we must first solve the problems of synodality and then go out into mission*' (Caribbean). Synodality and mission are two closely related aspects, because synodality enriches mission and mission animates synodality.

58. In the regional assemblies it was mentioned that the ecclesial tendency to focus on itself can be the result of '*fear and doubt about how to go out into daily life and life with the people*' (Bolivia). There is also '*the fear of losing power and the desire to control, which leads to intolerance and rigidity, preventing the taking of concrete and courageous steps to fulfill the evangelising mission of leading people to their encounter with God*' (Caribbean). This creates a strong tension between a pastoral of mere preservation, which secures the spaces and times of community, and a Church that not only enlarges its tent to welcome, but also goes out to meet others where they are.

59. In this sense, a question arises that gives rise to various accents: to what extent and in what way should the Gospel penetrate cultures? It is a challenge to discern how to carry out the task of evangelisation in the present context of diversity, multiculturalism and interculturalism, in order to learn to live the faith in great diversity. '*This inculturation must also influence the construction of liturgical spaces to make them more adequate to the theology of synodality*' (Cono Sur).

60. Evangelisation takes place through the witness of personal and community life. Faith grows through the attraction of God's grace, values individuals and peoples as subjects, and recognises the evangelising heritage of indigenous and Afro-descendant peoples who live the faith in their own way. Another '*challenge for the Church in its evangelising mission is sectarianism*' (Cono Sur), understood as the division and internal struggles of sectors closed in on themselves, which is an anti-witness.

61. We are also called to '*move from an evangelisation centreed on sin to a perspective of the Good News, like the doctor who, instead of focusing on the illness, focuses his work on health; (in this way) we can move from lamenting to being concerned with what we can do*' (Bolivariana). On the other hand, it is necessary to always remember what the purpose of the evangelising mission is, because sometimes it is reduced to one of its processes, such as the administration of the sacraments, instead of promoting a true encounter with Christ that initiates and strengthens a path of following and growing in faith.

62. The meetings highlighted the role of the lay faithful, especially women, in the transmission of the faith. Catechists and evangelisers who work with passion and hope in distant places and difficult contexts are a gift from God for which we are grateful and cherish. However, it was also mentioned that sometimes there is a perceived tension with the clergy who assume the responsibility of directing all evangelising action in the community. *'The support, proclamation and witness of missionary women must be valued. And this is fundamental in a synodal Church'* (Bolivariana).

V
SYNODALITY: SOCIO-ENVIRONMENTAL COMMITMENT IN A FRAGMENTED WORLD.

63. Synodality motivates the Church to go out from herself and to place herself, with all her mission, at the service of society. As the syntheses show, there are synodal experiences of a Church that accompanies the peoples of Latin America and the Caribbean on their journey. Several contributions affirm that in many societies of our region, there is great ethnic, cultural, and social diversity. This is a richness, but it can also be perceived as a threat. It manifests itself in multiple fragmentations, in great inequalities, in marginalisation and exclusion of different groups in the continent. Our societies also suffer from strong ideological and political polarisation; in several countries, we are concerned about the weakening of democracy as a system of representation and government. In these contexts, a synodal Church is called to renew its preferential option for the poor and to emphasise the social dimension of evangelisation, because *'if it is not properly explained, there is always the risk of distorting the authentic and integral meaning of the evangelising mission'* (EG 176).

64. During the meetings, attention was drawn to what is observed in many places: *'the distance of the local Churches from the reality, from the cries coming from the lands and peoples, from the diverse realities of people in vulnerability, from the peripheries'* (Southern Cone), be they geographical, territorial, social or existential peripheries. The poor have many faces: faces of women, of indigenous and Afro-descendant peoples, of people

in vulnerable situations such as migrants and refugees, of people with disabilities, of children and the elderly, and many others.

65. A synodal Church is called to be '*a more prophetic and Samaritan Church. A prophetic and missionary Church that truly goes to the geographical and existential peripheries and listens to the cry of the poor and of creation' (Bolivariana).* It is important that in the synodal process, we dare to bring up and discern great themes that are often forgotten or pushed aside, and to meet the other and all those who are part of the human family and are often marginalised, even in our Church. Several appeals remind us that, in the spirit of Jesus, we must '*include the poor, LGBTQI+ communities, couples in a second union, priests who want to return to the Church in their new situction, women who have abortions out of fear, prisoners, the sick*' (Cono Sur). It is about '*walking together in a synodal Church that listens to all kinds of exiles, so that they feel at home*', a Church that is '*a refuge for the wounded and the broken*' (Cono Sur). This requires availability to '*go out to meet, to give our attention, to commit ourselves. Because synodality is not waiting for people to come, but going out to meet them*' (Cono Sur).

66. The Church offers her Samaritan love and service in solidarity, learning to walk with those who also serve the suffering, seeking alternatives to the throwaway culture, and confronting the various forms of violence that have increased in recent years. These include the violence associated with social inequalities, drug trafficking, organised crime, human trafficking, and the abuse of women and children. In this journey together, the Church discovers different ways of being synodal in alliances with social and popular movements and other people and institutions committed to the promotion of all, such as the Global Education Pact.

67. Some contributions ask: '*Listening to the cry of the peoples and the earth is a commitment to the Gospel, which calls us to be allies of the peoples in the defense of life and their territories*' (Cono Sur). This is especially true for the Amazon, which is threatened by ecological collapse, with catastrophic consequences for the life of the earth and its peoples. There is a feeling from the Amazon that points to '*the abandonment of our indigenous peoples; the lack of a real presence among the Amazonian peoples*' (Bolivariana). There is '*a pending matter: to reach the original peoples, marginalised by their different language, culture, and cosmic vision; and [...] to reach the [other] peripheries, to approach and welcome those in need, those with different beliefs and customs*' (Cono Sur).

68. The socio-environmental service that the Church is called to serve in the light of the Gospel and the Social Doctrine of the Church is strengthened in an ecumenical and interreligious dialogue that leads to common action. In many countries of Latin America and the Caribbean, there are Interreligious Councils in which representatives of various Christian Churches and multiple religions present in our region actively participate. They jointly carry out activities in favor of society from a shared commitment to the promotion of human rights, justice, peace, and the care of the common home.

69. Several contributions express that a synodal Church lived as a field hospital, must give a central place to young people. To be close to them, to heal their wounds, and to accompany them in their search, the Church must '*adapt its language, its symbols, to their concrete reality. We must think of new ways to attract and rescue the presence of young people in the Church, going where they are and walking with them. It is important that 'they, and we too, become aware of the leading role they have to assume in the Church and society*' (Cono Sur).

70. The request for listening, integration, and participation in decision-making on the part of young people is reiterated. The prayer that a group of them made at the Southern Cone meeting resounds, expressing why their friends had left the Church and concluding with a heartfelt prayer: '*God, Mother, and Father, hear our cry in prayer! Blow strongly so that the Church does not forget the young people, that it may embrace their lives as they come, with their dreams and desires, and accompany them in the task of spreading and promoting synodality.*'

71. Many young people show great sensitivity to social and environmental problems, with great creativity in generating solutions from their spaces. As '*digital natives*,' they have much more knowledge and skills to help the Church discover the digital potential for evangelisation, networking, and the creating a synodal culture in these spaces.

72. The participation of representatives of the Digital Synod in the Assemblies has generated interest in a more active and proactive presence in this area. The need to accompany the digital evangelisers more closely was also felt.

VI
SYNODAL CONVERSION AND RESTRUCTURING REFORM

73. The Second Vatican Council conceives the Church as an institution in need of permanent renewal. In continuity with the Council, Pope Francis refers to the Church as *Ecclesia semper reformanda*, which requires the conversion of the entire ecclesial community. The Latin American and Caribbean Church understand this call as a permanent pastoral conversion that requires the revision of *'personal and community practices, relationships of equality and authority, and structures and dynamics'* (SD 30). The regions consulted stated that *'synodality requires a personal, communitarian, ecclesial and structural conversion' (Southern Cone), and that 'a change of mentality, a change of structures'* (CAMEX) is urgently needed.

74. This call is not exempt from challenges and tensions. We find people and groups who want to separate the change of mentality and personal conversion from the reform of structures, just as there are those who do not want the reform of the Church. Therefore, these changes must be part of a process of *'active conversion, for a true transformation of mind and heart, since we have all been formed in different times and have many ingrained practices'* (Cono Sur). From this follows the need for the local Churches to create processes and spaces for listening, dialogue and discernment that deepen the fundamental question of the synodal journey: *'How is this journey together being lived today in our own particular Church? What steps does the Spirit invite us to take?'*

75. The response to these questions involves the whole People of God. It is necessary to take the step towards an authentic Synodalisation of the whole Church, which will entail *'spiritual, pastoral and institutional reforms'* (DA 367) to form a new institutional model. The regional consultations recognise that to achieve this, *'new pastoral options must emerge from a change of mentality and a renewal of existing structures'* (Caribbean). In this context, the challenge of reforming seminaries and houses of formation arises, especially when some institutions have not outgrown their Tridentine form. Many see *'seminaries as closed houses that do not contribute to the vision of a ministerial priesthood'* (CAMEX). It is necessary to continue with the updated reform of the *Ratio fundamentalis institutionis sacerdotalis*. Families, laity and consecrated men and women must be involved in the formation of candidates for the priesthood. This was emphasised by all the Regional Assemblies.

76. The whole process of renewal towards greater synodality in the Church requires more formation. It was asked that the itineraries of formation and catechesis should be integral and shared by the members of the People of God. It was emphasised that families, as domestic Churches, and parish and educational ecclesial communities should be the first sphere of formation in synodal communion. At the same time, it was asked that parishes be renewed according to the model of a community of communities, thus revitalising small communities.

77. Various horizons and areas emerge among the numerous proposals and requests for formation expressed in the assemblies. As an outstanding theme: '*we believe in the importance of synodal formation and therefore we would like to contribute some ideas for an integral formation: learning to work collaboratively; growing in a culture of discernment; implementation of transparency in the various areas of ecclesial life; acquisition of digital and radio skills to be permanently connected with the needs of the parish; showing experiential experiences to make visible the relevance of synodality*' (Bolivariana).

78. A transversal axis in all ecclesial areas is the formation of a culture of respect for all persons and the prevention of any kind of abuse.

79. The regional consultations mention that there is a need to prioritise the obligation to form the various councils promoted by the Second Vatican Council: Presbyterian councils, economic councils (diocesan and parochial), and pastoral councils (diocesan and parochial). They also ask that '*they be a space of inclusion, dialogue, transparency, and discernment, not only at the national and regional levels but also in the basic communities, parishes and dioceses, prelatures and vicariates, following the process of communion and participation*' (Cono Sur). It is recognised that the Councils are '*permanent environments for the exercise and promotion of communion and synodality*' (ITC, Synodality, 80) but that their formal implementation is not enough. It is asked that each Council '*not only be a consultative space but that we ensure that it weights decisions about the mode of government and changes in structures*' (CAMEX).

80. A Church structured on the basis of a network of councils would make it possible to establish institutional procedures of accountability and transparency, starting from the communities, that would help to eradicate abuses of conscience, power, spiritual, psychological, sexual, and economic abuse. This requires the creation of institutions and protocols for prevention, reparation, and justice (cf. AE 355). This would respond to voices that see *'a tension between the desire for a more transparent Church and a culture of secrecy'* (Cono Sur) and that call for a greater *'commitment to care for and listen to victims of abuse'* (CAMEX). These and other aspects will require *'openness to possible changes in canon law that give juridical form to synodal practice; in particular, that synodal institutions be recognised by law and that the law help to guarantee and promote greater transparency'* (Cono Sur).

81. The Synod challenges ecclesial reconfigurations and invites us to imagine new structures. Some have already emerged, such as the Ecclesial Conference for the Amazon (CEAMA) and the first Ecclesial Assembly of Latin America and the Caribbean. However, the concern has arisen to see how to articulate episcopal collegiality and synodal ecclesial, which invites us to reflect on how to integrate elaboration and decision-making, because *'the synodal dimension of the Church must be expressed through the realisation and management of processes of participation and discernment capable of manifesting the dynamism of communion that inspires all ecclesial decisions'* (ITC, Synodality 76). In the same way, these new structures confront us with forms of organisation and functioning that must know how to articulate the sense of the faith of all the faithful, episcopal authority, and the service of theology, because the Holy Spirit speaks through the whole People of God and not only through some (the bishops) or one (the Bishop of Rome, who has the primacy). *'If the People of God were not a subject of decision-making, there would be no synodality. If the People of God does not constitute an organism which makes decisions for the whole Church, this organism is not synodal'* (CEAMA-REPAM). In all that has been said, it is understood that it is necessary to *'renew and rethink the structures of the Church to respond to the challenges of today's world, interpreting the signs of the times [and] one step towards this is the reform of the Code of Canon Law'* (Bolivariana).

VII
VOCATIONS, CHARISMS AND MINISTRIES FROM A SYNODAL PERSPECTIVE

82. *'Synodality is the art of valuing, welcoming and knowing how to articulate all the gifts and charisms that the Lord has given us so that they flow and become a channel of grace and blessing; therefore, it is important to value the different vocations'* (Bolivariana). The Church is a prophetic people, priestly and royal service where all its members are subjects of the theological life towards holiness. They receive from God diverse charisms to serve the common good (Cf. AE 171).

83. The richness of the diversity of charisms and ministries was repeatedly mentioned in the regional meetings. It is expressed both in the gifts that enrich the consecrated life and in the very diverse gifts of the various lay faithful. It is, therefore, necessary *'to review the structure of the Church so that it may be a community of communities, recognising the unity in mission with the diversity of ministries which the Holy Spirit gives through gifts to each of its members according to his vocation, so that the charismatic dimension is not opposed to the institutional dimension'* (Bolivariana).

84. However, a 'ministerial Church' is not necessarily a 'ministerial instituted Church.' Legitimately there are many ministries that spring from the baptismal vocation, including spontaneous and other recognised ministries, which are not instituted and others that are instituted with their training, mission and stability. Some indigenous peoples even pointed out that they have their own ministries, which are already being lived, but are not recognised by the ecclesial institution.

85. A profound communal discernment is needed as to what ministries, especially among the laity, need to be created or promoted in the light of the signs of the times. These ministries should not only respond to the internal needs of the Church but also be *'a response and service to the world'* (CAMEX), since *'the mission of Christians is above all in the world'* (CEAMA-REPAM). Here we hear the voice of Pope Francis who, in the exhortation, *Querida Amazonia*, speaks of *'a markedly lay ecclesial culture'* (QA 94). We must value and promote *'the service of the laity in the building of the world, in the economy, in politics, in the sciences, in the arts, etc.'* as an essential dimension so that *'the Church may be a prophetic, priestly and kingly people'* (Caribbean, CEAMA-REPAM).

86. A central issue is to promote the participation of the laity, especially women and young people, in decision-making scenarios. There is a majority presence of women because *'they are the ones who support the Church the most'* (CAMEX), but on the other hand, they are the ones who *'must be open to inclusion and participation in decision-making spaces'* (Cono Sur). Some contributions point out that these spaces already exist in some of our local churches, but others have *'the feeling that women are 'cheap labor' within the Church'* (Cono Sur) and it is *'necessary to create and institute new ministries, especially for women'* (CEAMA-REPAM). Many voices consider urgent the institution of the diaconate for women, recognising what is lived in several communities.

87. The priestly ministry has undergone a profound process of renewal since the Second Vatican Council. Nevertheless, the denunciation of clericalism, understood as an expression of clerical authoritarianism, as a deformation of the ministry in the abuse of power, continues to be heard. This does not only concern the ordained priesthood but is also a temptation for all the ministers of the Church including the laity. *'We see the need to think of a conversion within the Church that overcomes the clericalism and machismo that exclude women from the processes of discernment and decision-making, and this is something cultural that we must face, even if we have to go against the current. Fraternity and sisterhood are what must be cultivated'* (Cono Sur, CEAMA-REPAM).

88. For this reason, it is important *'to take steps to overcome clericalism in the laity and the clergy, starting our mission from the principle of subsidiarity as a synodal way of proceeding'* (Bolivariana). The Church is more synodal when she walks with all the baptised and encourages them to live the mission, recognising the common dignity as the basis for the renewal of ecclesial life and with ministries in which authority is service. *'Authority as service builds interdependence (neither dependence nor independence) from the common vocation of discipleship'* (Bolivariana).

89. The revaluation of baptismal life and dignity, as the primary source of all ministries, demands a new institutional model that counteracts the pyramidal model that facilitates clericalism. Synodality offers the appropriate interpretative framework for thinking about the renewal of the ordained ministry, which supposes, among other things, *'discerning the ministeriality of the entire People of God in co-responsibility'* and living *'ministeriality as a covenant with the poor'* (Cono Sur).

90. This also implies a rethinking of the model of ordained ministry. There are those who say that in their communities there is a '*conflict between the common priesthood and the ministerial priesthood*', as well as '*forms of priesthood that do not respond to the needs of the People of God*' (CAMEX), '*we do not know how to articulate lay and ordained ministry*' (Caribbean). Thus, if we want a more synodal and missionary Church, '*it is necessary to rethink the profile of ministries, especially of ordained ministers, so that they exercise their ministry "in" the community and not "on" it*', with a formation '*in close relationship with the pastoral processes and the life of the people they will serve*' (CEAMA-REPAM).

91. In this area of ordained ministry, several voices have stated that '*we need an open and sincere dialogue on whether the question of celibacy and its relationship to priestly ministry is still useful*' (Caribbean). In addition, the possibility of ordaining permanent deacons to the priesthood has been positively considered, and some have raised '*the ministry and inclusion of married priests and members of consecrated life who have left their institutes*' (Cono Sur).

92. Hence, it is requested that the General Assembly in October address this theme and promote the revision of the theology and forms of a ministerial church, the formation and profile of ministers, both instituted and ordained, and the opening of some ministries to women

93. The consecrated life present in the Regional Assemblies is aware of the action of the Spirit and feels a strong call to walk in communion with the Church, which is a community of equal disciples, baptised, sharing ministries, vocations, and charisms for the building up of the Kingdom of God. It is born and grows in the Church and is called to bear evangelical fruits in the living communion of the faithful People of God, for which reason it longs '*to continue to nourish the experience of synodality and to be a motor for its animation in the various contexts and local communities of belonging, in which it is constitutively called to be a prophetic synodal presence expressed in community meetings, chapters, assemblies, pastoral services, etc.*' (Caribbean). Consecrated men and women are committed to living as a Church that goes forth and is centreed on the Gospel, and therefore – poorer, missionary, rooted in the contexts, pneumatocentric, and in constant dialogue with reality.

94. Synodality and consecrated life are interlinked in the journey of conversion, listening, and mission, with the criteria of participation and

co-responsibility, which also define the identity and nature of the Church itself. The hierarchical and charismatic gifts go together to *'unlearn and eradicate all attitudes of dependence, submission, and silence in communities, Churches and society; and to eliminate the clericalism introduced in the way we relate to other members of the Church. For this reason, we try to rescue and value the synodal experiences that have been lived for a long time in some Churches of Latin America, to apply them in a renewed way in our here and now'* (Bolivariana).

VIII
CONTRIBUTIONS OF THE LATIN AMERICAN AND CARIBBEAN SYNODAL ITINERARY

95. In the narrative of the regional assemblies and in the introduction to this synthesis, we point out the peculiarities of the synodal journey of the Latin American and Caribbean Church. In the development of the seven previous themes, we have gathered the main contributions of the assemblies and syntheses for the Instrumentum laboris. Now, as a projective recapitulation, we raise four central questions.

96. (I) Both the text of our first ecclesial assembly and the document for the continental phase promote a missionary synodal church. The first question concerns the mutual relationships between ecclesiality, synodality, ministeriality and collegiality. Throughout the Assembly process, we have felt the mutual fruitfulness and positive tension between synodal ecclesiality and episcopal collegiality. The recent journey of the People of God among us, the discernment of the voices and expressions of the *sensus fidei fidelium*, the responsible and co-responsible participation of all, provide the appropriate interpretive framework – theoretical and practical – for listening, dialogue and discernment together, starting from the common dignity received in the filial and fraternal grace of Baptism. Our experience shows that in this horizon of communion the exercise of the episcopal ministry is enriched as a pastoral service to the People of God. We are learning that the ministry of the bishops, if it is not situated in a synodal ecclesiality, can be impoverished because it does not receive the fruits of a broad exchange and because it feels threatened, as if synodality were a democratisation that challenges the hierarchical institution of the Church. In a process lived in synodality, the elaboration and decision-making of the competent authorities gain legitimacy and are more positively received by the community.

97. In this context, a question arises that should be analyzed in the next Synodal Assembly with spiritual discernment, theological depth and pastoral sense. It is about the mutual relationships between ecclesiality, synodality, ministeriality and collegiality. This can be deepened on the basis of the central role of the Spirit of God in the life and mission of the Church. The theology of the sacraments, especially Baptism and Holy Orders, the reciprocal relationships between the common priesthood and the ordained ministry, and the reforms to the ministries and structures of the Church, including the reform of the ministry of the Successor of Peter, can be analyzed from a synodal perspective.

98. (II) The emergence of a renewed synodal ecclesiality raises the challenge to imagine synodal reforms in ecclesial mentalities, attitudes, practices, relationships and structures. The novelties of the Ecclesial Conference for the Amazon and of the First Ecclesial Assembly of Latin America and the Caribbean show that it is not enough to create new institutions, but that they must be accompanied by an awareness and formation that help to articulate communion in new forms of communal participation, organic and dynamic. Without a spirituality of synodal communion it is not possible to realise the movements of the Spirit for the Church of the third millennium.

99. We need to assume in a synodal way the orientations of the Second Vatican Council for a permanent renewal of the Church in her fidelity to Jesus Christ and her evangelising mission to the peoples. The conciliar exhortation to be an *Ecclesia semper* reformanda (UR 4, 6), or an *Ecclesia semper purificanda* (LG 8), are a source of inspiration for the next Assembly to renew synodality as communion, participation and mission. In the new synodal context, the Latin American and Caribbean Church continues to receive that conciliar call as a path of pastoral and missionary conversion.

100. In this process, questions arise which are not new, but which take on a new relevance: What is the magisterial value of the results of the ecclesial assemblies? Would they not be more valid and acceptable if they were presented as guidelines and documents of the whole People of God in a region, since they are the fruit of listening, dialogue and shared discernment? What would happen if some decisions of an assembly were rejected by the episcopal authority? When, how and where should deliberative and consultative votes take place? Is it possible to dream of a synodal configuration of episcopal conferences and continental

structures such as CELAM? Certainly, spiritual discernment, theological foundation and canon law must be articulated here.

101. (III) Since the Second Vatican Council, based on the method of the Pastoral Constitution *Gaudium et Spes*, a great contribution of the Church of Latin America and the Caribbean has been the way of reflecting on the faith and orienting evangelisation, not only through the service of bishops and theologians, but also through the contributions of the synodal tradition of the People of God. The teaching of recent Popes directs us to learn from the *sensus fidei* of all the faithful, while at the same time upholding the ministry proper to those who teach the faith of the Church with apostolic authority. It seems to us that the Synod should take into account the admirable exchange between the Magisterium of the People of God, pastors and theologians.

102. The method of seeing – judging – acting has acquired citizenship in the Latin American and Caribbean Church, as expressed in the Aparecida Document (cf. DAp 19). It has been refined, and now it has been enriched with the method of Spiritual Conversation, at the same time that eliminate the former enriches the latter. In this context we speak of the circular and progressive process configured by the respective moments of seeing – listening – contemplating, judging – discerning – interpreting, and acting —responding – projecting.

103. The background of our hermeneutical method is the conviction that God communicates himself in history and has spoken fully through his Son Jesus Christ, that his Word is transmitted in the Sacred Scriptures received and handed down in the Tradition of the Church, and that God continues to speak through historical events especially through the signs that mark the present time. In the Magisterium of Latin America and the Caribbean, history, theology and pastoral care are mutually enriching.

104. The Synodal Assembly could deepen synodically the communitarian discernment in listening to the Spirit and the historical-pastoral hermeneutic in the light of the Gospel of Christ, at all levels and in all ecclesial subjects, in conformity with the conciliar teaching (cf. GS 11, 44).

105. (IV) The Church on pilgrimage in Latin America and the Caribbean is recognised as a Church of Churches and a community of communities.

In the Councils and Synods of the First Evangelisation and in the post-conciliar Conferences of our Episcopate, there have been valuable exchanges between local Churches, episcopal conferences and regional bodies, promoted by CELAM. In his teaching, Pope Francis speaks of local, regional and universal synodality, and at this moment we are going through a process that begins in the local Churches, is enriched in the national conferences, now takes on continental dimensions and is lived in the Assembly at the level of the whole Church. In his encyclicals, exhortations and speeches, Francis incorporates the local ecclesial experience and the teaching of the bishops' conferences, such as the document of Aparecida (cf. EG 25, 122).

106. The call to live and act in synodality urges us to redefine the mutual implications between the particular and the universal, the value of the ecclesial experience in the peripheries and its impact on the whole, the just and tense balance between local, national, regional and global priorities, and the challenge of opening ourselves to harmony, the work of the Spirit. The next assembly can focus on these questions: How to integrate the particular riches into the beauty of the whole? How to respect the rhythms and demands of those who walk more slowly? How can a predominantly vertical practice, in which particular Churches seem subordinate, be overcome by a true communion of churches in universal Catholicism?

107. The text of the Ecclesial Assembly teaches: '*From the beginning of our American ecclesial history the Mother of God sustains the hope of the people in the continent and is the great spiritual bond in all America*' (AE 224). Our believing people, spiritually and effectively Marian from its Guadalupan origins and in all its local expressions, feel and know that '*there is a Marian style in the evangelising activity of the Church. This dynamic of justice and tenderness, of contemplating and walking towards others, is what makes her an ecclesial model for evangelisation*' (EG 288). From the heart of faith and piety of our Church we ask the Virgin Mother to sustain us in the hope of the synodal journey because she is '*queen and mother of mercy, our life, our sweetness, and our hope.*'

MIDDLE EAST

'The Word Became Flesh and Pitched His Tent Among Us'

(Jn 1:14)

'AND THE WORD BECAME FLESH AND PITCHED HIS TENT AMONG US' (Jn 1:14): THE CONTINENTAL SYNODAL ASSEMBLY IN THE MIDDLE EAST

Souraya Bechealany and Mirna Abboud Mzawak

Introduction

The Catholic Churches in the Middle East held their Continental Synodal Assembly in Harissa, Lebanon, from 13 to 17 February 2023.[1] One hundred and twenty-five people gathered to pray, listen and discern together what the Spirit is saying to the Churches today in the Middle East. The Assembly did so under the guidance of the Word of God: 'And the Word became flesh and pitched his tent among us' (Jn 1:14). The official Report submitted to the Secretariat of the Synod in Rome enlightens the reader on the specificities and challenges of synodality as confessed and lived today by the churches in the Middle East. The present study takes on the task of describing the broader and immediate context in which this Assembly emanates. It describes the biblical, theological, spiritual, technical and organisational dimensions that contributed to its success.

Context

The Middle East is a rather diverse and multi-faith region, home to different religions, rites and ethnicities. Christian communities are an integral part of the region. Although the majority of the region's inhabitants are Muslims, these communities play an important role in the life of many societies and countries in the region, both in religious, social, cultural, educational and health terms.

Today, this region suffers from instability and faces a multitude of socio-economic, political and religious challenges which have a considerable impact on the populations, particularly Christians. This includes the wars in Syria and Iraq which have had devastating consequences for the local communities that have been displaced, persecuted or killed. There is a massive presence of refugees in certain countries such as Lebanon. It creates existential and economic problems for the country, as the number of refugees has reached almost half of the number of its original population. There are economic and

1 All information about the Synodal Assembly of the Middle East including its final report can be found at: https://beirut.synod2023.org/

financial crises, sometimes unprecedented in contemporary history, such as the ones currently being experienced in Lebanon, but also in Syria, where the populations in their various socio-economic and professional categories are no longer able to meet their primary and basic needs; where elections and political changes often do not respect the founding principles of democracy. Youth that are well educated in secondary schools and universities are leaving their countries in large numbers. As a result, the Churches are not only decreasing in number, they are also in danger of ageing. The youth no longer believe in a future in these countries. On top of it all there are disasters such as the explosion of 4 August, 2020, in Lebanon which killed hundreds of people and destroyed a large part of Beirut and its port, as well as the devastating earthquakes that took place in Turkey and Syria on February 6, 2023.

Churches in the Middle East are affected by this complex geopolitical and socio-economic context and face a multitude of challenges, including the migration and exodus of their sons and daughters. Yet they seek to keep their focus on their mission and search for the meaning of their presence in the Middle East as an ongoing dynamic, which is the raison d'être of their continental synodal assembly held in February 2023.

Nature of the Continental Assembly

The Patriarchal Churches come from a long tradition of synods. Each Patriarchal Church holds regular synods in which only the bishops and major superiors of the religious orders participate. Patriarchal assemblies meet in each country (Lebanon, Syria, Palestine, Holy Land, Iraq and Egypt). However, these assemblies have only a consultative role. Each Church remains free to implement the resolutions or not. Hence the great importance of the few assemblies that gather all Catholic Churches in the region. This goes in particular for the Middle East Council of Churches (MECC), which brings together all the Churches in the region: Orthodox, Catholic and Evangelical.

Holding continental gatherings is not foreign to the churches in the Middle East. The current continental Assembly occurred within n a longer tradition of gatherings that dates back to the 1990s. In fact, shortly after the meeting of the Continental Synodal Assembly in Beirut, the fourth Assembly was celebrated in Cyprus from 20 to 23 April, 2023. This tradition is mentioned in the Continental Document of the Middle East (CD/ME): 'All our Eastern Catholic Churches, with the exception of the Latin Church, were instituted according to a patriarchal and synodal structure (see *Orientalium Ecclesiarum*, 7-11)' (CD/ME[2], n.13). In fact, in 1991, Conseil des Patriarches Catholiques d'Orient (Council of Catholic

2 The acronym adopted in this article: CD/ME.

Patriarchs of the East - CPCO)[3] was born as a sign and instrument of patriarchal collegiality and communion between the Catholic Churches of the East within the universal Church. The Council enjoys moral authority personality and it respects all the rights and privileges of the Synods of Bishops of each Patriarchal Church as well as those of the Assemblies of the Hierarchs in each country. The goals are

- 'receive' the Second Vatican Council (this is the primary goal);
- reflect together on the situation of Catholics in the East in order to promote Christian life;
- coordinate the pastoral activity of the Catholic Churches of the East;
- give the Catholic Churches of the East the possibility of expressing their point of view and of studying the questions that concern their faithful and their countries;
- strengthen the future of Christianity in the East as a priority, in the conscience of the Eastern Churches themselves, in the solicitude of the universal Church, and in the national and international bodies to consolidate the link between the faithful of the Diaspora and their Churches in the East;
- foster ecumenical and inter-religious dialogue;
- ensure the active participation of the Catholic family in the work of the Middle East Council of Churches (MECC);
- promote justice, peace, development, respect for human rights, especially those of women, and of the family in the countries of the region and in relations between peoples.

The CPCO holds meetings every two years. The first General Congress of the Catholic Churches was held at Notre-Dame du Mont in Lebanon in 1999. The theme was: 'The Eastern Catholic Churches on theThreshold of the Third Millennium.' Pope John Paul II's Apostolic Exhortation for Lebanon (1997) was a strong incentive for this historic congress. It implied that the seven synods of the seven patriarchal Churches of the East met for the first time. More than 200 people took part. The focus was on four themes: communion between the Churches, the relationship with fellow Muslims, the emigration of Eastern Christians and human rights (especially women's rights). Prepared since 1997[4], this congress followed a synodal process, following the pattern of the Special Synod Assembly created by Pope Paul VI. The final communiqué describes the main moments of the congress as well as its view on the mission of the Churches and their coordination structures. The ecclesial diversity is also reflected in

3 It is composed of the Patriarch of Antioch and all the East for the Maronite Church; the Patriarch of Antioch and all the East, Alexandria, and Jerusalem for the Melkite Greek Catholic Church; the Patriarch of Antioch and all the East for the Syrian Catholic Church; the Patriarch of Babylon for the Chaldean Catholic Church; the Coptic Catholic Patriarch of Alexandria; the Armenian Catholic Patriarchate of the See of Cilicia, and the Latin Patriarch of Jerusalem. It has its seat in the Maronite Patriarchate at Bkerke, Lebanon.

4 John Paul II, Apostolic Constitution 'A New Hope for Lebanon', 1997.

the moments of prayer celebrated in the different rites of the participating Churches. The recommendations of the congress were to be discussed by each Church, which has sovereignty in deciding how to receive them and how to implement them effectively. This sovereignty, however, is exercised within the framework of a 'co-responsibility' implied in the very nature of the Church, which is 'communion', and in the requirement of unity for mission.

The second congress took place only thirteen years later, from 3 to 5 December, 2012, in Harissa-Lebanon, motivated this time by the apostolic exhortation of Pope Benedict XVI, *Ecclesia in Medio Oriente* (14 September, 2012). It gathered 120 participants who reflected on seven themes: the Church in the Middle East, the service of the Word, the service of charity, the family, ecclesial communion, inter-religious dialogue, and political transformations in the Middle East.

From 12 to 18 February, 2023, Catholic Churches in the Middle East held their third Assembly. It is connected to the 2021-2024 Synod on 'For a Synodal Church: Communion – Participation – Misson.' This continental step marks a new stage in the long synodal experience of the Churches in the Middle East. It focuses on seven themes. They are listed in the official report:

> The summaries prepared and presented by the churches during the synodal assembly, as well as the deliberations in the reflection and Working Groups, unanimously underlined the crucial importance of the following issues: Unity in Diversity; The Liturgy is our Life; A Call for a Creative and Revitalised Ecumenism; The Church of Openness to the Different Other; Communion and Hope in the Midst of Suffering: Towards a Humble Church; In Favour of the Renewal of Structures for a More Synodal Church; The Media, Digital Culture and their Contributions to Making the Church More Synodal. (CD/ME, n.18).

The dynamic, as well as the content, is reminiscent in many ways of the two previous Assemblies (1999 and 2012) and anticipated the fourth Assembly which was held in Nicosia-Cyprus, from 20 to 23 April, 2023. This fourth Assembly, known as a symposium, celebrates the tenth anniversary of *Ecclesia in Medio Oriente*. It has as theme, 'Rooted in Hope', and concentrates on four subjects: 1) From ISIS to human Fraternity, ten years after the Apostolic Exhortation *Ecclesia in Medio Oriente;* 2) Freedoms and rights, between affirmations, aspirations and practices; 3) The Christian engagement within the socio-ecclesial space; 4) Challenges and opportunities for the Catholic institutions in the Middle East: support of the Universal Church.

The Symposium brought together 250 people, the highest number of participants since 1999, thanks to the initiative of Dicastery for the Eastern Churches and massive participation of members of the agencies and works of the *Riunione delle Opere di Aiuto alle Chiese Orientali*[5] (ROACO). The Symposium gathered the seven Patriarchs of the Catholic Churches in the Middle East, nuncios, bishops, priests, deacons, religious, laity, as well as ambassadors and diplomatic representatives.

What conclusions can be drawn from these four Assemblies in which the recent continental Assembly on synodality took place? First of all, the challenges reported in 1999 remain the same in 2023, with some variables. They indicate a stagnation, if not a worsening of the geopolitical situation in the Middle East, and a paralysis in the ecclesial structures. The lay faithful are increasingly suspicious of synodal processes, feeling uninvolved (particular synods of each Church, synod for Lebanon in 1997, synod for the Middle East in 2012, synod on synodality and symposium in 2023). The People of God are expressing the need for a new Pentecost that converts and renews mentalities, well before discourses and structures. The synodal process that gives voice to all the baptised could become this place of renewal.

Secondly, it is clear that the Catholic Churches in the Middle East hold patriarchal synods. But they only hold joint regional assemblies at the initiative of the universal Church: they occur because of the Popes Paul VI, John Paul II, Benedict XVI and Francis, their apostolic exhortations and of their official visits to the region.

Pope Francis' visits to the United Arab Emirates, Iraq and Bahrain aim to consolidate the presence of these Churches as part of the Middle Eastern societal and cultural fabric. Above all, his visits mark his commitment to promoting peace, inter-religious dialogue and cooperation between the different religious communities in the Middle East. The 2019 Declaration 'Human Fraternity for World Peace and Living Together'[6] is at the crossroads of the above-mentioned initiatives and lays the foundations and milestones for a new stage of collaboration between Christian and Muslim believers. Pope Francis and Grand *Imam* Ahmad Al-Tayyeb, one of the most venerable Sunni leaders, signed it in Abu Dhabi on 4 February, 2019.

This Declaration holds a perspective and a goal. It lays the foundations for a serious reflection and a new method for considering crucial and thorny issues concerning 'fraternity' as a principle and foundation, and 'otherness' as a concept that underlies and extends it. In order to be received in the life of the respective communities, this Declaration requires

- a great deal of patience and trust in the other,
- a great deal of work to adopt a new human and spiritual attitude,

5 ROACO (Reunion des Œuvres d'Aide aux Églises Orientales) is a committee that brings together agencies and works from various countries of the world that are committed to providing financial support in different sectors, from places of worship to scholarships, from educational institutions to social and health assistance.

6 https://www.vatican.va/content/francesco/en/travels/2019/outside/documents/papa-francesco_20190204_documento-fratellanza-umana.html

- a new social positioning, and
- a new intellectual posture in order to build societies where fraternity, justice and peace reign.

This choice is obviously very demanding. It requires from all, as Christians, the courage to hope for the other as a brother/sister and the will to commit oneself with him or her in reflection and in action in the service of humanity, where God calls to deification, revealed as the only way to a fulfilled humanisation.

Participants

The Continental Synodal Assembly of the Middle East consisted of 125 participants. It was characterised by the diversity of its participants, who belong to different Churches and represent a wide range of roles and responsibilities within their respective communities. Their varied backgrounds testify to the cultural and spiritual richness of Eastern Christianity and contribute to enriching the debates and exchanges during this Assembly. The official report speaks of this in the following terms:

> 'These Churches took part with delegations from Egypt, Palestine, the Holy Land, Lebanon, Syria, Jordan, Iraq and the Arabian Gulf countries. Cardinal Mario Grech, Secretary General of the Synod of Bishops, Cardinal Jean-Claude Hollerich, Rapporteur of the Synodal Assembly 2021-2024, and Sister Nathalie Becquart, Under-Secretary of the Synod, also took part. In addition to the Patriarchs, the delegations included bishops and priests, religious men and women, lay men and women of all ages. The total number of participants was one hundred and twenty-five' (CD/ME, n.1)

Each Church was represented by ten to fifteen representatives, respecting the diversity of ecclesial and pastoral profiles. They were chosen by the Patriarch in consultation with the coordinators of the synodal process in his Church. There were 95 representatives of the seven Churches and countries, including the seven Patriarchs, the Executive Secretary of the Council of the Catholic Patriarchs of the East (CPCO), twelve bishops, including the six coordinating bishops of the ecclesial synods for the local stage, and the five executive secretaries of the five national ecclesial assemblies (ACHE, ACOHL and LECAR, ACHS, ACPBL[7]), and married and celibate priests. It is worth noting the participation of ten celibate and married men and forty women who are either religious, married or single, as well as the active presence of twenty young people (under the age of 30) and two young persons with disabilities who brought their remarkable testimony to the Working Groups and the

7 ACHE: Assembly of the Catholic Hierarchy in Egypt; ACOHL: Assembly of Catholic Ordinaries in the Holy Land; LECAR: Latin Episcopal Conference for the Arab Regions; ACHS: Assembly of the Catholic Hierarchy in Syria; ACPBL: Assembly of Catholic Patriarchs and Bishops in Lebanon.

plenary sessions. In addition, two young agnostics also joined the daily wrap-up sessions at the Assembly and participated in the discussions, and five guests from other Churches and a young Orthodox woman representing the Middle East Council of Churches were actively involved in the Assembly and its work. Members of the steering committee (SC) also took part in the work of the Assembly. Representatives of Muslim denominations took part in the opening session. Around twenty people supported the event without participating directly; they were active in the secretariat, reception, logistics and/or media.

The patriarchs and bishops participated in all the plenaries and all the Working Groups according to the instructions of the facilitators of the groups. As for the text of the official report sent to Rome, they participated in the same way as all the other participants. Moreover, no patriarchal or episcopal meeting was held after the Assembly to discuss the text; it was accepted without any amendments or modifications (see section on Drafting Team below).

Programme and Method

The Assembly took place from 13 to 17 February, 2023, in the church residence of Beyt 'Anya, in Harissa, Lebanon. All meetings, liturgical celebrations and meals were held there. For lodging, the participants were welcomed on site and in the surroundings.

The Assembly was inaugurated on the evening of 13 February with words of welcome and a solemn celebration of the Eucharist in the Basilica of Our Lady of Lebanon with the participation of the People of God in attendance as well as by live streaming media.

The programme from 14 to 17 February was designed and led by the Steering Committee (SC) in a flexible and dynamic way. It was marked by morning prayers and an evening Eucharist. No keynote speakers were invited and no conferences were held during this Assembly. The time was devoted to the 21 meetings, in plenary and in groups. Personal time was also provided. The evenings were reserved for cultural activities, except for one evening dedicated to the Adoration of the Blessed Sacrament.

The Working Groups were composed of patriarchs, bishops, priests, religious men and women, lay men and women, young people and people with disabilities. All were coming from different Churches and several countries. On the first day only were the groups were divided by country, to discuss the report that each country presented on the Working Document for the Continental Stage.

The official language was Arabic, with simultaneous translations in Arabic and English during the plenary sessions. The group of representatives of the Secretariat of the Synod in Rome, of the Latin Church in the Holy Land and of the Gulf spoke in English.

The success of the programme was also due to the hard work of the secretariat team. Its members were responsible for the accommodation and reception areas. They also attended to the assembly's package for each participant, which contained a list of participants, general information, group lists, translation of Arabic-English documents, distribution of tasks, etc.

The Assembly chose the method of Spiritual Conversation for the Working Group sessions. Already before the Assembly, the method was explained to all the participants of the Assembly by way of a document in Arab and English, as well as explanatory and subtitled videos, was sent and published on YouTube through links.[8]

In addition, through several online and face-to-face meetings, the facilitators of the groups had been trained in advance by a Jesuit priest. During the Assembly, there was a daily follow-up to fine-tune the methodology according to the difficulties encountered and the opportunities that had arisen through the groups.

The SC adopted the method of Spiritual Conversation for the Working Groups for several reasons: to foster dialogue, value diversity, discern God's will and strengthen communion. The method followed the classic process adopted elsewhere: preparing before engaging in Spiritual Conversation; invoking the Holy Spirit; sharing authentically with honesty and humility; listening respectfully; discerning together; synthesising and acting together.

During the third day this dynamic caused tensions, hesitations and desolation in the groups as well as in the plenary. The SC took the opportunity to refocus the members of the Assembly on the objectives of the meeting, which had been spelt out in the Preparatory Document n.2, and recalled in the Document for the Continental Stage n.2: 'How is this "journeying together" which takes place today on different levels (from the local to the universal one) allowing the Church to proclaim the Gospel in accordance with the mission entrusted to Her; and what steps does the Spirit invite us to take in order to grow as a synodal Church? What is the Spirit saying to the Churches?'

In many respects this question was not foreign to the Churches of the Middle East. It found strong resonance in the consciousness of the Churches, because this question has challenged them in a continuous manner ever since the Second Vatican Council and in all their Assemblies (1991-2023). It finds reflection in the respective exhortations of the Popes, the communiqués of the Assemblies and the pastoral letters of the Patriarchs.

8 https://youtu.be/mzoKQiDyAeg; https://youtu.be/PIHPR_MEeYg; https://youtu.be/MifV7opM_vU

Biblical and Liturgical Dynamics: 'The Word who pitches his tent (σκηνόω) among us' (Jn 1:14)

The biblical and liturgical dynamics were entrusted to a team of nine experts, representatives of their Churches (5 priests, 3 nuns and 1 lay woman). The design of the biblical framework was entrusted to entrusted to Maryse Saghbini, a female biblical scholar who discussed the aspects with the team. Subsequently, the project was discussed and validated by the Steering Committee. The programme of liturgical celebrations was then distributed to the Churches and movements according to a pre-established format and the following 5-day calendar:

- Eucharistic Liturgy: Maronite Church, Melchite Church, Syriac Church, Coptic Church and Chaldean Church.
- Morning Prayer: Armenian Church, Latin Church, Office for Women's Pastoral Care in the Maronite Church and Our Lady's Team for Couples.
- Four cultural evenings: Jordan, Iraq, Armenians, and Faith and Light (movement for people with disabilities).
- An evening of adoration of the Blessed Sacrament: Young people of the Maronite Church.

A pilgrimage was organised on Wednesday 15 February to the monastery of Saint Maron, 'Anaya' (place of Saint Charbel). It allowed the groups to take a distance from their work and seclude in contemplation..

This dynamic was supported by a liturgical setting entrusted to an expert who was a young Christian involved in youth ministry. He designed a tent above the altar, with five veils bearing the five sub-themes. This tent was moved from the altar to the middle of the church during Adoration when it housed the Blessed Sacrament. On the last day, it was placed at the exit of the church from which at the end of the Eucharist people were send forth: the tent of the Church is enlarged and opened to the world.

The Assembly was supported by prayers of the contemplative cloistered religious communities and by the People of God who accompanied the event through the media.

'The Word pitches his tent among us' (Jn 1:14). This is the literal translation of the Greek verb σκηνόω or 'Tabernacle'. In the Old Testament, the tent made by humans refers to the presence and residence of God among them. In the new era, the only-begotten Son actually attained this mystical presence by becoming incarnate. The act σκηνόω does not come by chance in John's Gospel, but rather sums up God's purpose with his people: from the image of the tent of promise or tent of meeting, to the book of Revelation, where God pitches his tent in the new Jerusalem. And the centre of this process, from Genesis to Revelation, is the term 'incarnation', or 'the tent among us'. Indeed, in Revelation, the act σκηνόω symbolises not only the work of God and his presence in the midst of his people, but also the work of his people who also pitch their own tent in heaven: 'Rejoice, you heavens, and you who have pitched your tents in heaven' (Rev 12:12).

Why this joy? Because the accuser has lost all authority over the brothers. 'They have conquered him by the blood of the Lamb and the word of their testimony' (Rev 12:11).

This theme was divided into five areas:

- *Day 1 – God walks with us/with his people*: 'IHWH walked with them by day in a pillar of cloud to show them the way, and by night in a pillar of fire to give them light, so that they could walk by day and by night' (Ex 13:21). And there was evening and there was morning, the first day...
- *Day 2 – Listen together to the Word of God*: 'Shmah Israel! Listen, Israel: IHWH our God is the only IHWH' (Deut 6:4). And there was evening and there was morning, the second day...
- *Day 3 – Discerning together in the light of God's Word*: 'Beloved, do not put your faith in every spirit, but test the spirits to see if they are of God, for many false prophets have come into the world' (1Jn 4:1). And there was evening and there was morning, the third day...
- *Day 4 – Communion and Participation*: 'They were all with one heart in prayer with some of the women, including Mary the mother of Jesus, and with his brothers' (Acts 1:1). And there was evening and there was morning, the fourth day...
- *Day 5 – Towards a synodal missionary Church*: 'Go therefore and make disciples of all nations' (Mt 28:19). We are coming to the end of the current steps in the synodal journey but it is only the beginning. Christ has walked with us and shown us the way. He has spoken to us on the way and we have listened to His Word to the point where we have felt our hearts burn within us. We discerned His Word together, so that we could live in communion in love, bearing together our common responsibility in the Church. And today he returns and sends us out again together, renewed by the Holy Spirit, bringing the joy of the Gospel to all people, as a missionary synodal Church. And there was evening and there was morning... Eternal day!

Steering Committee

The Assembly was prepared and structured by the Steering Committee (SC). This team was formed by the executive secretary of the CPCO, Father Khalil Alwan, Maronite, Lebanese Religious – who was responsible for the first two congresses – and the representative of the task force of the Secretariat of the

Synod in Rome, Father Gabriel Hachem, from the Melkite Church. This core group was surrounded by fourteen experts from all Churches and countries (2 bishops, 5 priests, 1 nun, 5 lay women, and 1 one lay man). The SC met for the first time on 27 October 2022. Between 27 October 2022 and 12 February 2023 meetings were held regularly in-person and online. The SC decided on the place and date of the Assembly, as well as on the number of participants, both Catholic and non-Catholic. It set the theme, the dynamics and the programme of the Assembly according to the guidelines of the DC.

Six sub-committees were set up to prepare the meeting: 1) Scripture and liturgy; 2) facilitating the Spiritual Conversation Method; 3) drafting of the final report; 4) communication and media; 5) secretariat and 6) reception and decoration.

Each sub-committee was coordinated by members of the SC who were joined by volunteer experts. About twenty people supported the SC in its mission. A WhatsApp group was set up for continuous contact.

In addition, the SC coordinator explained the process and dynamics of the Assembly to the Synods of Bishops respectively.

On 20 December, 2022, the SC organised an online meeting for all participants to inform them about the programme and introduce them to their role. A second WhatsApp group was created on 19 November. Announcements and documents were shared in three languages (Arabic, French and English).

The SC secretariat provided Arabic translation of all documents received from Rome, and those of the Assembly.

The SC's mission ended with the submission of the official report to the Secretariat of the Synod in Rome on 31 March, 2023.

Drafting Team and Report

The SC appointed the drafting committee/team from among its members: the representative of the Synod task force as coordinator, three priests who are the executive secretaries of three national assemblies (APECL, AHCS, AOCT), two other lay women members of the SC and a nun from the Assembly. The selection was made on the basis of two criteria: 1) Representatives of churches, countries, men and women; 2) Experts in synthesising, group work and drafting.

The drafting committee/team was officially constituted on 15 February (third evening of the Assembly). It collected the reports and drew up a first outline, which it presented to all the participants at the plenary session on the evening of Thursday 16 February. Comments were collected and a second detailed plan was presented at the last plenary session on Friday 17 February. It was voted on and validated unanimously by all the participants in the Assembly.

The official report was sent to the Secretariat of the Synod in Rome on 31

March, 2023. No extraordinary patriarchal and episcopal meetings were held after the Assembly to discuss it. The text was sent to each patriarch on 1 April, 2023. All accepted it and congratulated the executive secretary and as well as individually the steering committee members. Therefore, no official meeting was held by the seven patriarchs to discuss the conclusion of the assembly or to execute any amendments or modifications. Only after this approval the document was posted on the site of the synod. It was mid-April.

Working Method of the Drafting Team

- *February 15, evening (third Assembly day):* Constitution of the drafting team. Distribution of the work among the seven members. Collection of Working Group summaries, country reports and post-it notes on the walls. Analysis of the reports and texts. Putting them into tables, then into a plan.
- *February 16:* Development of a detailed plan by the coordinator. Consultation with the team.
- *Plenary session on the evening of the 16th:* The coordinator proposes the detailed plan to the Assembly. Debates and collection of remarks were held. SC meeting and consultation.
- *February 17:* Amendment of the detailed plan by the drafting team in light of the comments received.
- *Plenary session on the evening of the 17th:* Presentation of the detailed plan and vote by the Assembly.
- *20 February–20 March:* The coordinator and the executive secretary of APECL drafted the text in Arabic.
- *20–30 March:* Two experts translate the report into French.
- *31 March:* The two editors and a lay woman from the drafting committee checked the French version, added quotations and finalised the editing. The text was forwarded to the Secretariate of the Synod in Rome.
- *1 April–10 April:* The SC coordinator sent the report to the seven patriarchs, to the members of the Assembly. The text received the approval of the seven patriarchs in order to be officially published on the official Vatican website of the Synod (www.synod.va).
- *Mid-April:* The Secretariat of the Synod in Rome officially posted the Assembly's conclusions in French on its webpage.
- *End of April:* The English version was finalised.
- *Mid-May:* All three version in different languages (Arabic, English and French) were available on the Vatican webpage.

Press and Media

The SC appointed the coordinator of the Press and Media sub-committee, Huguette Salameh, a female lay expert. She called on six professionals from various Middle Eastern countries to develop the strategy and action plan.

A coherent communication and media strategy was put in place. It encompassed the three moments of the event (before, during and after), with a diversification of television, radio, print and social media platforms in Lebanon and in the Middle East countries. The media strategy was designed along three lines: announcing and promoting the event through media interventions; ensuring media coverage on various platforms; presenting the participants of the Continental Synodal Assembly, their roles and responsibilities towards the Churches and the countries they represent.

Five objectives guided this strategy: to explain the synodal process 'Journeying together'; explain the ecclesial and theological dimension of this process; highlight the role of women, young people and the most vulnerable; communicate the synodal message to the greatest number of people; create new media platforms to continue the synodal process beyond the continental stage.

An action plan was put in place:

- Visit of the Lebanese Minister of Information to request cooperation from Lebanese TV, the National Media Agency and Radio Lebanon.
- Launch the work of the Assembly with a press conference held in Beit Annaya, in coordination with the Catholic Media Centre. Transferring it live to Christian television channels. Broadcast it on all media platforms.
- Production and broadcasting of television advertising on Christian and other television channels.
- Coordination with Vatican Radio, Arabic section, whose reporter was on site; and the Catholic Media Centre in Lebanon and the Coptic Catholic Centre in Egypt.
- Coordination of the direct broadcast programme between TV channels.
- Launch of the Continental Synod website in cooperation with the Vatican website.[9]
- Preparation and dissemination of a daily report on the Assembly's activities to various platforms.
- Regular documentation of media coverage.
- Taking photos of all activities and distributing them to participants via the Assembly's WhatsApp page.

9 https://beirut.synod2023.org/

- Organisation of a live stream for the final communiqué.
- Organisation of a live streaming media roundtable for the SC, the day after the Assembly.
- Organisation of post-event talkshows on TV channels to harvest the fruits of the Assembly.

Accredited journalists were on the scene 24-hours-a-day. Two specialised studios of two Christian TV channels were set up on site with live streaming. The interviews were offered to all participants without control and in total freedom, without instruction or recommendation, and no censorship. These interviews were shared simultaneously on official and personal social media.

Conclusion

The People of God in the Middle East live in a state of continuous insecurity and trial. With each new Church assembly, they return to the path of hope; a source from which they quench their thirst in order to continue their journey together, however difficult the road may be.

This contribution was completed when the Symposium of the Churches of the Middle East had just been concluded in Cyprus. It had the fitting theme: 'Rooted in Hope'. This virtue was highlighted by Pope John Paul II in his 1997 post-synodal Apostolic Exhortation *A New Hope for Lebanon*.[10] The Patriarchs have never ceased to recall it in their pastoral letters (nine times in the first letter in 1991, seven times in 1996…). Let the word be given to them here:

> 'We want to conclude with a word of hope. Our hope is not based on the human but on God. He has always been present among us in the past. This presence in the past is the guarantee of his presence among us today and in the future. Our churches are churches of hope. The Spirit acts and awakens in them a new awareness of their identity, their existence, their vocation and their mission. We can only listen to what the Spirit is saying today to our Churches in the East, so that they may be renewed and continue their earthly pilgrimage, responding to the calls of the world that challenges them'.[11]

In the continental report of the Middle East the word 'hope' appears eleven times. Number 10 reads:

> 'Our Synodal Church is the Church of the Arab East, as portrayed by the late Father Jean Corbon: a Church that announces the mystery of Christ and is a faithful witness of the Good News, even to the point of martyrdom. It is true that she carries the deposit of faith and

10 https://www.vatican.va/content/john-paul-ii/fr/apost_exhortations/documents/hf_jp-ii_exh_19970510_lebanon.html Editor; the Document is in French and Italian only.
11 Conseil des Patriarches Catholiques d'Orient, *Le Mystère de l'Église*, 4e lettre pastorale, 1996, n.65 (conclusion). See https://www.lpj.org/cached_uploads/view/2020/06/11/4e-lettre-pastorale-des-conseil-des-patriarches-catholiques-d-orient-1591874002.pdf

transmits it in 'vessels of clay' (2 Cor 4:7), enduring suffering, fragility and fear, yet she keeps the spirit of hope.

And n.48k writes:

'In order for our Churches to incarnate the Church of Hope in the Middle East, there is a need to revive the prophetic spirit that listens to the Will of God and works for its realisation, for God is the true Master of History. This is how the witness of Hope remains until the end of time.'

Listening to the voice of the Spirit today and living according to His commandment is what is required of the Churches so that their witness remains in the Middle East until the end of time!

Middle East ACRONYMS AND REFERENCES

ACHE	Assembly of the Catholic Hierarchy of Egypt
ACOHL	Assembly of Catholic Ordinaries in the Holy Land
ACPBL	Assembly of the Catholic Patriarchs and Bishops of Lebanon
CASP	Continental Assembly of the Synod, Plenary Session
CCCS	Council of Catholic Churches in Syria
SC Dulcis	Spiritual Conversation...
CChI.	Chaldean Church, Iraq
SCI.	Syriac Church, Iraq
YACPBL	Youth, Assembly of Catholic Patriarchs and Bishops in Lebanon

CONCLUSIONS OF THE CONTINENTAL ASSEMBLY OF THE SYNOD OF CATHOLIC CHURCHES IN THE MIDDLE EAST

Harissa, Lebanon

'The Name of the Church is Synod'[1]

FOREWORD

1. The Catholic Churches in the Middle East (Coptic, Maronite, Greek-Melkite, Syriac, Chaldean, Armenian and Latin) held their Synodal Continental Assembly in Bethania (Harissa, Lebanon) from February 13 to 17, 2023. The participants were from Egypt, the Holy Land, Lebanon, Syria, Jordan, Iraq, and the Arabian Gulf. Cardinal Mario Grech, General Secretary of the Synod of Bishops, Cardinal Jean-Claude Hollerich, General Relator of the 2021-2024 Synod on Synodality, and Sister Nathalie Becquart, Undersecretary of the Synod, were also present. In addition to the Patriarchs, the delegations included bishops and priests, religious men and women, and laypeople of all ages. The total number of participants was 125, including 40 lay and consecrated women (married and single) and 40 laymen (adults and young people of all ages, married and single), as well as people with disabilities. The Assembly was also attended by friends from the Orthodox and Protestant Churches and the Middle East Council of Churches (MECC), as well as agnostic men and women. Some representatives of Muslim denominations also took part in the opening session.

1. John Chrysostome, *Explicatio in Psalmum* 149: PG 55, 493.

2. The Synodal *Document for the Continental Stage* mapped the path of this Synodal Assembly. It was a Pentecostal moment during which all its members allowed themselves to be guided by the Holy Spirit, so much so that prayer was the foundation on which the axes of daily reflections were built, both during the plenary assemblies and the group work. Mutual listening was the reference paradigm, while participation reflected the spirit of communion that reigned among the members of the Assembly. This communion reached its fullness in the Eucharist, which was celebrated each day according to one of the rites of the Eastern Churches and crowned each day's work. Moreover, the meditation of the Word of God and the Spiritual Conversations created an atmosphere of fraternity, trust, courage and responsibility during the deliberations, through which the participants attempted to shed valuable light on the fundamental question: '*How can the Church become more synodal?*'

3. The careful and meticulous organisation of the Assembly created a relaxed and serene atmosphere that constituted a valuable motivation for hard and serious work. The credit for this goes to the immense effort made by the General Secretary of the Council of the Catholic Patriarchs of the East, in collaboration with the organising committee and other committees that prepared and accompanied the work of the Assembly.

I
'HE PITCHED HIS TENT AMONG US' (JN 1:14): THE WORD OF GOD AMID HIS PEOPLE

4. The presence of the Incarnate Word among us and in us did not cease, from the opening prayer until the end of the proceedings, to guide our steps during this Synodal Assembly. We listened to and celebrated the Word, and we meditated on what His Holy Spirit inspired us to do today. We realised that the People of God living in the Middle East are constantly being called to walk under the guidance of the Word and in the strength of the Spirit, in the midst of challenges, changes and misfortunes, animated by the hope of seeing this world transfigured into the Kingdom of God, a kingdom of peace, justice and joy, where God's love is bestowed, without distinction, on all human beings.

5. God invites His Church to form first and foremost a single community, who listens to His Word, who walks under His guidance, who discerns what the Word reveals in order to share it when the Church goes out to meet every human being, and who remains faithful to their mission. Going out

into the world is the reason for the Church's existence; it is her vocation. The Word precedes the Church, and traces for her the path according to which, thanks to the inspirations of the Spirit who leads her, apprehends the needs of her People and of the world. In the first chapter of the Gospel of St John, the Word emanates from the Father and 'pitches His tent' among us; indeed, He pitches His tent in us – in His People and in His Church. Through His incarnation, the only begotten Son accomplished the sacramental presence of God, making it real and tangible, for God's dwelling place is no longer restricted to any one place: it has become concrete in His mystical Body and in the union of its members. The more this Body remains united, harmonious and open, the more it allows the 'Word' that is in it to come out to meet every man and woman.

6. The expression 'pitching His tent' sums up God's entire journey with His people, from the metaphor of the Ark of the Covenant or the Tent of Meeting in the Old Testament, to the Book of Revelation, the crowning book of the New Testament, where God pitches His tent in the New Jerusalem. God's journey with His People is thus completed in glory, as He spreads His tent above His People and in their midst, once and for all and until eternity, by the virtue of His Incarnate Word. In turn, the Church also pitches her tent, in response to God's presence and action in her, and moves on until she reaches her dwelling place, which is, as we learn in the Book of Revelation 12:12, the heavenly house: 'Therefore rejoice, you heavens, and you who have pitched your tents in them!' This exhortation to joy recapitulates the celebration of salvation and the praise of the hymn of ultimate victory, as a sign of Christian hope, overcoming all our fears, anxieties and uncertainties, and transcending all tangible, perceptible and visible reality.

7. Throughout the history of salvation, God accompanies His people and offers them His Word and Spirit – all that He has and possesses. However, in the New Testament, God's journey with His people is accomplished in an unprecedented way: through the incarnation of His Son, who manifests God's indefectible and undeniable love to mankind. There lies the eternal covenant, the perennial communion, because through Jesus Christ the union between God and human is completed once and for all (*Ephapax*). The synodality that we aspire to live fully will only reach its paroxysm through the communion by which God introduces us, as His People, to His divine Trinitarian life and to our communion with one another, provided that we gather around the Word and the Body of the Risen Lord, and that we work according to the inspiration of the Holy Spirit, in order to achieve

communion with the world through the proclamation of the Good News and the bond to the cause of human dignity.

II
THE SYNODALITY OF THE CHURCH: NATURE AND SIGNS

8. Synodality is not a casual thing in the life of the Church. It is a sign inherent in her nature. True synodality is, for us, as members of the mystical body of Christ, identification with Christ and imitation of His way of life. Since Christ is risen, He 'being, in very nature, God, did not consider equality with God something to be used to His own advantage; rather, He made himself nothing by taking the very nature of a servant, being made in human likeness. And being found in appearance as a man, He humbled himself by becoming obedient to death – even death on a cross!' (Phil 2:6-8). It was among us that He pitched the tent of His divinity and His humanity, and led us from death to resurrection, thus opening the way to divine life. He accompanied us on the path of life and was attentive to our trials, sharing our joys and offering us His love to the end. For us, Christ is the Way (Jn 14:6). That is why the first Christians were called 'fellow companions', 'followers of Jesus' (*sequela Jesu*, the following of Jesus).

9. The Church is synodal through her very nature, for it is not only an institutional and juridical body, but first and foremost the mystery of Christ who works among and in those who believe in Him (*Lumen Gentium*, 1-5). This work is guaranteed by the Holy Spirit, who was given to the Church on the day of Pentecost to accompany her in her mission and to direct her 'with hierarchical and charismatic gifts' (*Lumen Gentium*, 4). In this way, the faithful walk in the footsteps of the Risen Christ, listen to His word and unanimously discern His will in the light of the Holy Spirit, agreeing in dialogue on the modalities of its accomplishment *hic et nunc*, according to the context and the requirements of the Kingdom.

10. The synodal Church is the Church of unity, catholicity, holiness and apostolicity. These four signs constitute the Church of God in a place, in a '*humus*', i.e., in history, geography, culture, language, challenges, traditions, poetry, stories, etc. Our Synodal Church is the Church of the Arab East, as it was portrayed by the late Father Jean Corbon: a Church announcing the mystery of Christ, and a faithful witness of the Good News, even to the point of martyrdom. It is true that she carries the deposit of faith and transmits it in 'jars of clay' (2 Co 4,7), enduring suffering, fragility and fear; yet she keeps alive the spirit of hope. It is undeniable that synodality consolidates unity, manifests catholicity, leads to holiness and safeguards the bond of apostolicity and mission. This can be seen in the common journey of a people united by the Word of God, His will and His divine economy; a people sanctified by the Holy Spirit, who constantly renews in them the life of the Risen Christ; a people that gathers without any distinction, because 'in Jesus Christ there is no longer slave nor free' (Gal 3:28), because the whole of humanity forms the family of God; a people who, throughout the centuries, has never ceased to bring the Good News from the Apostles and the Churches to the world in a flexible spirit of creativity that adapts to the changes of context and circumstances. Synodality is based on the work of the Holy Spirit, who transfigures us *hic et nunc* into the new People of God, the mystical Body of Christ, the living Temple of the Spirit.

11. Our Churches find themselves in the midst of a struggle for survival and active presence, in order to meet the challenges of unity in a world divided and undermined by egoism and self-centeredness; the challenges of holiness in a world that has lost its spiritual and human values; the challenges of catholicity in a world dominated by discrimination, and whose behavior is marked by unacceptable racism; the challenges of apostolicity in a world where over-mediatisation obscures the evangelical values of love, justice and peace. These challenges take on an extremely serious dimension in the Middle East, where armed conflicts, violence, hatred and war are exacerbated. A common journey of the Churches, in a spirit of authentic synodality, is the only way to guarantee the proclamation of the Good News and the coming of the Kingdom of God. This process requires a common journey of the People of God and an active collaboration in order to heal the wounds, to console the sorrows, to be in solidarity in the trials, to purify the memory, and to collectively elaborate decisions and put them into practice.

III
SYNODALITY IN OUR EASTERN THEOLOGICAL TRADITION

12. The theology of our Eastern Catholic Churches has always emphasised the meaning of synodality, referring to the mystery of the grace of salvation, the Trinitarian life and the earthly communion with the human race – a communion concretised in the summons of the People of God and their exhortation to gather in what was once called in Hebrew *Kahal*.

In His plan, God sees His People as partners; a people made up of men, women and children, of strangers, responding to God's call and flocking from all sides to worship Him, to listen to His Word, to discern His will and to act according to His precepts.

13. All of our Eastern Catholic Churches, with the exception of the Latin Church, have been established according to a patriarchal and synodal structure (see *Orientalium Ecclesiarum*, 7-11). However, synodality is first experienced, within these Churches, in the Liturgy, in the worship of the One and Triune God. No synod can be held if it is not inaugurated and closed by the celebration of the Eucharist – a sign of communion and unity, taking place in the presence of the People of God who explicitly approve and accept the resolutions taken. Unfortunately, for historical reasons, the synods of the Eastern Churches have become over the years simple annual assemblies limited to the participation of the bishops, following the example of the National Episcopal Conferences – although these synods are clearly distinguished from them by their nature, power and status conditioned by the reception of the whole People of God. It is undeniable, therefore, that the return to synodal practice, concretised by the presence of representatives of the entire ecclesiastical world, is more in keeping with the Pope's exhortation to revalorise the theology of the People of God, to rekindle the sense of faith (*sensus fidei*), and to assume common apostolic responsibility in accordance with what is recommended in the second chapter of the constitution *Lumen Gentium* (9-18). In virtue of such a return, communion, collective work and commitment to the common mission will be revealed in a more radiant clarity.

14. As we mentioned above, our Eastern Catholic Churches have their origins in synodality, namely in the regional councils or synods which, according to historians, appeared in the region of Asia Minor in the second half of the second century. Following the Council of Chalcedon, they were established as patriarchal churches according to the provisions of Justinian's Code in the sixth century. Over the centuries, patriarchal canon law evolved, especially following the restitution, from the eighteenth century onwards, of the union of our Churches with the Roman Apostolic See. Since the middle of the nineteenth century, this patriarchal code was considerably affected by the confessional regime or system of *Millets* (confessional communities), according to which the laity participated as members in synods. Nevertheless, the interference of politics and personal interests led to the exclusion of the lay faithful from the synods, which paved the way for the emergence of a form of clericalism that emphasised the grip on power and authoritarianism in the process of promulgating decisions. Today, thanks to the exhortation of Pope Francis, we intend to re-emphasise the decisive role of all the members of the same ecclesial body, thus promoting the concrete application of synodality in all its dimensions.

15. Synodality in the East is indispensable for the management of plurality in all its forms. It is an ecclesiastical *praxis* approved in the synods of our patriarchal Churches, where the decision of the *protos*, or first, is conditioned by the assent of all, and where the outlook of all the members does not contradict the decision of the *protos*, in accordance with Canon 34 of the Apostles. This *praxis* also commands the Assemblies of National Catholic Patriarchs and Bishops who, in this region, work together to accomplish the same mission through the implementation of a common pastoral plan. The creation of the Council of Catholic Patriarchs of the East (CPCO) has strengthened this cooperation, and shows the importance of the process of common journey, which has been expressed above all in the Pastoral Letters addressed from 1991 onwards, to the faithful of the different Churches, revealing and analysing the most salient issues related to their presence and the proclamation of the Gospel in the Middle East. However, what characterises this process of common journey within our Eastern Catholic Churches is precisely their joining in 1990, as a united ecclesial family, through the Middle East Council of Churches (MECC), in order to live in communion with all their Christian brothers and sisters of the region, to engage together in addressing the difficult challenges they face and in common dialogue with Muslims, Jews and other parts of Middle Eastern society, and to journey together towards a worthy and effective proclamation of the Gospel.

16. In this common journey, our Churches were nourished by the universal Church and their communion with the Roman Pontiff. They thus contributed to the building of the catholicity of the Church, enriching it, thanks to their ecclesiastical, theological, patristic and cultural patrimony, by their presence, contribution and participation in the Roman Catholic councils and assemblies. They constantly reminded us of their value as a witness to the unity of Christ's Church, thus evoking the motto coined by Pope John Paul II: 'The Church must breathe with her two lungs [the East and the West]!' (cf. *Ut unum sint*, 54). Indeed, our Churches can find in the synodal process a unique opportunity to renew themselves in fidelity to our Master, the Risen Lord, and in submission to the inspirations of the Holy Spirit and to what He breathes into them today.

IV
THE EXPERIENCE OF THE CONTINENTAL SYNODAL ASSEMBLY

17. The participants in the Synodal Assembly expressed the difficulty of communicating under the harsh conditions that have affected, and continue to affect, the countries of the region, especially in terms of disruption, conflict and war. Taking charge of the priorities related to the survival and safeguarding of the Christian presence in the Middle East had a profound impact on the synodal process, common reflection, mutual listening, and especially the attention given to those who seem to live on the margins of ecclesial life, in conditions of estrangement and distance. To take a recent example, the earthquake that devastated parts of Turkey and Syria, and which has afflicted the minds and hearts of all the members of the Assembly – who carried the inhabitants of these devastated regions in their prayers and reflections, throughout their meeting with their representatives. They also did everything possible to express their communion and solidarity with the victims and their families. Today, the Synodal Assembly has rekindled hope for a new impetus to our Churches and their members to take up, with renewed vigor, a common journey of witness and mission, especially in a context of diverse cultures, religions, currents of thought, and the conditioning of each country, society, and people. Where its directives have been observed, the synodal process has enabled the members of our Churches to experience a common journey, to encourage mutual listening and freedom of expression, especially on the part of women and young people (ACPBL[2], §1.1, p3).

18. The syntheses prepared and presented by the Churches during the Synodal Assembly, as well as the deliberations in the reflection and Working Groups, unanimously underlined the crucial importance of the following issues: Unity in Diversity; The Liturgy, Our Life; The Call to a Creative and Revitalised Ecumenism; A Church of Openness to the Other and to Differences; Communion and Hope in the Midst of Suffering: The Journey Toward a Humble Church; Renewal of Structures for a More Synodal Church; and finally the Media, Digital Culture, and their Contributions to Making the Church More Synodal.

2 See List of Acronyms and References, p. 252.

4.1 Unity in Diversity: A Source of Wealth or an Obstacle?

19. Since its birth, the Church of Antioch has experienced a diversity of ecclesial and liturgical ways of life, and has been open to the civilisations of the peoples who have taken up residence there, to their languages and traditions. Similarly, the Churches of the region have lived their unity in diversity, placing themselves at the service of the proclamation of the Gospel and the witness of the faith (ACPBL, §1.5 -p4). Their unity did not mean uniformity and fusion (E. Ch. I, p3). Rather, it meant a real sharing of the same good, a concerted response to the issues raised, and a common facet of the challenges to be met (ACHE, p1). The foundation of this unity is the same baptism, communion in the same body of Christ and the call to the same mission (ACPBL, §1.4, p4). Consequently, the one and plural Church is a Church constantly renewed by the Spirit of God, who confers upon it all kinds of charisms, ministries and structures, and strengthens it by the unity of initiation accomplished in its midst and by the integration of all members, without any exclusion (ACHE., p2).

20. Within the Patriarchal Church, unity in diversity is manifested in the communion of the same synod, where the dioceses assume, in sharing, the responsibility of management and pastoral care, and cooperate in the care of the People of God, through the unity of liturgy, history, identity and hierarchy. This unity extends to communion with the Catholic Churches of the same country and region, resulting in the establishment of structures of synergy and partnership, such as the Assemblies of Catholic Patriarchs and Bishops established in each of the countries of the region, or the Council of Catholic Patriarchs of the East. The aim is to foster cooperation in a common pastoral space, in the service of the same Gospel proclamation, and without losing each of the Churches' identity, historical, and illustrious tradition, which ratify unity in diversity, manifest the richness of plurality and its decisive role in the expression of the same faith, and concretise the catholicity of the Church, whether it be at the level of the Eastern Catholic Churches, with the Roman Catholic Church, or with the Orthodox and Protestant Churches of the Middle East.

21. Men and women, sons and daughters of our Churches, are competent beings, endowed with various charisms and talents which they willingly place at the service of the unity of the Church and its renewal (S. C. I., §17, p3). For this reason, it is incumbent upon the ecclesiastical authority, in close collaboration with the whole people, to discern well the various charisms and ministries surrounding them, so that all people may assume a common responsibility in different areas of ecclesial life (E. Ch. I, §21, 23 p10-11). In this regard, the role of the charismatic movements in Egypt was highlighted, especially their impact on the consolidation, through common worship and prayer, of fraternal bonds among young Catholics (ACHE, p2). Others praised the efforts of religious orders to live authentically the evangelical virtues (E. Ch. I, §5 p4), recommending appreciation of the ministry of priests at its core value, especially in the present difficult circumstances (S. C. I., §15, p3). They also spoke of the mission of married priests and its positive impact on the family, children and youth. A request was made to re-examine the requirements for the preparation of married men to the reception of Holy Orders, and to reconsider its theological, juridical, pastoral, human and social aspects (ACPBL., §3.13, p8).

22. However, maintaining unity in diversity is not easy; rather it is the gift of the Holy Spirit. In order to manage diversity within unity, enormous efforts and sacrifices must be made in a spirit of humility, fraternity, repentance and fidelity to Christ. The members of the Synodal Assembly had to point out certain grievances that are detrimental to the achievement of unity within each Church, leading to the dissension of the People of God and its dispersion, such as the tensions felt between clergy and laity and the aggravation of the gap that separates them from one another (A. P.E.C.L, §1.7, p4), as well as the abuses and ethical transgressions committed by the clergy, consecrated persons and laity in search of a life of luxury and wealth. These behaviors caused many young people to leave the Church (ACPBL., §2.3, p. 5-6), provoking a state of weariness and despondency among the priests who, because of the constraints, are seeing their numbers decrease (ACPBL., §1.7, p. 4).

23. Failure to address certain tensions would eventually lead to the disfigurement of this rich diversity, as well as to the misuse of hierarchical power, and thus turn us away from a spirit of communion and sharing. The exercise of ordained and non-ordained ministries is intended to build up the body of Christ harmoniously. Where power is not exercised in a spirit of service, trust between the faithful and clerics is eroded (C.C.C.S.., §6, p2), and so the clerical spirit will prevail to the extent that bishops, priests and consecrated persons begin to abuse their power (ACHE., p3). Assembly participants expressed dissatisfaction with ecclesiastical authorities who monopolise power and make decisions without consulting the faithful (S. C. I., §21, p4), and complained about the lack of coordination between ordained ministers and their lay partners (C. Ch. I., §8, p5). Others also noted the lack of coordination and cooperation between religious orders and dioceses (C. Ch. I., §4, p5). Such things lead to the exacerbation of a negative spirit, the alteration of the spiritual sense of communion (ACHE., p3), and the questioning by the faithful of the relevance of the decisions issued by the ecclesiastical authority, when the latter monopolises the power of decision to the detriment of the spirit of service, thus hindering the understanding of unity in diversity.

4.2 The Liturgy, Our Life

24. The Pastoral Constitution *Sacrosanctum Concilium* affirms that 'the liturgy is the summit toward which the activity of the Church is directed; at the same time, it is the font from which all her power flows. For the aim and object of apostolic works is that all who are made sons of God by faith and baptism should come together to praise God in the midst of His Church, to take part in the sacrifice, and to eat the Lord's supper.' (SC 10). Indeed, Liturgy is the life of the Churches in the East; its celebration constitutes the fundamental axis of ecclesial life (C. Ch. I., §13, p8). The high point of liturgical celebrations is undoubtedly the Eucharist, for it builds up the Church, the Body of Christ (1 Cor 12).

25. While recognising the splendor of the liturgies and spiritualities proper to the Eastern Churches (A.C.O.H.L.), the reports underlined the tensions created because of the sometimes-literal practice of the traditional liturgical rules, to the detriment of the faithful and their active participation in the work of adoration and prayer, as well as in the sacraments. Among these tensions pointed out were the emergence of aberrant devotions of religiosity and unhealthy phenomena related to apparitions (C.C.C.S.., §3, p3); the problem of any form of renewal of traditional liturgical models (S. C. I., §17, p3); the non-adherence of the new generation to the convictions related to the liturgical rites and symbols (C.C.C.S.., §1, p4), because of a deficiency in liturgical formation (S. C. I., §16, p3). In addition, the divergent sensitivities concerning whatever order governing the liturgical celebration sometimes led to dissensions that weaken communion and erode confidence in the Church's maternal love. There is also the problem of the style, content and purpose of the homily; the disharmony in the choice of hymns; the absence of an inspecting body to verify the content of the texts and define the nature of their use in the Church in the form of recitation and song. Some participants recommended abandoning liturgical puritanism, being open to the process of evolution of liturgical prayers and their adaptation to the aspirations of the faithful, especially the young (ACPBL, §1. 2, p3), thus emphasising the need for a liturgical reform capable, on the one hand, of taking into consideration the safeguarding of tradition and, on the other hand, of opening up to modernity (ACPBL, §2.4, p6). Hence the urgency of allowing the Liturgy to adapt to the emerging realities and their context, in order to be able to regenerate it (C. Ch. I., §2, p3; (ACHE, p5) in conformity with the requests involved in the process of returning to the roots.

4.3 The Call to a Creative and Revitalised Ecumenism

26. The synodal Church is ecumenical because it is the accomplishment of the common journey of the People of God (C. Ch. I., §19, p10), a journey that cannot be completed without encountering the brothers and sisters of the other Churches (ACPBL, §1.3, p3-4). 'In the East, we shall be Christians together or not be' (CPCO, 1st pastoral letter, 1991). For the Christian presence is dependent on the witness of each faithful and each Church, based above all on the common witness of Christians as a whole. It is undeniable that the ecumenical movement in the Middle East has contributed to the emergence of a dialogical reality that favours collaboration and dynamic interaction between the Churches (E.S.I., §6, p2), as well as a common human pastoral care in the service of charity, through the deployment of concrete spiritual and ecclesiastical experiences (ACPBL., §3.7 p7). Some participants saw the experience of mixed marriages as a positive factor that could consolidate relations between the Churches (E.S.I., §6, p2), while others saw it as a risk factor and a source of conflict (Coptic Church). The participation in the Assembly of some Orthodox and Protestant friends was an enriching experience that confirmed the importance of living together and of the untiring search for visible unity.

27. For the Christians of the East, unity is a matter of life and death (Patriarch Maximos IV). Therefore, the adhesion of the Catholic Church to the Middle East Council of Churches (MECC) was a clear expression of her desire to achieve unity in diversity, through gathering and collaborating in various areas of ecclesial life, especially the *diakonia*, and also through coexisting with other citizens of different religions and confessions. The Council contributes greatly to the spreading of an ecumenical spirit among the Churches, the accentuation of rapprochement and of a common pastoral work, and the strengthening of a common witness. For this reason, the ecumenical movement in the Middle East is seen as the unique model of a common journey that transcends the frameworks and limitations of the single church family; a model also of commitment to

communion among the Churches, in all their diversity and despite their doctrinal, liturgical and canonical differences.

28. The withdrawal into the confessional identity, the fear of opening up to a different otherness (S. C. I., §3, p1), the lack of transparency (A.C.C.H.L., §5, p2), and the spread of proselytism, exercised especially by certain new evangelical communities under the pretext of offering financial, medical and food aid in the midst of the economic crisis that is acutely affecting the standard of living, are dark realities which disrupt inter-church relations and are detrimental to the ecumenical spirit (ACPBL., §2.8, p6). In addition, there were tensions and discordances affecting the relations between the Churches of the West and the Churches of the East (C.E.C. S, §2, p3); the problem of ecclesiastical canon law, which is torn between unity and decentralisation; political interference in ecumenical affairs (Latin Church), leading some participants to evoke the metaphor of the 'ecumenical winter' (ACHE, p4), following the ecumenical golden age that prevailed in the sixties and seventies of the past century.

4.4 A Church of Openness to the Other and to Differences (Enlargement of the Tent Space)

29. In the Middle East, which is experiencing serious political, security and social tensions due to the Sunni-Shiite conflict in Iraq, Yemen and Syria and the hegemony of fundamentalist movements and organisations in some countries, Christians feel the danger of being uprooted, deportation and the threat of annihilation of their heritage (ACPBL., §2.11, p6). The reports provided by the Catholic Churches in the Middle East and coming from the work of the Synodal Assembly highlighted the emergence of various tensions: fear of renewed violence (S. C. I., §2, p1); risk of dissolution into the predominant Muslim culture (S. C. I., §13, p3); impact of religious extremism on Christian presence (C. Ch. I., §9, p3); inability to create new methods and strategies to listen and break down barriers (C. Ch. I., §10, p6); lack of an environment conducive to dialogue (E. Ch. I, §11, p7); indifference and loss of interest in the other (C. Ch. I., §24, p11); unfruitfulness of attempts at dialogue and rapprochement in certain cases (E. Ch. I, §18, p9) ; and the problem of the settlement of Palestinian refugees and displaced Syrians with a Muslim majority, leading to a dysfunctional experience of freedom of faith in general, and of the free and regular practice of Christian religious rites in particular (ACPBL, §2.10, p6). However, despite all this, the openness of the local Churches to others, whether different in faith, culture, concepts and/or choices was clearly reaffirmed. Emphasis was also placed on the need for listening, dialogue and coexistence, because the tent, i.e., the Church, which God has set up in the heart of mankind and the world, is wide enough to welcome all, without any exclusion.

30. The concept of the other is not limited to women and men who belong to other Churches, nor to other religions! The 'different other' could be the one closest to each person. Through her fidelity to Christ, the Church pursues the same work of redemption, insofar as she manifests her love to every human being without distinction or discrimination. She cannot exclude anyone, because if she does, she would lose her identity and her mission to pursue redemption through Christ. The participation of the faithful with special needs, either in prayer or in reflection groups, was an eloquent expression during this Assembly of the size of the Church's tent. In this regard, the participating members, among those with special needs, emphasised the characteristic of their participation in the life of the Church and her mission, according to their own capacities (ACPBL, §1.11, p4). In any case, it will be necessary not only to safeguard the dignity of these persons, but also to organise formation and awareness sessions in parishes, schools, institutes and universities. Hence the importance of training competent guides and counselors capable of accompanying these people and their families.

31. The Church will become more synodal as she strives to promote coexistence and dialogue with other religions, in order to manifest the true and unique face of God (C. Ch. I., §6, p5). Listening is the first step in welcoming the different other (C. Ch. I., 9, p6). In this regard, the reports and deliberations of the Working Groups paid tribute to the initiative of Pope Francis and Sheikh Ahmed el-Tayeb, Grand Imam of the al-Azhar Mosque, who signed and published together the *Document on Human Fraternity*. Its positive concrete repercussions were welcomed, as was the impact of the meeting of the Holy Father Francis with Ayatollah al-Sistani in Najaf (S.I. § 13, p. 3), and the crucial effect produced by the visits made by Pope Francis to the countries of the Middle East, manifesting the positive and promising character of the dialogue with Muslims.

32. The opportunities for dialogue are intensified and consolidated through the participation in institutions and colloquiums promoting understanding (C. Ch. I., §18, p10), meetings and gatherings of the faithful belonging to different religions, and the collaboration with all religious bodies aiming at establishing common bases for dialogue (ACHE, p2). Emphasis was placed, therefore, on the importance of formation in dialogue, of promoting initiatives of openness to the faithful of other religions, of concretising human fraternity (ACPBL, §1.5, p4), and of the importance of creating new methods of dialogue that could contribute to transferring it from administrative offices to parishes and to realities of every day (ACPBL, §4.2, p8).

4.5 Communion and Hope in the Midst of Suffering: Toward a Humble Church (The Mustard Seed, Mk 4:30-32)

33. The Churches of the Middle East were born amid suffering and persecution, and it is in blood that their history was written. The hagiography of the martyrs formed the largest part of the *Synaxarium*, and became a source of inspiration for many believers, who drew from it an energy of hope to survive and persevere. Their relics remain to this day a source of blessings and miracles. Yet, this reality also provoked the emergence of tensions and challenges, the first of which is emigration (C. Ch. I., §3, p4), and which were raised frankly by the consultations within the Churches and the syntheses of the Working Groups throughout the Synodal Assembly. The reports and interviews denounced a fundamental problem from which our Churches suffer, and which is becoming more and more critical and dangerous, namely the massive emigration of young people, which leads to the emptying of the Churches of their capacities and resources (ACPBL., §1.7, p4), and to the dispersal of families (C. Ch. I., §2, p1). This problem has degenerated into an existential threat (ECS, p1-2)

34. Despite the tireless initiatives taken by Pope Francis to safeguard Christian presence in the region, and despite the efforts of their Beatitudes the Patriarchs and bishops to maintain the best relations with civil authorities and leaders of other religions, fears are growing about the return of waves of violent fundamentalism; the resurgence of emigration; the challenges of welcoming immigrants and displaced people (A. H.C.E, p4); the preservation of the identity of immigrants, their traditions and rituals, as well as their ecclesial belonging on the one hand and the relationship with the Latin Church and their integration in the countries of immigration on the other hand (ACPBL, §2.9, p6). Some of the participants also raised sensitive issues faced by believers living in Middle Eastern countries, among others those of armament, compulsory military service, liberation theology (C.C.C.S., §2 p4), as well as the fidelity of Christian leaders to spiritual values in the exercise of their political function, especially when making decisions about war and peace (ACPBL, §3.6, p7).

35. The recommendations presented in the reports and the work of the various teams can be summarised in three points:

- For the Church, to open up to others and to listen to different opinions have broadened horizons of hope, united Christians in the witness of their faith and nourished their sense of belonging to the Church (ACPBL, §1.1, p3);
- To trust in the initiatives of local Churches and National Assemblies, without waiting for solutions from abroad (C.A.S.P of 14.02.2023);
- To witness that consecrated life offers a good model for living in integrity and hope amid suffering (S.C. Dulcis).

4.6 In Favour of a Renewal of Structures for a More Synodal Church

36. It has become clear to the Assembly that the Eastern Churches are synodal in structure. For these different structures to be put at the service of communion, partnership and mission, they must be constantly renewed, especially by activating them at different levels: the Pastoral and Diocesan Councils, the National Assemblies of Patriarchs and Bishops, and the Council of Catholic Patriarchs of the East. This way, these structures can become more contributive, professional and transparent, and will not hinder the transmission of the message of the Church to all. Some laypeople proclaimed their desire to live in partnership within the Church, to share the responsibility and burden of mission with their bishops and priests (ACPBL, §4.4, p8). They recommended that the work of the financial committees and those who are responsible for providing relief and assistance to the needy, the poor and the afflicted be monitored (C. Ch. I., §11, p22).

37. To answer the call of His Holiness Pope Francis to build a more synodal Church, the Eastern Catholic Churches are working to approach cultural pluralism with greater awareness and esteem for the other, especially as they accompany young men and women who feel estranged from the Church, so that this feeling does not turn into indifference over time. Several participants in the Assembly spoke of the reluctance of laypeople to participate at times in the life of the Church, because of lack of transparency and tyranny of authoritarianism of some clergymen (ACPBL, §1.8, p4). Other participants also pointed out the predominance of the institutional character within the Church, which at times alters the foundations of ecclesial, priestly and monastic service, because of their deviation from the spirit of free mission and personal witness. Some ecclesiastical institutions have sometimes acquired an organisational character from which the rich have benefited more than the poor

(ACPBL, §2.6, p6). Some have thus expressed the need for the Eastern Catholic Churches to review the concept of ecclesiastical leadership, its tasks and principles, and to adopt modern foundations of administration and governance. The renewal of ecclesiastical structures requires special attention and must grant greater attention to the pastoral care of families, women and youth.

Pastoral Care of the Family

38. The participants in the Assembly saw the need to educate families; to teach children how to pray, how to read the Holy Bible and how to listen to the Word of God (ACPBL, §4.1, p8). In this education, it is with boldness and transparency that the new ethical questions must be given the attention they deserve (ACPBL, §4.4, p9). To this end, the participants recommended that special programs be devoted to married and engaged couples (C. Ch. I., §5, p5), and that the Church accompany spouses and families who encounter difficulties because of cultural changes. The Church will thus be committed to dealing with the phenomenon of family disintegration, and will work to protect and strengthen the family, for it is the nucleus of the Church and society (ACPBL., §3.2, p7).

39. Churches have recently observed an increase in the number of separated couples, of those who prefer to change their denomination or religion to divorce, and of women who resort to abortion (ACPBL, §2.13, p7). They see the LGBTQI+ community sometimes participating in the transfer of ideas and concepts from Western society and the spread of gender theory in the world of electronic communication and social networks, as well as their impact on youth (ACPBL, §2.12, p6).

40. Access to the sacraments in some of the above-mentioned cases is often a problem in the Churches. The question is how to properly discern in such situations in the light of the Word of God and according to the elements offered by the Church's teachings. Some believe that for the Catholic Church, it is necessary to define the concept of sexuality and the moral issues that go with it, while others emphasise topics that help to avoid problems and difficulties, by finding new ways to support families through ecclesial institutions (C. Ch. I., §14, p8), providing appropriate preparatory programs for the sacrament of marriage (C. Ch. I., §17, p10), communicating with families who are away from the Church (C.C.C.S.., §1, p4), and seeking to exclude no one in the synodal process.

opposing concepts and ideas that offend human dignity, nourish the spirit of estrangement from God and contribute to the spread of moral decadence (ACPBL., §3.18, p8). The need to train experts in the field of Christian communication and media was also confirmed (ACPBL, §4.3, p8). The conclusions of the Churches and the debates of the Assembly warned against the repercussions abuse of social media can have on the faithful, in particular on young people (ACPBL, §2.7, p6).

V
HOW CAN OUR EASTERN CATHOLIC CHURCHES BECOME MORE SYNODAL?

47. 'The name of the Church is Synod.' This definition sheds light on how we might understand the very nature of the Church, as well as the unity of her members and the complementarity of their roles, and their union in Jesus Christ through the action of the Holy Spirit. The Church is, in history, the People of God that walks together towards the accomplishment of the Father's Kingdom. But how could this synodality develop? And what would be the means of its accomplishment?

48. During the Synodal Assembly, through prayers, Spiritual Conversations, debates and discussions, proposals that could help the Churches to be more in line with their deepest nature and to become more synodal emerged. Here are the most important ones:

a. *To bring about a change in the mentality of all*, laity and clergy, in order to assume the universalism of salvation through Christ and to provide all with the adequate means to better understand and accomplish it. This requires that each baptised person live and recognise themselves as a member of the People of God, through word, committed action, example of life and witness.

b. *To recognise the complementarity between the common priesthood and the ministerial priesthood* (diaconate, presbyterate, episcopate), both of which participate in the one Priesthood of Christ and are interrelated (*Lumen Gentium* 10). To adopt spiritual discernment as a method to promote listening, walking together and the ability to recognise God's will.

c. *To affirm that every baptised member of the faithful has a 'sense of faith'* and that the Church carries out her mission through the universal call to holiness, until Christ is 'all in all' (1 Cor 15:28). To commit ourselves to walking together, despite all that this requires in terms of stripping ourselves of all our possessions, and to be open to others to accept them as they are.

d. *To work for the renewal of liturgical life in the Churches*, taking care to preserve the essentials of the Holy Tradition and at the same time to adapt the liturgical offices to the present needs of the People of God, which are dependent on the contexts and circumstances proper to the different countries and societies. Insofar as the life of the whole People of God is organised around the Liturgy, it is imperative to uphold the designated roles of each member and align their formation and development with their individual gift and ministry.

e. *To purify the ministry of priests of all weaknesses* and shortcomings present in some of them, because they are incompatible with the holy vocation and service in the image of Christ, the Servant *par excellence*. This purification requires a review of the means and criteria for choosing candidates for the holy orders of deacon, priest and bishop. This implies not being satisfied with merely ascertaining their scientific and theological competence, nor their managerial and administrative know-how, but above all their capacity to respect their holy commitment and to live a life of virtue that is a sign of pastoral commitment and love of Christ to the point of martyrdom.

f. *To make an irreversible commitment to the restoration of the visible unity of the Church*, and to promote ecumenical relations between the Churches and ecclesial communities in the Middle East. In addition, to develop new initiatives towards other Churches, especially in the areas of cooperation and common witness. To improve the efficiency of the role of the Catholic Churches in the Middle East Council of Churches and to seek to unify the dates of feasts (Spiritual Conversations). The experience of the pastoral agreements regarding ecclesial identity, common catechism, solemn communion and mixed marriages (Agreement of Charfet-1996) could be considered a model for such initiatives, especially for the unification of the date of the celebration of Easter.

g. *To recognise the value of religious, cultural and human diversity in the Middle East*, and to confirm the choice to live together in order to open a new page in relations with Muslims and Jews, as well as with adherents of other religions, agnostics and those who declare themselves not to belong to any particular religion, philosophical trend or ideology. To work for the purification of memory and to engage in authentic and bold dialogue based on charity and mutual respect. Only in this way will our Eastern Churches be able to contribute to the pastoral care of reconciliation for the common good and the future of the peoples of the region.

h. *To abandon any form of exclusion of women from participation in the life of the Church*, especially in making ecclesial decisions. Our respective Churches should begin to reflect seriously on the re-establishment of the diaconate for women. The conclusions of the Synod for Women, initiated and implemented by the Maronite Church, are eagerly awaited, with the objective of enabling women to be more active and present in the life of the Eastern Catholic Churches.

i. *To trust young people and believe in their gifts and capacity to contribute to the various responsibilities of the Church*, especially in the service of proclaiming the Good News. This requires pastoral accompaniment that consists of listening attentively to them, accompanying them and assisting them in the discernment of their vocation.

j. *To have faith in the participation of people with disabilities and in the value and importance of their constructive role in the life of the Church.* Their human and spiritual experience should be welcomed, as well as the expression of their hope, which can inspire the healthy.

k. *To adopt the principles of good governance and transparency in the administration of Church institutions.* Many voices have been raised among the faithful of the Eastern Catholic Churches to re-examine the methods of governance and administration, especially in processes of decision-making. These voices have called for a vision of power as one of the concrete expressions of charity and service.

l. *To avoid minority complexes and to banish the fear associated with it*, due to multiple hardships suffered through persecution, immigration and other difficult situations, in order not to succumb to temptations and to preserve Faith and Hope. To work to enable Christians to take root in the territories of their respective countries and to contribute to stemming the current process that is emptying the East of the Christian presence and risks changing its demographic identity. This requires close cooperation with the civil authorities. Furthermore, for our Churches to incarnate the Church of Hope in the Middle East, there is a need to revive the prophetic spirit that listens to the Will of God and works for its accomplishment, for God is the true Master of History. This is how the witness of Hope can remain until the end of time.

VI
PRIORITIES

49. From all these synodal conclusions, three priorities emerge that deserve, from the point of view of the Eastern Catholic Churches, to be presented at the first plenary assembly of the next Synod (October 2023):

a. To help the particular Churches to promote the catholicity of the Church in a harmonious relationship between Unity and Diversity, while preserving the specificity of each of them. To reflect and act on the contribution and role the Eastern Catholic Churches can have in the communion of all the Churches.
b. To clarify the structures of communion and the juridical links between the Catholic Patriarchal Churches and the Successor of Peter in the See of Rome. To reconsider the nature of their relationship with the various dicasteries of the Roman Curia, which are at the service of communion within the universal Church.
c. To define and promote the most appropriate structures and mechanisms to concretise synodality in the life of the Church and of the People of God, while considering the multiplicity and diversity of religious and socio-cultural contexts throughout the world.

CONCLUSION

50. In the joy of a meeting that celebrated the One Church, and despite the sadness provoked by the loss of many after the deadly earthquakes in Turkey and Syria, we were given the grace to celebrate the Continental Synodal Assembly of the Catholic Churches in the Middle East and the Arabian Gulf. Together, we listened to each other and to the message that the Spirit is giving us today. All the participants in this Assembly expressed their joys and hopes, as well as the fears and the challenges they face. This has encouraged them to undertake concrete initiatives for which they have invested themselves in their respective Churches. Moreover, their participation made synodality a tangible experience and a space for free expression, especially for women and young people, as well as for many people whose voices were no longer heard; or for people with disabilities; and finally, for all those who found themselves on the margins of pastoral life. The experience of this Synodal Assembly has been a kind of remedy for many difficult situations within each Church, and for strained relations between the different Churches. It clearly recognised two dimensions without which the Church would lose the reason for her existence and her soul in the East: the ecumenical dimension, which concerns relations with sister Churches, and the dialogical dimension, which ensures openness and encounter with other religions.

51. It is clear that the People of God in the Middle East are called to be witnesses to their faith, through their life and their Hope, despite the complexity of the present context. The call to renewal, to journey together, to dialogue and to discernment is an urgency that admits of no postponement. To gather, without delay, the fruits of synodality, is done in view of the constant commitment to walk together behind Christ and under the guidance of the Holy Spirit, as the People of God, animated by the will to promote human fraternity. This is how the Eastern Catholic Churches will succeed in responding to the call of His Holiness Pope Francis to achieve what God wants for His Church in the third millennium: to be more synodal.

NORTH AMERICA

‘A New Experience of Discerning Together’

A NEW EXPERIENCE OF DISCERNING TOGETHER: OPPORTUNITIES AND CHALLENGES IN THE NORTH AMERICAN CONTINENTAL MEETINGS

Kristin Colberg and Gilles Routhier*

I
THE PROCESS OF THE NORTH AMERICAN CONTINENTAL ASSEMBLIES

Kristin Colberg

The Catholic Church in North America gathered between December 2022 and March 2023 in response to Pope Francis' invitation to continue the work of the 2021–2024 Synod: *For A Synodal Church: Communion, Participation and Mission.* The People of God in this region met to listen to and reflect on the voices of the local Churches as expressed in the Document for the Continental Stage (DCS) and deepen discernment of what the Holy Spirit is saying to the Churches (Rev. 2:7) in this time and place. The North American continental assemblies consisted of representatives from two episcopal conferences, the United States Catholic Conference of Bishops (USCCB) and the Canadian Conference of Catholic Bishops (CCCB). While Mexico is geographically a part of North America, the church of Mexico participated in the synod's continental phase as part of the Latin America and the Caribbean region, given their long history of partnership and on-going work on different Encuentros with CELAM. Thus, whereas for example the European continental assembly was comprised of thirty-nine episcopal conferences, Oceania of four conferences but twenty-one countries, North America was comprised of only two countries and episcopal conferences. While this makes North America the continent that included the smallest number of episcopal conferences, these meetings represented a huge number of people in that there are over seventy-seven million Catholics in this region (66.8 million in the United States and 10.8 million in Canada). Also, although there were only two episcopal conferences participating in these

* Since neither author participated in the whole Synodal gathering in North America, they each write about the part in which they participated.

assemblies, observers should not make the mistake of assuming that there was only minimal diversity of views and experiences represented in these meetings; on the contrary, there is tremendous diversity within the Catholic Church in North America

Virtual Assembly Meetings

Early in the development of the synod's continental stage, North America made the decision to conduct its assemblies virtually. The USCCB and the CCCB agreed that a virtual programme would accommodate the widest participation by the People of God by promoting greater accessibility for those unable to travel due to health or work, placing less financial stress on dioceses and eparchies, allowing for meetings to be held in multiple languages, and enhancing the possibility that all bishops would be able to participate. Concerns about the on-going effects of the COVID-19 pandemic also influenced the choice to gather the delegates virtually. While the meetings would be held over Zoom, it was a priority from the very beginning that these assemblies would maintain a synodal style including prayer, Spiritual Conversation and reflection. Another priority established by the North American synodal team was that the work of the continental stage would not be limited to involvement from particular delegates, but it would be a time for the entire People of God in the United States and Canada to engage in continued synodal listening and, in particular, in sustained reflection on the content of the DCS. The hope was that the delegates would bring the fruits of these continent-wide conversations to the continental assemblies.

Twelve (12) Virtual Assemblies (sessions) were held between mid-December 2022 and late January 2023. These sessions included seven (7) in English, three (3) in Spanish, and two (2) in French. The bishops of each of the 296 dioceses and eparchies in the US, and the 72 dioceses and eparchies in Canada, were asked to identify four to five delegates to participate in one of these gatherings. Although the choice of delegates was left to the discretion of the bishops, there was a desire to follow the encouragement voiced in the DCS that these assemblies represent the diversity of the People of God and 'pay special attention to the presence of women and young people (laymen and laywomen, consecrated men and women in formation, seminarians); people living in conditions of poverty or marginalisation, and those who have direct contact with these groups and persons; fraternal delegates from other Christian denominations; representatives of other religions and faith traditions; and some people with no religious affiliation' (108).[1] The chosen delegates, along with the bishops themselves, were asked to register for one of the twelve virtual assemblies.

1 Document for the Continental Phase of the Synod (DCS), 108.

Participants and Method

In the North American process, a distinction was made between delegates and bishops. This distinction, as we will see, is reflected in several parts of the process and was supported by some as a way of highlighting the unique role of the bishops in this process and critiqued by others who thought it hindered important opportunities for sharing. Ultimately, 931 delegates participated, with an almost equal split between women and men (50.2% / 49.8%, respectively). The 931 delegates ranged from a variety of vocations, with 391 lay women, 235 lay men, 148 priests (diocesan and religious), 77 women religious, and 4 non-ordained men religious. The statistics provided do not indicate the number of deacons who participated. In addition 146 bishops participated in one or more of the virtual assemblies. Almost 90% of the dioceses and eparchies in the United States and Canada (236/267) were represented at these meetings.[2]

The North American virtual assemblies were planned to correspond to the Spiritual Conversation Method encouraged in the DCS by the Secretariat of the Synod. At the heart of each assembly was time for small group listening circles. The composition of these small groups was established in advance to ensure that they represented the diversity of North America. Each group was comprised of six to eight individuals and consisted of a mix of delegates from Canada and the United States, from various dioceses and eparchies, included both men and women, representing multiple generations, and diverse cultural backgrounds. The bishops who participated in these assemblies were generally placed in separate listening circles comprised only of bishops. This was to allow bishops an important, and somewhat rare chance, to get to know one another and share their experiences of the synodal process. However, some questioned whether the value of allowing space for such conversations outweighed the benefit of including bishops in listening circles with the rest of the People of God so that there could be some important exchanges and chances for listening. A member of each group was named the facilitator and was tasked with keeping time and ensuring that all members were invited to contribute. Another individual in the group was charged with serving as the reporter who would share the fruits of the conversation in the plenary. Prior to each assembly, the delegates were introduced to one another via email. In this exchange, they were asked to share their name, diocese or eparchy, and how they had been engaged in the Synod thus far. This introduction allowed participants to see that there would be a range of experience represented in the conversation, from planning and facilitating listening sessions in their parish in the Diocesan Stage, to the virtual assemblies being one of their first encounters with the Synod.

2 The *Final Document* for the Continental Stage in North America contains an excellent introduction which provides these statistics and many other details of the process referred to here.

In the weeks leading up to the assemblies, each participant was sent a *Delegate Participation Guide* to orient them to the plan for these sessions and introduce them to the Spiritual Conversation Method. This guide led the participants through four steps: read, pray, reflect, and discern. As a first step of preparation, all delegates were asked to read the DCS. Additionally, it was recommended that participants read the national syntheses for both Canada and North America. The virtual version of the preparation guide provided the appropriate links for these documents in French, Spanish and English. The second step was to pray with the framing scriptural text of the DCS, Isaiah 54:2: 'Enlarge the space of your Tent, spread out your tent cloths unsparingly; lengthen your ropes and make firm your pegs.' The guide asked the participants to reflect on the following questions: 'What are the gifts and strengths of the Synod and the DCS? What are the challenges and the weaknesses of the Synod and the DCS?' The third preparatory step offered to the participants was to reflect on the DCS with three questions adapted from DCS 106.

1. What aspects of the *Document for the Continental Stage* resonated with what you heard in your diocesan and/or regional listening sessions?
2. The DCS reports some tensions as well as some joy; what substantial tensions or divergences emerge as particularly important for the Church in North America?
3. From what you heard and read, what are the priorities, recurring themes and calls to action that can be shared with other local Churches around the world and discussed during the First Session of the Synodal Assembly in October 2023?

Delegates were asked to note the main themes arising out of their personal prayer and reflection so that they might bring these insights to the continental assembly. The final step for delegates was to discern together, when possible, with the bishop, members of the local Church, and the other delegates from their diocese using the Spiritual Conversation Method. Delegates were asked to note the main themes arising out of their personal prayer and reflection so that they might bring these insights to the Continental Assembly.

The Twelve Assemblies

All twelve of the North American continental assemblies were conducted in two parts.

Part one began with a brief welcome and the *Adsumus* prayer, followed by few moments of reflective silence. The majority of this first part was anchored in the small group listening circles (147 in total). The listening circles met for fifty-five minutes and comprised of three rounds adopted from Appendix B, nr. 8 of the *Vademecum*.

1. **Round One**
   a. Open with the *Adsumus* prayer and a moment of silence.
   b. Everyone takes equal turns to share the fruit of his or her prayer, in relation to the reflection questions.
   c. There is no discussion in this round.
   d. Participants listen deeply to each person and attend to how the Holy Spirit is moving within oneself, within the person speaking, and in the group as a whole.
   e. Round One ends with a brief time of silence to note one's interior movements.
   f. Total time: 25 minutes.
2. **Round Two**
   a. Participants share what struck them most in the first round and what moved them during the time of silence.
   b. The same spiritual attentiveness is maintained.
   c. Round Two ends with a brief time of silence.
   d. Total time: 20 minutes.
3. **Round Three**
   a. Participants reflect on what is resonating in the conversation and what moved them most deeply.
   b. New insights and unresolved questions are noted.
   c. Prayers of gratitude can conclude the conversation.
   d. Total time: 10 minutes.[3]

At the conclusion of the listening circles, participants were invited to take a five-minute recess so that they could step away from the screens and take a break as needed.

Part two of the continental assemblies brought all the participants together as a large group to share, and reflect on, the fruits of the listening circles. The second part began with a prayerful reading of DCS 25-26 followed by a period of reflective silence. Then, a facilitator for each group was given three minutes to share two or three themes that emerged in the listening circle and a brief reflection on the conversation as a whole. Notetakers were present in the plenary sessions to record common themes and quotations from the large group sharing. However, participants were also invited to send in notes from their conversations to supplement what was recorded by the official notetakers. The time for this process of sharing was varied depending on the number of groups present, but typically it lasted an hour. One thing that stood out in these meetings was how many of the themes that arose in particular listening circles were shared by the group as a whole. After three or four of the groups shared the fruits of their sessions, the other groups would often begin by saying 'we talked about many of the same

3 Delegate Preparation Guide for the North American Virtual Continental Assemblies.

things that have already been mentioned.' Each session concluded with words of thanks from one of the organisers and a prayer, typically offered by Bishop Daniel Flores of Brownsville, Texas who led the synod process for the USCCB.

After the completion of all twelve virtual assemblies, representatives from each session met virtually early in December with the North American Synod Team for a 'Debrief Session'. A primary purpose of this meeting was to help prepare the North American Synod Team for the work of writing the final report. At this 'Debrief Session' the representatives shared the fruits of each of the twelve assemblies and then there was time to discuss common themes and experiences. In contrast to the virtual assemblies, the 'Debrief Session' allowed the Synod team to ask follow-up and clarification questions of the delegates. What emerged from the assemblies was a recognition that there are strong tensions within the Church, but that the delegates predominantly felt hope and encouragement and a desire for the synodal process to continue.

II
THE PROCESS OF WRITING THE CONTINENTAL DOCUMENT FOR NORTH AMERICA

Gilles Routhier

A Representative Group of the People of God?

The drafting team for the final document of the North American continental assembly met in Orlando, Florida from February 13-17, 2023. It was composed of 18 people: 11 from the United States and 7 from Canada. In addition, there was a representative from the General Secretariat of the Synod and an envoy from the Vatican Press Office. The US delegation consisted of six bishops from various parts of the country, four USCCB staff members, which included a priest and the moderator of the proceedings, and only one other person not attached to the USCCB. Or to put it differently: there were eight men and three women, one of whom was a religious sister. While this delegation was diverse in origin, with many having roots in the Latino community, its ability to represent the whole People of God in this country remained weak. The bishops formed the majority of the participants. In addition, the USCCB staff members – who can be considered clerics in the sociological, not ecclesiastical, sense of the term[4] – represented more than a third of the participants. This left only one

4 This is an employee in a law firm or an officer in a ministerial office. A notary's clerk, for example. The term is used especially in the field of law to designate an employee working in the office of a public or ministerial officer; secretary of a person, a group of persons, an official body. They are at the service of an institution. The term became specialised in the Middle Ages and came to designate those who performed services or functions in the Church. For the sociologist Max Weber, the cleric is the one who represents the institution. The cleric has a charisma of function that legitimises him.

person, a religious sister, who did not represent the institutional dimension of the Church. The Canadian delegation, made up of people from three of the four regions of the country (there was no one from the Atlantic), was composed of two bishops, two priests, one nun and two lay people. Four of the seven persons (two bishops, one priest and one lay person) were attached to the Canadian Conference of Catholic Bishops, hence the majority.

The composition of this group, in spite of the good will of the participants, often led to a lack of balance during the exchanges. The composition of the group and the choice of the invited persons had undoubtedly been decided by those in charge, in both countries, of the synodal process. Similarly, the decision to have a USCCB staff member serve as moderator for the process must have been made in the same way. It is noted that the composition of the group would not have met the indications given by canon law for the composition of bodies promoting the synodal life of a particular Church, notably the pastoral council of the diocese. Indeed, canon 512 § 2 states that 'The Christian faithful who are designated to a pastoral council are to be selected in such a way that they truly reflect the entire portion of the People of God which constitutes the diocese, with consideration given to the different areas of the diocese, social conditions and professions, and the role which they have in the apostolate whether individually or joined with others.' It cannot be said that the eighteen persons assembled in Orlando faithfully reflect the entire portion of the People of God who live in Canada and the United States of America, taking into account the various regions, social and professional conditions, and participation in the apostolate.

The Distant Voice of God's People

The voices of the 931 delegates from the North American dioceses who had participated in the virtual continental assemblies were present at this retreat through a document which synthesised the extensive notes that had been taken by the notetakers and submitted by participants. This synthesis of the zoom sessions, very well done, totaled 57 pages (verbatim).[5] These pages allowed the writing team to hear from the delegates at the twelve zoom meetings. In addition, the experience of the 'Debrief Session' and the reflections shared there were also helpful in discerning a sense of what the People of God in North America had said during this consultation. In my opinion, we were able to develop a spiritual climate at the 'Debrief Session' that was not achieved at the five-day writing retreat in Orlando. The spiritual atmosphere was possible, not because prayers were recited and a biblical text read; rather it was possible because an atmosphere of deep listening came about. In Orlando, we frequently recited prayers, we multiplied the signs of the cross – often done in a hurry – we recited again and

5 North American Continental Assembly. Plenary Notes, 57 pages.

again the *Adsumus*, which began our work sessions or interrupted them, but did we develop a spiritual atmosphere, which is not the same as reciting prayers?

This seems to me to be the crucial element. Furthermore, there was a great distance, not only in the atmosphere, but also in the content of what was said, between the 'Debrief Session' and the writing retreat. In this preparatory zoom session of debriefing, the eighteen people charged with writing the text that would conclude the continental phase of the synodal journey in North America hardly spoke at all. They made room for the nineteen delegates, listening to them tell the stories of walking with others. They welcomed these stories with great respect, as echoes of the field and of the life of the People of God. Then, about ten days later, in Orlando, the members of the writing team found themselves alone, isolated. It was no longer an assembly that allowed the portion of the People of God of the Churches in North America to be truly present – albeit by being reflected on, according to the various regions, social and professional conditions and their differentiated participation in the apostolate – as determined by the *Code of Canon Law* for the diocesan pastoral council. In practice, only 'clerics/clergy', in a sociological or ecclesial sense of the word, were left to write a text. All that remained of the words of the People of God, in all their diversity and complexity, were the 57 pages that reported the exchanges held during the zoom meetings, and the echo of the living words of the nineteen delegates heard on 1 February. These words became inert, buried in memories and mere ink on paper. It was necessary to constantly try to bring them to life, to give new life. From then on, the 931 participants in the zoom meetings of December 2022 and January 2023 were absent. We had gone into retreat, as expressed in the name of this meeting, the 'Continental Writing Retreat'. Who says retreat, says separation, distance, isolation. We never spoke of a 'Continental Assembly', but of a 'Continental Writing Retreat'. There was only one group left to write a text, isolated, separate and in retreat. This was, in my opinion, the 'original sin' of this process that hindered its ability to succeed.

Left alone, without any interaction with this portion of God's people living in North America, the challenge was to continue to listen to these people and lift up their voices. The temptation was great to write a text that expressed our own convictions, our own ideas, what we thought was right, etc. Over and over again, the group of writers had to be brought back to what the People had said. They needed to be reminded that their words should not be forgotten. However, the writers' group no longer had a living contact with the members of God's holy people in their diversity. There were not even small groups, scattered across the continent, with whom one could keep in touch and interact, if only at a distance and occasionally, through the myriad means of communication available today. No face-to-face meetings, not even at a distance.

The Conversion Called for By the Listening to the People of God

The Continental Writing Retreat was designed to be a retreat behind closed doors. It fostered an 'inter-self'. The development of the document followed a process led by the retreat moderator, presented at the first meeting. If a doubt was raised or an objection formulated during the process, the answer came spontaneously: 'Trust the process'. This was not, strictly speaking, the synodal process, but the process devised to lead eighteen people to a final document. What was most demanding in this process was to pay attention to what people had said, to return to it again and again and to be faithful to it. In short, not to speak for ourselves, but to carry the insights verbalised by the 931 people who had spoken at the zoom meetings.

This conversion to 'listening to the other' – which represents one of the greatest challenges of the synodal process – is not simply a matter of good will on the part of each other. It also has structural and methodological dimensions. On the one hand, the capacity to listen was linked to the greater or lesser knowledge and appropriation of the minutes of the plenary sessions of each zoom meeting (57 pages). If the notes had not been read, reread and pondered by the members of the team responsible for writing the document, it would become difficult to echo them. This, then, is also a matter of methodology. What is the starting point of the reflection? What is the source material from which to work? What do we have to keep coming back to and who should measure the results of our work? Finally, what interaction do we have with participants outside the Working Group and who can validate the fidelity of our development with regard to what had been said by so many people, who at times had expressed feelings of hurt or suffering? Regardless of their willingness or goodwill, members of the writing team encountered all three of these obstacles along the way, resulting in real confusion. Because the writing team did not have living contact, even remotely and intermittently, with members of God's people who would have been able to challenge the isolated writing team, the group of writers remained existentially cut off from the most important source for their work.

Impasse as a Stage in the Synodal Process

After three days of exchanges and discussions, the impasse was obvious. The outline proposed by some small groups on the three themes of the synodal journey (communion, participation and mission) added to the perplexity of many. As if in a theological treatise, an infinite number of questions related to the communion of the faithful in the Church (up to cloistered nuns and permanent deacons) were addressed, all of which had not been dealt with by the participants in the zoom meeting. Clearly, the work had to be taken up again.

A few interventions, caucuses on the sidelines of the meeting, and a night of sleep led to an initiative to break the logjam. The morning of the final day was led by one of the bishops present who attempted to build consensus, based on what the participants in the zoom meetings had said. This change in leadership led to the development of consensus around a new plan. The small Working Groups went back to work, gathering what the zoom meeting participants had said on various topics. It was now too late to expect a final document by the end of the retreat. We had to resign ourselves to leaving without having produced a conclusive document of the North American continental meeting. At least this time we had materials and *lineamenta* for a document that was more in line with what the 931 participants in the zoom meetings had expressed. The commitment to foregrounding the voices of the delegates was now accepted by all.

Putting the Work Back on Track

With the exception of the bishops, the participants left the next morning. As planned, the bishops met behind closed doors and offered some suggestions for breaking the deadlock. It was a turning point. As at Vatican II, after most of the documents drawn up during the preparatory phase had been rejected at the first session, significant efforts had to be made during the first intersessional period of the Council. In this process, too, the document and the plan for completing it had to be re-envisioned. It was agreed that the text had to be significantly reworked and this effort was entrusted to a very small group: a bishop and a few members of the staff of the two conferences. This new phase, at a distance, was to last from the last week of February until 27 March, and involve several back-and-forth meetings between the small group in charge of the drafting and the entire drafting team. A new draft of the text was presented on 3 March, a substantially reworked and already much better text. Team members were given until 8 March to comment. At this stage, a novelty was introduced: delegates who had shared their thoughts with the writing team following the zoom meetings before the team went into isolation (1 February – Continental Stage Debrief Session) were again reintroduced to the writing process. They were presented with the draft text on 14 March and their reactions were expected on 17 March. Twenty-five delegates from both countries provided feedback on this version of the text, with a view to improving it. After a series of back and forth discussions, the text was submitted to the drafting team for a final reading on 27 March, with the bishops holding a special meeting before the full team met. It was at this final meeting that the text was approved.

It was then sent for approval by the councils of the two episcopal conferences. Eventually there was a French version of the text, which had been requested for a long time, without ever obtaining satisfaction. In fact, the linguistic diversity of the continent had not been taken into account until during the writing phase. At the time of the zoom meetings (October-December), the issue of languages had been given consideration by offering separate meetings, in English, French and Spanish. Yet, because these meetings did not provide simultaneous translations, there was no exchange between people of different linguistic groups, which implied that there was no opportunity for an intercultural enrichment.

The Decisive Role Played by the Bishops

The bishops (six from the USCCB and two from the CCCB) played an important, positive and constructive role throughout. They were the only ones who had the authority to break the deadlock. This was particularly the case on Thursday, 16 February and Friday, 17 February. When, on the Wednesday evening of the writing retreat, it became clear that the proposed plan was unacceptable, some of the bishops listened to the members of the group who were expressing their dissatisfaction and fears about the impasse. They provided crucial positive leadership. The next day, one of them took over the leadership of the team, trying to turn the situation around. A modified plan was developed as a group and, most importantly, the team members were put back to work, this time explicitly asking them to write up the feedback from the zoom sessions held in December and January. The 57-page report regained the importance it should always have had. The dynamic was changed. However, we were at the eleventh hour and it was not possible to arrive at a text in the remaining short time: available was only half a day of effective work. Already, however, the text improved; it reflected more faithfully the outcomes of the virtual assemblies.

Throughout the revision process, a question of concern arose: should the 'Bishops' Reflections on the Experience of Synodality in North America' be inserted into the text itself, and if so, where in the text should it appear, or should it be a separate document? It was decided to include their reflections, because under the circumstances it seemed most useful for the Christian people 'to know' how Bishops see the synodal process.

A Non-event

The role of the press was marginal in this process. It is true that zoom meetings do not favor media coverage. Moreover, who would be interested in a meeting of eighteen people in an isolated retreat centre? Since there was no real assembly, there was no event or media coverage, except for a sporadic curiosity on the part of the Catholic press, which had heard about a continental meeting that was not announced. As with the other continental assemblies, a representative of the Vatican Press Office attended and reported on the Orlando meeting. Otherwise, it was a private meeting, with no media coverage and no influence in its environment or in the Churches. The Orlando meeting was not broadcasted by streaming and no one other than the small team of eighteen people cloistered in their retreat could participate.

While there were challenges in this process, there is consensus in North America that the final document is able to give voice to some important fruits reaped during the continental process. The *Final Document* for the Continental Stage in North America highlights three themes that capture the heart of what was heard during these continental assemblies. These three themes are:

* *Called and Gifted Through Baptism*: Implications of the dignity and responsibilities of our common baptism.
* *Communion with Christ and One Another*: Recognising the stresses on our ecclesial communion in North America and discerning ways forward.
* *Sent Forth on Mission*: Living out our communal baptismal call to bring the Good News to the world.

The introductory part of the document sums up North America's contribution as follows:

> This report from the Continental Stage is North America's contribution to the larger, global discussion and discernment stage of the 2021-2024 Synod. The North American participants felt that the DCS reflected much of what the participants expressed during the diocesan and national stages of the Synod. The conversations at the Continental Stage focused on the intense need for the Church to become even more synodal. In summary, what was shared and what was heard at the Continental Stage was that by our common baptism, we are each called by God and gifted by God with dignity. This common baptism places us in communion with Christ and one another. The synodal journey thus far has made us more conscious of where the stresses on our communion lie. But it also has revealed that, as one delegate described it, 'the more we become missionary disciples the more we will address these challenges' (Debrief Session). Our baptismal dignity is inseparable from our baptismal responsibility, which sends us forth on mission. 'Many times, we focus on the negative and forget the joy; the Spirit we experience in our core is to be missionary' (Debrief Session) (nr. 13).

NORTH AMERICAN FINAL DOCUMENT FOR THE CONTINENTAL STAGE OF THE 2021-2024 SYNOD

Orlando, Fl. USA

I
INTRODUCTION

***He said to them, 'Come, and you will see.'* (John 1:39)**

1.1 The Invitation

1. Time and time again, the invitation from the Holy Father to the People of God to participate in the *2021-2024 Synod: For a Synodal Church: Communion, Participation & Mission* elicited a range of responses. Profound joy and enthusiasm were experienced by many, while resistance, suspicion, and anxiety were aroused in some. In the Continental Stage, the delegates accepted the invitation; they came, and they saw. As one delegate remarked, *'The Holy Spirit is at work! This is only the beginning; we don't know where the Holy Spirit is taking us. We are coming to a deeper understanding of what it means to be Catholic'* (Session X Group 1). The experience of the Synod demonstrated that many Catholics in North America are committed to the communal discernment necessary to discover where the Holy Spirit is guiding the Church in the present moment.

2. There was great gratitude for being together with other Catholics, who come from different parts of the continent, who are lay, religious, and clergy, each with their own ideas and views, yet all part of the one Church. As one group mentioned, *'The synodal process gives us life and also gives life to the Church; we are grateful for that gift'* (Session IV Group 8). The overwhelming sentiment from those who participated in the

local, national, and now continental stages was an optimistic hope and uplifting joy at being able to participate and contribute. As one group noted, *'The word that kept coming up in our group was* joy – *to share, to listen, and to be together'* (Session III Group 10). The experience of being able to share and express both disappointments and blessings was seen as a real fruit of the synodal process. *'People would start with pains and resentments, but at the end of the process the Holy Spirit had opened people up'* (Session II Group 7).

1.2 The Virtual Continental Assemblies

3. The Continental Stage in North America consisted of twelve virtual assemblies (sessions): seven in English, three in Spanish, and two in French. Attending these assemblies were 931 delegates, with an almost equal split among delegates between women and men (50.2% / 49.8%, respectively). The 931 delegates ranged from a variety of vocations, with 391 lay women, 235 lay men, 76 deacons, 148 priests (diocesan and religious), 77 women religious, and 4 non-ordained men religious. There also were 146 bishops who participated in one or more of the virtual assemblies. Almost 90% of the dioceses and eparchies in the United States and Canada (236/267) were represented in the assemblies. As one group reported, *'There was a lot of participation and diversity, yet there was still lots of convergence. The Spirit is at work'* (Session III Group 6).

931 Delegates

Women 50.2%

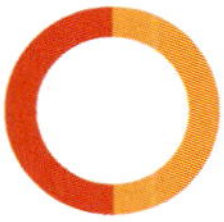

Men 49.8%

391 Lay Women | 235 Lay Men | 76 Deacons | 148 Priests

77 Women Religious | 4 Non-ordained Men Religious

4. The virtual format for the Continental Assembly was chosen to accommodate as many delegates as possible, including those who were unable to travel due to health or work, and to minimise financial burdens while maximising participation of the dioceses and eparchies in the United States and Canada. The ongoing COVID-19 pandemic also influenced the decision to hold virtual assemblies. Feedback from the assemblies revealed mixed opinions on the value of a virtual format. Some were appreciative that the virtual assemblies allowed for greater participation. *'Some of the groups I attended were easily able to engage in a prayerful manner in Spiritual Conversation and the questions. There was a possibility of significant dissonant voices to be heard'* (Session I

Feedback). Others felt that the Spiritual Conversations suffered due to the lack of in-person engagement. *'Zoom is a great tool and made it easier for more participation as travel may have limited those who could attend, but in-person is always so much better'* (Session II Feedback).

5. Each Ordinary was asked to select four to five delegates to be part of the Continental Assembly. These delegates, along with the bishops themselves, were then asked to register for one of the twelve virtual assemblies that would be the main component of the Continental Assembly. For each assembly, small listening circles were formed in such a manner that they consisted of a mix of delegates from Canada and the United States, dioceses and eparchies, men and women, generations, and cultural backgrounds. To aid the preparation for these assemblies, each delegate was sent a *Delegate Preparation Guide* (Appendix C) that outlined the format of the assemblies and the *Spiritual Conversation Model*.

6. A week before each assembly, the delegates were introduced to one another via email. In this exchange, they were asked to share their name, diocese or eparchy, and how they had been engaged in the Synod thus far. There was a range of experience, from planning and facilitating listening sessions in their parish in the Diocesan Stage to the virtual assemblies being one of their first encounters with the Synod. Many exchanged warm wishes along with their hopes and prayers for the upcoming assemblies. While not always effective, overall, these introductions were helpful.

7. Each of the twelve virtual assemblies began with the *Adsumus* prayer, followed by time together in small group listening circles (147 in total). These small groups followed the Spiritual Conversation Model, as suggested by the Secretariat for the General Synod. After the small group discussions, everyone returned to the larger group to share the fruits of the conversations, there was a reflection from DCS #25-26, and there was a period of silence (Appendix D). While some delegates noted that the Spiritual Conversations had the potential to be more enriching if they had been in person, many others observed that the Spirit was present in the virtual assemblies. *'I am very grateful for the opportunity to participate in the synodal process and truly appreciate the efforts of those who organised the virtual gatherings. While there certainly were limitations because the sessions were virtual, nevertheless, I do believe it was a good experience and could sense the Holy Spirit at work'* (Session III Feedback). *'The very real feeling of the guiding presence of the Holy Spirit is its greatest strength'* (Session VIII Feedback).

8. The North American Synod Team (see Appendix A), in a spirit of co-responsibility, relied upon the delegates to facilitate and report back the fruits of the listening circles at the plenary portion of the Continental Assemblies. This process achieved varying degrees of success, depending on the preparation of the participants. Nonetheless, the methodology offered the delegates an opportunity for formation in synodality. All of the delegates were given resources explaining the Spiritual Conversation Model, and a webinar on this topic was offered to those who volunteered to facilitate a listening circle; a recording of the webinar was made available to others.

9. The listening experienced by the delegates during the Spiritual Conversation was greatly appreciated. Many spoke of it with admiration, acknowledging that they had been transformed. Not only did the synodal experience create a space for them to speak freely, but it also provided an opportunity to be heard. For many it was a discovery, an illuminating experience. It filled them with joy, hope, and gratitude. '*The methodology that has emerged from the synodal process – particularly the Spiritual Conversations – is so important. We have learned that we can learn from listening. We hope this will continue! This is an empowering way to reach out and to attend to places of hurt*' (Session XII Group 2).

1.3 The Continental Debrief Session

10. After the completion of all twelve virtual assemblies, representatives from each met with the North American Synod Team, which was tasked with writing this report. At this 'debriefing,' the representatives shared the fruits of each of the twelve assemblies; common themes and experiences naturally emerged and were further discussed. In contrast to the virtual assemblies, the Debrief Session allowed the Synod Team to ask follow-up and clarification questions of the delegates. As will be seen below, what emerged from the assemblies was a recognition that there are strong tensions within the Church, but the delegates predominantly felt hope and encouragement and a desire for the synodal process to continue. At the Debrief Session, one delegate shared that she '*was very encouraged by the small groups; people are modeling synodality for themselves, and I can see that as a fruit of the process*' (Debrief Session).

1.4 The Continental Writing Retreat

11. For the composition of this document, the North American Synod Team began with a weeklong retreat. A word that frequently surfaced during the team's discernment at the retreat was 'messiness.' Synodality is not always easy to comprehend; it can also be seen to be a complicated

process. As a participant at one of the virtual assemblies noted, '*People don't know what the Synod on Synodality is for. They don't understand the purpose, couldn't grasp what was trying to be achieved*' (Session XI Group 14). Yet, there was the simultaneous acknowledgement that trust in the Holy Spirit is crucial for the fruitfulness of the Synod. '*Maybe we need to admit that we're stuck here and that we don't exactly know where we're going, but it's okay because we're following the Holy Spirit! We must allow the Holy Spirit to take the lead to guide us to where we are meant to go!*' (Session XI Group 14). When there were moments of uncertainty, the Synod Team chose to trust the Holy Spirit and each other. Openness to the Spirit is essential to being fruitful companions on the synodal path.

1.5 The North American Final Document

12. What follows is based on what was heard at the virtual assemblies. The North American Synod Team was composed of laity, priests, religious, and bishops from both Canada and the United States, who met together to reflect on what was shared and to discern not a plan or a project, but simply what has arisen from this journey so far. In order to further ensure that the *Final Document* was faithful to what was shared during the Continental Assembly and to foster co-responsible discernment, the Synod Team invited comments and reflections on a draft of this document from 25 delegates from Canada and 25 delegates from the United States. The document was subsequently revised in light of their contributions. Bishops designated by each episcopal conference validated and approved the *Final Document*.[1]

13. This report from the Continental Stage is North America's contribution to the larger, global discussion and discernment stage of the 2021-2024 Synod. The North American participants felt that the DCS reflected much of what the participants expressed during the diocesan and national stages of the Synod. The conversations at the Continental Stage focused on the intense need for the Church to become even more synodal. In summary, what was shared and what was heard at the Continental Stage was that by our common baptism, we are each called by God and gifted by God with dignity. This common baptism places us in communion with Christ and one another. The synodal journey thus far has made us more conscious of where the stresses on our communion lie. But it also has revealed that, as one delegate described it, '*the more we become missionary disciples the more we will address these challenges*' (Debrief

1 This included the CCCB Executive Committee and the USCCB Executive Committee.

Session). Our baptismal dignity is inseparable from our baptismal responsibility, which sends us forth on mission. *'Many times, we focus on the negative and forget the joy; the Spirit we experience in our core is to be a missionary'* (Debrief Session).

II
CALLED AND GIFTED THROUGH BAPTISM

14. Expressed over and over in the Continental Assembly of North America was the need to grow into a more synodal Church, starting with the recognition of the dignity of all the baptised. *'Walking together and expanding the tent envelops everyone. All the baptised have a right to be there'* (Session IX Group 2). Every human person possesses the dignity that comes from being created in the image of God. Through baptism, Christians share in an exalted dignity and vocation to holiness, with no inequality based on race, nationality, social condition, or sex, because we are one in Christ Jesus (*Lumen gentium* 32; cf. Gal 3:28, Col 3:11). *'Synod was a good way for laity and clergy to realise that we are all the Church and that we have a co-responsibility for expanding the tent. If we aim to do that it will take all of us!'* (Session VIII Group 3).

15. In the Continental Stage in North America, the joy of the participants was based in large part on their baptismal dignity being acknowledged through the synodal path. This awakened a desire for a greater recognition of, and opportunities for, co-responsibility within the Church and her mission. *'One of the challenges was the need to keep discovering and keep seeing what our baptismal call is inviting us to do'* (Debrief Session). At the same time, many of the conversations, like those held during the diocesan and national stages, referenced times when the Church's members failed to recognise this shared dignity. These failures place stress on our communion with one another. *'Responding to Christ's message requires that we talk the talk and walk the walk. We all must respond to our universal call to holiness'* (Session VIII Group 10).

2.1 Co-responsibility

16. Our personal call to holiness arises from our baptismal dignity. We are called to a particular state of life and simultaneously to share in the mission of the Church. The call to holiness includes and endures for all the baptised, no matter their state in life. *'We should release the gifts of everyone'* (Debrief Session). As several delegates in the North American Continental Stage explained, this universal call to holiness is lived out in particular ways of service to the wider mission of the Church. *'We cannot always be all things to all people; some people have certain charisms and we need to divvy up the work'* (Debrief Session).

17. Frequently in the Continental Assembly, there was the desire for greater co-responsibility among the laity and the clergy, including bishops. *'We need to ground ourselves in the equal dignity of baptism. This is an entry point for co-responsibility'* (Session XII Group 2). An emphasis on our shared baptismal dignity allows us to see in each other a co-laborer who can be formed, equipped, and encouraged for mission. *'We are called to act co-responsibly in a synodal fashion, not to wait until we know how to do everything perfectly, but to walk together as imperfect people'* (Session II Group 6). When Church structures and practices are dynamic and able to move with the Holy Spirit, everyone is able to *'use their gifts in service of the Church and of each other'* (Session XII Group 4).

18. For many delegates, the experience of the synodal path was one that reignited their call to discipleship. *'Through the synodal process the Church is being lived out right now in front of us and we are experiencing it! We are excited about this. The Holy Spirit is moving in this process and giving us a common spirit of mission worldwide!'* (Session III Group 2). This co-responsible Church will challenge each of us and necessitate greater collaboration and communication among all the People of God. *'We must... reach out to everyone from every walk of life. The responsibility of ministry is not just for priests, but for each baptised person. This is a real space where we can allow women and some of the more marginalised folks in the Church to really take up leadership roles'* (Session XI Group 7).

2.2 Women

19. There can be no true co-responsibility in the Church without fully honoring the inherent dignity of women. The continental delegates recognised the crucial work women do to keep the Church *'alive and healthy'* (Session IV Group 8). Nonetheless, delegates also named women as a marginalised group in the Church. *'We have come a long way, but we deplore the fact that women cannot invest themselves fully'* (Session V Group 4). While clarity is still needed around exactly what a fully co-responsible Church looks like, delegates proposed the examination of a variety of aspects of Church life, including decision-making roles, leadership, and ordination. Central in the discernment of these questions is the faithful acknowledgment of women's baptismal dignity. A frequently heard call was that *'more space needs to be opened for them, especially at decision-making tables'*

(Session IV Group 8). The Church in North America was encouraged to *'recognise, discern, and promote the role of women . . . so that they may have a greater presence in the Church'* (Session IV Group 5).

2.3 Youth / Young People

20. Authentic acknowledgment and respect for the gifts and talents of young people is another vital aspect of a co-responsible Church in North America. *'We are often perceived as the future, but we are also the 'now' of the Church'* (Debrief Session). Many delegates lamented the absence of young people both in their parishes as well as in the Continental Assembly. *'We are concerned that young people are not at the table and we wonder how they are going to be represented in Rome. Not only people who work with young people but the young people themselves. They know their reality the best'* (Session VI Group 1). Empowering young people to more fully live out their baptismal dignity requires that we confront tensions within our communion as the Body of Christ. The *'gifts of young people are not always fully appreciated by older generations. We should appreciate the creativity and the ingenuity of young people'* (Session I Group 6).

2.4 Formation

21. The People of God participating in the Continental Stage in North America expressed a great longing for formation as the key to living out both their baptismal dignity and their duty in a co-responsible Church. Especially as a response to ongoing challenges – as well as the desire to further engage in the practice of synodality – formation arose as a fundamental requirement. *'The answer to that question that surfaced was the need for formation – formation for synodality, for listening deeply; formation for stretching as is alluded to in widening the tent'* (Session I Group 9). Delegates expressed the desire for the Church to further *'develop formation in order to know our faith better'* (Session V Group 7). There also was a special concern to better accompany youth throughout their formation process, fostering a bold curiosity about the Christian faith. *'Children who go through religious education come out wondering if there is even a God. Are they afraid to ask questions? If they are afraid to ask questions, they may be stunted in their ability to grow in their faith'* (Session VIII Group 7). This desire was intimately linked to the dignity of our baptism and the responsibility it entails. *'In sharing our faith, we – who are in the pews – we have to not only be able to share our faith but to understand it'* (Session I Group 5).

22. Delegates expressed a desire for formation that is life-long and offered to all members of the communion of the baptised, whatever their vocation. This includes not only formation in the fundamental teachings of our faith, but also formation for synodality, co-responsibility, welcoming, and going out to the peripheries. *'A deeper formation allows us to present the beauty of our faith, rather than a list of rules. To go deeper and underneath it and be formed in a way that allows us to present the hows and whys'* (Session XII Group 6). Delegates were insistent that deeper formation is central to our ability to live out our baptismal dignity and strengthen communion with Christ and each other. *'How do we go about becoming a people that have a disposition of listening, of being synodal, of putting listening first?'* (Session III Group 8).

III
COMMUNION WITH CHRIST AND ONE ANOTHER

23. During the Continental Assembly, the North American Synod Team heard over and over again of the need within the synodal process to maintain the centrality of Christ, with whom we are all united by baptism. *'Jesus Christ* [is] *at the center of the tent'* (Session II Group 9). *'The Eucharist is the center of our lives'* (Session XI Group 4). *'The center of our faith is the person of Jesus Christ'* (Session XII Group 8). *'Jesus is the center pole of the tent that we must never lose sight of in what we do'* (Session III Group 16). Through baptism we are made members of the Body of Christ and are drawn into communion with one another.

24. Yet the synodal process of discernment in North America has revealed that the Church, like the larger society, is experiencing polarisation and a strong pull towards fragmentation. This was a major theme throughout the diocesan, national, and continental stages of the Synod. As one delegate commented, *'The call to communion is something we need to make present in us and in our communities'* (Session XI Group 15). There was a recognition that we cannot fully live out our baptismal dignity and responsibility without addressing the areas where our communion with one another, and thereby our communion with Christ, is stressed almost to the breaking point. Several themes emerged that were common among all the virtual assemblies.

3.1 Trust and Credibility

25. A significant threat to communion within the Church is a lack of trust, especially between the bishops and the laity, but also between the

clergy in general and the lay faithful. One of the major areas of tension in North America is the clergy sexual abuse crisis and its effects, which have created a loss of trust that cannot be overstated. Many people continue to carry the wounds of abuse and many others have lost their trust in the clergy and in the Church's institutions. To this reality, one must add that the historical wrongs found in the residential/boarding schools for indigenous people, which also included abuse of all kinds. This only compounds the woundedness of the Church and the lack of trust in its leaders. *'The sexual abuse crisis and the residential schools are so much a part of the reality of the Church; we have to be able to engage those questions and face those situations'* (Session II Group 9). Although it was acknowledged that Church leaders have done much to promote healing and prevent future abuses, it is apparent that more needs to be done to rebuild trust. As one delegate commented, *'There are different levels and degrees of engagement within the Church as an institution, but it has to start with healing and trust-building'* (Session II Group 8). Many of the listening sessions of the Synod called for a cultural change in the Church with a view to greater transparency, accountability, and co-responsibility. *'Synodality,'* it was seen by many, was *'a beautiful way to build trust through dialogue'* (Session XII Group 4).

3.2 Greater Inclusivity

26. In the Continental Assembly, as in our national reports, there was a deep desire for greater inclusivity and welcome within the Church. In fact, one of the major factors that was seen as breaking down communion was the experience of many that certain people or groups feel unwelcome in the Church. The groups named during the Continental Stage included women, young people, immigrants, racial or linguistic minorities, LGBTQI+ persons, people who are divorced and remarried without an annulment, and those with varying degrees of physical or mental abilities. While the reasons for experiencing the Church as inhospitable may vary, what is common is the Church's need to authentically honor the baptismal dignity of everyone. As one participant explained, *'we think we are welcoming, but we know that there are people who feel "outside" the Church'* (Session III Group 12). Another suggested that this is because *'we get caught up in the minutiae of evaluating the worth of people on the margins'* (Session VIII Group 14). *'There is a need to differentiate between the importance of teaching and the need to welcome those into the Church, especially as it relates to our LGBTQI+ brothers and sisters'* (Session II Group 4).

27. Some participants in the synodal process reported on the profound sense of suffering of those prevented from receiving the Eucharist. While there are a variety of reasons for this reality, perhaps preeminent among them is Catholics who are divorced and remarried without an annulment, and others whose objective situation in life contradicts the beliefs and teachings of the Church. Additionally, some delegates spoke of those wounded by the limitations placed on the pre-conciliar Latin rite. Unfortunately, liturgy is not always experienced as unifying. '*We could find our unity in common prayer, but liturgy is one of the things that is divisive in the Church and we must break through that*' (Session X Group 18).

28. The listening sessions also produced ample examples of the longing to incorporate young people more fully in the life of the Church. As one group stated simply, the youth '*are indispensable*' (Session V Group 4). Practically all of the synodal consultations shared a deep ache in the wake of the departure of young people and viewed this as integrally connected to becoming a more inclusive Church. One group noted that there is a '*generational divide in communities – tension between younger and older members of the Church. This is something to pay attention to*' (Session XI Group 9). The desire to be a more inclusive Church resonated throughout all the virtual assemblies. One delegate said, '*The Church must know how to be the family of God, to be open and receptive*' (Session IV Group 7).

3.3 Listening

29. Alongside the desire to be a more inclusive and welcoming Church was the need to understand how to be more hospitable, while maintaining and being true to Church teaching. '*There is tension between welcoming and formation in Church teaching. We need to keep in mind that Church teaching comes from the gospel – work must be done in that kind of hospitality*' (Session III Group 6). A key to solving this problem was seen in the ability to listen. One delegate reminds us that '*listening doesn't always mean you get the answer you are looking for*' (Session X Group 6), while another pointed out that listening helps us understand the perspectives of others and thereby welcome them (cf. Session III Group 12). Another proposed that we '*need to be inclusive and to love people enough to meet them where they are, but to love them enough not to leave them there*' (Session III Group 7).

30. A frequent theme heard during the assemblies was that '*tension is a part of life and will never be completely resolved. We must keep listening,*

but tension will always be part of our life. We need to be okay with that and allow the Holy Spirit to guide us through that' (Session XI Group 11). The delegates reported that the Synod was an experience of both being heard and of listening. It is important that *'people have a chance to speak but also to be heard and validated, recognised'* (Session III Group 11).

3.4 Formation in Synodality

31. In the virtual assemblies there was discussion about the stress placed on our communion within the Church. There was a consensus that more formation in synodality is needed. *'We need formation on how to listen and accompany; resources that will help us grow as people'* (Session VI Group 4). The majority of the delegates agreed that in order to become a more listening Church, one that bolsters communion, more formation in how to be a synodal Church is crucial. *'How do we continue training ourselves, converting ourselves and others, to this synodal way?'* (Session 1 Group 12) was a frequent question.

32. Synodality is a great source of hope for renewing and strengthening communion. The hope is that by becoming more synodal, the Church, as one delegate described, would create *'safe places where people can ask their real questions about Church teaching without judgment or punishment'* (Session X Group 8). In describing the experience of the Synod, one delegate said, *'The most beautiful thing about this was that from every stage of listening, people responded in an extraordinary way. People felt listened to very well. We believe that the concept of synodality is a concept that must continue, that must become a way of life. We thank God for these fruits'* (Session VII Group 3). Such formation not only would aid the development of deeper bonds of communion within the Church, but also would be a stimulus for evangelisation and mission. As was discussed in one of the assemblies, *'We want our faithful to know that they are needed and wanted . . . Listening is the first part of evangelisation; we are accompanying folks, meeting them where they are'* (Session VIII Group 2).

IV
SENT FORTH ON MISSION

33. Throughout the Continental Stage in North America, delegates recognised the duty of the communion of the baptised to go out on mission to the peripheries to proclaim the Gospel and care for those who are wounded and downtrodden. *'How beautiful the Church got to* *be by the wounded and the hurt! When the Church reaches out in times of disaster, that is a reminder that the Church is a place of compassion and care. Caring for people is a good way to welcome them in'* (Session I Group 4). Many recognised that the Church is at its best when walking alongside those forced to the margins of our society. It was recognised that for the Church to be truly missionary – to go out to the peripheries and to evangelise – what is needed is holistic formation in our baptismal dignity and calling, in co-responsibility, and in synodality. It also was recognised that in order to proclaim Christ effectively and clearly, the Church must be united. *'We must find the balance to proclaim Christ to others and be united as a Church rather than being fragmented into separate groups'* (Session VIII Group 8). With God's grace, this, in turn, will make for a stronger communion, allowing the Church to be a credible witness to Christ and a Church *en salida* (Spanish) or *en sortie* (French), i.e., a Church that 'goes forth' (cf. *Evangelii Gaudium* 24).

34. As noted in an image from Isaiah 53, the Church *en salida* or *en sortie* requires us to leave the tent – to not just welcome people where we are but to seek them where they are. As one participant noted, *'We want to respect everyone's inherent dignity and meet people where they are. We want to do all this while remaining faithful to the teachings of the Church.'* (Session X Group 13). Delegates expressed the desire to *'nurture the joy of discipleship'* (Session X Group 2) by accompanying those who experience alienation in our society. *'We are called to accompany marginalised people. How can we give the truth with compassion and get rid of the fear that parishioners have to go out and evangelise?'* (Session VI Group 3). For some, this means living even more deeply the truth of the Gospel. *'These people have not left the Church, but the Church has left them. How do we go out and minister to them and exude that joy?'* (Session II Group 8). The North American Synod Team heard repeatedly that central to this mission of accompaniment is Jesus Christ. *'This whole process of synodality must all be centered around Jesus Christ. It is Christ we are trying to live out in all our listening, accompanying, worship, participation'* (Session III Group 16).

4.1 Moving Out of the Tent

35. For many delegates, being a Church on mission is the natural outgrowth of synodality and co-responsibility. *'There is hope in trusting the Holy Spirit as we apply synodality to the local community. We are being called to have that missionary mindset to see the love of Christ and then go out and walk in friendship with those who are feeling marginalised* *and accompany them. . . What do co-responsibility and synodality look like in our lives to bring people to Christ?'* (Session II Group 11). It was precisely the experience of synodality that, for many, renewed this call to discipleship and evangelisation. *'All people are called to mission and have something important to contribute to the life of the Church and the world. This is our opportunity to go out and share with others'* (Session X Group 3). It also was expressed that moving forward, the Church in North America needs to *'engage synodality as a missionary movement. Synodality leads to an encounter with the Lord and with truth'* (Session I Group 15). For the Church in North America, synodality is inseparable from becoming a Church sent forth on mission. A delegate spoke of *'the importance of authentically listening to each other and to reaching out to the peripheries, expanding our tent and embracing the reality that there is a place for everyone in this Church and that Jesus wants everyone to know him and receive his love'* (Session I Group 10).

4.2 A Church in the World

36. Throughout the Continental Stage in North America, the tensions present within a Church sent out on mission in the world were apparent. *'Consumerism and secularism have provided answers to questions we didn't know we were asking in ways that feel fulfilling but that really aren't. This false fulfillment will collapse and crumble, but the Church offers true fulfillment that will last. Economic/political upheaval are doing great damage, but as we all come – broken and sinful – to the Church, everyone must feel welcomed and at home'* (Session XI Group 7). For some delegates, this tension created feelings of fear and discomfort. *'There are tensions between letting the popular culture enter into the life of the parish. There is a tsunami of culture threatening to overwhelm us'* (Session III Group 15). For others, this tension was understood as an opportunity to collaborate with other people of faith. *'We don't live in Christendom anymore! We need to recognise that so that we can move forward. This should involve partnering with others. What does ecumenism look like right now? How can we work with people of other faiths?'* (Session VIII Group 8). Delegates from the Continental Stage in North America are ready to embark on mission, while tending to inevitable discomfort. *'Tension is conversion; it leads us to the openness of listening to the other, welcoming the marginalised, not rejecting those who come in the tent and receiving them. It creates tension; to want to receive people brings up the question of those who feel distant. How can we have this gift of helping them to approach without fear about their process of conversion to the teachings of the Church? We*

need to look for ways to help them' (Session VI Group 6). Navigating this tension is an important task for mission and evangelisation in North America today.

4.3 Formation for Mission and Catholic Social Teaching

37. Proper formation is the key to embracing our baptismal call to go out on mission. As one delegate put it, we need to *'recognise the importance of faith formation for our ability to be a missionary Church. We have to be adequately formed in our faith to bring it to others'* (Session XI Group 11). There also was a desire among delegates to understand more deeply the social mission of the Church. *'There is a need for formation at all levels (clergy, laity, etc.). We need to be formed to understand our Catholic Social Teaching, to be leaders, and to be evangelisers'* (Session XII Group 7). This formation in evangelisation and Catholic Social Teaching is crucial to walking the synodal path. *'We must embrace a missionary mindset and reach out to everyone from every walk of life. The responsibility of ministry is not just for priests, but for each baptised person'* (Session XI Group 7). The duty to know and live the teachings of our Catholic faith, including the Church's social teaching, flows from our baptism, but it is not always easy and requires intentional formation. *'This isn't so much about the* what *as about the* how' (Session III Group 4).

V
BISHOPS' REFLECTIONS ON THE EXPERIENCE OF SYNODALITY IN NORTH AMERICA

38. This *Final Document* presents the response of the People of God in North America who participated in the Continental Stage of the Synod. As baptised members of the People of God, many bishops participated actively in this process. Many, however, particularly the lay faithful, expressed a longing to know how this synodal process was viewed by their bishops. Furthermore, in accordance with the methodological guidelines for the Continental Stage, bishops were *'invited to meet at the end of the Continental Stage to collegially reread the lived synodal experience from the perspective of their specific charism and role'* (DCS #108). Accordingly, what follows is an insight into the reflections and experiences of the many bishops who participated during the Continental Stage of the synodal process, as well as those who participated in the drafting of the *Final Document*.

39. During the course of the Continental Stage, 146 bishops from Canada and the United States participated in at least one of the virtual assemblies. Of these, with rare exceptions, they shared in the full two-and-a-half-hour session, which included Spiritual Conversation in small groups. Some participated in small groups by being dispersed at random into the general mix of participants. The great majority, however, participated in small groups made up of other bishops from Canada and the United States. The bishops who participated in the small group Spiritual Conversations also participated in the plenary portion of the Continental Assemblies, heard what the other groups shared, and reported back to the wider body the fruits of their own Spiritual Conversations as bishops.

40. Some of the bishops commented that it would have been preferable for all of the participating bishops to have been placed in the randomly mixed small groups, as it would have provided another opportunity for bishops to listen and share within a setting more representative of the full body of the Church. Other bishops, however, commented on their appreciation of having a sustained time of small group reflection with other bishops about their experiences of the synodal process thus far. It often was mentioned that it has been rare for bishops to have an opportunity to listen to and share with other bishops about their synodal experiences. Further, it was frequently noted that the opportunity to hear and discuss with bishops from both Canada and the United States together was a tremendous grace, unique in the history of the two episcopal conferences.

41. In addition, the eight bishops from the United States and Canada who were members of the North American Synod Team had an opportunity to prayerfully reflect together on the experience of collegiality and synodality in North America. These reflections will be summarised at the conclusion of this section.

42. During the Continental consultations, the bishops expressed their experience of synodality at the Diocesan Stage as a great grace, although often challenging, and as a learning experience. They frequently expressed their joy at participating in their home dioceses by prayerful listening and dialoguing with their own people. In this sense, the bishops shared in the joy that the wider body of participants also expressed. '[We are] *grateful for the opportunity for fraternal dialogue. This echoes the positive reaction of the faithful to the listening process*' (Session X Group

18). Likewise, many bishops expressed the same kinds of uncertainties and ambiguities about 'where all of this is going' that many participants at all levels of the consultative process mentioned. *'Many of our people expressed gratitude at being asked to participate.* [But they asked] *what are the next steps? Where do we go from here?'* (Session XII Group 8).

43. The participating bishops conveyed appreciation for the pathway of patient listening and the dialogue it opened. *'Small groups make* such *a huge difference, even among bishops, because this is where dialogue can begin. This must continue!'* (Session VIII Group 16). *'For some people, a listening session was the first opportunity they had ever had of speaking directly to a bishop!'* (Session X Group 15). Yet there is a general recognition of the challenges that still face us. *'This is a great process for us all to participate in; there is still a need for the wider Church to understand what synodality is all about'* (Session III Group 16). Indeed, the listening sessions in the local Churches caused bishops to reflect on the structural challenges that make it difficult to sustain this style in a consistent way. *'Has the Church been so organised that it becomes difficult to speak to it? The Church has organisationally isolated itself from the People of God'* (Session III Group 17). *'Synodality is the way forward, but it is not an easy way'* (Session III Group 18).

44. Concerning the DCS, some bishops remarked that it provided a rare window for the Church in North America to hear voices from the Church experiencing great trials and even persecution. *'We feel gratitude that the process has helped us to see the witness of the whole Church, the suffering Church that is persecuted in other countries'* (Session VI Group 6). *'Our concern should be for the Church around the world, not just our own dioceses'* (Session VI Group 6). This made the sharing of common concerns across very different global situations all the more striking. *'The synodal documents expanded our consciousness about the realities of life in the Church in different places in the world. Also bringing our attention back to our own situation in the local Churches and to see the commonalities we all share'* (Session XI Group 15).

45. The bishops reflected frequently on what they heard during the various consultative phases, from the diocesan through the national and continental stages. They noted gratefully the resonances that were shared throughout the synodal process. This included the joy of the baptised at being asked to participate and share their perspectives, as well as the call to co-responsibility. It also included hearing the many

pains and tensions expressed by participants. This has been of immense value. *'The openness that the synodal process should bring about for everyone is to listen and hear what is hurting people and what needs healing.* [We should be asking] *what is helpful and what does this mean for reconciliation?'* (Session XI Group 16). *'People of God have concerns across the board and we need to listen and accompany better'* (Session III Group 18).

46. *'The great opportunity we have now as bishops is to transmit, to share our experience of conversion. Our faithful see the process as something difficult, [but] we must reflect on whether we are giving witness of conversion for the laity. We can continue to grow as a synodal Church, have the gift of being able to dialogue and change the culture of the Church, listen to the voice of the Spirit in order to walk together'* (Session VI Group 6).

47. The week-long writing retreat offered the participating bishops from Canada and the United States an opportunity for a sustained reflection on the synodal experience in North America. For them the continental retreat was a valuable experience of collegiality. It was a fruitful challenge for these two countries to address common experiences as well as to explore the many nuances and varieties of circumstances in each one. Through this challenge there has been growth in mutual understanding and in the sense of having a unique ecclesial bond. The bishops openly wondered, however, about how it might have been a further grace also to have walked and worked together with the Episcopal Conference of Mexico. While it is clearly understood why Mexico collaborated on the Continental level with the countries of Central and South America, it was acknowledged that the North American ecclesial context is deeply impacted by the faith and practice of the Church in Mexico, and the Church in Mexico is deeply affected by the Church in the United States and Canada.

48. During their meeting on the final day of the writing retreat, the bishops observed that *'our people are interested in where we are going with this. Synodality is an adventure and we aren't very familiar with it. We do have the experience of parish pastoral councils, presbyteral councils, and diocesan pastoral councils, but this is different, bigger. How can we teach it and learn it? We need to do more with our people – listen to them more to aid our discernment; sit down with them and discuss the religious life in the diocese. We cannot just sit in the office and make important decisions* *by ourselves.'* The bishops were grateful for the Spiritual Conversations and prayer that were present throughout the synodal endeavor. They also noted that this aspect, and its relation to ecclesial discernment, is vital for living the *way of the Church* that avoids the polarising habits of the wider society in North America. *'If we are going to be people of dialogue, we have to first have a dialogue with God; synodality needs to be based on a dialogue with Scripture and the Lord.'* The bishops also stated a desire to promote much-needed formation in Scriptural prayer and discernment. *'Much of the anxiety around the Synod comes from a misunderstanding of what discernment actually entails.'*

49. The bishops also noted that the great majority of our people had little or no direct contact with the synodal process and are unsure of their role in it. Likewise, many are unsure of the discerning role of the local bishop and the college of bishops in union with the Pope as the process unfolds.

50. As a learning experience, the bishops noted that *'we are recalibrating; how can we do the synodal process better?'* This flowed from a recognition that the process undertaken with great generosity and creativity also revealed our weaknesses. We can and must do better in consulting those who are poor, migrant communities, indigenous peoples, and racial minorities in our communities, and the many others who are wounded in the Church and in society.

51. The relative absence of priests also was noticeable in this process. The bishops acknowledged that it is their responsibility to address this in the future, both by example and by conveying the transparency and spiritual/pastoral fruitfulness of synodality. *'We need to be more intentional in working with our priests and parish leadership on synodality.'* The circumstances are somewhat different in the northern dioceses of Canada, where *'the majority of bishops have [a very small number of] priests in the diocese . . . So the relationship between bishops and priests and bishops and the people is closer. Under these circumstances, the bishop can't just do what he wants to do with a parish. He must do it together with the clergy and the people.'* Bishops need to do a better job of modeling synodality by listening, conversing, and discerning together.

52. There is a concern about the danger of false or unrealistic expectations regarding what the synodal process is meant to be and to 'produce.' Western, North American culture automatically thinks in terms both of measurable results and of winners and losers, and the Church's voice can be drowned out by that competitive impulse. Nevertheless, the bishops felt that they must show a different way, one that promotes our common baptism, our communion in the Lord, and our will to work together to address the challenges we face, which is led by the Spirit and is faithful to the Lord Jesus. *'Bishops must simply do the best we can in the synodal process and be authentic and honest. We must be transparent. Bishops need to reveal themselves more. We need to recognise the need for conversion all the way around (bishops, priest, laity). We can't control the outcome of this process. Bishops cannot regain credibility without acting credibly.'*

53. The bishops noted the importance of the national syntheses as well as this continental *Final Document*. They view them as documents that serve to reflect back to our local communities what was said and heard in the synodal consultations. This is especially important in acknowledging that as the Church in Canada and the United States, we heard those who feel wounded or cast aside by the Church. This does not solve the issues or heal the wounds, but it is an important beginning. *'The Indigenous want to know that the Church knows. This needs to be in the document. We must let them know that we understand the issues they are dealing with in their daily lives, and we are listening to them.'* A woman who is a leader in her Indigenous community told a Canadian bishop, *'Don't give up on us. Yes, we are grieving and, yes, we are angry, but don't give up on us.'* This aspect of the synodal experience also applies in addressing the anger and distrust caused by the ongoing effects of the sexual abuse crisis. The bishops ask also that the people not give up on us.

VI
PRIORITIES DIRECTED TO THE OCTOBER 2023 GATHERING OF THE SYNOD IN ROME

54. The Church in North America has experienced a significant moment of joy and hope in the journey along the synodal path. Gathered in a spirit of prayerful listening, local communities in our dioceses have expressed their joys and their anxieties. The path led initially to shared Spiritual Conversations in each of our countries, and then to similar, mutual conversations by delegates from the United States and Canada. During the Continental Assembly, many resonances and tensions were expressed, all of which were spoken out of a great love for Christ Jesus and his Church. The North American Synod Team labored to give a synthetic account of the richness of the conversations. The Synod Team has gathered the principal themes that emerged from our Continental Assembly and now propose them for further consideration at the Synodal Assembly to be held in Rome in October 2023.

I. **Integration of synodal consultation in the local Churches. This would include formation both in synodality and in the spirituality of discernment.** Although the synodal way was experienced with such joy on our continent by those who participated, we acknowledge that it is just the beginning. Much work remains to be done to integrate the synodal style of consultation at the level of the local Churches, as well as at the national and continental levels, to increase participation and reach many in our communities who have not yet even heard of synodality. This includes particular attention to the spiritual formation necessary for personal and communal discernment. We also urge that formation in the synodal style be encouraged and guided, so that it may be properly understood. Many who chose not to participate conceive of it as a competitive model, opposing laity to clergy. Others see it as insufficiently clear in its methodology, ecclesiology, and aims. Nevertheless, there is the practical matter of rethinking our diocesan and national ecclesial practices and/or structures in a way that truly prioritises the synodal style.

II. **The challenge of welcoming those who feel excluded from participation in the life of the Church in a manner that is authentic and faithful to the Gospel and the Catholic faith weighs heavily on the hearts of our people.** This tension in individuals and in communities was spoken of often. Our people perceive that welcoming and serving the wounded and isolated in the world and in the Church is an essential aspect of the mission given to us by the Lord Jesus; yet they also observe that the new complexity of issues before us requires discernment, because it implies both new pastoral initiatives and fidelity to the kerygma that we are to announce publicly. Hence, many asked what is meant by 'radical inclusion,' and what are its pastoral and even doctrinal implications? The term itself elicited widely divergent reactions during our consultations. There also is a need for formation in how to be more welcoming of one another.

III. **Co-responsibility.** A plea for renewed consideration of the mission of all the baptised, with specific attention given to particular vocations, was frequently mentioned. The discernment of how baptismal co-responsibility for the Church's mission should be appreciated and achieved demands a better understanding of the roles of the laity in general, and of women and young people in particular. The theme of co-responsibility also touches the frequently raised issue of shared decision-making and the desire for more transparency in Church governance. Discerning a practical way forward on these issues will require a consideration of current canonical norms and ecclesial structures. Intimately connected to this theme is the need for more integral formation for the whole of Christian life.

IV. **Addressing the unity and communion of the Church in the midst of various kinds of polarisation and division.** Some polarisations arise within the Church, whereas others originate in the wider society and are transposed into the Church. Discernment is needed so that local Churches are better able to promote the ecclesiology of communion, rooted in baptism and nourished by the Eucharistic sacrifice. These must be seen as primary sources of our identity and unity as the People of God, and prior to any racial, ethnic, social, economic, political, or ideological differences. This is a challenge for our immediate future.

V. **A Church that goes out to the peripheries.** Much of the conversation in the Continental Assembly concerned the internal workings of the Church, but we also are called to be outward looking. Our people speak often of having heard the call of Pope Francis to go out credibly to the margins. On our continent there is always a danger of forgetfulness of, and indifference to, those who are poor and ostracised. The North American Synod Team heard through the synodal consultations that our people are asking for more robust formation in this kind of missionary activity. It is vital that the local Churches hear the call to assist the needs of the poor and marginalised churches around the world. This is a concern of the whole Church and should be articulated with greater urgency on the level of the Universal Church.

VI
CONCLUSION

***They were all in one place together.* (Acts 2:1)**

55. At the very beginning of the Church, at the time of Pentecost, there was confusion and fear and yet expectation and hope as well. This is true of every age, including our current time. The response of the Holy Spirit was to gather the Church together *in one place* and give them the ability to hear and understand the Gospel message. As the Church in North America continues to journey on the synodal path, we must imitate Mary, who was present at the first Pentecost and continually said 'yes' to the invitation to contribute to the building up of the Kingdom of God. '*We want to be like Mary*' (Session I Group 2).

56. The gift of being gathered together in the Holy Spirit was experienced again by the Church in Canada and the United States during the Continental Stage. There was great gratitude for being in *one place,* that is, being (virtually) together with other Catholics, who come from different parts of Canada and the United States, who are lay, religious, and clergy, each with their own ideas and views, yet all part of the one Church. '*I am thankful for the time and effort taken to facilitate this process. It gives me hope that we can move forward to healing and rebuilding trust with the Church and among our brothers and sisters*' (Session II Feedback).

57. The gift of being together *in one place* and listening to each other is perhaps the best lesson learned during the Continental Stage in North America. As one participant said, '*People enjoyed sharing, rather than just being talked to – there is no going back*' (Session III Group 4). The benefits of being intentionally synodal was a common theme. As was mentioned by a bishops' group, '*The synodal process has not been perfect, but it has been good*' (Session XII Group 8).

* *Editorial comment: for readability the editors inserted a numbering of the sections of the document. The Appendices mentioned in the document can be found on the website: https://www.usccb.org/synod*

OCEANIA

OCEAN

'Care for People and Planet'

OCEANIA

OCEANIA

CARE FOR PEOPLE AND PLANET: DISCERNMENT FROM THE CONTINENTAL SYNODAL STAGE IN OCEANIA

Susan Pascoe and Ormond Rush

1. Introduction

The vast continental region of Oceania encompasses one fifth of the planet, with large and small island states surrounding the Pacific Ocean. It is a region rich in biodiversity and vibrant cultural and linguistic heritage, alongside varied stages of economic development. There are considerable logistic challenges to maintaining communication, including large distances, remote islands and highlands, interrupted information and communications technology, and constrained budgets. The region is dramatically impacted by the world's ecological crisis – it is an existential threat to those island states which will disappear as sea levels rise.

On a global comparison Oceania has a small number of local Churches with four episcopal conferences in communion with the Eastern Catholic Churches – some of which have jurisdiction across the region. The Federation of Catholic Bishops Conferences of Oceania (FCBCO) comprises the four episcopal conferences – the Catholic Bishops Conference of Papua New Guinea and the Solomon Islands (CBC PNGSI); the *Conferentia Episcopalis Pacifici* (CEPAC); the New Zealand Catholic Bishops Conference (NZCBC) and the Australian Catholic Bishops Conference (ACBC) – as well as the representatives of the Eastern Catholic Churches. The Oceania region consists of four episcopal conferences covering almost 20 countries – from small island states to large land masses. There are more than 70 archdioceses, dioceses and ordinariates across Oceania. There are also five Eastern Catholic Eparchies, the heads of which are members of the Australian Catholic Bishops Conference, and Eastern Catholics who do not have their own Ordinary. There are, therefore, almost 80 'local churches' that make up the Catholic Church in Oceania.

2. Context

During the conduct of the local and continental stages of the Synod on Synodality, Archbishop Peter Loy Chong of the archdiocese Suva, Fiji was FCBCO President from 2018 till 2023. He had a well-communicated agenda – to strengthen the FCBCO through a proposal to create a permanent secretariat, and to agree on a pastoral plan for the region. The three themes for the February 2023 Assembly were: Care for the Oceans; Becoming a more Synodal Church; and Formation for Mission. There was synergy with the discernment process on the Document for the Continental Stage in Oceania, as all three themes were also highlighted in the Oceania submission. Archbishop Loy Chong is a climate activist for *Laudato Si'* in Oceania, and ensured that the ecological crisis was a focus for the Assembly.[1]

The largest country and episcopal conference in the region is Australia. The ACBC agreed to hold a Plenary Council in 2016 with a four-year synodal journey planned from 2018 to 2022. There was an initial stage of listening and discernment,[2] followed by two Assemblies of the People of God. The COVID-19 pandemic had an impact on the timelines, with the first assembly moving to an online event in October 2021. The delayed second assembly was face-to-face and occurred in July 2022. It is noteworthy that the ACBC decision to hold a Plenary Council was made during the five-year public inquiry from 2012 to 2017 into child sexual abuse in Australian institutions.[3] While the Royal Commission was an inquiry into the sexual abuse of minors in all Australian institutions, there were dedicated sections on the Catholic Church, and specific recommendations.[4]

The pandemic also impacted the timing of the FCBCO Assembly that had been scheduled for Suva, in Fiji, as a regular episcopal meeting in their four-yearly cycle of terms of office. There is a practice of the FCBCO President being elected at the regional assembly and an agreed rotation of which country assumes the presidency. Unlike larger continental federations which tend to send delegates to their scheduled meetings, the FCBCO invites all the bishops of the region to their fraternal gathering each four years. There was reluctance by the FCBCO Executive to change the mode of the delayed Suva Assembly to

1 The 2015 Encyclical, *On Care for Our Common Home*, alerted the Catholic and global community to the urgent need to attend to the effects of environmental degradation and its differential impact on the world's poorest. See **Laudato si' (24 May 2015) | Francis (vatican.va)**.

2 17,500 submissions were received from groups and individuals comprising some 250,000 people.

3 The Royal Commission into Institutional Responses to Child Sexual Abuse (RCIRCSA) was a very high-profile inquiry with sections of the final report focused on the Catholic Church, as well as specific recommendations.

4 The ACBC and the peak body of religious women and men (Catholic Religious Australia) created a number of dedicated initiatives to deal with the RCIRCSA recommendations, including an Implementation Advisory Group, a Governance Review Project Team, and a Working Group to investigate the adequacy of the Church's safeguarding mechanisms. Each of these groups was responding to the recommendations from the public inquiry and providing advice to the ACBC and CRA.

accommodate the timelines of the Synod's second stage of discernment on the Working Document for the Continental Stage. The primary intent of the Assembly was the consideration of a Pastoral Plan for the Continent. Rather than consider a further delay to their episcopal assembly, it was instead agreed that there would be two discernment sessions on the Document for the Continental Stage at the Assembly.

3. The Federation of Catholic Bishops Conferences of Oceania

The FCBCO was created on 28 July, 1992 as a structure to enable the four episcopal conferences in the Pacific region (Oceania) to collaborate in collective pastoral action as agreed by the members. It is a forum to enable member bishops to share their insights, experiences and concerns, and to take joint action when agreed. It aims to promote and defend the common good, give visible expression to unity in diversity, and to deepen collegial spirit and strengthen solidarity amongst the members.

The countries in Oceania vary in size from large island nations such as Australia to small atoll-based countries such as Niue. They are: American Samoa, Australia, Cook Islands, Fiji, French Polynesia, Guam, Kiribati, Marshall Islands, Micronesia, Nauru, New Caledonia, New Zealand, Niue, Northern Mariana Islands, Papua New Guinea, Samoa, Solomon Islands, Tokelau, Tonga, Tuvalu, Vanuatu, Wallis and Futuna.

While Christianity is the dominant religion in the region, there is considerable variability in the proportion of the population which is Catholic and the degree of secularisation in each country (Table 1).

Oceania

Region	Australia	Eastern Catholic Churches	Pacific (CEPAC)	New Zealand	Papua New Guinea / Solomons
Population	24.4m	N/A	2.3m	4.9m	8.9m in PNG and 732k in Solomons
Catholic Population	19.9%	N/A	31%	10%	25% in PNG 20% in Solomons
Number of dioceses	28 + 2 ordinariates	5	14	6	19 dioceses in PNG 3 dioceses in SI

Table 1: Total population in Oceania by regions, with percentage of Catholics and diocesan numbers

Countries such as New Zealand and Australia were occupied by the British in the eighteenth century, and today are economically advanced, politically stable, and prosperous. Both countries are working toward full justice and reconciliation with their indigenous peoples. Both countries have significant migrant populations and while predominantly Christian, are home to many cultures and religions.

The island states in the Pacific, including Papua New Guinea and the Solomon Islands, are rich in biodiversity, and cultural and language diversity. However, many face systemic challenges such as interrupted telecommunications, inadequate infrastructure, and underdeveloped health and education systems. Hence there is a reliance on aid from wealthy donor countries. There are significant geopolitical tensions, with both China and the United States vying for strategic dominance, using aid and development grants and loans as one means of achieving this.

The region is particularly prone to natural disasters, ranging from deadly cyclones and earthquakes in the Pacific, to catastrophic fires and droughts in Australia. The accelerating effects of climate change mean that rising sea levels are threatening the very existence of small island states.

4. Organisation of the Discernment on the Document for the Continental Stage

There were initial logistical challenges with the organisation of the discernment period for the Document on the Continental Stage, the first being establishing contact with the FCBCO. There was no permanent Secretariat and communication was difficult. Efforts were made to contact the Suva-based FCBCO President (who also chaired its Executive Committee), such as flying at short notice to meet him when he was visiting Australia, and seeking the assistance of the ACBC Secretariat to maintain contact. Once contact was established it was possible to organise an online meeting on 24 August 2022, for the members of the FCBCO Executive with the Secretary General of the Synod in Rome, Cardinal Mario Grech, in order for him to speak with them, explain the purpose of the Continental Stage, and seek their active support.[5] A Draft Proposal on the approach to discernment in Oceania was discussed and agreed at this meeting. This included approving the membership of the Oceania Taskforce. The lay women Susan Pascoe, already a member of the Roman commission on methodology of the Synod on Synodality, was appointed as Oceania Taskforce Chair by the FCBCO Executive at this meeting.

The timing of the discernment period for the Document on the Continental

5 This meeting occurred on 24 August 2022, and provided a sense of the Continental Stage being launched.

Stage was particularly challenging for the FCBCO whose member countries are predominantly in the Southern hemisphere. For all Christian Countries, Advent and the lead in to Christmas preoccupies the local Churches. For countries in the Southern hemisphere, it is also the end of the school year, and the start of the summer holiday period when many businesses and schools shut down throughout January.

One advantage in being a member of the Synod Taskforce planning the Continental Stage was an alertness to the timing challenges. The Oceania Taskforce had its first meeting on 7 October 2022, ahead of the release of the Working Document for the Continental Stage on 27 October. This meant that those responsible for coordinating the organisation of discernment within episcopal conferences were alert to the time pressures and able to start planning immediately. Deadlines were agreed for finalisation of discernment sessions within episcopal conferences, synthesising across them, and submitting to the Oceania Taskforce – all before Christmas. All meetings of the Oceania Taskforce were held online. They were scheduled at the outset with agreement to cancel any unnecessary meetings. This happened – particularly towards the end of the process.

Ahead of this discernment process within episcopal conferences, the FCBCO Executive agreed to the creation of a Discernment and Writing Group, to be comprised of nominees of the four episcopal conferences and the Eastern Catholic Churches, selected by them to be broadly representative of the full membership of the People of God.

Having agreed to the timelines for discernment within Oceania, the approaches were left to the discretion of local churches, to enable a fit with their cultural context. One of the episcopal conferences struggled with completing the task within the agreed timeline, and as a consequence provided a partially completed report. It was agreed to enable verbal elaboration of their issues during the process of synthesis across Oceania.

One further element added to the complexity and uniqueness of the approach in Oceania. In anticipation of their four-yearly Assembly, the FCBCO Executive created the Suva Assembly Taskforce. This group was chaired by theologian and academic, Dr Sandie Cornish, and had been meeting for eighteen months when the Oceania Taskforce was established. The role of the Suva Assembly Taskforce was to plan the programme for the FCBCO Assembly and to support the organisation of the Assembly. The key aim of the programme was to reach agreement on a pastoral plan for the Oceania region by the end of the Assembly.

Once it was clarified by the FCBCO Executive that they did not want to change their scheduled episcopal meeting into an ecclesial meeting to accommodate the discernment process for the Working Document on the Continental

Stage, it was clear that some accommodation of the existing programme was required. The Chairs of the two Taskforces worked together and recommended two discernment sessions as part of the Suva Assembly, and the use of the same facilitator for the Spiritual Conversations for the Discernment and Writing Group and the Suva Assembly. This was agreed by the FCBCO Executive.

5. Discernment and Writing Group

The role of the Discernment and Writing Group had an elevated significance in Oceania compared to the processes in those continents where the Assemblies were fully ecclesial, not only episcopal. As already described, there were logistical and timing imperatives which persuaded the FCBCO to retain the format of its delayed episcopal assembly in Suva in February 2023. As a result, efforts were made to ensure the Discernment and Writing Group was broadly representative of all echelons and roles in the Latin and Eastern Churches, as their task assumed a symbolic dimension as a demonstration of the ecclesial breadth.[6] Given that this was essentially a Working Group, there were no observers or people of other Christian denominations present.

The Discernment and Writing Group undertook their task of discernment, synthesising and drafting during 8–13 January 2023 in Melbourne. A small sub-group of four presented the Draft Oceania Submission to the FCBCO Assembly in Suva during 5–10 February for their reflection and feedback and for any re-drafting required. Once final changes were made following the FCBCO Assembly, the full Discernment and Writing Group presented the final version of the Oceania submission to an online meeting of the FCBCO Executive on 22 March 2023 for validation. The FCBCO President then sent a copy of the submission to the Secretary General of The Synod, Cardinal Mario Grech before the deadline of 31 March 2023.[7]

The overlap in membership of the Discernment and Writing Group and the Oceania Taskforce was constructive as they had a ready established a collegial *modus operandi*. They shared the same chairperson and administrative officer.[8] This assisted a smooth transition from operating as a Taskforce with a planning, liaison and organisational role, to becoming a Discernment and Writing Group with a spiritual, discernment and drafting role.

There was a considerable administrative load in organising pre-meetings; drafting and consulting on the programme of discernment with the Oceania Taskforce; identifying a suitable venue for the week-long discernment and

6 The Discernment and Writing Group comprised 9 women and 11 men. Amongst this group of 20 people were an archbishop, two bishops and six priests; a deacon and a religious brother; and nine lay women from a variety of academic, advisory and administrative roles.

7 The newly appointed FCBCO President is Bishop Anthony Randazzo, of the Broken Bay Diocese in Australia.

8 One of the co-authors, Susan Pascoe, chaired both groups. All work for the synod was done on a pro bono basis.

writing process; and establishing travel arrangements and protocols.

Funding had been successfully negotiated for the continental stage of the Synod by Sr Nathalie Becquart XMCJ, Undersecretary at the Synod Secretariat, who liaised with funding bodies. As Oceania does not have a permanent secretariat, the Taskforce chair negotiated with the ACBC to become the financial clearinghouse for the grant. This required a legal agreement, and the establishment of accountability protocols, so the funding could be adequately acquitted to the funding bodies. The volume of work required – and the mix of administrative, planning, process and relational elements – was significant.

The Catholic Leadership Centre in East Melbourne opened a week early to accommodate the Discernment and Writing Group.[9] The venue had been a Catholic primary school and was co-located with a Church. It was well-appointed for retreat or conference groups and had the facilities for plenary and small group work. A modified Frascati process was adopted with initial time for participants to get to know one another, and to engage in group and personal prayer.[10] There was daily Eucharist and symbols present in meeting rooms. Participants had read the five submissions ahead of meeting as a group and were either familiar with the Spiritual Conversation Method, or quickly became so. The key difference between the Oceania and Frascati processes was that in Oceania the programme for the entire period was released in advance in draft, and the writers in Oceania were drawn from the participants instead of having dedicated writers.

What quickly emerged was a camaraderie amongst the participants, a positive collegiality, a shared spirituality, and a commitment to faithfully producing a document which reflected the voices of the People of God in the region. Like those involved in the Frascati process, the Oceania Discernment and Writing Group said they felt privileged and humbled to be involved. They shared a similar sense of responsibility to those who had contributed to the discernment in local churches to ensure their voices were clearly heard.

The FCBCO Executive originally agreed that a group of consultant theologians would be available for the FCBCO Assembly in Suva. However, the Discernment and Writing Group that was later created included three theologians (Rev. Dr Ormond Rush, Dr Therese Lautua and Dr Sandie Cornish), a canon lawyer (Fr Sijeesh Pullankunnel), a Church historian (Rev. Dr Max Vodola), and a philosopher (Prof. Renee Kohler-Ryan), as well as episcopal and clerical members with postgraduate credentials. Ormond Rush and Max Vodola

9 Australia is the easiest country for the majority of Pacific participants to access, due to the number of flights. Considerable effort had been put into identifying a venue in Brisbane or Sydney as these are preferred destinations for those flying in from a range of Pacific locations, but due to the holiday period, none were available. Hence the location in Melbourne, the capital of the southern state of Victoria.

10 The process of discernment developed for the synthesising of the submissions from stage one in local churches was implemented in a monastery outside Rome in the small town of Frascati. It has become known as the Frascati process. It involves prayer, Eucharist, listening, reflection, and dialogue in a process of communal discernment.

are both specialists in Vatican II.[11] While all members of the Discernment and Writing Group brought expertise and skills, it is also noteworthy that Trudy Dantis, Director of the ACBC National Centre for Pastoral Research, was a member.[12] Given the calibre of members, it is unsurprising that the group did not need to engage with the team of consultant theologians.

There were two streams to the core work of the Discernment and Writing Group – the spiritual discernment process and the drafting of the Oceania submission. Very beneficial was the expertise brought by Br Ian Cribb SJ who was appointed to facilitate the Spiritual Conversations for the Discernment and Writing Group and for the FCBCC Assembly.[13] The week-long process was guided by the Oceania Taskforce Chair, Susan Pascoe. Ian Cribb is a recognised expert in the Spiritual Conversation Method, and skilfully guided members to reflect on the submissions they had read, listen to each other's responses, and then dialogue with one another. This was particularly helpful at the start of the week when the focus was on identifying common themes and issues, areas of difference, and gaps. As the focus moved to putting these reflections into writing and agreeing on priorities, a more conventional process of moving to consensus was used. The interplay of the two approaches assisted in finalising an initial draft by the end of the week.

Amongst the observations from the week-long discernment is that it took time for some participants to fully understand the process, and the Spiritual Conversation Method. For the first day and a half some of the participants referred back to their submission from Stage One of the Synod, or wanted to introduce ideas of their own, not contained in the submissions. Some had to be reminded that their task was to faithfully discern the voices from the submissions to the continental stage, remembering that this exercise was itself a deep discernment on the Document for the Continental Stage through the lived experience of being Church in Oceania. In addition, the discipline of listening uninterrupted for the first round of the Spiritual Conversation was a challenge for some, who wanted to immediately move to dialogue. Gentle coaching moved them into the disposition and method suited to spiritual discernment, so that rich reflections emerged in the plenary sessions.

The second core task was the drafting the FCBCO submission for Oceania, noting that guidelines had been issued from the Synod Secretariat as to the length, structure and format of the submissions. When volunteers were called for the writers, five women offered. This was a somewhat ironic reflection of the critique of institutional Church that women typically do the work for the

11 Ormund Rush had agreed to be the coordinating writer for the drafting of the Oceania submission.
12 Trudy Dantis had responsibility for organising the synthesis of the 17,500 submissions to Australia's Plenary Council held from 2018 to 2022, and contributed to the Plenary Council as Secretariat Chair and as a writer.
13 It was beneficial having someone of Ian Cribb's expertise for establishing the process as one of spiritual depth and integrity, and of ensuring continuity between the two exercises.

consideration of men. The inclusive, scholarly style of the coordinating writer generated a genial and productive approach within the team of writers who forfeited discretionary time to complete their writing task. It was readily agreed that all findings would be sourced in the submissions to add integrity to the process and to avoid the possible criticism of either sloppiness or personal bias. The team of writers worked diligently with the goal of completing a first draft by the end of the week. This was achieved.

The draft FCBCO Oceania submission was circulated to Discernment and Writing Group members in the following week, adjustments made, and then put into a report format by the ACBC. The submission was provided to the FCBCO two weeks ahead of their Assembly to give bishops time to read and reflect upon it. Unfortunately, it was not distributed ahead of the Assembly. With the pressure of finalising Assembly arrangements, the submission was not sent out.

6. FCBCO Assembly

Despite the FCBCO comprising only four episcopal conferences and representatives of the Eastern Catholic Churches, their numbers are significant when they meet in assembly, as all Bishops from the four episcopal conferences are invited to attend, and most do. Two local people were co-facilitators of the Assembly – Fr Asaeli Raass SVD and Susan Sela. Sr Nathalie Becquart, Undersecretary for the Synod Secretariat, was present for the entire Assembly and spoke on synodality – a topic on which she is an expert. Cardinal Michael Czereny SJ, Prefect of the Dicastery for Integral Human Development, presided at the opening Mass, spoke twice at the Assembly and stayed for four days. Other significant people in attendance were the General Secretary of the Pacific Conference of Churches (Rev. James Bagwan);[14] representatives of The River above Asia Oceania Ecclesial Network (RAOEN);[15] representatives of the funding body Misereor;[16] two staff representatives of the Dicastery for Integral Human Development; and a representative from Portugal involved in the July 2023 World Youth Day. Each had the opportunity to speak, to attend sessions and liturgies, and to mix with delegates.

The environment at the Assembly was fraternal, notwithstanding the variability between the wealth and size of Australia and New Zealand in comparison with the island nations in the Pacific, the Solomon Islands and Papua New Guinea, which are at varied stages of economic development and

14 Pacific Conference of Churches is an ecumenical organization representing Christian churches in the Pacific region.

15 RAOEN is a network dedicated to raising understanding of ecological issues in Oceania and Asia so that Church agencies can better care for the earth and the oceans. Rev. Pedro Walpole SJ spoke at the Assembly and coordinated a statement from the Bishops on the Environmental Crisis in Oceania.

16 Misereor is the German Catholic Bishops' Organisation for Development Cooperation.

subject to geopolitical contest for influence in the region.[17] Australia and New Zealand are donor countries with prior colonial relationships in the region, and many of the island nations are reliant on aid programmes and foreign commercial operators. The language of the Assembly was English, which is a second language for many, including the nations which are French-speaking.[18] These differences can create a climate similar to the recent colonial past, if not well managed, where the voices from the wealthy countries dominate.

The two discernment sessions on the Draft Oceania submission scheduled for the Assembly were expanded to five as the draft document had not been distributed ahead of the Assembly as planned. It was agreed to give most of the first session to time for the bishops to read and digest the document. As they had done with the Discernment and Writing Group, Ian Cribb SJ and Susan Pascoe shared the facilitation with Br Cribb taking the bishops through a process of spiritual discernment, and Susan Pascoe introducing them to the Draft submission, and facilitating the process of finalisation. Four members of the Discernment and Writing Group were in attendance to redraft the submission following episcopal consideration.

The unexpected death of Emeritus Cardinal George Pell on 10 January 2023, just a month ahead of the FCBCO Assembly, may have impacted the dynamic. While Emeritus Cardinal Pell was living in Rome, he was still an influential person in his home country, Australia, and in the region. He wrote an article for *The Spectator* which was published on 11 January 2023, describing the Synod on Synodality as a 'toxic nightmare', hostile to the apostolic tradition, and 'an outpouring of New Age good will'.[19] On the first morning memorial cards for Cardinal Pell were found at the seat of each delegate, although no mention was made of their placement.

Two of the delegates wrote to their fellow bishops with critiques of synodality, and of the draft FCBCO submission. One of these critiques was of synodality itself. The more detailed critique, felt that some areas, such as LQBTQIA+, had been overemphasised and that there was a misunderstanding of Church teaching in other areas. The representatives of the Discernment and Writing Group went through each criticism that had been made and respectfully responded. Given that the critique of the Draft Oceania Submission in two other submissions had been circulated, and the unfamiliarity with the method of the Spiritual Conversation for some bishops, additional sessions were scheduled to enable adequate time for discernment. Each evening there was a meeting of the core organising committee to review the day and to make any adjustments

17 Attempts to exert influence are particularly intense between the US and China.

18 Vanuatu, French Polynesia, New Caledonia, and Wallis and Futuna are French-speaking. One challenge at the Assembly was the realisation that some French-speaking delegates were struggling to keep up. They had been offered interpreters by the Suva Assembly Taskforce, but at the time, did not think the service would be needed.

19 See https://www.spectator.co.uk/article/the-catholic-church-must-free-itself-from-this-toxic-nightmare/

to the programme for the following day. Ian Cribb SJ was a member of the group and Susan Pascoe was added, as it quickly emerged that additional time would be needed to get to consensus on the Oceania Submission.

Two observations are relevant here – one is the flexibility of the organising committee, and the second is the congruence between the core elements of the proposed Pastoral Plan for Oceania and the Draft FCBCO Submission. Given that the original aims of the assembly were to strengthen the FCBCO and to reach agreement on a Pastoral Plan for Oceania, it was impressive that additional time was found for discernment on the Draft submission. The core elements of the Pastoral Plan were listed as: Care for the oceans; becoming a more synodal Church; and formation for mission – all priorities in the Oceania submission. This overlap between the two documents likely assisted in the flexible reshaping of the Assembly programme. The topics of care for the earth and the oceans, synodality, and formation were in both documents.

During the Assembly, the bishops were assigned to tables to ensure there would be mixing across episcopal conferences. The location of the tables in the conference room was changed daily, but not the membership of each table. Like the experience with the Discernment and Writing Group, there were initial difficulties for some bishops in understanding the nature, genre, and status of the FCBCO submission and their task in receiving it. There was a concern from some that elements of the submission were at odds with the magisterium, and from others a concern that the critical voices in the submission might reflect poorly on the Church in Oceania. The two facilitators explained that the submission was based on a faithful discernment of the issues raised in the submissions from their episcopal conferences, which themselves were a deep discernment on the issues raised throughout the universal Church written into the Document for the Continental Stage, and reflected through the lived experience of the People of God in Oceania. It was helpful that each finding was sourced back to the submission/s.

For the sequencing of sessions on the Draft Oceania submission, the initial approach was to use the Spiritual Conversation Method. Individuals provided comment in a plenary style for the initial sessions.[20] Given that some voices were more vociferous than others, the two facilitators decided to seek responses from tables, as this would better enable all voices to be heard, and require them to reach consensus as a small group. As a result, for the third session the tables were asked to report back on three elements – what they agreed with in the submission, what they found troubling, and any specific improvement they would like. There was a real sense of purpose in the room, and the reports from each table were rich and candid. As there were remaining tensions with some

20 The programme each day began with a celebration of the Eucharist, and was followed by some formal presentations (such as the addresses by Cardinal Czerny) as well as small group work (including the Spiritual Conversation Method), and plenary sessions.

bishops regarding the status of the Oceania submission, the Discernment and Writing proposed to them that they finish the submission with a Pastoral Reflection. This was agreed and a Draft was developed by those members of the Discernment and Writing Group who were present. This draft was based on the issues raised from small group discussions in tables in session three.

The creation of a Draft Pastoral Reflection proved to be a positive means of reaching consensus and giving a sense of ownership of the FCBCO submission. Prior to this, for a vocal minority of bishops there was a sense that they were being asked to 'rubber stamp' the Draft Oceania submission, and a frustration that they were unable to change the contents of the summary. They did have considerable impact on the emphasis in certain sections, on language, and on the addition of one more priority in the last section of the document. Having a statement of their own, and confidence in the process, meant they could be at peace with the document. The final two sessions were devoted to finalising their Pastoral Reflection. There was a sense of camaraderie and achievement when their Pastoral Reflection was finalised.

Once again, the ACBC secretariat provided the final editing and typesetting of the document. The ACBC Communications team also helped support the local media person at the FCBCO Assembly. The Media Director from the Archdiocese of Suva, John Tabore, was supported by Gavin Abraham, the ACBC Media and Communications Director, Neil Helmore from the Australian Diocese of Townsville and Sr Bernadette Reis from Vatican Media. There was live steaming, interviews, podcasts and reflective pieces. This communication was an important immediate means of involving those interested people who were not there in person. It is a dimension of transparency and inclusion when any of the broader can participate vicariously.

7. Concluding Comment

After reflection on the Oceania discernment on the Document for the Continental Stage, three points emerged as significant for the ongoing synodal process.

1. **Significance of the Continental Stage**
   The current synodal journey (2021–2024) is much more than these continental meetings, leading up to the two sessions of the Synod in 2023 and 2024 in Rome. But the Continental Stage, while it is not the only stage, has been found to be vital. The novel introduction of a continental stage into the synodal process is a highly significant element for understanding the dynamic of synodality. The 2022 Document for the Continental Stage (DCS) might well have been

the end point before preparation of an *Instrumentum Laboris* for the 2023/2024 sessions of the Synod—a process that had started at the local parish/diocesan level and moved to the level of episcopal conference, and then towards a global synthesis from all the episcopal conferences and other international levels. However, the Document for the Continental Stage was then sent back to the local dioceses for further discernment, and then on to a continental discernment and synthesis. In other words, synodal discernment is not a one-way street, from local to universal. It is a back-and-forth from local to universal, and back again, in a circular ecclesial listening to the Spirit of God. What began as a global listening process, and then synthesised at its various local/national/universal levels, is sent back to local levels for their further discernment, confirmation, or critique. This model highlights the ecclesial process as one of ongoing *dialogue*, rather than that of *monologue*.

2. **The Genre, Purpose, and Status of the Synthesis Documents**

Much unnecessary smoke has been created by those misunderstanding the very genre, purpose, and status of the 'listening documents' along the way of the synodal process. Whether it be the syntheses from listening, dialogue and discernment documents at the local parish, diocesan, episcopal conferences, or world-church level, these multi-phased syntheses do not at all claim to be 'theological treatises' nor indeed 'magisterial statements', let alone claim to be covering each and every aspect of the *Catechism of the Catholic Church*. Rather, these 'listening documents' are attempts to capture how committed Catholics are receiving, in the complex reality of their lives, the official teaching of the magisterium. Under the 'canopy' of the wings of the Holy Spirit, as fashioned by the prayerfulness created in Spiritual Conversation, these documents present opportunities for the church to learn—from the Spirit-aroused 'sense of the faith' of all the faithful—new perspectives that may require development of the church's teaching regarding doctrine and morals as it stands at the moment.

3. **Still Learning to be Synodal**

In retrieving synodal practice from the early Church (as called for by the Second Vatican Council) and applying it in contemporary settings across the universal Church, we are encountering some of the hurdles to full synodal practice. Hence the priority in the Oceania submission that those teachings, structures and aspects of culture which impede synodality be examined in the two sessions of the Synod in Rome in 2023 and 2024. Furthermore, that as evidence of genuine synodal practice called for in the Document for the Continental Stage, the two sessions of the Synod should find ways for greater involvement of all members of the People of God – lay people, religious, deacons, priests.[21] In this regard, the Oceania assembly was itself not fully representative in its composition. An observation can be made regarding the difference between the continental assemblies in Asia and Oceania.[22] While the bishops in Oceania were genuine in their engagement with the draft FCBCO Submission, those in Asia were sitting at tables with lay people, priests and religious, and hearing at first hand their responses as part of the discernment process. There is a difference between receiving and discerning upon the written word as a single ecclesial group , and considering it in person as a group across ecclesial roles. One exercise can be cerebral, the other inevitably engages head and heart. This is a lesson for future discernment processes.

This account of the experience of synodality in the Continent of Oceania illustrates the movement of the Spirit amongst the full People of God as we strive collectively to be Church, and individually to be fully Christian.

21 DCS para 108.
22 Due to her role on the Synod Secretariat's Taskforce for the Continental Stage, Susan Pascoe accompanied both the Oceania and Asian processes.

OCEANIA DISCERNMENT ON THE WORKING DOCUMENT FOR THE CONTINENTAL STAGE

Suave, Republic of Fiji

I
INTRODUCTION

This document reflects the voices of the People of God in Oceania in response to the Working Document for the Continental Stage. It includes a Pastoral Reflection by the bishops of Oceania gathered at the Federation of Catholic Bishops Conferences of Oceania (FCBCO) Assembly in Fiji (5-10 February 2023), on what they have heard from their people.

1.1 Description of Oceania

1. The vast continent of Oceania is a sea of islands, large and small, situated in the Pacific Ocean, which occupies one third of the planet. Oceania has a unique feature that no other region shares. The international dateline passes through the middle of this continent. The position of the dateline means that each new day begins and ends in Oceania. The prayer of the Church, the first Masses of the day, happen in Oceania, each day. The last prayers and activities of daily life also happen in the countries of Oceania.

2. Oceania is rich in diversity. There are 21 countries, from small island states to large land masses, with a wide range of ethnic, cultural and linguistic groups. The region is rich in a natural abundance of flora,

fauna and marine life. There is wide variance in access to resources, communications and community infrastructure across the region. For all countries, the impact of the ecological crisis is a considerable threat and preoccupies the political, economic, social and ecclesial discourse. The global commercial expansion in and around the region poses a threat to the survival and existence of the livelihood, culture and home of the many diverse and unique minority indigenous groups of people in Oceania.

3. Rising sea levels threaten the very existence of the small island states in Oceania and, increasingly, catastrophic floods, cyclones and fires are a reality in many countries. Our region is the focus and location of geopolitical conflict between world powers and is impacted by colonial and neo-colonial dynamics driven by transnational economic entities. Like all other continents, the COVID-19 pandemic caused a significant impact on lives and livelihoods, as well as Church life.

4. The Federation of Catholic Bishops Conferences of Oceania (FCBCO) comprises four episcopal conferences – the Catholic Bishops Conference of Papua New Guinea and the Solomon Islands (CBCPNGSI); the *Conferentia Episcopalis Pacifici* (CEPAC); the New Zealand Catholic Bishops Conference (NZCBC); the Australian Catholic Bishops Conference (ACBC); and representatives of the Eastern Catholic Churches (ECC).

5. The countries in Oceania are: American Samoa, Australia, Cook Islands, Fiji, French Polynesia, Guam, Kiribati, Marshall Islands, Micronesia, Nauru, New Caledonia, New Zealand, Niue, Northern Mariana Islands, Papua New Guinea, Samoa, Solomon Islands, Tokelau, Tonga, Tuvalu, Vanuatu, Wallis and Futuna.

II
CONTEXT OF EPISCOPAL CONFERENCES AND EASTERN CATHOLIC CHURCHES IN OCEANIA

6. Common organisational and ecclesial principles coexist alongside the richness and diversity in the episcopal conferences across Oceania. In the Eastern Catholic Churches there is a variety of administrative arrangements with some operating within a single country and others in multiple countries, or across the continent. Our region includes both

developed and developing countries – as a result, there will inevitably be different issues to be addressed, pastorally and as a matter of urgent advocacy.

2.1 Australian Catholic Bishops' Conference (ACBC)

7. According to the 2021 Census, Australia's population was around 25.4 million, of which almost 5.1 million (20%) identified as Catholic. In recent years, the number of Australians not identifying with any religious group increased to almost 10 million in 2021, and now comprise 38.9% of the population.

8. Almost one in five Australian Catholics (19.9%) were aged 65 and over, while 17.9% were aged under 15. Twenty-seven per cent were born overseas, of whom four in five were from non-English-speaking countries. Just over one in five Catholics (21.5%) spoke a language other than English at home. Around 2.7% of Australian Catholics – or almost 136,000 people – identified as Indigenous Australian.

9. The Catholic Church in Australia comprises 28 geographical dioceses, seven of which are archdioceses. There are also five Eastern Rite eparchies and two ordinariates, each of which covers all of Australia, and beyond, in some cases. All bishops, eparchs and ordinaries meet twice a year, working through 11 episcopal commissions and are supported by numerous advisory councils. There are around 175 religious institutes whose members live in community and adhere to a way of life under vows. Most are governed under their own constitutions, but in some cases by the local bishop. They work in a diocese with the consent of the bishop.

10. A particular feature of the Catholic Church in Australia is the range of ministries it undertakes and for which it has responsibility. It is the largest non-government provider in welfare and education, with Catholic schools educating just over one in five Australian children, and Catholic hospitals and aged care facilities caring for the sick, vulnerable and elderly. Increasingly, the governance of these services is by Ministerial Public Juridic Persons (MPJPs) – entities established in canon law with a specific function, such as stewardship for ministries. They have been created by religious institutes who have transferred their ministries to canonical stewards.

2.2 Episcopal Conference of the Pacific (CEPAC)

11. CEPAC comprises 16 jurisdictions – 14 dioceses (five of which are archdioceses) and the Prefecture Apostolic of the Marshall Islands and *Missio Sui Iuris* of Funafuti and Tokelau are also members of CEPAC. There are 750,000 Catholics in a region of some 2.3 million people. This Catholic population is supported by 485 priests and 126 deacons (some of whom are affiliated to religious orders), 133 brothers and 666 religious sisters.

12. The tradition of Basic Christian Communities (BCC) is alive in many parts of the Pacific with groups gathering to pray and read the Bible – often with sparse contact from a priest or religious due to seasonal and geographic challenges.

13. The Catholic Church coexists alongside majority Protestant and evangelical Christian communities in many Pacific countries.

2.3 Eastern Catholic Churches (ECC)

14. The Eastern Catholic Churches of Oceania comprise five Eparchies (dioceses) — the Ukrainian, Melkite, Chaldean, Syro-Malabar and Maronite Churches. There are also other Eastern Catholic Churches who do not presently have an Ordinary of their own churches, including the Coptic, Armenian, Russian, Syriac and Syro-Malankara Catholic Churches. The Eastern Catholic Churches collaborate on exercises such as a response to synodality, but are not formally associated in a single entity comparable to an episcopal conference.[1]

15. There is a wide array of experiences amongst the Eastern Catholic Churches in Oceania.[2] They operate as autonomous entities and are flourishing. They are made up of diverse liturgical and theological heritages, in both the Antiochian-Syriac and Byzantine traditions. Each of the Churches also presents unique cultural perspectives. This diversity is marked by the different components that form the identity of each of these Eastern Catholic Churches including:

a. special liturgical and theological heritages,
b. Chalcedonian Churches faithful to 'the mystery of salvation';
c. Patriarchal Churches, many with a unique ascetic and monastic aspect; and
d. Churches in full union with the Apostolic Roman See.

1 In addition to being members of the Episcopal Synod of their respective *sui iuris* Churches, the Eastern Catholic Bishops are also members of the Australian Catholic Bishops Conference.

2 In 2016, the Australian Catholic Bishops Conference issued a document on the presence and reality of the Eastern Catholic Churches in Australia, and how the wider Church can relate to them – https://www.catholic.org.au/images/pdf/2016_Eastern_Catholic_Churches_in_Australia.pdf

16. In the Eastern Catholic Churches in Oceania there are:

- Two Eparchies of East-Syriac Liturgical Rite:
  - Syro-Malabar Eparchy of St Thomas the Apostle of Melbourne for the Syro-Malabar faithful (13 Parishes, 82,000 Catholics).
  - St Thomas the Apostle of Sydney for the Chaldeans (7 Parishes, 70,000 Catholics).
- Two Eparchies of the Byzantine Liturgical Rite:
  - St Michael the Archangel of Sydney for the Melkite Catholics (13 Parishes, 52,000 Catholics).
  - Sts Peter and Paul of Melbourne for the Ukrainian Catholics (10 Parishes, 7,046 Catholics).
- One West-Syriac Rite: St Maroun of Sydney for the Maronites (14 Parishes, 161,370 Catholics).

2.4 New Zealand Catholic Bishops Conference (NZCBC)

17. There are almost half a million Catholic-affiliated people living in Aotearoa New Zealand, making up 10% of the total population. The Catholic Church is the largest Christian denomination and largest faith group. New Zealand is an increasingly secular country; in the last Census, undertaken in 2018, almost half of all people in New Zealand stated they had no religion (48.6%), compared to 34.6% in 2006.

18. The population of New Zealand is increasingly diverse, with a large migrant population. Māori, the indigenous population, make up 16.5% of people, with the Asian population 15.1% and Pacific peoples 8.1%.

19. There are six dioceses in New Zealand. The Archdiocese of Wellington is the metropolitan Archdiocese. The Catholic Church in New Zealand also consists of many Catholic religious orders and lay organisations, some that are undertaking significant pastoral ministries. NZCBC has embraced the bicultural relationship (Māori and Pakeha [non-Māori]) in respect of the mana [authority, spiritual power, mandate] of the people of the land.

20. Within the territory of the dioceses of New Zealand, there are also Eastern Catholic parish communities that fall under the pastoral care of Eastern Catholic Eparchies in Australia.

2.5 Catholic Bishops Conference of Papua New Guinea and the Solomon Islands (CBCPNGSI)

21. Papua New Guinea (PNG) is an island country in the southwestern Pacific Ocean. It encompasses the eastern half of New Guinea, the

world's second-largest island. It is a diverse country with more than 800 languages and 640 islands. The spectrum of PNG society now ranges from traditional village-based life, dependent on subsistence and small cash-crop agriculture, to modern urban life in the main cities.

22. It has a total population of 8.9 million (Worldometer of United Nations Data) out of which 95.5% are Christians. Catholics comprise 25.1% of the population and are the largest church.

23. The neighbouring country of Solomon Islands (SI) has a population of 732,000 (Worldometer of United Nations Data) and 20% are Catholics. There are 63 distinct languages in the country, with numerous local dialects. English is the official language, but Solomons' Pidgin is the lingua franca for the majority of people.

24. There are 19 dioceses in PNG and three dioceses in SI. Both countries belong to one Catholic Bishops Conference of Papua New Guinea and Solomon Islands (CBCPNGSI).

25. Both PNG and SI have a mix of expatriate and local priests and religious working in parishes and other ministries such as schools and hospitals.

III
DISCERNMENT PROCESS IN OCEANIA

26. In the first stage of the Synod on Synodality from 17 October 2021 until 15 August 2022, there was an open invitation to all the baptised to engage in a process of prayerful discernment, Spiritual Conversation, reflection and deep listening using a Preparatory Document and *Vademecum* (Guide) prepared by the Synod Secretariat. In Oceania, each of the episcopal conferences, the Eastern Catholic Churches and many religious institutes, lay movements and other groups and individuals contributed to the local discernment. Each episcopal conference and the Eastern Catholic Churches prepared a response which reflected the discernment process and outcomes in their jurisdiction.

27. Of the 114 episcopal conferences around the world, 112 submitted a national synthesis to the Synod Secretariat by the deadline of 15 August 2022. In addition, over 1,000 responses were received from religious institutes, lay movements, other groups and individuals. To discern the issues in these responses, some 30 people from a range of backgrounds and expertise were invited to a monastery in Frascati outside Rome from September to October 2022 for two weeks together of prayer, reflection, discernment and synthesis. At the end of this process, the Council of Ordinaries, which governs the Synod Secretariat, joined the Frascati group to familiarise themselves with the Working Document for the Continental Stage (DCS), and approve it.

28. The release of the DCS on 27 October 2022 was the start of the second stage of the Synod: the Continental Stage. In preparation for this stage, the FCBCO created the Oceania Taskforce. This Taskforce worked alongside the Suva Assembly Taskforce to ensure the two planning processes were integrated. The Oceania Taskforce requested that the FCBCO also create a Discernment and Writing Group (DWG) to take the fruits of the responses from the five jurisdictions and create a draft submission for episcopal consideration at their Assembly scheduled for early February 2023. The DWG comprised a diverse range of people from across ecclesial, geographic, age, sex and experiential backgrounds.

29. The four episcopal conferences and the Eastern Catholic Churches in Oceania were well prepared, despite the concurrence of the discernment period with Christmas and summer holidays in the Southern Hemisphere. In addition, the FCBCO had been planning their regional assembly for some years which had been delayed by the COVID-19 pandemic. It was rescheduled to 5-10 February 2023 in Suva, Fiji, and the FCBCO agreed to include discernment on synodality as part of their program, necessitating a draft submission in time for their consideration ahead of the Assembly.

30. From late October to mid-December 2022, the episcopal conferences and Eastern Catholic Churches undertook a discernment process with representatives of the People of God (with an emphasis on reaching those at the margins). The prayerful process enabled participants to discern the DCS through the lens of their lived experience of the Church in Oceania. A process of discernment and synthesis was conducted in each jurisdiction in mid-December, and responses were sent to the Oceania Taskforce by late December.

31. Similar to the approach taken in developing the DCS, the Oceania Discernment and Writing Group gathered in a retreat-like mode to authentically and prayerfully discern together the common themes

across the five responses from Australia, New Zealand, the Pacific, Papua New Guinea and the Solomon Islands (PNG/SI) and the Eastern Catholic Churches (ECC) and to identify differences, gaps and priorities for the consideration and finalisation of the FCBCO members at their Suva Assembly. Some members of the Oceania Taskforce attended the FCBCO Assembly to present the draft submission and support the episcopal discernment process, leading to the bishops' pastoral reflection on the document.

32. The Oceania submission was finalised at an online meeting of the FCBCO Executive and the members of the Discernment and Writing Group prior to sending the submission to the Synod Secretariat by the deadline of 31 March 2023.

IV
EXPERIENCE OF SYNODALITY

33. Responses to the DCS were generally positive in relating people's experience of synodality as God's will for the Church in the third millennium. There were, however, a few negative views, but with quite different reasons for this negativity.

34. There was fundamental resonance that synodality is grounded in the primary sacrament of Baptism, noting that 'Baptism is not an abstract concept but identity. The synodal process is further encouraging and aiding towards this experience to a more deep and enriching level with the emphasis to create an environment where every baptised individual and people of good will feel at home in the Church. The synodal way is a way for the Church to reach out to everyone and it is a way to create a welcoming atmosphere for all its children' (PNG/SI, 2.2). The very opportunity to participate in responding to the DCS was experienced with gratitude: 'There was great gratitude for the [synodal] process, being able to speak freely and to be listened to. "Young and old, women and men, so glad to have this chance – they must be heard." The participation of so many people was commented on by many' (New Zealand, 10).

35. The ancient vision and practice of the Church as synodal was affirmed: 'Synodality has been a large part of how the Eastern Catholic Churches have functioned for a long time. There is much to be learned from the Eastern Catholic Church about synodality' (ECC, 6). Another element of

the positive experience of discerning the DCS was people encountering the global nature of the Church (for some for the first time); it expanded their view of 'Church' and of the many common issues across the Universal Church.

36. There were, however, some negative responses regarding synodality. For some, this disquiet expressed itself in doubts that the bishops would in fact consider the fruits of discernment and with that a fear that the synodal work would not make any real difference in the end. For others, there was concern that synodality will harm the Church. Both these reasons were captured in the New Zealand document: 'There were some fears and cautions expressed during the process. People are waiting to see if their voices have been heard, or if they will be lost as the process reaches the Rome Assemblies. Some are anxious and even angry about people talking about change and see the synodal process as potentially 'wounding the Church' (New Zealand, 14).

37. The breadth of experience is reflected in another response: 'Many participants were greatly impressed by the global calls for a synodal Church. This resonated with local experiences because some dioceses and parishes are growing in synodality by listening to diverse voices, being open to new approaches, and including a diverse range of people in leadership and ministry. At the same time, other regions remained 'inward-looking', with a passive laity and clergy' (Australia, 32).

38. On the whole, however, all regions of Oceania saw the DCS as capturing a truly global experience of synodality. This was seen as a welcome direction for the Church's inner life and mission in the third millennium: 'The synodal process of prayerful discernment, Spiritual Conversation, deep listening, and respect for each person and their views is a powerful process. Most people see synodality as the way to move forward in their own spiritual journey, individually and collectively, and agree with the DCS: 'In fact, it is the way of being Church. The Holy Spirit is asking us to be synodal [DCS, 3]' (New Zealand, 15). This positive embrace of synodality is also captured in the report of one diocese of the Pacific: 'Reflecting on the Working Document for the Continental Stage, it is clear that the Church needs to make a radical decision to bring a sense of welcome and inclusion among its members, even those outside of the faith. The Synod can be the catalyst ... to promote collegiality, unity, and synodality in our Church and society' (Pacific).

V
FRUITS OF THE DISCERNMENT

5.1 Common Themes, Issues, Insights

Tent Metaphor

39. In the larger countries of Oceania, the image of the tent (Isaiah 54:2) was received with enthusiasm and joy, seeing it as very relevant for a Church which is deeply wounded by the abuse crisis. 'The tent is a much humbler building than great edifices, such as cathedrals, so enlarging space in the tent is a very good image to use' (Australia, 58).

40. The tent image did not have the same resonance among the Eastern Catholic Churches in Oceania, as some of their people have been 'forced by difficult circumstances, including war, persecution, and economic hardships, to settle in other countries' (ECC, 2). For some of their members, tents are associated with impermanence, lack of safety, and even refugee camps, while they seek safety and permanence in their new lives in Oceanic countries.

41. The tent also did not have a strong resonance in the Pacific countries of Oceania. For people who live on small islands, the DCS description of the Church 'as a tent, indeed as the tent of meeting, which accompanied the people on their journey through the desert: called to stretch out, therefore, but also to move' does not accord with their experience as *tagata o le moana*, people of the sea, who have travelled throughout history in boats as they moved through their region (Pacific).

42. Care is needed to ensure that continuing with the image of the tent does not exclude people for whom the tent has little resonance, or for whom it may be an unwelcome image because of their life experiences.

43. The DCS description of the tent as an image of the Church means that all those who are baptised are inside the tent, whether they are active participants in the tent community or not. People such as those in an irregular marriage situation are not able to take part in aspects of the sacramental life of the tent community, but they are not excluded from the tent. Similarly, people who do not participate in Sunday Masses are not outside the tent. All the baptised are in the tent, whether they are active participants in the community or not.

44. There are many reasons for non-participation: 'Many Church members such as gay and lesbians, feel that they are outsiders and not part of the Church. The poor, because they cannot afford decent clothes, are also scorned. Some feel unwanted because they are not members of the ruling clique in the parish. New people in the Church feel they cannot help in the Church as it is taken over by selected families' (Pacific).

45. In parts of Oceania there is a very visible gap between the poor and the rich, between ethnic groups, between migrants and those who consider the country to be theirs, and between people from different islands in the same country or diocese. These societal issues are experienced within the Church: 'The gap between the poor and the rich is visible and emphasised even more by priests who offer special treatment to the rich and well-dressed. Different races compete for dominance in parishes, making it almost impossible for racial minorities to participate. Discrimination because of gender seems to be a lingering struggle within the Church, particularly towards the LGBTQI+ community' (Pacific). There are concerns in the responses about 'gatekeepers' in the Church who are perceived to exclude, either overtly or in more subtle ways, those they deem unacceptable.

46. Reflection upon the tent image has sharpened our focus on barriers to participation and inclusion. In doing this it has exposed and named the reality of the situation the Church is facing globally: 'The DCS reports a rather inconvenient truth about the Church: her children are divided and scattered, some are lost, and some intentionally walked away. Walls seem to separate people making it harder for everyone to live in true communion with God and people' (Pacific).

Baptism and Sacraments

47. The responses affirmed that Baptism is the source of common identity, that this needs to be recognised as such, and that Baptism calls all members of the Church to communion, participation and mission. 'People are gaining a deeper appreciation of the sacrament [of Baptism], not just as their entry point to the Church, but as the basis of their participation in ministry and mission' (New Zealand, 36).

48. Some responses also argued that the call for all the baptised to be recognised is as yet unrealised: 'There is a yearning for the acceptance that all the baptised are called to full, active, and equal participation in the Church' (New Zealand, 38). 'One theme that resonated with many

was the growing recognition of the baptismal dignity of all, as well as the realisation that the Church's mission of making Christ present was a responsibility shared by all the baptised; however, greater formation for a deeper understanding of this reality was critical to empower people' (Australia, 34).

49. Obstacles to the full realisation of our baptismal call were recognised in the responses. For instance, some argued that greater participation is needed for the laity, especially women. The New Zealand response argued that the Second Vatican Council emphasised Baptism as the source of our communion and participation (New Zealand, 36). This fruit of the Second Vatican Council, however, has not been realised because the understanding of 'The Church as the People of God... was undermined by structures that did not facilitate this new model' (New Zealand, 37).

50. The responses highlighted the centrality of the Eucharist to the experience of community and what it means to be Church. The ECC highlighted their 'common love of the liturgy – which is steeped in beauty, richness, and authenticity (ECC, 10)', in which participants 'experience our Lord in a mystical and monastic way' (ECC, 18). The Pacific response emphasised: 'The liturgy, especially the Eucharistic Liturgy, the source and summit of Christian life, which brings the community together, making communion tangible, enables the experience of participation and nourishes the momentum towards mission with the Word and the Sacraments' (Pacific).

51. The Australian and Pacific responses noted 'calls for a more synodal and participatory style of Eucharistic celebration, liturgies that are inclusive of other cultures and relevant to young people, a broader understanding of what it meant to be Eucharistic in essence, and a greater outreach to Catholics who have lost appreciation for these rituals' (Australia, 35; Pacific).

52. There was a statement that ecumenical relationships are affected by Church teaching. There was a view that 'there needs to be more Eucharistic hospitality to members of other churches in place of the exclusive line currently practised' (New Zealand, 70).

53. The Australian and New Zealand responses noted the desire by some for the Third Rite of Reconciliation to be used (Australia, 52; New Zealand, 71). Some women said that the Sacrament of Penance places 'a lay person in an inferior position to the priest' (New Zealand, 71).

54. The PNG/SI response noted that while there were calls in other parts of the world for greater recognition of same-sex relationships, 'Same-sex marriage (DCS, 39) is disturbing the Catholics and those who consider it a sin. LGBTQI+ is not accepted by the tradition and the society of PNG' (PNG/SI, 3.2).

55. Eucharist and marriage coalesced around the issue of communion for the divorced and remarried, particularly in the New Zealand response, which said that 'Although *Amoris Laetitia* opened potential pathways for the divorced and remarried to receive communion, these are perceived as narrow and difficult' (New Zealand, 69). The Australian response referred to the exclusion that the divorced and remarried feel (Australia, 44; 57) and the need for greater compassion.

56. Finally, lay prison chaplains in New Zealand observed that, having accompanied 'some of our most disadvantaged people on a life-changing faith journey [they then] have to step back when sacraments are required' (New Zealand, 85).

57. Polygamous marriages are a social reality in some parts of our region and need attention, whereas this is not the case in other parts (PNG/SI, 4.3). Issues related to marriage appeared in various ways throughout the responses. The Australian response recognised that there was a gap in the DCS: 'the absence of any mention of the role of marriage and family, particularly in the transmission of faith' (Australia, 26).

58. It noted that 'A number of participants called for a re-examination of the Church's position on married men becoming priests, and on the requirement for celibacy.' It also raised concerns about the 'lack of understanding of the [permanent] diaconate' (Australia, 49). While the issue of women's ordination was raised in the Australian response, the New Zealand response noted that 'there was no request for the consideration of ordination of women as priests, although one group asked for their [women's] ordination as deacons' (New Zealand, 65).

Inclusion

59. All the responses supported calls for the Church to be more inclusive, particularly of those whose relationships present challenges to participation in the Eucharist. They also desired a more inclusive approach to people living with disabilities, migrants and refugees, and others who were marginalised and neglected, such as the elderly, terminally ill, street children, orphans, criminals, addicts, prostitutes, widows, and victims of

rape, abuse and domestic violence. There was also a desire to welcome those with 'diverse thinking', 'non-practising Catholics and unbaptised people' (Australia, 44).

60. There was particular emphasis on the need for the inclusion of the poor in the Pacific region, where poverty was seen as a discernible force dividing the Church: 'In many cases, the poor are sometimes reduced to an opportunity to raise funds for seasonal outreach and photo opportunity to make the Church look good' (Pacific; PNG/SI, 2.4).

61. Lack of inclusion of people with diverse experiences of sexuality and gender appeared to affect community life even in small island nations: 'The LGBTQI+ community resonates very strongly in the Mariana Islands, a reality that was not evident in the past' (Pacific).

62. However, as noted in para 54, people with diverse experiences of sexuality and gender are 'not accepted by the tradition and the society of PNG' (PNG/SI, 3.2). Nevertheless, many responses called for greater inclusion of people in this group, particularly 'to recognise and give them a space for ministry, for participation, and involvement in the life of the Church' (Pacific).

63. In Australia, the inclusion of First Nations peoples was named as a priority: 'Our listening needs to include the Uluru Statement, our Church elders [to] include our Aunties and Uncles caring for Country' (Australia, 46).

64. From the perspective of Eastern Catholic Churches, the call to being inclusive meant creating an environment of hospitality and welcome within their churches to invite Catholics from other liturgical rites to experience their liturgy, theology and disciplines (ECC, 18) as full and complete expressions of the Catholic faith. However, this call to hospitality to include other Catholics in experiencing the venerable Eastern Christian traditions also means that Eastern Catholics must hold on to what is truly theirs and not assimilate rituals. The Eastern Catholic Churches have a duty to show that to be Catholic does not mean one has to be Latin.

65. While all the responses called for the Church to focus on inclusion and representation of those in the excluded groups, there were calls for 'radical inclusivity' from a few groups, urging the Church to be 'brave, bold and innovative', rejecting the notion of being 'a gate keeper', excluding

those Christ would welcome into the tent' (Australia, 28). However, challenges were identified in the call to proclaim authentic teaching (PNG/SI, 4.5), alongside being called to respect others, avoid judgment and take a compassionate and pastoral approach (Australia, 44).

Church Teaching

66. Some participants raised concerns that 'the rules and regulations of the Church were at odds with the Gospel message, and that greater weight should be given to the "primacy of conscience" and supporting people in a compassionate and pastoral manner to develop a more mature relationship with God' (Australia, 54).

67. There was also a 'call for the Church to reform some areas of its theology, teaching and dogma related to the formation of seminarians and the professional supervision, development and support of priests' while, for some participants, the priority was to 'address afresh the whole concept of the priesthood in the Church, including that of the laity' (Australia, 75).

68. While there was consensus on the need for an enhanced role for women in the Church, the issue of women's ordination was only explicitly raised in one submission, so that 'acting on the inequalities of women called for equal, just and full participation of women in Church governance, mission and ministry' and 'recognising their admissibility to any role, such as deacon, priest, or representative on decision-making councils' (Australia, 60). The New Zealand submission noted that 'there was no request for the consideration of ordination of women as priests, although one group asked for their ordination as deacons' (New Zealand, 65).

69. Some aspects of Church teaching were perceived as 'exclusionary or hurtful' and understood to 'cause people to walk away from the Church or deter them from returning'. These include teaching on sexuality, contraception, the situation of the divorced and remarried, and intercommunion with other Christian denominations whose Baptism we recognise (New Zealand, 117).

Authority and Decision-making

70. A synodal Church needs a cultural and structural change in Church leadership (Australia, 61; New Zealand, 79; PNG/SI, 4.1). Leadership in a synodal Church must be re-thought, lest the current problems with clerical power and authority are simply transferred to lay people who are participating in shared decision-making. To avoid this trap there must

be 'formation of individuals as leaders dedicated to God's Word, who can facilitate dialogue, are trained to listen and discern, and are appointed to serve rather than assume power over others' (Australia, 62).

71. In the responses from the Oceania conferences there were many comments from participants who expressed their love for the faith and their desire to continue to belong. They were grateful for the pastoral care they received from clergy and were aware of the challenges they faced: 'We are grateful for all the Church has given us and the way we have been supported' (Australia, 36).

72. There were also deep concerns about governance and decision-making in the Church, at parish, diocesan, national and global levels. The renewed emphasis on Baptism in the synodal process revealed 'a deep desire for acceptance that all the baptised are called to and capable of full, active and equal participation in Church' (New Zealand, 76). There was a perception that canon law creates a power imbalance between bishops, clergy and lay people which could undermine the embedding of synodality as the way of the Church in the future (New Zealand, 82).

73. Shared governance and decision-making, involving both laity and clergy, were seen as necessary if we are to be a truly synodal Church. Current governance structures and the power they give bishops and priests are seen as 'one of the mechanisms which exclude lay voices, and women's voices in particular' (New Zealand, 80).

74. Dominance of governance and decision-making by the ordained is seen by some as fostering clericalism and impeding laity in the exercise of their gifts. 'Clericalism separates the clergy from the lay people and gives the clergy a superior role over the lay people, limiting the full participation of lay people in the decision-making in the parishes, dioceses and higher levels of the Church hierarchy' (PNG/SI, 2.5).

75. Frustration was expressed by some lay people at being shut out of decision-making, especially when they often have a better understanding of the needs of the people. 'Our attitude needs to shift from hierarchical to communal. For example, a priest may have a theoretical knowledge of raising a family, but parents are the ones who live out this life' (Pacific).

76. Clericalism and abuse have triggered distrust among the people towards the hierarchy of the Church. Greater openness and accountability have

allowed the people 'to see the truth about the Church, that bishops, priests, religious, and lay workers are flawed. However, they do whatever they can to do good and become responsible workers in God's vineyard' (Pacific).

77. Clericalism is not confined to the ordained but is also found among lay people who support and facilitate the exercise of power by the clergy. That power and 'superior role' the priest assumes is the antithesis of the servant leadership people yearn for and need from their priests: 'Their servant leadership should lead to humble service' (PNG/SI, 5.1). The people know a good pastor when they have one: 'The people's desire is to witness a true pastor moulded in the heart of Christ' (Pacific). This can be particularly the case in traditional ceremonies following priestly ordination where the newly ordained priest is accorded treatment befitting that of a high chief (Pacific).

78. The effects of clericalism are widely felt in dioceses and parishes: 'Clericalism in clergy and lay people perpetuates abuse of power and isolates groups, stymies evangelisation efforts, and impedes youth engagement, servant leadership development and the implementation of necessary change' (Australia, 30).

79. The challenges for ministry reported by clergy and religious include 'grief and powerlessness' in the aftermath of the clergy sexual abuse crisis, the increasing demands on their time due to the pressure of priest shortages and the experiences of 'loneliness, isolation and burnout', particularly among 'the elderly, those in country dioceses and those who come from overseas' (Australia, 31).

80. There was a call for leadership to be more participatory with 'a less exclusive role given to bishops' (New Zealand, 81). The selection process for bishops is considered to be opaque (PNG/SI). 'People want to know how the current process works and want to ensure that the selection is the product of genuine discernment involving a wide range of people, clergy and lay. There is a desire for specific scrutiny of a potential bishop's record on abuse, and a close examination of his attitude towards abuse' (New Zealand, 81).

81. It was noted that 'people see canon law, not Church teaching, creating a power imbalance between bishops, clergy and lay people which has major effects in relation to authority and governance in parishes and dioceses. People are aware that there have been changes to canon law in recent years and know that this is possible' (New Zealand, 82).

82. In the absence of a priest, lay people have shown in Oceania that they can take ownership of both the pastoral ministry and governance of their local Church. For example, 'during the crisis of Bougainville (PNG), for almost 10 years the families and the Basic Christian Communities kept the faith alive in absence of effective clerical presence' (PNG/SI, 2.12). The importance of the Eucharist in Basic Christian Communities and family life was emphasised: '[Basic Christian Communities] can empower and strengthen the families through the holy presence of Jesus in the Eucharist' (PNG/SI, 5.4).

The Challenges of Mission

83. There are multiple challenges in Oceania for 'bringing God's kingdom to a contemporary world' (Australia, 40). A primary difficulty is the lack of agreed understanding about what mission is and the vast number of perspectives on its meaning: 'The word "mission" was mentioned many times, but as in earlier parts of the synod process it is not clear what "mission" means when people talk about it. It does not seem to have a concrete or active form for many people. There is a need for shared understanding, and work needs to be done in this area' (New Zealand, 104).

84. There was a strong emphasis on 'mission' being the responsibility of all the baptised: 'The Diocesan Synod creates in each one of us a mission-driven and mission-focused attitude and spirit. Mission is no longer a monopolised endeavour of the clerics and religious, but a shared journey within all peoples. This shared journey implies sharing in the brokenness and woundedness of others' (Pacific). The Church was seen as 'a mission-driven institution that Jesus Christ himself designed' (Pacific).

85. The mission activity of the Church was hindered by 'discrimination based on matrimonial/relationship status, financial status, customs/traditions (gender and age status), and disability status' (Pacific). The lack of formation in understanding the baptismal call to evangelise and proclaim God's love in unity with others was also a barrier to transition from a 'maintenance Church' to a 'missional Church' by establishing communities that 'join with all humanity in journeying together' (Australia, 69).

86. The diversity of liturgical rites and cultures in Oceania was seen as important to our unique contribution to the mission of the Church: 'The Eastern Catholic Churches in Oceania must preserve their identity and

be recognised by the wider Catholic community as being more than just ethnic communities, but rather, *sui iuris* Churches who through their rich spiritual tradition can contribute to the mission of the Church' (ECC, 19).

87. The richness of the synodal experience should ultimately 'lead us to experience the person of Jesus within the Church and to share this good news to others; it leads us to mission; mission to evangelise; to preach the good news' (PNG/SI, 5.7).

Ecological Crisis

88. The ecological crisis was emphasised as an urgent issue for the whole Oceania region, for all of humanity and for the earth community. 'If we are people of the Tent then we must understand the importance of the earth as our common home, respecting the ground, the sea and the environment within which we assemble the Tent' (New Zealand, 93).

89. From the Torres Strait Islands of Australia to the Solomon Islands, and the small island states of Micronesia and Polynesia, the ecological crisis and rising sea levels are a real and present existential threat: 'Islands in the Pacific are relatively smaller and scientifically proven to be getting even smaller due to the rising ocean water level. Climate change, the driving force that ignites catastrophic typhoons, heatwaves, drought and flooding, directly affects people' (Pacific). Highland and inland communities in our region are also directly affected by these phenomena.

90. The responses from New Zealand acknowledge that integral ecology and care for creation 'is not an area in which the Church's teaching is lacking' but note that 'there is a need for formation and prophetic witness, and encouragement to act' (New Zealand, 93). Australian respondents also relayed concerns regarding the Church's responsibility for 'stewardship of creation'; however, some 'reported on the work being undertaken in their particular community' (Australia, 50).

91. As Pope Francis presents in *Laudato Si'*, the interconnectedness of ecological, social and economic justice means the 'mistreatment of our planet disproportionately affects the poor' (New Zealand, 92). The People of God in Oceania want to listen to the cry of the earth and the ocean, the land and waterways, as well as the cry of the poor, and to 'collaborate with others who share a common purpose' (New Zealand, 95).

92. The ecological crisis must be understood as a mission field in which the whole Church, globally and locally, must be engaged given the 'urgent struggle to preserve our planet and its life, and to provide economic justice for its people' (New Zealand, 114). The fact that the 'threat to human life posed by climate change to the island nations in the Oceania region caused significant anxiety to some participants' in Australia is a promising sign of solidarity and a renewed understanding of mission (Australia, 50).

Inculturation and Localisation

93. Oceania is expansive, yet the numerous nations and cultures flourish in their connectedness to the land, ocean, creatures and indigenous spiritualities. While numerous Catholic missionaries to the region have shared the gift of their faith, this has sometimes undermined the contribution of the local culture to the Gospel. The Church in Oceania today is both encouraged and challenged by inculturation as Christianity and Indigenous Spiritualities often co-exist in the everyday lives of people.

94. Inculturation of the Christian faith positively impacts liturgical celebrations: 'Cultural differences connect strongly as well among the islands in the Marianas, and the Pacific in general. This is visible in churches during Eucharistic celebrations. The colours, music and language freely shift to celebrate the Lord through various faith expressions' (Pacific, 10). Others in Australia have similar experiences: 'Some groups described positive and enriching experiences of Church and parish life such as multicultural engagement' (Australia, 36).

95. Indigenous perspectives are also used to re-envision and contextualise the meaning of Church. For example, *a Te Ao Māori* worldview could see the Church as *tūrangawaewae*, a place to stand 'where we feel connected, empowered and accepted' (New Zealand, 13).

96. There are challenges when people are unable to see the compatibility of traditional cultures with Catholicism: 'How can the Church keep her reverence to the sacredness while at the same time make it accessible for the faithful? In our culture, our sacred sites are kept away from the people to maintain its sacredness. Likewise in the Church, we try to keep the sacredness from being profaned. The question is how to keep the sacredness of the Church while at the same time making it accessible to the people' (PNG/SI, 4.4).

97. Real difficulties emerge when specific indigenous ways of being are in stark contrast to Church teaching: 'Cultural beliefs and traditional practices such as sorcery and polygamy continue to be a big challenge to Christian values and teachings. For example, cultural polygamous marriages are still practised in PNG while the Church is against it' (PNG/SI, 4.3). In some parts of Oceania, the Church is also severely lacking in its genuine engagement with indigenous peoples: 'The Church's role in recognition of and reconciliation with indigenous peoples was highlighted. In particular, the need to ensure that attention was paid to the spiritualities of the indigenous peoples of Australia and in Oceania was prominent' (Australia, 46).

98. Overall, it is important to emphasise the importance of cultural diversity to the life of the Church: 'We must start by being fully ourselves. It is only in our distinctiveness that we can make any kind of contribution to the larger society. It is only by being what we are that we retain a reason for existence at all' (ECC, 16).

Women

99. The theme of women's roles and participation in the Church resonated strongly across Oceania, though women's experiences varied across the region. The DCS was praised for naming global concerns about women's roles and vocations in the Church, and many groups in Australia and New Zealand expressed strong concern about the lack of women's participation in Church leadership and governance structures, including the diocesan marriage tribunal (New Zealand, 41-42). A minority concern was expressed that women were still barred from the permanent diaconate and ordained ministry. Although many women serve in leadership and governance roles that do not require ordination, this was a significant issue affecting Church life in these countries.

100. Other groups stated that they had not experienced a lack of equality for women in the Church. One group of young lay women, for example, saw themselves as equals with a unique role in the Church, whereas a group of priests described their experiences with women being present and influential in parish bodies and ministries (New Zealand, 41). Similarly, the PNG/SI response stated that women play a 'very active role in the life of the Church' and that there is a growing positive change in terms of equal participation in Church work (PNG/SI, 2.6).

101. Some responses were concerned about women being treated as 'cheap labour' (DCS, 63) and two responses called for women to be adequately remunerated for their work (Australia, 29; PNG/SI, 2.6). Other issues identified in the responses affecting women in the region included family and domestic violence, abuse, sorcery-related violence, divorce and remarriage, women being shunned for crimes that men are forgiven for, those alienated by Church teachings on sexuality, and misogyny and sexism particularly perpetrated by the clergy (Australia, 47).

102. Many responses reaffirmed the call for Catholic women to be valued as equal members of God's People, stating that 'the continued exclusion of women from aspects of Church life was disempowering' (Australia, 29). There was a call for more emphasis on 'using the gifts and experience of women in discerning and providing advice, guidance and challenge in decision-making beyond the managerial and parish roles many women occupy' (New Zealand, 42), as well as a need for greater listening, particularly to the realities and needs of poor, marginalised and neglected women (Pacific).

Young People

103. The absence of young people participating in the Church features in nearly all of the Oceania responses, which reveal great anguish and profound worry about the future: 'We are only ever one generation from dying. It only takes one generation to say NO. The Church is fragile. Our young people – God is on their hearts, but they don't feel drawn to the Church ... They have their prayer groups in their *whares* (houses)' (New Zealand, 45-46). There was also reference to young people who are very committed participants in their faith communities. 'Irrespective of the challenges that our Church is conflicted with during unprecedented times, it remains a home, providing strength, warmth, and optimism. This would not be possible without the leaders and volunteers who are constantly ready to serve' (ECC, 11).

104. Our baptised young people are in the tent, but many are not participants in the life of the tent community. Reasons given for this vary. Some young people feel they are inside the tent, but invisible and ignored. Others feel unable to participate due to a fear of being judged or not fitting in (New Zealand, 47). Their local parish can appear to be 'owned' by older people, with power being exercised in ways that make young people feel that it is not a place for them (Australia, 37-38).

105. The response from PNG/SI spoke about young people leaving their parish communities to join other churches (PNG/SI, 2.13), and others 'being pulled away from spiritual and faith programs by the strong attraction of the secular activities, social media and modern technology, which is causing distraction to the traditional youth formation programs in BCCs, parishes and dioceses' (PNG/SI, 4.7).

106. Young people see the urgency of the ecological crisis, which is of intense interest and concern to them, but do not see its urgency being recognised in their local Church. Many also struggle with aspects of the Church's teaching on sexuality: 'LBGTQIA+ issues are also of intense interest to young people, who have to work through them at a personal level and among their friends. Responses have indicated that the Church's teaching on this and other aspects of sexuality are a major barrier for many young people in maintaining their connection to the Church' (New Zealand, 49).

107. There are very few ideas about how to respond to this genuine crisis for the Church. Nevertheless, one Pacific diocese has found a way to engage with marginalised young people: 'Some young, marginalised, excluded and some of those who are not in good standing with the Church are welcomed in choirs, prayer groups and catechesis as catechist assistants. Young people are listened to more today because there are more youth groups in parishes' (Pacific). Other suggestions included accompaniment and formation for leadership using 'platforms that allowed them to utilise their skills and passions' (Australia, 76).

108. In contrast to those who feel the Church needs to 'modernise' to remain relevant (Australia, 38), some young people are seeking a stronger proclamation of the faith of the Church. They believe that personal conversion is needed rather than institutional change (New Zealand, 55). In the Eastern Catholic Churches' response, a young woman described her faith journey and the support she had received at all stages to share her gifts and to remain faithful and engaged with her Church community (ECC, 11). In other responses, some young people described feeling persecuted and alone while promoting strong faith-based values (ECC, 13; Australia, 38).

109. Concern was expressed by some young people about feeling excluded by the language of the DCS: 'The DCS is largely inaccessible to young people, in terms of language, process and practical application. New

terms such as, "dialogical sharing", "fraternal conviviality" and the Eucharist as a "generative tension" are not accessible to young people' (New Zealand, 47).

110. While there is a deep concern about the loss of young people as individuals, their disengagement from the Church in numbers is also seen as preventing the embedding of synodality as the way of the Church: 'How do we impart synodality to the young, as the future of the Church, when there are so few young people in the Church today?' (Australia, 48).

111. There was a call to investigate 'how the faith needs of young people could be met and how youth could be better formed and provided with platforms that allowed them to utilise their skills and passions' (Australia, 76).

Formation

112. There are calls for formation of various kinds throughout the region. The formation of seminarians and priests received special attention, with the observation that this needs to be holistic: 'spiritually, socially, psychologically, mentally, emotionally and economically' (PNG/SI, 5.1). In some dioceses, women already do work in this area (Australia, 66; New Zealand, 102). Formation for marriage and family life is also a fundamental need (ECC, 18; Australia, 77; PNG/SI, 5.3). Catholic educators need 'more appropriate' formation (Australia, 77). Formation for young people is essential, but difficult to achieve (Australia, 76; New Zealand, 44). We also need to provide formation to respond to Pope Francis's call to missionary discipleship.

113. It is unclear whether 'formation' meant the same thing across the documents. Formation in a general sense involves shaping the way that people respond to the world around them. At times the word 'formation' refers to training (PNG/SI, 5.1) and at other times, to personal faith development (Australia, 77). While the desire was expressed that Catholic Social Teaching be the basis for formation across the Church (Australia, 65), formation is possible and perhaps also desirable in other areas and works best when addressing an identified need in the light of Scripture and Church teaching.

114. As our Church becomes more synodal, ongoing formation is needed for all (New Zealand, 100). A synodal Church will need participants formed

in listening and dialogue (Australia, 62). Furthermore, leadership in the Church will require a different mode of formation, so that there is 'servant leadership at all levels' (PNG/SI, 5.1).

5.2 Tensions and Differences

115. As indicated earlier, the Oceania region includes both developed and developing countries, and so there are different pastoral issues to be addressed as a matter of urgent advocacy.

116. A 'tension' is an area of differing views that need further discernment or attention. The sections above have already identified some tensions. These are:

a) Different attitudes toward those with diverse experiences of sexuality and gender in the region.
b) The roles of women in the Church.
c) Some voices in the responses call for change in Church teaching, according to a 'dying and rising' cycle (New Zealand, 52-56). Others asserted the need to retain teaching and provide formation in unchanging Church teaching of the present (ECC, 18).

117. In some areas of the region, the wounds of sexual abuse within the Church are not as much to the fore: 'The scandal of sexual abuse by the clergy and abuse of minors ... is a growing issue of concern. Although there are a few abuses, the scandals do not greatly affect the faith of the people yet' (PNG/SI, 3.1). In other areas, the scandal is clear and public. The ongoing wound for the whole Church, not only those of the victims and survivors of abuse but also their families and parish communities and other clergy, needs attention directed toward ongoing healing.

118. There is a tension in understanding the issue of inculturation, where a local Church adopts local customs and cultural expressions. Some regard the traditions of the universal Church as a kind of imposition on local culture, and even a form of colonialism. Others consider God present in every culture so that every culture already expresses Christian truths. Another view is that Christians cannot adopt and adapt some pre-Christian cultural practices. For instance, when a priest takes on the symbolism of the chief of a village, the priest becomes a symbol of power rather than of service (Pacific).

119. Questions about Church teaching, or the application of Church teaching, were raised by many participants. While there was a desire to remain faithful to Church teaching, there was also a desire to embrace the paschal cycle of 'dying and rising' (New Zealand, 51).

120. Some participants said that while the Church might appear to be dying 'we are meant to die and rise. This is the cycle of the life of Christ in us. Some things are brought to death so that other things may rise. We need to let go and go with the dying and rising. This is what this moment is asking of us' (New Zealand, 52). For others, the Church was seen as 'an unchanging rock in a sea of social change' and the 're-statement of its teaching and further catechesis' is the 'necessary response to this change' (New Zealand, 55).

121. Meanwhile, the Eastern Catholic Churches suggest that 'our position on Catholic teachings is not to be compromised by potential external forces that require a change in the Church for their agenda rather than accepting the truth, love and beauty that the Church offers to all people' (ECC, 18).

5.3 Gaps and Omissions in the DCS

122. In the lived experience in Oceania, the following areas were identified as gaps, or matters inadequately dealt with, in the DCS:

a) The ecological crisis including the threat of rising seas and environmental and marine degradation in Oceania, also being experienced in other parts of the world, should be amplified in the *Instrumentum Laboris*. This includes loss of cultural identity, psychological stress and for some a sense of hopelessness.
b) Religious life, including the contribution of religious men and women and the exemplar of relevant spiritualities, good governance and shared leadership in many of the religious institutes warrants further reflection.
c) Greater acknowledgement of the vocation of marriage and the role of families in faith formation would be valuable (Australia, 26).
d) In the DCS, the absence of lay men from sacramental programs and decision-making is not explored adequately.
e) The ongoing effects of the sexual abuse crisis have not received adequate attention in the DCS. During the life of the synodal journey launched by Pope Francis in April 2021, there have been further damaging revelations of mishandling of sexual abuse cases within the Church. This needs to be acknowledged, alongside a reflection on whether existing Church structures impede or enable adequate safeguarding, good governance and fair redress.

For some parts of Oceania and more broadly, this would also include a positive recognition of the efforts in local churches to improve professional standards and safeguarding.

f) Beginning-and end-of-life issues such as abortion and euthanasia need greater attention than given to them in the DCS.

g) Growing restrictions on religious liberty is a concern that has not been adequately addressed in the DCS.

Voices not Heard or Under-Represented in the Oceania Representation

123. Many voices could not be heard directly for reasons such as remoteness and lack of access to information and communications technology, or due to disabilities or language differences. Accordingly, 'advocacy' was implied throughout the five responses — advocacy for diverse groups of people in the Church or wider society which could not be directly part of a synodal listening, dialogue, discernment and decision-making process. For example: 'The plight of the poor and the marginalised people, disabled, elderly, street children, orphans, criminals, prostitutes, widows, divorcees, victims of abuses, victims of sorcery-related violence and refugees is a great concern for the Church' (PNG/SI, 2.4).

124. The decrease in the number of young people in the Church was lamented in the documents. Their voices have not been sufficiently heard in the synodal process.

125. Another problematic issue that was raised was the issue of inaccessibility for many countries in Oceania. This is related, first of all, to the geographical isolation of many ecclesial communities, either due to mountainous terrain, the distance between islands or the lack of roads. Also, many areas lack the technological infrastructure that would facilitate access to the internet and online communication. All these factors impeded responses from people in these regions.

126. For a variety of reasons, CEPAC was unable to submit a synthesis document.

127. Other voices that were identified as missing or inadequately represented from all countries in the region were: the voice of West Papuans; the adequate representation of migrants; the voice of those affected by 'neo-colonialism' (the workers of the multinational extractive companies), the voice of those still affected by 'the old colonialism' and the Church's role in colonialism; lay men; members of other Christian churches; religious

movements; and victims of domestic violence and human trafficking, slavery, exploitation and other abuses.

128. It was also noted that the voices of bishops in some parts of the region were missing, not only for hearing their perspectives on the style of synodal leadership but also about isolation and other challenges that they experience in their pastoral ministry.

VI
PRIORITIES AND CALLS TO ACTION

129. Many themes, issues and insights emerged as the fruits of the discernment process in Oceania, and the 11 key themes outlined in the earlier sections of this document. These are the priorities that emerged from the five syntheses which the People of God in Oceania consider appropriate for consideration at the First Session of the Synod Assembly in October 2023. In doing so, we have concentrated on those matters which are more properly considered by the Universal Church (such as Church teaching) and left other matters for consideration at the level of continental, episcopal conference or local Church. Other important topics such as the relevance of the tent metaphor, the centrality of baptism as our identity and forming the baptised to understand their call to mission may be helpful in the writing of the *Instrumentum Laboris*.

6.1 Mission

130. Mission was identified as a key priority in each of the responses, with a strong sense that the mission which Christ entrusted to the Church is truly linked to the inclusion of all the baptised. Below are the issues for the Synod Assembly to consider:

a) Ways of more effectively engaging the whole People of God in their baptismal invitation to participate in God's mission (Pacific).
b) Making a transition from a 'maintenance' to a 'mission-focused' Church (Australia, 69).
c) Inviting and encouraging all Catholics 'to accept their baptismal call to evangelise and proclaim God's love in unity with others' (Australia, 69).
d) In the absence of priests, validating and strengthening lay pastoral ministry in prisons and hospitals to ensure that people receive the healing ministry of Jesus (New Zealand, 116).
e) Recognising the Eastern Catholic Churches in Oceania as *'Sui iuris* [self-governing] Churches who through their rich spiritual tradition can contribute to the mission of the Church' (ECC, 19).

6.2 Ecological Crisis

131. As a sea of big and small islands, Oceania is uniquely impacted by the devastating consequences of the ecological crisis – from rising sea levels threatening the very existence of island communities to catastrophic cyclones, floods, fires and droughts and the resultant loss of human life and biodiversity. While acknowledging that the DCS made reference to the climate emergency, the Synod Assembly should consider this as an urgent existential global issue:

   a) Stand in solidarity with those communities severely impacted by the ecological crisis, noting the differential impact on the poor and vulnerable.
   b) Promote *Laudato Si'*s integral ecology as critical to our care for the earth and for the oceans and urge local churches and ministries to implement action plans.
   c) Consider the ecological crisis as a mission field in which the whole Church, globally and locally, should be engaged in the 'urgent struggle to preserve our planet and its life, and to provide economic justice for its people' (New Zealand, 114).

6.3 Church Teaching

132. Questions about Church teaching, or the application of Church teaching, were raised in the Oceania responses. There are differences in the region about whether change is needed in Church teaching in some areas, and about whether Church teaching can change or develop. These issues listed below need to be addressed for the sake of our unity in diversity.

   a) Those aspects of Church teaching which are perceived as 'exclusionary or hurtful' or understood to 'cause people to walk away from the Church or deter them from returning' (New Zealand, 117). These include teaching on sexuality, diverse sexual relationships, contraception, the situation of the divorced and remarried, intercommunion with other Christian denominations whose Baptism we recognise, priestly celibacy and the restriction of ordination to men.
   b) Improved communication of Magisterial teaching, in accessible language and modes for the People of God.
   c) Liturgical reforms to implement the teachings of Vatican II on inculturation and reflect contemporary theology, such as 'a better translation of the Missal, inclusive language, lay people giving homilies, flexibility in different contexts ... Overall, it was agreed that liturgy should always allow for active participation and be inclusive and open to all' (Australia, 68).

d) Liturgical norms which enable and facilitate local cultural approaches to worship (Pacific).

6.4 Becoming more Synodal

133. The majority of respondents valued the experience of synodality and expressed a desire for the Church to become more synodal. This was seen as a priority in each of the responses. The Synod Assembly should consider ways of embedding synodality in the life and teaching of the Church:

a) Using discernment processes in Church decision-making, which requires that 'those in leadership positions listen to the Holy Spirit and try to seek the will of God in affairs of the Church' (Pacific).
b) 'Developing further resources for discernment and synodality in the ordinary life of the Church' (New Zealand, 113).
c) Shifting attitudes and practices within the Church to be more communal (Pacific).
d) Transforming the culture of Church leadership to emphasise 'the importance of accountability, transparency and openness at all levels of the Church, for parishes, dioceses and Church agencies and for the bishops themselves' (Australia, 61).
e) Embedding 'synodality as the "way of being Church" at every level' (New Zealand, 113) by identifying 'those bodies in the Church at all levels which are synodal by nature' (New Zealand, 113), and 'establishing forums at all levels of the Church' where they are lacking (Australia, 61) in order to promote 'subsidiarity within the Church' (Australia, 61).

6.5 Authority and Decision-making

134. Discernment in Oceania revealed a common view that a synodal Church needs a cultural and structural change in Church leadership, including shared governance and decision-making, involving both laity and clergy, to reduce the possibility of a culture of clericalism and enable the laity in the contribution of their gifts.

The Synod Assembly should consider:

a) Ways of embedding a culture of servant leadership for those in leadership positions – clerical, religious and lay people.
b) Changes to current governance structures to enable shared governance and decision-making, involving both laity and clergy.
c) Those areas of canon law which do not enable lay women and men to participate in appropriate forms of decision-making, while not derogating from episcopal authority.

d) Removing provisions that restrict certain diocesan and tribunal roles to clerics to allow qualified lay people to take up these roles (New Zealand, 116).
e) How initiatives to improve transparency and accountability in the Vatican might be modelled in the local churches.
f) Investigating 'pathways for people from diverse backgrounds to be trained in governance roles, such as pastoral councils or other areas of governance' (Australia, 67).

6.6 Young People

135. The discernment across Oceania revealed a common concern regarding the disconnection and absence of many young people in the life of the Church and a keenness that the Assembly give them priority:

a) Listening and 'investigating how the faith needs of young people could be met and how youth could be better formed and provided with platforms that allowed them to utilise their skills and passions' (Australia, 76), including documents in a language they can understand (New Zealand, 47).
b) Accompanying young people in discerning the gifts and talents 'that they can offer for the growth of the Church' (Pacific).
c) An increased focus on 'a union of family, parish and school to work together' to enrich the Catholicity within Catholic schools (ECC, 20).
d) More pastoral activities and faith formation programs that cater to young men's and boys' unique perspectives (PNG/SI, 5.6).

6.7 Women

136. The role and place of women in the Church was a uniform concern in Oceania. The Synod Assembly should consider the experience of women in the Church:

a) Hearing directly from women on all matters under consideration during the Synod Assemblies.
b) Ensuring the spirit of synodality continues to cause the Church to listen to those women who do not feel sufficiently recognised in the Church (Pacific).
c) Change the perception of women in the Church as being homogenous in their views, the way cultural influences impact them at a local level or their way of life (New Zealand, 118).
d) Full and just participation of women in Church governance, decision-making, mission and ministry (Australia, 60; New Zealand, 118).

e) A just remuneration for lay women working in the Church and 'religious women, especially in the pastoral field' (PNG/SI, 2.6).
f) A greater involvement of women in the formation of seminarians and priests (New Zealand, 118).

6.8 Formation

137. In the five responses from the region, formation was seen to be essential. As this was seen as a priority, the Synod Assembly should consider:

a) Creating a formation framework for all the baptised to help them participate in a synodal Church and be courageous missionary disciples.
b) Ensuring that formation identifies needs within the light of Scripture and Church teaching, includes Catholic Social Teaching, and addresses the reality of people's lives.
c) Prioritising formation resources for ecological conversion and specific resources for the formation of young people in the faith.
d) Ensuring that there is an adequate emphasis on formation for catechists and other lay leaders.

VII
CONCLUSION

138. The experience of synodality became for many people a new experience of Church. During the process people recognised the presence of the Holy Spirit in listening to one another, in the joy and freedom they experienced and in the common ground they found. Those who reflected upon the DCS found the emergence of clear themes across the world amazing – evidence of the Holy Spirit at work in the Church. 'The experience with the DCS has given many people a global perspective of the Church which they did not have before, which has induced a sense of wonder at the diversity and breadth of the Church to which we belong' (New Zealand, 13).

139. As the *Instrumentum Laboris* is prepared for the Synod Assembly, we note that the many people who have taken part have already been changed by this process. An outpouring of people's hearts has taken place which has created new bonds and strengthened people's understanding of their shared identity as members of Christ's Church. Many lay people now have a deeper knowledge of their Baptism and what it means, and a strong desire to act upon that new knowledge.

140. People are awaiting with interest the next stage of the global process. There is great hope that the First Synod Assembly in October 2023 will be aligned with the synodal process, Christ-centred and Spirit-led, focused on God's call to us at this point in the Church's history. To be truly synodal the lay and religious participants need to reflect the diversity of the People of God.

141. There have always been 'experts' and 'auditors' at Assemblies of the Synod of Bishops in the past. We invite the Synod Secretariat to discern carefully how those people are chosen for this Assembly and recommend a transparent process be adopted. The 'experts' should have expertise in areas such as pastoral care, missionary work and synodality, alongside theology, ecclesiology and canon law. 'Auditors' should include people such as migrants, the poor, priests and religious who work among the marginalised, and survivors of abuse. Whether the traditional roles of 'experts' and 'auditors' are retained, or a modified structure is adopted, women, lay men, young people and indigenous people should participate with the bishops in the Assembly, and some of these should be from Oceania.

142. The title of the Working Document for the Continental Stage is Enlarge the Space of your Tent. The People of God need the Assembly to heed this call as we continue the synodal journey.

VIII
PASTORAL REFLECTION BY THE BISHOPS OF OCEANIA GATHERED AT THE FCBCO ASSEMBLY, ON THE OCEANIA RESPONSE TO THE DCS

143. As we considered this Oceania document, we had a sense of a very real confidence in the presence of Christ in the Church, and that He is moving the Church forward. The document captures the hopes and concerns of our people, and this might give the impression that the Church is in disarray. However, it is precisely in places and times of pain and suffering that Christ reveals himself. This confidence and faith in His presence can guide us in our response. We seek the guidance of the Holy Spirit as we continue our synodal journey.

144. We trust the process and the people we appointed, who have collated well the responses of the People of God to the questions posed in the Document for the Continental Stage of the Synod. We believe that this document is a fair representation of the reality of the People of God who participated in this synodal process. However, we acknowledge that this document is not a census of all Catholics in Oceania but an expression of the views of those people who responded to the invitation to discern on the DCS. Acknowledging the limited participation due to time pressures, we hope for broader participation as the synodal process unfolds.

145. We noticed in the people's responses a desire for practical applications of synodality in the present moment. However, we also realise that while we are a synodal Church, giving practical expression to synodality will take time. It will be a long journey, both in Oceania and in the Universal Church. This document is not a catechetical or magisterial document. It is more like a postcard at this point in our journey, showing where we are now.

146. We do not want to build a different Church, but rather to renew and revitalise the Church which we love. This renewal and revitalisation will begin with personal conversion, and it will also find communal and structural expression. A renewed and synodal Church seeks not to leave anyone behind. In such a Church we will walk together, loving one another.

147. Reflecting on the responses of the people, we were pleased to see they appreciate that their Baptism is foundational and that it receives great attention in this document. However, we noticed that Eucharist is less prominent.

148. For Catholics, the Eucharist is central. Through Baptism, we gain entry to the Eucharistic community gathered at the Table of the Lord. With Christ, we as a people are invited to die to self and rise again with Christ as we participate in his sacrificial self-emptying and self-giving. The Lord Jesus gives us Himself as food for the journey until we share in the banquet of heaven. He gives us priests, whom He calls to have a shepherd's heart to care for their people, proclaim the Word of God, celebrate Eucharist with and for them, and so nourish the Church as she strives to fulfil her mission for the life of the world. Similarly, the Sacrament of Penance reunites the sinner with the Eucharistic community.

149. Not every bishop found every part of the document wholly convincing or complete, and some had doubts and concerns about where this might be leading us. Jesus appeared to the disciples with their pain, shame, loss and shattered hopes. In the same way, we bishops feel doubts, anxieties and fears about certain parts of this document. We also feel joy and hope. The crucified and risen Christ showed his wounds to his disciples and despite their shame, doubts, and fears, they were filled with joy and hope. His words were 'peace be with you'. He invites us bishops to trust in his mercy and proclaim the truth with love, as Jesus did.

150. In the face of our doubts and fears, Jesus sends us to a broken world. We receive the griefs and anguish, the joys and hopes of the people of Oceania expressed in this document. With trust in the Holy Spirit, we will continue to journey together, people and pastors, as the pilgrim People of God. Jesus Christ is walking with us in our synodal journey, offering us His peace and urging us to have courage.

151. Our sharing of the Gospel in Oceania takes place in quite varied contexts. This document is an example of the voices of the peoples of our nations revealing the contexts of our mission. The document has a lively sense of mission, which is at the heart of the laity being Church in the world.

152. We have a desire and responsibility to listen to and accompany our young people and assist them to draw on the life-giving Gospel in responding to the challenges they face in their search for meaning, hope and healthy relationships. We are conscious that reaching out to our young people in more courageous, creative and engaging ways is an essential aspect of mission for our Church in the context of our world today.

153. We are also committed to our shared responsibility expressed in this document to better care for and advocate for our common home. In our region, the ecological crisis is an existential threat to many people and communities. It is experienced in sea level rises, the acidification of the oceans, droughts, flooding rains, and more frequent extreme weather events. The destruction of some island nations becomes increasingly likely as the melting of the Antarctic ice cap on our southern periphery continues with global warming. Ecological conversion is an urgent mission priority.

154. Formation for all members of the Church, including the bishops, will be essential to support our journey of becoming a more synodal Church.

155. Having reflected on this document together at our Assembly, we feel peace and joy. We also feel called to be prophetic. The apostles were accepted by Jesus even though they had let him down. He offered them peace. We are called to be ready to sacrifice ourselves in the process of being prophetic. We need to model ourselves on the love we proclaim. We are sent forth just as Jesus sent forth the apostles.

ON SYNODALITY

After the explanation of the three key words of the synodal process – communion, participation, mission – the people in the village shouted confidently and loudly, 'We are synodality! We are synodality!' Why? 'We are doing it ever since we became Catholics.'

(Balimo Village, Papua New Guinea, became a parish 27 years ago and people are NO READ, NO WRITE)

When the explanation went on to emphasise the idea of 'WALKING TOGETHER', they said, 'Every day we ONLY WALK and all the time we walk in numbers because it is strange walking ALONE and CAR ride not possible for we don't have road!'

If synodality expressed the Church-people's ordinary way of living and working, then I must say, people in Balimo are right in one sense in their simplicity as Church and in their display of faith practice.

Bishop Joseph Durero
7 February 2023

CONTRIBUTORS

Bechealany, Souraya, a Maronite from Lebanon, is professor of ecclesiology and ecumenism as well as Director of the Center for Research in Religious Studies, at the Faculty of Religious Sciences, Saint Joseph University of Beirut. She is a former Secretary General of the Middle East Council of Churches. She participated in the 2022 Frascati meeting which developed the *Document for the Continental Stage* and served on the steering committee and the drafting committee of the Continental Assembly in the Middle East (February-March 2023). She is member of the strategic committee of the synodal process on woman in the Maronite church and part of its drafting committee. She serves as a member of the International Joint Commission for Theological Dialogue between the Catholic Church and the Oriental Orthodox Churches. She co-authored the 2021 document on the Mission of Christians in the Middle East: 'We choose Abundant Life. Christians in the Middle East: Towards Renewed Theological, Social and Political Choices'. She is a lay woman.

Abotcha-Boni, Marie-Laure Josée, is the National Administrator of the Catholic Media of Ivory Coast. She is the President-Founder of THEOS, a Christian initiative at the service of God, the Church and man, with the ambition to promote Christian values in the temporal realities of society. She is a former representative of the Catholic Church in Ivory Coast on the Board of Directors of the Biblical Alliance of Ivory Coast, and served as Deputy General Treasurer of this Board. She is a former member of the Scientific Committee of the Pontifical Mission Societies (PMS) for the Missionary Congress. She is a founding member of the Catholic Community of Divine Love. She was a member of the Synod's National Contact Team on Synodality in Ivory Coast, served on the Methodology Commission within the Synod's National Contact Team on Synodality and participated in the 2023 African Continental Synodal Assembly. She is married and mother of two children.

Candelario, Jessica Joy is a lay theologian from the Philippines and a member of the Philippine National Synod Team. She is presently the Pastoral Programme Coordinator of Bukal ng Tipan (Wellspring of Covenants), a pastoral center that works towards the vision of a more synodal church in the world. She participated at the Asian Continental Assembly as a Philippine representative. She was also involved in the FABC as executive secretary for the Youth Desk and continues to be engaged in collaborative work within the region. She completed her MA and PhD in Practical Theology at the Catholic Theological Union in Chicago and St. Thomas University in Florida.

Colberg, Kristin is an associate professor of theology at the College of Saint Benedict and Saint John's University and School of Theology in Collegeville Minnesota (USA). She holds a doctorate in Theology from the University of Notre Dame. She is a member of the Theological Commission for the Synod on Synodality and served on the team in Frascati, Italy that drafted the *Document for the Continental Stage* in 2022. She was a minute taker at a number of the digital meetings of the continental sessions of the synod held in the USA / Canada. Her research focuses on Vatican I, Vatican II, ecclesiology and ecumenism. On behalf of the Dicastery for the Promotion of Christian Unity she serves on the Anglican-Roman Catholic International Commission (ARCIC).

González Sánchez, Ricardo, a priest of the diocese of Zamora, Michoacán, Mexico, holds a licentiate in dogmatic theology from the Gregorian University in Rome and a doctorate in systematic theology from the Boston College School of Theology and Ministry. He is a founding member of the Mexican Academy of Theology, member of the Council for Continuous theological reflection within the Mexican Bishops' Conference and of the theological reflection team of CELAM. He was part of the drafting team of the final document of the Ecclesial Assembly of Latin America and the Caribbean. He participated actively in the regional meeting of Central America and Mexico (CAMEX) for consultation and discernment of the Working Document, and later, in the drafting of the document of the Continental Synthesis of Latin America and the Caribbean for the Synod on Synodality. Currently he serves as Professor of Dogmatic Theology and Dean of the Faculty of Theology of the Pontifical University of Mexico.

Gracias, Oswald has been the archbishop of Mumbay (India) since 2006 and a Cardinal since 2007. Pope Francis appointed him on the Council of Cardinals in 2013. He served as president of the Catholic Conference of Bishops of India (CCBI – Latin Rite only), of the Catholic Bishops' Conference of India (CBCI – all rites) and of the Federation of Asian Bishops' Conferences (FABC) for several terms. He also serves on the Council of Bishops for the Synod on Synodality, which has as task to assist in preparing the synod. In this function he closely attends to the development of the Synod on Synodality. Cardinal Gracias participated in the 2022 Frascati meeting which prepared the *Document for the Continental Stage* and in the 2023 Continental Assembly Meeting of the Synod in Asia held in Bangkok, Thailand. He is a voting member of the October 2023 Synod on Synodality.

Join-Lambert, Arnaud is a professor practical theology and liturgy at the Catholic University of Louvain (UCLouvain) in Belgium. He is head of the Centre for Practical Theology and director of the EcclesiaLab. He is a former president of the International Society of Practical Theology (SITP). He is director of the international journal *Lumen Vitae*. His research focuses on changes in parishes and the ministry of priests, new forms of Christian presence and mission in society, rituality and liturgy in a post-modern context, synodality in the churches. He was an expert theologian for the Provincial Council of Lille and for several diocesan assemblies and synods in France, Belgium and Germany. He is a member of the Methodology Commission for the Roman Synod on Synodality (2021-2024). He was a member of the Redaction Committee at the 2023 European Continental Assembly of the Synod in Prague. He is married and has three children.

KHENG, Christina is a laywoman from Singapore and teaches theology and pastoral leadership at the East Asian Pastoral Institute in Manila. She also provides accompaniment for organisational renewal and communal discernment by ecclesial entities, including formation and facilitation for Spiritual Conversation. With regard to the Synod 2021-2024, she is a member of the Methodology Commission which drafted the Vademecum. She served also on the team at Frascati which saw to the *Document for the Continental Stage*, as well as a moderator and speaker at the Asian Continental Assembly in Bangkok. She holds a PhD in theology from the Australian Catholic University and a Masters in Public Administration from Harvard University. She participates as a facilitator in the October 2023 Synod on Synodality.

KLÖCKENER, Martin was a full professor of liturgical studies at the bilingual German / French University of Fribourg (Switzerland) from 1994 until 2022. He obtained his doctorate with a thesis on the liturgy of synods and councils. He is the chief editor of 'Archiv für Liturgiewissenschaft', of the Handbook for liturgical studies 'Gottesdienst der Kirche' and of the 'Spicilegium Friburgense'. He authored in particular studies on the history and theology of liturgy. He held numerous ecclesial mandates in Switzerland and on an international level.

MZAWAK, Mirna Abboud is professor and head of social sciences at the Holy Spirit University of Kaslik in Jounieh, Lebanon and associate Dean for Research and Director of the IDEES Research Laboratory. She is the coordinator of the Women's Pastoral Office at the Maronite Patriarchal Curia in Bkerke and of the Synodal process on women in the Maronite Church. She is part of the committee of the Maronite Patriarchal Synod (2003-2006) and coordinated research on the reception of the said Synod. She was a member of the Steering Committee of the Continental Synodal Assembly of Churches in the Middle East (2022-2023).

Pascoe, Susan AM is Adjunct Professor at the University of Western Australia, a Trustee of St John of God Health and a Board member of Mercy Health. She assists the General Secretariat of the Synod as a member of the Methodology Commission for the Synod on Synodality, participated in the 2022 discernment and writing group in Frascati, and was a member of its Taskforce for the Continental Stage. The Federation of Catholic Bishops' Conferences of Oceania appointed her to chair its Continental Taskforce and its Discernment and Writing Group. She also participated in the Continental Assembly in Asia. She has served in senior roles within government and the Church including as Australia's inaugural Charity Commissioner and as Chief Executive of the Catholic Education Commission of Victoria. She participates as a facilitator in the October 2023 Synod on Synodality. Susan Pascoe is a married and a mother and grandmother.

Routhier, Gilles, a priest of the archdiocese of Quebec, Canada, serves currently as a member of the Theological Commission of the Synod on Synodality. He was part of the team that drafted the North American *Final Document for the Continental Stage of the Synod 2021-2024.* He was an expert to the Canadian delegation to the 2001 Synod of Bishops on the 'Bishop: Servant of the Gospel of Jesus Christ for the Hope of the World.' He is a Professor of Ecclesiology and Practical Theology at the Faculty of Theology of Laval University (Quebec), and specialises in the history, teaching, hermeneutics and reception of the Second Vatican Council. He is a fellow of the Royal Society of Canada and holds honorary doctorates from the Dominican University College (Ottawa) and University of St. Michael's College in the University of Toronto. He participates as an expert in the October 2023 of the Synod on Synodality.

Rush, Ormond, a priest of the diocese of Townsville, Australia, is a fundamental theologian who specialises on the *sensus fidelium*. He is an Associate Professor and Reader at Australian Catholic University, Brisbane campus. He was a member of the Bishops' Executive Committee planning of the 2021–2022 Plenary Council in Australia, and was a *peritus* at the Plenary Council's two assemblies (in October 2021 and in July 2022). He is a member of the Theological Commission of the Synod on Synodality. He was a member of the writing group in Frascati, which prepared the *Document for the Continental Stage*, and also a member of the writing group that drafted the working document for the Oceania Continental Assembly in Suva, Fiji. He is an expert at the October 2023 Synod on Synodality.

Tirimanna CSsR, Vimal is a Redemptorist priest from Sri Lanka who serves as professor of moral theology at the Pontifical Alphonsian Academy, Pontifical

Urbaniana University and the Pontifical Beda College in Rome, and also at the National Seminary of Our Lady of Lanka in Sri Lanka. From 1996 to 2012, he was a member of the Office of Theological Concerns of the FABC (Federation of Asian Bishops' Conferences), and from 2002 to 2012, he was the Executive Secretary of the same Office. Through conferences, seminars and spiritual retreats he has given inputs to the numerous Asian bishops and priests. From 2011 to-date, he has been a member of the Catholic delegation of the Anglican-Roman Catholic International Commission (ARCIC). He is a member of the Theological Commission for the current Synod of Synodality. He participated in the Frascati meeting in the Autumn of 2022 that produced the *Document for the Continental Stage*, and also in the Asian Continental Ecclesial Assembly in February 2023. He is a voting member in the October 2023 Synod on Synodality.

Weiler MMS, Birgit, belongs to the Congregation of Medical Mission Sisters. Born in Germany, she left for Peru more than 35 years ago. She is professor for systematic theology at the Department of Theology at the Pontifical Catholic University of Peru and specialises in intercultural theology. She was a member of the commission of the Bishops' Council of Latin America and the Caribbean (CELAM) which prepared the document for the discernment of the signs of the present time, done through a broad process of listening to each other before the First Ecclesial Assembly of Latin America and the Caribbean. She coordinated the commission to draft the document for discernment, based on the results of the process of listening, at the Ecclesial Assembly. As a member of the Group for Theological Reflection of CELAM, she was involved in the drafting of the Document of the Ecclesial Assembly. She also participated in drafting the *Working Document for the Continental Stage* in Frascati as well as in writing and editing the Synthesis of the Continental Stage of the Latin America and the Caribbean Synod.

Wijlens, Myriam, born in The Netherlands, holds a licentiate in systematic theology (Nijmegen) and a doctorate in canon law (Ottawa) and a Habilitation in canon law (Münster). She has been a full professor of Canon Law at the University of Erfurt (Germany) since 2005 and served her university as vice president (2008-2011). She is a honorary professor of 'Canon Law and Ecumenism' at Durham University (UK). She is the co-moderator of the international research group 'Peter and Paul Seminar' which attends to reforms on canon law in light of Vatican II. On behalf of the Dicastery for the Promotion of Christian Unity she serves on the Faith and Order Commission of the World Council of Churches (2008-2030) in which she moderated the Study Group 'Moral Discernment in the Churches' and participates in the Study Group 'Nicea 325-2025'. She also serves as an expert on the Anglican Roman Catholic International Commission

(ARCIC). From 2018-2022 she served on the Pontifical Commission for the Protection of Minors (PCPM). In 2021 Pope Francis appointed her as Consultor to the Synod of Bishops. She serves on the Coordinating Committee of the Synod on Synodality. She was a member of the Redaction Committee of the Continental Ecclesial Assembly in Europe and participates as an expert in the October 2023 Synod on Synodality.

ACKNOWLEDGEMENTS

The following document in this book is reprinted from the website: https://www.synod.va/en/resources/official-documents.html

Secretaria Generalis Synodi, *Enlarge the Space of your Tent (Is. 54:2)*: Working Document for the Continental Stage, Vatican 2022 (also known as 'Frascati Document').

The official logo of the Synod 2021-2024 is taken from:
https://www.synod.va/en/what-is-the-synod-21-24/the-official-logo.html

The following documents in this book are reprinted from the website:
https://www.synod.va/en/synodal-process/the-continental-stage/final_document.html

Africa: Symposium of Episcopal Conferences of Africa and Madagascar (SECAM), *Document of the African Synodal Continental Assembly*, 1-6 March 2023.

Asia: Federation of Asian Bishops Conferences (FABC), *Final Document of the Asian Continental Assembly on Synodality*, 16 March 2023.

Europe: Council of Bishops' Conferences of Europe (CCEE),, *Synod 2021-2024, European Continental Assembly, Prague 5-12 February 2023 Concluding Dossier*.

Latin America and Caribbean: Consejo Episcopal Latinoamericano y Caribeño (CELAM), *Synthesis of the Continental Stage of the Latin America and the Caribbean Synod*, 2023.

Middle East: *Conclusions of the Continental Assembly of the Synod of Catholic Churches in the Middle East*, 13-18 February 2023.

North America: Canadian Catholic Conference of Bishops (CCCB) & United States Conference of Catholic Bishops (USCCB), *Final Document for the Continental Stage in North America*, 2023.

Oceania: Federation of Catholic Bishops of Conferences of Oceania (FCBCO), *Oceania Discernment on the Working Document for the Continental Stage*, 2023.